The Rothschilds

Virginia Cowles

The Rothschilds

A FAMILY OF FORTUNE

ALFRED A. KNOPF   New York   1973

This is a Borzoi Book
Published in New York by Alfred A. Knopf, Inc.

© Crawley Features, 1973

*All rights reserved under International and Pan-American
Copyright Conventions. Published in the United States
by Alfred A. Knopf, Inc., New York. Distributed by
Random House, Inc., New York. Published in Great Britain
by George Weidenfeld and Nicolson, London.*

Library of Congress Catalog Card Number: 73-3663
ISBN: 0-394-48773-7

Designed by Trevor Vincent; filmset by BAS Printers
Limited, Wallop, Hampshire, England.
Printed in Italy LIBREX Milano
First American Edition

*Dedicated to my dear children
Andrew, Harriet and Randall
who, I feel sure, would have won
the approbation of Mayer Amschel Rothschild
for their devotion to one another when
not locked in physical combat*

Sources of Illustrations

The author and publishers would like to express their gratitude to members of the Rothschild family for their generous help at every stage of this book and for their permission to photograph their houses and objects in their collections. They would like to thank in particular: in France, Baron and Baroness Élie, Baron and Baroness Philippe, Baron and Baroness Guy, Baroness Cécile, Baroness Édouard and Mme Armand de la Baumelle; in England, Mrs James de Rothschild, Lord Rothschild, Mrs Miriam Lane, Mr Evelyn de Rothschild, Mr Edmund de Rothschild and the Hon. Jacob Rothschild.

They would also like to thank the Earl and Countess of Rosebery for their permission to photograph some paintings at Mentmore; Sir Cecil Beaton for his permission to reproduce the portraits of Baroness Cécile on page 292 and Baroness Élie on page 293; Mr David Rutherston for his permission to reproduce his Beerbohm caricature of Alfred de Rothschild (photograph Eva Reichmann; by courtesy of Sir Rupert Hart-Davis in whose book, *A Catalogue of the Caricatures of Max Beerbohm*, published by Macmillan Ltd, it appears); and Captain R. Eggers, camp and security officer at Colditz Castle, 1940–5, for his permission to publish the photograph of Baron Élie on page 257, taken from his *Documentation on Oflag 4C, Colditz Castle*.

The following photographs were taken for Weidenfeld and Nicolson by Werner Forman: 34, 44, 51, 52b, 69, 72, 77, 80, 114–5, 159, 160, 195, 222–3, 224, 258–9, 260, 287b, 288, 294; and Derrick Witty: 20, 33, 52t, 61, 68e, 68r, 78–9, 93, 122, 133, 141, 196, 250.

In addition the author and publishers would like to thank the following collections for the use of their photographs: Agence d'Illustrations pour la Presse, 266, 281; Archiv Gerstenberg, 17, 27, 71, 108, 136; Bibliothèque Nationale, Paris, 10; Roland Bonnefoy, 257; British Museum (photo A. C. Cooper), 31, 61, 86, 87, 91t, 126, 134, 137t, 137b, 139, 140, 155, 165, 167, 180, 190, 215, 279; Camera Press (photo Patrick Ward), 256, 264, 278; J. Allan Cash, 245; Central Press Photos, 263; Central Zionist Archives, 205; *Country Life* (by courtesy of the National Trust, Waddesdon, and Mrs James de Rothschild), 177; Mary Evans Picture Library, 48, 54, 94, 101, 111, 153, 163; Frankfurt Staatsbibliothek, 90; Gunnersbury House Museum, 93, 171; J. Hillelson Agency (photo I. Yeomans) 143, 172b, 173, (photo Ian Berry) 284t, 284b, 289; A. F. Kersting, 157; Keystone Agency, 273; London Museum, 91b, 117; Mansell Collection 12, 211b, 216r; National Portrait Gallery, 92; the National Trust (by courtesy of Mrs James de Rothschild) 178, (by courtesy of Mr Evelyn de Rothschild) 222–3, 224; Österreichisches Nationalbibliothek, 187, 188t, 216l, 228; Paul Popper, 64, 20, 204, 229; Radio Times Hulton Picture Library, 8, 40, 55, 58, 66, 82, 107, 109, 123a, 124, 138, 170, 174, 189, 198, 213, 222; *Réalités – Connaissance des Arts* (photo R. Guillemot), 116, 142, 287t, 290; H. Roger – Viollet, 98, 122b, 127, 150, 185, 199, 209, 211a; Georges Sirot, 145t, 145b, 152, 154; Snark International, 76, 182.

Contents

1   The Jew and the Prince (1763–1806)   9

2   The Rothschilds and Napoleon (1806–15)   28

3   Five Brothers in Five Capitals (1815–25)   53

4   Uneasy Times (1825–36)   70

5   Supremacy (1836–49)   92

6   The Challenge (1849–68)   112

7   Victorian High Noon (1860–80)   140

8   Magnificent Brothers (1880–1901)   164

9   End of an Era (1898–1918)   190

10 The Years Between (1918–39)   208

11 The Second World War (1939–45)   234

12 The Rothschilds Today: The Bankers
    (1953–73)   253

13 The Rothschilds Today: The Others
    (1953–73)   274

    Family Tree   294–5

    Notes   296

    Index   299

Chapter 1

The Jew and the Prince

(1763–1806)

*W*HEN THE SEVEN YEARS WAR CAME TO AN END IN 1763, two young men at opposite ends of the social scale, one a Prince, one a Jew, both twenty years old, returned to the great imperial city of Frankfurt on the Main. The Prince had never heard of his lowly contemporary: yet their paths were destined to cross and recross until the fame of the Jew and his sons had spread across Europe, eclipsing the importance of the Prince so completely that his name is remembered only as an incident in the rise of the Rothschild family.

Mayer Amschel Rothschild was a tall, spare man with piercing black eyes and a slightly quizzical smile. His inky beard was small and pointed and he wore a wig which, as a Jew, he was not allowed to powder. On his coat was sewn the yellow patch compulsory in Frankfurt for members of his race. When he crossed the bridge over the Main he had to pay Jew tax; and as he walked through the city streets more than one urchin jeered: 'Jew, do your duty.' Almost automatically and with remarkable good temper he removed his hat each time and bowed.

There was no mistaking the ghetto. Although it was nothing more than a street twelve feet wide, wedged between the city walls and a trench, it differed from other streets by its dramatic entrance: a pair of heavy iron doors, closed on Sundays, and Feast days, and an arch over which was written:
'Under the Roman Emperor's Majesty and the Holy Emperor's Protection.'

The 2,800 inmates of the ghetto had to pay high taxes for this fictitious protection. The custom had been instigated in the thirteenth century after a pogrom which had wiped out the two hundred Jewish inhabitants of Frankfurt, whose ancestors had lived in the city since the days of Charlemagne. Although in those times the Jews were not confined to a ghetto and enjoyed the same rights as the Christians, the current Emperor, Frederick II, had seized upon the idea of 'protection' to raise extra revenue. But nothing stopped the periodic pogroms which always seemed to spring from a wave of utterly irrelevant hysteria. In 1349, when the Black Plague was raging, bands of Flagellants burst into Frankfurt accusing the Jews of poisoning the wells. When the citizens ignored these provocations the Brothers secretly set fire to several houses and ran through the streets crying: 'Now the Jews are burning down your houses.' This resulted in a general massacre.

The Judengasse in Frankfurt.

Yet it was not for another hundred years, in 1442, that the Holy Roman Emperor bowed to pressure from the Church and ordered the Jews to remove themselves to a specified quarter of the city. The Judengasse, or Jews' Alley, offered enough space for the 150 inhabitants, but by 1760 nearly three thousand people were crammed into three hundred houses. The street was almost always deep in mud and garbage, and the stench unbearable. The heavily-bearded, Oriental figures in caftans and stove-pipe hats rooting through the stalls of second-hand junk alarmed young Goethe who grew up in Frankfurt. 'The limited area, the filth, the crowd, the accent of an unpleasant language, all combined to produce a most disagreeable impression,' he wrote, 'even if one merely looked in as one passed the gates.'[1] Not only disagreeable but frightening for *Gottfried's Chronicle*, read by German schoolboys, claimed that Jews spirited away Christian children and offered them as human sacrifices. Yet to Mayer Amschel Rothschild the jostling and the bargaining brought back nostalgic memories. He had grown up in the Judengasse with its welter of cheap merchandise, as had his father and grandfather before him. Despite the insistence of many writers, Jews were not denied the right of a surname; indeed, the fact that they clung to Oriental habit, referring to their male children as Sons of So and So, was a source of irritation and confusion to the authorities who eventually forced them to conform to Christian practice. Until this happened, however, many families, identified themselves by nailing a picture or a sign over their front door. In 1585 records show that Mayer's forbears had lived in a house with a red shield – hence the name Rot-schildt.

But now home meant a small, damp dwelling known as the House of the Saucepan, which Mayer shared with his two brothers, Moses and Kalmann. The boys had lost their parents in a smallpox epidemic in 1755 when Mayer was eleven years old. The father had been a small trader, and as a child Mayer liked nothing better than to accompany him on journeys in the surrounding countryside, walking behind a donkey laden with samples. Although the man and the boy rarely covered more than ten or fifteen miles a day, they frequently passed through several principalities, for the Holy Roman Empire, the system under which Central Europe had lived for a thousand years, still encompassed most of Germany. As an institution it was almost moribund; indeed Voltaire inquired caustically in what sense it was either Holy or Roman or an Empire. Its elected Emperors, almost always chosen from the Habsburg family, were no more than honorary presidents of a loose confederation which, by the middle of the century, consisted of over three hundred independent states. Governed by absolute rulers ranging from imperial knights to sovereign abbots, from landgraves to dukes, from electors to princes and kings, almost all of them were feudal and military.

As each state had its own treasury, and each treasury minted its

An early nineteenth-century caricature of Mayer Amschel Rothschild: 'Blueshield, Travelling Salesman for Merchants, makes deals in all branches of commerce.'

own coins, Mayer Amschel was taught the intricacies of money at a tender age. He not only learned to translate gold and silver into the copper coins in common use, but to calculate with lightning speed the exchange rate between thalers and ducats and florins and gulden. He became so proficient that when his father opened a money bureau in the ghetto he often left his youngest son to mind the shop. The many picturesque and obsolete coins that passed through Mayer's hands awakened the collector's instinct; and before long the child had an array of rare specimens coming from such faraway places as the Palatinate and Russia and China.

When Mayer was ten he was sent by his parents to a *yeshiva* – a Jewish religious school – near Nuremberg to study to be a rabbi, a calling which several of his ancestors had adopted. The ghetto was famous for its scribes and scholars and no occupation commanded more respect than the pursuit of knowledge. Mayer was thought to have the application for such a life, but after a few months the boy became restless. The jingle of coins not only conjured up ancient lore but sang a song of freedom and power that was heady music to a· ghetto boy.

Mayer remained at the school for eighteen months after his parents' death but finally persuaded one of his mother's relations that he was not cut out to be a scholar. Although he was only thirteen in 1757, he was sent to live in Hanover with a cousin who got him a job as an apprentice in the famous Oppenheimer bank. Here life was far from dull as the Seven Years War was in progress and the city crowded with troops. The conflict had begun when Frederick the Great of Prussia had grabbed Silesia from Maria Theresa of Austria. The latter persuaded Russia, Sweden and France to support her and soon almost all the states of the Holy Roman Empire were drawn into the quarrel. Frederick aptly compared himself to 'a stag pursued by a pack of kings and princes'. Although most of his battles took place in eastern Germany, one of his few military allies, Duke Ferdinand of Brunswick, with an army made up of Hessians and Hanoverians subsidized by Britain, fought the French in and out of Hanover, Frankfurt and Cassel.

Very little is known of Mayer Amschel's life in Hanover except that the city was invested several times, and that he made the acquaintance of General von Estorff, an ardent numismatist who was so impressed by the boy's rare coins that he employed him to help with his own collection. The general does not seem to have been very active in the war; but he followed Duke Ferdinand's fortunes closely, as much of the fighting took place in the principality of Hesse-Cassel, not far from Hanover, which was owned by his friend, the Landgrave Frederick II.

Indeed, when peace was signed in 1763 the general accepted an invitation to join the court of the Landgrave's son and heir, Prince William, who had been fighting in the Duke of Brunswick's army.

Although William's father ruled from Cassel, which had been occupied by the French for several years, the Prince had inherited a property from his grandfather in Hanau, on the outskirts of Frankfurt, where he had the power of life and death over fifty thousand people.

A few months later Mayer Amschel followed in the general's footsteps and made his way south. Some biographers puzzle as to why he left Hanover, where Jews had a tolerable life, for the oppression of the Frankfurt ghetto. But the truth was that the city on the Main vibrated with energy and excitement, and offered more hope of riches than any other place in Germany. Lying as it did, close to the Rhine, it was brash and competitive, and one of the great centres of Europe. For centuries its merchants had exploited its geographical position by organizing fairs which attracted buyers from every part of the continent. Perhaps the most famous event was the autumn Trade Fair, started in the eighteenth century by the ambitious owner of a printing press. It drew a monster crowd of 400,000 people, and to this very day remains an annual fixture.

The Jewish community did everything in its power to increase Frankfurt's trade, as trade was one of the few occupations open to their race. They accelerated business by initiating bills of exchange, a novelty on the continent, the equivalent of the modern cheque. 'I

Frankfurt in the mid-eighteenth century.

don't think I exaggerate,' wrote a diarist, 'when I aver that, without the Jews, our city would not be as flourishing or as important as it now is.' Silver was heavy and dangerous to carry. The fact that visitors could buy without paying in cash not only increased sales but earned Frankfurt a reputation for modern methods.

Apart from being drawn by the city's magnetism, Mayer Rothschild was eager to exploit his acquaintanceship with General von Estorff and to establish a link with Prince William of Hesse. The latter was a rich man and if a Rothschild succeeded in winning his confidence there was no telling what the future might hold.

The German princes of the eighteenth century were famous for their unsatisfactory family relationships; and the Hesse-Cassels were no exception. The son of the Landgrave, Frederick II, was estranged from his wife, and rarely saw his sons and daughters. The trouble had started when he abandoned the Protestant faith and became a Roman Catholic. His consort, a daughter of George II of England, was so outraged that she had packed her belongings, scooped up her children from the nursery and left her husband's roof never to return. As the Hesse family owned a great many houses she was not homeless; but any suggestion that her offspring should come into contact with their father's pernicious ideas threw her into such hysterics that the notion was always abandoned. Supported by her father-in-law, the ruling Landgrave at that time, she sent her two sons to Copenhagen to be educated under the vigilant eye of her sister, the Queen of Denmark. The eldest boy, Prince William, struck up a friendship with his cousin, Princess Caroline, whom he wed years later when he was twenty-one. His younger brother obediently followed suit and married Caroline's sister.

Meanwhile the old Landgrave had died and the unrepentant Catholic convert, Frederick II, moved to Cassel where he resided without family in solitary splendour. From this small capital, 120 miles north of Frankfurt, he ruled over an area fifty miles square, containing 330,000 inhabitants. As much of his territory had been ruined by the fighting in the Seven Years War, his main task was to restore prosperity. He revised the land laws, instigated a new system of weights and measures and introduced the potato, hitherto unknown in Germany. He lived very frugally in an ugly palace and attended mass twice a day, praying to God to have mercy on his soul.

His son, the Crown Prince William, was a very different kettle of fish. He was neither religious nor conscientious. He lived in a beautiful schloss at Hanau, ten miles from the centre of Frankfurt, which had been left to him by his grandfather. He had a talent for stitching and carpentry and a good eye for buying pictures. The only trait he seemed to have inherited from his father was thrift, which in middle age turned to avarice and in old age to miserliness. As a young man he cared about only two things, both odd for the times: making

money and siring illegitimate children. As a bride Caroline of
Denmark was a bitter disappointment. She was so repelled by the
sexual act that she screamed when William approached her. However, she submitted long enough to give him three children. Not
surprisingly he turned to more sensual ladies for comfort, and
apparently was so potent that almost every woman he slept with
became pregnant. Some biographers claim that he fathered seventy
children; others set the figure at forty; the most conservative at
twenty-one.

The Prince's sexual activity did not preclude love. After fathering
half a dozen bastards by a woman who has faded into oblivion, he
became greatly attached to the daughter of an apothecary, Fräulein
Ritter, who became his mistress in the early 1770s and bore him
eight children. As she presided over his table and ran his household,
he took the trouble to write to the Holy Roman Emperor to secure
for their joint progeny patents of nobility; and for the lady herself
the respectable title 'Frau von Lindenthal'.

William threw himself into the business of making money with
the same fervour as in procreation. He studied the investment market
each day and loaned out his gold to those who could couple security
with high rates of interest. Unlike the Christian burghers of
Frankfurt he admired the Jews for their financial acumen and learned
as much as he could from them. He was receptive to any scheme that
would increase his capital. Indeed in 1765 when General von Estorff
convinced him that rare coins would appreciate in value he decided
to begin a collection, and he welcomed the suggestion that Mayer
Amschel Rothschild be summoned to the schloss to show his wares.

No one knows whether or not the Prince and the Jew met on this
occasion. Romantic story tellers insist that William was playing
chess with Estorff when Mayer was ushered into the room. The Jew
stood watching the game in silence. Suddenly His Highness looked
up. 'Do you know anything of chess?' Mayer pointed to the board.
'Perhaps if Your Highness moved this piece . . .' Defeat, of course,
was turned to victory and William congratulated the general on
sending him 'no fool'.

Although some biographers scoff at the account, arguing that it
was most unlikely that a Jewish pedlar would be admitted into the
presence of a prince, it seems equally unlikely that such a keen
bargainer as William would allow his underlings to buy coins for
him. Whatever the truth of the matter two facts are clear: Mayer
Amschel sold coins to the Prince for the next four years at ridiculously low prices, and in 1769 claimed his reward by submitting to his
'lofty Princely Serenity' a humble petition 'for the advantage of
being appointed Crown Agent to the Prince of Hesse-Hanau'.

I am making so bold as to beg for this with more confidence in the
assurance that by so doing I am not giving any trouble; while for my part

such a distinction would lift up my commercial standing and be of help to
me in so many other ways that I feel certain thereby to make my way and
fortune in the city of Frankfurt.[2]

Mayer was not asking an outrageous favour. The designation
merely signified that the merchant had done business with the
royalty in question; and that the royalty was willing to advertise the
fact. It corresponded to the modern practice of displaying a coat-of-
arms with the fiction: 'By special appointment'. And yet, because it
was not automatic, it was an honour.

Although Mayer showed a certain amount of effrontery in pushing his claim on the basis of having sold a few coins to His Serene
Highness, his extreme candour was refreshing. Moreover he knew
his Prince; and his Prince clearly intended to continue to snap up
coins at bargain prices, as the request was granted. Mayer celebrated
the news by investing in wig and pigtail, donning a three-cornered
hat and pinning a lace jabot under his coat front. He was right to
array himself as splendidly as possible for he was the first Jew to tack
the Crown Agent's sign on the front of his house, and the event
created a stir in the ghetto. Not only were the neighbours impressed
but the Rothschild's landlord suddenly relented and allowed Mayer
to buy the freehold of the House of the Saucepan, something he had
been trying to do for seven years. Most important of all, Wolf
Schnapper, a well-to-do merchant who lived in the Judengasse
decided that he could fare worse than have Mayer Amschel for a
son-in-law. Mayer was courting Wolf's shrewd, bright-eyed,
seventeen-year-old daughter, Gutle. The father gave the couple his
blessing and the marriage took place in 1770. Mayer's two brothers
moved into another house, and he used the space to set up a money
exchange bureau in one of the bedrooms. He also had an antique
coin catalogue printed which, in his new capacity as Crown Agent,
he sent to all the most illustrious gentlemen in the neighbourhood,
including Goethe's patron, Duke Carl August von Weimar, who
apparently showed no interest.

Yet Mayer Rothschild had no intention of remaining an antique
dealer all his life. He was an odd mixture of the philosopher and the
entrepreneur, a perfect reflection of the two strains that ran through
the ghetto. Because of his coin collection he had acquired an impressive knowledge of the customs of ancient times and liked to
discuss the medieval world with his erudite neighbours. Yet he was
anything but a cultivated man. The moment he opened his mouth he
branded himself as an uneducated ignoramus. Three years at school
had not taught him to master the German language; not only was he
unable to write it, but he could not speak it correctly. He talked in a
comical mixture of Yiddish-Deutsch, the dialect of the ghetto.

Apparently he was not troubled by these deficiencies for he had a gentle, courtly way about him that pleased and charmed his betters. His ambition was to make money, and his immediate aim to persuade the vastly rich William of Hanau to give him some business. Banking was in such an elementary state that men of property had to pay high commissions for the management of their cash incomes. Loaning out money often meant physically dispatching bullion to the borrower; collecting interest literally meant collecting the coin and bringing it to the lender.

Prince William employed a number of people to look after his affairs, including two old, established firms, the Bethmann Brothers and Ruppell and Harnier, as well as half-a-dozen Jewish middle-men who received generous commissions for their trouble. Yet although Mayer courted His Serene Highness year after year, selling his coins at ridiculously low prices, the Prince was satisfied that his investments were well handled and refused to employ newcomers.

So Mayer Amschel jogged along selling cloth and tobacco and wine, running his *Wechselstube* and hoping that the future would bring him a windfall of royal florins. Nevertheless, he earned a comfortable livelihood, something in the region of £4 a week, the same income that the prosperous Goethe family enjoyed. Encouraged by affluence, the Rothschilds produced a torrent of children in the 1770s, many of whom died. The survivors of this decade consisted of a daughter and three sons, Amschel, Salomon and Nathan; in the 1780s three more daughters and a son, Carl; and in the 1790s a daughter and a son, James.†

Meanwhile His Serene Highness, William of Hanau, and his father, the Landgrave were busy carving out a fantastic new fortune for themselves. Ever since the beginning of the century the rulers of Hesse-Cassel had hired out Hessian soldiers to the highest bidder. The Duke of Marlborough had been a customer; also Frederick the Great during the War of the Austrian Succession. Even in the Seven Years War the old Landgrave, William VIII, (Frederick's father and William's grandfather) had struck an amazing bargain with George II of England. His Britannic Majesty hired a regiment of Hessians whom he lent to the Duke of Brunswick, who, in turn, employed them to defend their Hessian villages against the French. The Landgrave could compliment himself, for it was not everyone who managed to make someone else pay for the defence of one's own hearth and home.

As George III's North American subjects began to make trouble in the 1770s more than one German prince smelled a chance of gain. According to Burke the sky above the British Treasury was alive with royal vultures; but no family struck such a fantastic bargain as

---

†Mayer Amschel gave all five sons the name of Mayer. Although they were always known as Amschel Mayer, Salomon Mayer, Carl Mayer etc., in order to avoid confusion for the reader Father Mayer will be the only Mayer of this period while the sons will be referred to by their distinctive names alone.

the Hesse-Cassels who were more experienced than anyone in 'trafficking in valour'. The new Landgrave, the Catholic Frederick II managed to conscript an army of seventeen thousand men which meant that one out of every three able-bodied youths were forced to join the colours. Thousands tried to escape impressment by fleeing to neighbouring states, but the princes prided themselves on solidarity and kept their eyes open for 'deserters' who were put in irons and quickly sent back to their rightful kingdoms.

Even Prince William managed to scrape up an army of two thousand men in tiny Hanau. He drilled the soldiers himself and was known as a stickler for shining buttons and boots. He insisted that the officers' pigtails should be of uniform length and frequently went down the lines on the parade ground with a measuring tape in his hands.

Although Hessian soldiers were not in the least extraordinary the Landgrave made history by driving the hardest bargain ever known for mercenaries with the British Government. He induced London to sign what he called 'a subsidy contract'; apart from a guaranteed flat sum, an extra fee was payable for each man wounded, and still another for each man killed. Furthermore the contract would not cease when the fighting stopped, but only when the Hessians had been back in Germany for at least twelve months. Altogether he was believed to have netted £5,000,000 from these arrangements. Indeed, huge sums of money were still flowing into his treasury in 1785, when he had a heart attack at his midday meal and died an hour later. Upon reading his father's will William learned to his great joy that he was the richest prince in Europe, with an inheritance in the vicinity of forty or fifty million thalers, (between £8,000,000 and £10,000,000), an almost unheard of sum for the times. The Prince moved his court, his officials, his mistresses and bastards from Hanau to Cassel; and because he was short of space commissioned an Italian architect to present him with plans for a fine new palace.

The House of the Green Shield to which Mayer Amschel Rothschild and his family moved in 1785.

The same year that Prince William moved to Cassel, Mayer Amschel Rothschild moved from the Saucepan to the House of the Green Shield. This new dwelling was a semi-detached residence, one half of which was occupied by the Schiff family, who had taken their name from the gay little boat painted on a sign over their door. Their descendants were destined to become distinguished American bankers who do business with the Rothschilds to this day.

As the ghetto was fiercely overcrowded it was a miracle that any house had become available and the Rothschilds regarded it as a direct portent of the Lord's favour. The new residence was not as damp as the Saucepan and had the rare advantage of possessing a pump. It was a three-storied house, narrow and dark, and almost unbearably small for a family which eventually consisted of five girls and five boys. All ten children had to share one bedroom, for apart from the sitting room, known as the Green Room because of the colour of the upholstery, there were only three rooms. One was occupied by the Rothschild parents, and one used as a money exchange bureau, the first Rothschild bank.

The great asset of the house was its much cherished terrace looking on to the back yard. As Jews were not allowed to set foot in the Frankfurt public gardens, the family could sit out of doors in the fine weather, Gutle sewing, Mayer talking about the carefully tended pots of flowers. Here under the ghetto stars they celebrated the Feast of the Tabernacles which must not be held under a roof.

The house had other excitements. Every time the front door opened a bell clanged, a feature introduced some years earlier when pogroms were frequent and even the police could be unfriendly. The wooden stairs creaked and every passage had hidden shelves and cupboards built to overcome the shortage of space. Across the back yard was a shed which covered nine square feet where the girls played house. When the children grew older Mayer Amschel turned the shed into a counting house. It contained a large iron chest which was so cunningly contrived that it would open only if the lid was lifted from the back near the hinges. The chest itself was a decoy, covering a trap door which led to an underground room quite separate from the cellar. Here Mayer Amschel kept his money and account books. In 1785 he could not know how precious his hiding place would prove to be in twenty years time.

The Rothschilds had no secrets from their children. Crowded together, life might have been intolerable; instead it was an adventure, for from their earliest days they were part of the family struggle. Mayer Amschel imbued everything he touched with a sense of urgency; for others success might mean fame or luxury but for them it would open doors to a new world. Solidarity was what mattered. As a member of a persecuted race he saw life as a challenge, not to the individual but to the whole. 'All the brothers shall stand together,' he taught them, 'all shall be responsible for the action of each one.'

Both Mayer and Gutle were deeply religious. Like other orthodox married women, Gutle cut off her hair and covered her head with a large wig on which she placed an even larger bonnet. At night Mayer took down the Talmud and hummed the sacred words while Gutle sewed and commanded the restless boys to listen. The young Rothschilds showed little taste for philosophy. Their attention wandered from a finely spun casuistical argument; only in the market place did their eyes come alive.

Like their father they rebelled agsinst school, and Mayer allowed each to enter the family business at the ripe age of twelve. Trading seemed to be in their blood for they could calculate before they could read, and their lives revolved around the maxim: buy cheaply, sell dearly.

The boys pursued their objectives with exhausting concentration, no doubt derived from the example of Mayer Amschel's dogged persistence with William of Hesse. For twenty years Mayer had tried in vain to capture a trickle of the Prince's mightly flow of business. When the latter became Landgrave in 1785, and moved north, it would not have been odd if Mayer, now a well-to-do merchant, had washed his hands of the whole unsatisfactory affair. Instead, in 1787 he made the long trip to Cassel to keep in touch with the court.

As usual Mayer sold the Prince antiques; but far from usual was the important new friend he acquired. Although William's wife, poor Caroline of Denmark, lived in the palace with her three children, William's mistress, Frau von Lindenthal, was also present with her eight children. These noisy little bastards, ranging in ages from fifteen to three, were tutored by a schoolmaster, Buderus; and Mayer learned that the man's son, young Carl Buderus, was the rising star of the Landgrave's treasury.

Apparently Carl had come to Prince William's attention two years earlier when he had pointed out that His Serene Highness' milk profit would be increased if he would cease to omit the fractions in his dairy accounts. As the Landgrave was becoming increasingly penurious, counting and recounting his money, and working for hours with paper and pencil figuring out rates of interest, Carl's scheme had thrown him into rhapsodies of delight. He not only promoted Carl over the heads of older men but he put him in charge of his private purse. The following year, when the Prince was complaining about the cost of his many offspring, Buderus suggested a Salt tax. This innovation not only proved an easy tax to administer but brought in so much revenue that after the children's requirements were met he had a delightful surplus. Buderus again was promoted and now was serving as the Landgrave's chief financial adviser.

Carl was amiable, serious and ambitious, not unlike Mayer Amschel himself. The two men seemed to understand each other at once. Mayer presented Carl with a rare and expensive coin as a gift and murmured that he would give him a cut of the profits if he succeeded in persuading His Serene Highness to favour the Rothschilds with some of his business. . . . Nothing happened until 1789 when Mayer paid a second visit to Cassel. Suddenly Buderus' influence made itself felt and Mayer was given £800 of bills to discount for the Landgrave.

Was this tiny episode the start of the Rothschild fortune? Or was it the momentous event of the French Revolution, which shattered the calm of Europe that same year, 1789? No one could know that the curtain was rising on twenty-five years of war, and that the war would create acute shortages which the Rothschilds would be in a unique position to exploit both for themselves and the Landgrave. As usual infant opportunity seemed to be the child of coincidence.

Yet for many, 1790 appeared to herald the end of the world. Prince William's court was crowded with French refugees who could talk of nothing but the Terror. The Landgrave became so fearful that the disease might prove contagious that he could not sleep at night. Envisaging a mob storming his palace and stealing his gold, he decided to delay no further in investing his money in bricks and mortar, much more difficult to displace. He accepted the plans of his Italian architect and commissioned a stupendous new palace on the scale of Versailles. The residence was called Wilhelmshöhe; and although some people said it was too heavy to be beautiful, it was set in a wonderful park, where it stands to this day.

The building took place during the tumultuous years from 1791 to 1798. Indeed, the troubled times seemed to begin as workmen walked onto the site, for in the summer of 1791 the Holy Roman Emperor, Leopold II, followed ministerial advice and met Frederick William II of Prussia to discuss what military action they could take against revolutionary France. 'If the cabinets of foreign courts try to stir up a war of Kings against France,' angrily cried the revolutionary Foreign Minister in Paris, 'we will stir up for them a war of the peoples against the Kings.'

Nevertheless Austria and Prussia took the field against the French in 1792; and for once the Landgrave pledged his whole-hearted support. In a letter to the Archduke Francis of Austria he observed that anyone 'blest by God with any possessions . . . must realize . . . that the war is a universal war declared upon all forms of private property . . .'

The war was fought badly by everyone concerned. The French invasion of Belgium was a fiasco; so was the Austrian-Prussian-Brunswickian invasion of France in the Champagne area. The French general, Custine, managed to cross the Rhine and for a time occupied Frankfurt. He pasted manifestos on the walls calling on the Hessian soldiery to forsake 'the tyrant and tiger who sold their blood in order to fill his chests'.

His Serene Highness was in Cassel, but when he learned of these developments he was so enraged that for the first and only time in his life he financed a few battalions with his own money and drove the invaders out of the city. Although he moaned about the costliness of the operation, he soon recovered what he had spent by signing a subsidy contract with Britain for eight thousand soldiers which the latter threw onto the battlefield.

Although the anti-French coalition grew in size the generalship was incredibly inept and in 1795, at the end of three years of desultory fighting, the Prussian King, a stupid blond giant very different from his uncle, Frederick the Great, left Austria in the lurch by making a separate pact with France. William of Hesse-Cassel, who had become a Prussian field-marshal, was glad to follow suit, as he found it much more lucrative to hire his soldiers to Britain than to

Prince William IX of Hesse–Cassel, wearing the uniform of a Prussian field-marshal.

employ them himself. The new Holy Roman Emperor, Francis II, was furious at what he regarded as a rank piece of treachery, but as he was very short of cash William managed to appease him by loaning him £120,000.

Meanwhile the Rothschild family business was expanding by leaps and bounds. By the 1790s they had half a dozen irons in the fire. Apart from their money bureau and their antiquities they acted as forwarding agents and did a good trade in wine. But the bulk of their business was importing manufactured articles from England, mainly cloth, for re-sale. As the wars continued and the continent became increasingly starved of essential goods, people showed their willingness to pay famine prices. Mayer Amschel doubled and tripled both his orders and his charges and profits soared.

At this point Mayer made a proposition to the enterprising Carl Buderus. England was paying the Landgrave large sums of money for the hire of Hessian soldiers; and the Rothschilds were paying England large sums of money for the goods they were importing. Why not let the two-way movement cancel itself out, and pocket the commissions both ways on the bills of exchange? Buderus agreed, and soon this extra string to the Rothschild bow was producing an impressive revenue.

Indeed every ill wind of the 1790s seemed to blow good to the Rothschilds. When the French invaded the Netherlands in 1795 and brought the Amsterdam Bourse to a close, every Frankfurt financier benefited, including Mayer Amschel; and when the French tried to cut off the Austrian army by bombarding Frankfurt, the Jews were freed from the ghetto. Over 150 houses on the Judengasse were destroyed, which gave the Christian burghers no alternative but to allow the Jewish population to live in the main part of the city. Mayer Amschel was quick to take advantage of the relaxation by renting warehouses and filling them with English imports.

When the 1790s drew to a close the Rothschilds had become rich and independent. The change had taken place in six short years. Until 1794 the family property had been assessed for twenty years at the constant figure of 2000 gulden a year (about £170). Mayer had paid annual taxes amounting to twenty-seven English shillings. Suddenly in 1795 – the year that Holland fell – the amount was doubled; and in the following year the family was placed in the highest category of those earning 15,000 gulden or above. This figure shrouded a fortune for by 1800 Mayer's capital lay in the region of £13,000, making his the eleventh richest family in the ghetto, and far richer than most of the Christian burghers who still smugly patronized them.[3]

Yet the tide had only begun to flow in the Rothschild favour. In 1798 a quarrel took place which must rank as the luckiest altercation in the family's history. If an important Lancashire cotton manufacturer had not annoyed Mayer's third son, the red-headed, hot-

tempered, twenty-one-year-old Nathan, the Rothschilds might
never have sprung into world prominence. As Germany was entirely
dependent on Britain for its cotton goods, English travelling sales-
men were often bad-mannered and arrogant. 'One great trader came
to Frankfurt who had the market all to himself', Nathan explained
years later. 'He was quite the great man, and did us a favour if he
sold us goods. Somehow I offended him and he refused to show me
his patterns. This was on a Tuesday. I said to my father: "I will go to
England". . . . On the Thursday I started.'[4]

Nathan arrived in Manchester with a few letters of introduction
and not a word of English. But he had something even more
valuable: at least £10,000 in cash and the promise from his father
that if he did well he would send him even more capital. Mayer
regarded Nathan as the cleverest of his sons. If anyone could buy
shrewdly it would be Nathan, although at the moment not much
discrimination was necessary as the continent was so starved of goods
that almost anything from England fetched a high price.

Despite the sellers' market, Mayer Amschel and the Landgrave of
Hesse, both in their fifty-seventh year, knew that their future prosperity depended on events outside their control. As the year 1800
slid into being, the name of the newly-created French First Consul,
Napoleon Bonaparte, rang through Europe. The two men watched
the march of events with fervid attention for the new decade, like
the old, was bound to drag them in its rough political wake, and
each nursed a deep concern; the Prince had a fortune to keep and the
Jew a fortune to make.

'As long as I am alive France shall have peace,' Bonaparte told his
ecstatic countrymen; yet within a few months France once again was
at war with Austria. 'Between old monarchies and a young republic
the spirit of hostility must always exist,' Bonaparte explained with
a charming lack of embarrassment. '. . . I believe that, while I fill
my present office, my destiny is to be fighting almost continually.'

Austria, however, was too exhausted to oblige him for long, and
a year later signed the humiliating peace of Lunéville which not only
recognized Napoleon as the master of Italy and the Low Countries,
but acknowledged his ownership of all German territory on the left
bank of the Rhine. In order to placate the dispossessed German
princes the First Consul announced that he would recompense them
at the expense of the Church. William of Hesse-Cassel was one of
the many Serene Highnesses who travelled to Paris for the 'Great
Auction' at which Napoleon wielded the hammer. He returned to
Germany with a large slice of Mainz in his pocket and the title
'Elector' which he had always wanted.

Yet William of Hesse was still unwilling to knuckle under to the
Corsican upstart. He had no wish to alienate England with whom
he did a roaring trade in soldiers, and where he had over £500,000

invested in securities and another £100,000 on loan to the Prince of Wales and the Dukes of York and Clarence. Furthermore, he was deeply impressed by the way in which Britain demonstrated the superiority of sea power.

Such an instance took place in 1802 when Napoleon inveigled Russia, Prussia, Sweden and Denmark into signing a pact of 'armed neutrality', directed against England. The British Admiralty sent a fleet into the Baltic and shattered the alliance in a single afternoon. The ships attacked the Danish flotilla which lay in Copenhagen harbour protected by seven hundred guns. The engagement was so fierce and bloody that the English Admiralty finally gave the order to 'discontinue the action'; but the second in command, Horatio Nelson, turned his blind eye to his telescope and sent out a signal, 'Engage more closely.' Although the British lost 943 men, the Danes suffered casualties of over 1,700 and had the humiliation of seeing many of their ships towed away to England.

The Danish King, a brother-in-law of William of Hesse-Cassel, felt himself badly used for he could not see why the British had picked on him rather than the Prussians or the Swedes. Danish bonds fell in value; and the King's private funds shrank so dramatically that his bankers put out feelers for a loan. But although the Elector of Hesse-Cassel had plenty of money he told Buderus that he was unwilling to lend it to his in-laws as he did not want them to know how rich he was.

Buderus repeated the story to Mayer Amschel who proposed lending the money anonymously. The Elector was delighted with this cunning suggestion and on Buderus' recommendation appointed two middlemen: Rothschild and a Hamburg Jew named Lawaertz. The latter made the approach to Copenhagen. 'The lender,' he wrote, 'is an exceedingly rich capitalist and exceptionally friendly to the Danish Court. It is possible that in the future even greater sums and better conditions may be obtainable from him.' The loan was concluded in September 1803 with instructions that the interest should be paid regularly to Rothschild.

After thirty-six years of persistence Mayer Amschel had done a major piece of business for the Prince. Although the transaction remained secret for many months, eventually he was allowed to alter his Crown Agent sign to read 'Hesse-Cassel' in place of 'Hesse-Hanau'. Mayer recognized, of course, that Buderus was responsible for his good fortune and now offered to make him a secret partner in his business. Carl was delighted. Not only did he like and trust Rothschild but he was only too well aware that he would never grow rich if he relied solely on his salary from the miserly Elector. It was good business on Rothschild's part for during the next three years the Elector made a further six loans to Denmark all of which were handled by Mayer.

Although Prince William paid the commissions promptly he was not an easy man to serve. The artistic impulses and intellectual curiosity of his youth had given way to a neurotic and querulous old age. He could think and talk of nothing but protecting his vast fortune against the uncertainties of war. He was safe while Napoleon was preoccupied in organizing a camp at Boulogne, in building two thousand barges and threatening the British. 'I do not say,' airily pronounced Britain's First Lord of the Admiralty, 'that the French cannot come. I merely say that they cannot come by water.' Apparently the First Consul finally reached the same conclusion for he turned his attention back to the continent; and among those on whom his glance fell was the fabulously rich Elector of Hesse-Cassel.

His Serene Highness squirmed, for he had hoped to remain unnoticed until the winning side had emerged so clearly that he could join it with impunity. Napoleon, however, was eager to enlist the opulent Prince as an ally, and asked him whether he would like to buy a slice of English Hanover. William politely declined, and Bonaparte then invited him to join the Union of Princes who were meeting at Mainz to discuss a Federation of the Rhine. Once again the Prince refused, this time pleading an attack of gout. 'On n'oublie pas,' the French ambassador observed menacingly, pointing out that history was favouring France. The prophecy seemed alarmingly accurate for in 1804 Napoleon proclaimed himself Emperor of the French; and Francis II, well aware that Napoleon's next move would be to supplant him as Holy Roman Emperor gracefully relinquished the title assuming the more modest appellation of Francis I, Emperor of Austria.

Poor William was caught in a cleft stick, for while he was being coerced by France, France's enemies were offering him inducements to join an anti-Napoleon coalition; the bait was a subsidy of £1,250,000 for every hundred thousand men put in the field. As Hesse-Cassel could raise an army of twenty thousand, it would mean a cool quarter of a million pounds in the Prince's pocket.

The fact that he was too frightened to accept this tantalizing offer, made William more irritable than ever. Even his mistress of thirty years, Frau von Lindenthal, could not stand his bad temper any longer, and ran off with a subaltern half her age. William consoled himself with a young Russian beauty, Caroline von Schlotheim, who tried to soothe him as he strode through his great palace, locking and unlocking the doors that led to his hundreds of treasure chests.

The trunks took up one whole wing of the palace and contained everything from jewels to *objets d'art*, from silver to pictures, from mortgage documents to porcelain. Half belonged to the Prince; the other half to borrowers who had been obliged to put up collateral. Apart from this he had some ten million thalers (about £1,800,000) in cash or bills of exchange.

In 1805 Mayer Amschel instructed his eldest son, thirty-two-year-old Amschel, to remain in Cassel so as to be on hand in case the

Elector had any sudden business impulses. But William was not in a
fit state to think clearly. He inveighed against the forces that
threatened his property; and when Austria, along with Russia,
joined the anti-French coalition, and announced that as she was short
of bullion in future she would pay interest on loans in paper rather
than specie, the Prince became hysterical. He wrote to Emperor
Francis II reminding him of his loan of £120,000 and begging him
to make an exception in his case. The Austrian ambassador, von
Wessenberg, advised the sovereign to try and pacify him as His
Majesty might want to borrow more money. 'Since avarice is the
Elector's greatest weakness,' he counselled Francis, 'to grant Frau
von Schlotheim the title of Countess without payment might be
the best way of quietening him.' The Emperor acted accordingly
but the Elector continued to rant and rave against his cruel fate.

Carl Buderus and Mayer Rothschild begged the Prince to loan
out more of his money, arguing that it was safer outside the country
than stored at Wilhelmshöhe. The Elector did not agree. Already
half the crowned heads of Europe were in his debt, as well as scores
of petty rulers. Altogether he had some thirty million thalers
(c. £6,000,000) out on loan – not to mention the pounds sterling in
England – and he insisted that this sum already was much too large
for complacency. Furthermore he was not sure that he wanted
Mayer to handle any more of his business. The Bethmann brothers
and Ruppell and Harnier had discovered that the 'ghetto firm', as
they called the Rothschilds, had ousted them from their profitable
trade. Ruppell and Harnier had started a whispering campaign
against old Mayer and the Elector was inclined to believe what was
being said. Buderus, of course, did his best to dispel the malicious
talk but William stubbornly clung to his own notions.

The truth was that His Serene Highness was so harassed by the
turn the war was taking that it was difficult to talk to him at all. He
clung to the hope that Russia and Austria might deliver a mighty
blow to Napoleon's Grand Army. Not only would such a development send the price of his English bonds soaring, but it would
encourage bankers to lend to Vienna, perhaps enabling him to call
in his loan from the Emperor. Unfortunately, his hopes were dashed,
for Napoleon attacked the Austrians at Ulm before the Russians had
time to come to their assistance, and the Russians at Austerlitz before
the Prussians made up their mind to join the coalition.

The guns of Austerlitz blew the anti-Bonaparte coalition to
pieces. The Russians made their way home; the Austrians sued for
peace; even Britain felt the blow. 'I, too, was hit at Austerlitz,'
murmured William Pitt before he died. Napoleon stripped Austria
of the German Empire and established a German Confederation of
the Rhine, composed of sixteen reigning kings and princes, with
himself as Protector.

Too late Prussia saw the danger and began to prepare for war,

The establishment of the German Confederation of the Rhine: the German kings and princes swear allegiance to their Protector, Napoleon.

frantically trying to draw to her side her traditional ally, Hesse-Cassel. But William was so overwrought that not even his Countess could comfort him. First he plastered his principality with signs saying '*Pays Neutre*'. Then he behaved like a lunatic in trying to ingratiate himself with both sides. He got in touch with the French Government and asked to be assigned the city of Frankfurt in exchange for his neutrality; at the same time he wrote to the Prussian King declining to be his ally but offering to hire him twenty thousand Hessian soldiers for the quarter of a million pounds he had itched to accept the year before. When his offer was accepted he argued that this piece of business in no way infringed his neutrality. Unfortunately both Prussians and Hessians were routed by Napoleon at Jena, then at Auerstadt. In October 1806 Bonaparte entered Berlin in triumph. When he visited the tomb of Frederick the Great with his aides-de-camp he said: 'Hats off, gentlemen – if he were still alive we should not be here.'

The French Emperor then turned his attention to the Elector of Hesse-Cassel; and by doing so unwittingly opened Aladdin's Cave to the Rothschilds.

27

Chapter II

The Rothschilds and Napoleon

(1806–15)

'*Y*OU WILL,' NAPOLEON COMMANDED MARSHAL MORTIER, who was moving on Cassel, 'seal up all treasures and stores and appoint General Lagrange as Governor of the country . . . . My object is to remove the House of Hesse-Cassel from rulership and to strike it out of the list of powers.'[1]

For the preceeding ten days Wilhelmshöhe had been plunged into feverish activity. Coaches carrying chests of gold and silver and guarded by a posse of soldiers left for Copenhagen and Prague. But there was no time to send away everything. Fifty trunks of jewellery, silver plate, antiques and the whole collection of coins and medals, to which Rothschild had contributed so many valuable specimens, were hidden under the stairs and in secret passages. More valuables, including mortgage documents and bonds, were concealed in Lewenburg Castle, which stood in Wilhelmshöhe Park, while further treasures were sent to Sababurg Castle in the middle of a remote forest.

Soon French troops were encamped on the heights surrounding Cassel. The Elector could see their camp fires from the windows of his castle, and, alternating between tears of despair and rage, he despatched adjutant after adjutant to Mortier begging to be given a hearing. But Napoleon was implacable. When the marshal eventually sent an envoy to the Elector, the latter carried a personal ultimatum from the Emperor significantly addressed: 'To the Elector of Hesse-Cassel, Field-Marshal in the service of Prussia.'

Although William returned a grovelling letter offering to throw in his lot with France and to join the Confederation of the Rhine, his pleas were in vain and he was given to understand that unless he left the country he would be made a prisoner of war. Indeed Napoleon was so determined to avoid a misunderstanding that he not only sent instructions to Mortier but to Lagrange himself. 'Have all the artillery, ordinance stores, furniture, statues and other articles in the palace of the Court brought to Mainz. . . . I shall not continue to suffer a hostile Prince on my boundaries, especially one who is practically a Prussian, not to say an Englishman, and who sells his subjects . . .'[2]

On the night before French troops swarmed into Cassel a member of the Elector's staff aroused the Austrian ambassador, Baron von Wessenberg, from his slumbers, and handed him for safe keeping a casket of jewels and envelopes containing £100,000 in valid bills of exchange. An hour later Carl Buderus banged on the Baron's door and delivered two chests crammed with securities which he begged the ambassador to look after. Meanwhile the Elector was fleeing the country in a coach and six. He reached one gate to find French soldiers on sentry duty but managed to escape by another. Late the next day he arrived at Gottorp, in Denmark, and moved into the palace of his younger brother, Carl. The latter had also married a Danish princess and was Resident Governor of the Duchies of Schleswig and Holstein, which he administered from Gottorp.

Buderus remained in Cassel and tried to soften the effect of the occupation. The new governor, General Lagrange, was a bluff and amiable soldier who liked the good things of life. He carried out the Emperor's orders and was successful beyond expectation. Within two days he had discovered all fifty chests of Electoral treasures hidden in the walls of Wilhelmshöhe. The silver table-ware was sent to Mainz to be melted down, while the collection of rare coins and antiques was dispatched to Paris for auctioning.

At this point Carl Buderus intervened. He called on General Lagrange and after a conversation filled with very obvious innuendoes, left 260,000 francs (£10,800) on the table and departed. The following day the general returned to the Hessian officials forty-two trunks containing securities, title deeds and ledgers. He then reported to Napoleon that the Prince's worth was about 10,000,000 thalers (£2,000,000) less than a quarter of the true value.

Nineteen of the chests were sent to the vaults of Preye and Jordis in Frankfurt, while another four, containing William's Privy Council minutes were despatched to the House of the Green Shield during the Spring Fair of 1807. The ledgers not only revealed the true extent of the Prince's wealth but contained a list of his debtors and the interest received from them. As Napoleon had instructed his officials 'to seize the Prince's revenue' it was essential to prevent the information from falling into the hands of the French. Mayer Amschel concealed the trunks in the secret cellar built to hide Jews from their persecutors.

Meanwhile Napoleon issued his famous decree establishing his continental blockade against England. He could not make himself master of Europe until he had brought the mistress of the seas to submission; and as invasion was impractical, he must conquer her by privation. If he could destroy the gold reserves of the Bank of England he believed that he would destroy the fabric of her industrial society. In his optimistic moods he envisaged an unemployed and starving population, and finally a revolution that would place in power a government amenable to Bonapartist ideas.

Napoleon overlooked the fact, however, that the continent needed British goods just as much as Britain needed continental markets. War-torn Europe was starved of everything from overcoats to shoes; from cottons and silks to sugar and coffee. Pressure from the public made the edict difficult to enforce and for the first few years the inconvenience lay mainly in higher prices.

Napoleon seemed bent on improving the Rothschilds' lot in life, for his actions of November 1806 – the seizure of Hesse-Cassel and the imposition of the continental blockade – resulted in extreme good fortune for the family. The Elector, cowering in Denmark, had no option but to entrust Carl Buderus with his finances; and Buderus immediately appointed Mayer Amschel his chief banker. The blockade was advantageous in two ways for it not only increased Mayer's Frankfurt business but opened new fields for Nathan in London.

This red-headed youth with the sagging lower lip and the bulbous blue eyes had done brilliantly during the six years he had lived in Manchester. In his father's shop he had known only one profession, that of distributor, but in England he began to buy semi-finished goods, had them dyed, parcelled them out for manufacture and finally sold the end product. 'I soon found there were three profits,' he wrote years later. By 1804 he had increased his capital to £50,000, and decided to move to London where he could extend his activities to the stock market.

Here he met Levi Cohen, a linen merchant who had left his native Holland in 1770 and opened an accounting house in Angel's Court, Throgmorton Street, and became the richest Jew in England. Apparently Cohen was greatly taken with the energetic Rothschild despite the fact that the young man spoke abominable English; almost as bad, Nathan admitted, as his German. But he excused himself by saying that there was no time for frills as there was too much to do. Levi had a surplus of beautiful daughters and was eager that all of them should marry well. He was therefore delighted when Nathan, who appeared to have an impressive bank account, asked permission to court Hannah Cohen.

Soon, however, the young man was gambling in gold bullion, leaping in and out of the market with exhausting enthusiasm. Now Levi began to wonder. Nathan's large, bulging eyes seemed a little wild. Could he be taking such chances with his own money? Or was he an irresponsible gambler, acting as a broker for someone else? Politely and prudently Levi asked Nathan for proof of his wealth, but the hot-tempered suitor angrily refused, snapping that Levi could not do better than to give him all his daughters in marriage. Father Cohen was amused by the effrontery, and the wedding took place in October 1806, a month before the blockade was imposed. Hannah did not come empty-handed. She brought Nathan a dowry of £10,000.

Nathan wrote to his father that he was confident that he could increase any funds entrusted to him and urged him to send whatever capital he could lay his hands on. Mayer passed the message to Buderus, who was leaving for Gottorp to pay his first visit to his

Nathan, or 'N. M.' as he was called, third son of Mayer Amschel Rothschild and founder of the English branch.

difficult master, all the more difficult now that he was in exile. On this occasion, however, the Elector was so overjoyed to learn that Buderus had managed to prevent large sums of money from falling into enemy hands that he raised him to the nobility with the title 'von Carlhausen'. He also gave him the equivalent of 'power of attorney', which meant that in future the latter could handle William's resources at his own discretion. However the Elector's temperament was alarmingly mercurial. One moment he was over-joyed, the next plunged into the depths of despair, complaining of his bad luck. He particularly resented the fact that when the Danish Crown Prince visited Gottorp he, William, was obliged to move out of the palatial apartment lent to him by his brother and accommodate himself in a miserable suite of rooms in the opposite wing.

Buderus remained with his master a week, outlining strategic plans for the future; but the old man could talk of nothing but the Countess von Schlotheim whom he referred to as 'my best friend for whom I wait yearningly'. At last the lady arrived with her child-ren in tow – she eventually had nine – and set about making her lover more comfortable. She rented a house, first at Rendsburg,

31

Two miniatures illustrating the
traditional story of the founding of
the Rothschild fortune: the Elector of
Hesse entrusting Mayer Amschel
Rothschild with his treasure and the
return of the chests a few years later.

then at Itzehoe, both spacious, and well staffed with servants. 'I feel almost at home again,' William wrote, a momentary change from his endless complaints.

His chief worry, of course, was his money and when Buderus took his leave he begged him almost piteously to do his best for him. As soon as the latter reached Cassel he sent a message to Mayer Rothschild in Frankfurt asking if he personally would undertake the collection of interest on the money that the Elector had out on loan. Very large sums were in the hands of German and Austrian princes and aristocrats. Mayer was determined to exploit a position which he had struggled to achieve for nearly half a century and readily agreed.

Yet the assignment was fraught with danger. The French were swarming over most of Germany, and Napoleon had announced that since Hesse-Cassel no longer existed all money owing to the Elector was to be paid to the French Treasury. There was certain difficulty in enforcing this imperious edict as the French officials did not know the name of the debtors. They suspected, however, that Mayer Rothschild of Frankfurt might have valuable information on the subject and went so far as to offer him 25 per cent commission on whatever debts he collected.

The old man nodded but remained scrupulously loyal to the Elector. Soon he had pressed all the members of his family into his subversive activities. His two eldest sons, Amschel and Salomon, were left in charge of the Frankfurt business which meant receiving and distributing smuggled goods; while he himself and his two youngest boys, eighteen-year-old Carl and fourteen-year-old James, travelled about Germany in a coach with specially constructed compartments, scooping up the bullion belonging to His Serene Highness. They had their own secret language, the usual jumble of Yiddish and German, and a code of pseudonyms. Mayer Amschel was known romantically as 'Arnoldi' while the Prince was judaized into 'Goldstein'. Occasionally Mayer made the seven-day journey to Schleswig to consult the Prince, but the constant jogging on the rough roads made him so ill that Carl Rothschild gradually took over as the principal family courier. Although at first some of the debtors protested against repaying William for fear of offending the invader the majority responded, for they knew that if they needed money in the future the Elector would be a better bet than the French Government.

Mayer Rothschild tried to lessen the dangers he was incurring by winning the friendship of powerful protectors. In 1807 Hesse-Cassel was incorporated into the kingdom of Westphalia, while Frankfurt became the capital of the Confederation of the Rhine, administered by a German primate, the Grand Duke Carl von Dalberg. Luckily for Mayer Amschel, the Grand Duke not only had liberal ideas but was a spendthrift. Mayer advanced him money on easy terms and

pressed him to relax the restrictions on the Jews. Dalberg finally granted the community political equality with the Christians, and the right to have their own governing body, but made them pay a huge price for it, half a million gulden (£48,000). Mayer Amschel himself put up half the sum demanded, a large chunk which went straight into von Dalberg's pocket.

Despite the high cost, the Duke's friendship stood Mayer in good stead, for during 1807 Napoleon's police spies became suspicious that Rothschild was acting as a banker to the Elector and demanded to see his accounts. As he kept two sets of ledgers he gladly allowed them to peruse the ones that had been written up by his daughter-in-law for their special benefit. Not satisfied, the police called on the Duke von Dalberg who assured them that Mayer was wholly law-abiding and most unlikely to be engaged in illegal pursuits.

In Cassel Mayer's close friend, Carl Buderus, was using the same methods of bribery to ingratiate himself with Napoleon's profligate brother, Jerome, the new King of Westphalia. Jerome had moved into the Elector's palace, Wilhelmshöhe, and complained bitterly of the frugal meals and provincial outlook of the local gentry. The miserly Elector was furious to think of such an extravagant man living in his palace and cried poverty to all who would listen, despite the fact that he had thousands of pounds in cash and regularly received large sums from Buderus, as part of the debts collected by Mayer.

Buderus was conscious of the great risks that his friend Rothschild was undergoing, and as a reward gave him the less arduous and equally profitable assignment of discounting the English and Danish interest payments which now came as drafts directly to Rothschild. As the Elector had £600,000 invested in England, his income from this source alone lay in the region of £2,000 a month.

Apparently this arrangement was deeply resented by Ruppell and Harnier, the rival bankers, who had formerly handled the bulk of the Elector's business. Bethmann Brothers, the other firm in a similar position, had bowed out gracefully but in June 1807 Herr Ruppell himself went to Rendsburg to lay his case before the Prince. He argued that although he had never failed His Serene Highness, he had been victimized by Rothschild who seemed to have some sinister hold over Buderus, perhaps blackmail. The Elector was always a prey to suspicion and became greatly agitated by the suggestion, particularly as he had just received a letter from his Hessian business manager in London, Lorentz, informing him that Nathan Rothschild had approached him for a loan. Upon being refused, Nathan had intimated that he would get the money anyway by writing to his father.

The jealous Lorentz intended this story to anger the Elector and was more successful than he could have hoped, as the Elector not only punished Buderus by entrusting Herr Ruppell with an import-

The palace of Wilhelmshöhe, built by William of Hesse between 1791 and 1798, on the slopes of the Habicht-wald.

35

ant financial transaction, but informed his Privy Councillor that the English and Danish cheques being cashed by Rothschild should be sent to him at his new residence in Itzehoe, untouched. 'I shall expect from you,' he thundered, 'an immediate acknowledgement of this decision and your compliance therewith.'[3] At the same time he wrote to Lorentz in London, and told him to give Nathan Rothschild no reply whatsoever if he should again venture to inquire into the Elector's financial affairs.

The Elector's actions came as a bombshell, particularly as Rothschild and Buderus were desperately anxious to transmit money to Nathan in London who assured them that he could guarantee the Elector the three or four per cent he desired, but in fact make ten or twelve per cent, entitling them to pocket the difference. Now not only were their immediate plans upset, but Buderus felt that his whole future lay in the balance. Nevertheless he did not hurry to re-establish himself with his master, for he had a shrewd understanding of the latter's character. He sent the cheques to Itzehoe as requested and delayed the trip to Denmark until September. When he finally confronted His Serene Highness he was a perfect picture of injured dignity.

The first evening the Elector did most of the talking. He told Buderus that he could not understand why he wanted to give all his business to a Jew of obscure antecedents, and that he was greatly concerned that Rothschild was employed to the exclusion of such respectable firms as Ruppell and Harnier and even more particularly of the Bethmann Brothers, whose prestige stood so high. Buderus did not reply until the next day when he had had time to assemble his arguments. He reminded the Elector of the risks that Mayer Rothschild had run for him, travelling around Germany collecting the Elector's interest payments. The very fact that his origins were obscure was in his favour; he had more to gain than the well-established Bethmanns and far surpassed them in energy and determination. Furthermore, the Bethmanns' financial resources had given out in 1806 when Prussia was overrun. The Rothschilds, he continued, were punctual with their payments; always quoted the exact rate of exchange prevailing on the day of a sale; and knew how to hold their tongues. 'And,' added Buderus, 'since I am unable to discover the smallest difference between a florin of Rothschild and a florin of Bethmann I thought that I was doing everything for the best. It hurts me, however, to observe that your Prince-Electoral Serenity, to judge by yesterday's verbal utterance, does not seem graciously to approve. I should therefore like to ask for definite instructions as to how the English cheques are to be disposed of in future.'

But before His Serene Highness could reply, Buderus added that he was in duty bound to say: 'Had your Prince-Electoral Serenity been most graciously content not to interfere in my business I could have sold £20,000 sterling at 141½. Today they are worth at least 6,000 florins less, and no human ingenuity on earth can now prevent that loss.'[4]

This last broadside demolished the Elector's defences. That money should be lost through his interventions was an anxiety he could not bear. He reaffirmed his faith in his adviser and once again empowered him to handle all his finances in whatever way he saw fit. He excused his behaviour by grief that his beloved Hesse-Cassel had been incorporated into Westphalia, and was being ruled by a parvenu and a wastrel.

A few months later Napoleon's army moved into the Duchies of Schleswig and Holstein and Prince William was once more forced to flee. Disguised as a woman, he travelled in a carriage piled high with bales made to look like cotton, but filled with treasures and money. The vehicle lost a wheel in a town swarming with the French and the passengers had to transfer themselves and their belongings to another carriage; but neither the Elector nor his companion, the Countess von Schlotheim, was noticed or molested.

William settled near Prague, in Bohemia, which was part of the Austrian Empire. He bought a Palace on the Kleinseite, where he maintained a household of thirty-six people, and a castle at Bubenetsch where he held courts. Nevertheless he pretended to be living on the bread-line and gave his guests disgusting food. 'Personal association with him is indescribably unpleasant,' wrote an official of the Prussian Government. 'The greatest patience is required to put up with his endless complaints and sudden outbursts.'[5]

Once again the Rothschild–Buderus axis swung into action but this time in a daring and unorthodox way. The partners began the operation that was to lay the foundation of the Rothschild fortune and to make Buderus a rich man. In his difficult interview with the Elector Buderus not only had restrained himself but had emerged with more authority than ever before. The Elector had to rely on someone, and Buderus had impressed him by his quiet dignity; so once again the latter filled the role of chief financial advisor.

But Buderus was not content to serve the Elector forever without a suitable reward. He had his own family to think of, and was greatly taken by Mayer Rothschild's enthusiastic insistence that if he could divert sufficient sums to Nathan in London, the boy could double and treble the money very rapidly to the benefit of all of them. Nathan lived in a sellers' market. Not only was the continent increasingly starved of merchandise, but the London stock market was rising steadily. Furthermore, silver coin and gold bullion were in such short supply that anyone with enough money to buy specie, and hold it, could not fail to make enormous gains. What the Rothschilds would have liked was to borrow money directly from the Elector at the current rate of interest, but Buderus understood his master well enough to know that he would never lend money to upstarts like the Rothschilds. The Elector was a snob and only liked to do business with kings or princes or aristocrats. Besides, what security could the Rothschilds offer him?

Nevertheless, Buderus was able to raise some cash without referring the matter to the Elector. He allowed Mayer Rothschild to retain at three per cent interest the debts he collected for the Elector; and Mayer of course forwarded the money to Nathan. Next, Buderus authorized Mayer to instruct the Elector's Dutch brokers in London, the van Trottens, that the interest payments on the Elector's £600,000, invested in British securities, was no longer to be sent to Frankfurt but to be paid directly to Nathan. Although Nathan would pay three per cent interest for the use of the money, the arrangement was to be kept secret from the Elector's London agent, Lorentz, and of course from the Elector himself. This was not easy for Prince William was demanding to see Buderus' accounts. 'It is surely most graciously known,' Buderus wrote firmly to William, 'that my papers are hidden away, so that I could not (even if I had the time) possibly work at my accounts.'[6]

Buderus' excuses were valid as both he and the Rothschilds lived in constant danger as the Elector's employees. Prince William had donated money to the Baron von Stein's League of Virtue, a Prussian organization formed to deliver the German states from the Napoleonic yoke. Letters were intercepted, and the Rothschilds and Buderus were denounced as accomplices. All of them were cross-examined by the police, but finally released through lack of evidence.

Meanwhile Buderus, at the instigation of the Rothschilds, was urging the Elector to double his investments in British gilt-edged securities. The consols not only paid a steady rate of interest but were bound to soar if Napoleon were defeated. This was sound advice: but there was more behind it than at first met the eye. No one knows who thought of the idea first, Buderus or Mayer or Nathan. If the Elector could be induced to divert large sums of money to London, the Rothschild-Buderus axis might 'borrow' the money for a few months before investing it, and the few months might be sufficient to accumulate a fortune. It took Buderus nearly a year to persuade the Elector to follow his advice. In the early months of 1809, however, the Prince sent £150,000 to Buderus with instructions that it be used to buy British consols quoted at 72. The money was despatched to Nathan who reasoned that as he had been asked to buy at 72 and consols had fallen to 60 he was within his rights to postpone the investment until the specified figure was reached.

In any age, this was sharp practice, but as the months passed no one could deny that Nathan Rotshchild made brilliant use of the money. Altogether, between 1809 and the end of 1811 he received £550,000 from the Elector, via Buderus, via his father. And not a penny was invested in consols. The most difficult aspect of the operation was how to fob off the Elector without producing certificates from the Bank of England proving that the purchases had been made. Prince William was a cynical man and however much he tried to place faith in his servitors he never wholly succeeded. Therefore he began badgering Buderus for the certificates and Buderus countered with a flood of excuses: the difficulties of travel; the danger of being caught with treasonable documents; the fear of being under surveillance from Napoleon's police.

This last contingency was more than likely, for Napoleon's blockade had set in motion a chain of action and reaction. The Papal States flatly refused to impose it, whereupon the French Emperor invaded Rome and took the Pope prisoner; Russia fumed because she could not send and sell her timber and hemp to England; and the Portuguese tried to think of some clever way that they could maintain their wine trade with London, whereupon Napoleon deposed the House of Braganza. Britain retaliated by sending troops to Portugal and Spain under the command of Sir Arthur Wellesley, later the Duke of Wellington.

In 1809, the Austrians, encouraged by huge subsidies from Britain, were ready once again to take up arms against the French. The Elector of Hesse offered the Emperor Francis four thousand troops, but at the last minute only supplied two thousand. He gave Mayer Rothschild the dangerous task of distributing the £30,000 necessary to keep his tiny army in the field; then he called upon his Hessian subjects to revolt against King Jerome. 'I come,' he wrote in a proclamation of April 1809, 'to loosen your bonds; Austria's exalted monarch protects me and protects you . . .'

Unfortunately Austria's exertions proved unsuccessful, and the Hessians failed to respond to their master's call. At this point, one of Mayer Rothschild's jealous rivals, a banker named Simon, is believed to have supplied the Westphalian police with the information that Mayer Amschel had served as Paymaster to the Prince of Hesse's army. M. Savagner, the Police Chief in Cassel, succeeded in obtaining a warrant for Rothschild's arrest and travelled to Frankfurt to conduct an investigation.

The Grand Duke von Dalberg was furious at what he considered an infringement of his sovereign rights. That the police from another province should poke their noses into Frankfurt's business was more than he could bear. Consequently, he warned Mayer Amschel to prepare himself for the visit. When Savagner arrived he found the old man ill in bed. He placed him under arrest in his own room and confined James and Salomon to the office below. Gutle, with her uncomprehending eyes and her rough hands, wept and wailed and drove everyone mad by asking repeatedly what it was all about. Mayer Amschel found an opportunity to slip Savagner a wad of bank notes and although the French report described the family as 'exceedingly wise and cunning', the only positive information gleaned was the fact that Amschel was in Prague advising the Elector on his investments.

The Elector was busy bemoaning his own misfortunes so that he scarcely noticed the danger to which his servitors were subjected. The unsuccessful campaign of 1809 had resulted in the retirement of the Austrian Foreign Minister, Count Stadion, and the promotion of Count Clemens Metternich, destined to play a major role in the fortunes of Europe in the next forty years. The Elector immediately wrote to Metternich requesting him 'to restore to his orphaned subjects their native Prince, whose presence they so ardently desire'. At the same time he wrote furiously to the out-going Stadion:

> So many worthless people relying on French protection are enabled to sin against me with impunity, and nobody now feels that he has any duties toward me; everybody does as he pleases and is actuated by base and selfish motives. I have thus lost more than two-thirds of a fortune that was never very considerable. That is hard, but harder than everything else is my present condition.[7]

All of this was completely untrue. By the end of 1810 the Elector had sent £450,000 to England for investment. Although he had badgered Buderus relentlessly for certificates the latter still prevaricated. The Elector now lost his temper and threatened to turn really nasty, but fortunately for Buderus and the Rothschilds, Napoleon chose this moment to try to put an end to black market activity and enforce his blockade. He strode to a map and placed his fingers squarely on Frankfurt as a hot bed of subversion. The French army was ordered to search the warehouses for illegal goods.

Once again Dalberg tipped off Mayer Rothschild, enabling him to empty his storerooms before the inspectors arrived: '. . . several French regiments with artillery have come into the town as well as a host of Customs officials,' Buderus wrote from Frankfurt to the Elector in Prague. 'All the gates have been occupied, and nobody is allowed to pass out without being closely inspected; all warehouses have been sealed and an intensive search for English and colonial goods have been instituted, severe penalties being inflicted when such goods have been discovered.'[8] Thousands of pounds' worth of goods were publicly burned, and over two hundred tradesmen fined. Although some were made to pay nearly a million francs, the Rothschilds, sixty-eighth on the list, were fined only 19,000 francs.

This was a pittance to Mayer Amschel who by now was one of the richest men in Frankfurt. He revealed his prosperity in expensive black suits, lace jabots, and wigs made of the best quality human hair. In the summer of 1810 his mounting fortune prompted him to prepare a new deed of settlement. The firm was renamed M. A. Rothschild und Söhne and the partnership drawn up between the four sons in Frankfurt. Nathan was still excluded as he was residing in enemy territory, but Mayer, now 67 years old, made it clear that his

Mayer Amschel Rothschild: an idealized drawing showing him dressed in the black suit and lace jabot he affected after his fortune was established.

ROTHSCHILD (Mayer-Anselme).

own share was earmarked for him. The deed recited that:

> ... with the help of the Almighty, Mayer Rothschild had, through the industry which he had shown from his youth upwards, through his discernment and through a tireless activity continued to an advanced age, alone laid the foundation of the present flourishing state of the concern, and thereby provided for the worldly happiness of his children.

But Mayer was thinking of something more than fleeting wealth. He dreamed of founding a dynasty and pondered the rules as carefully as though he were the head of a royal clan. Rothschild solidarity must not be diluted by outsiders brought into the family by marriage.

The deed emphasized that female Rothschilds who married non-Rothschilds were to be excluded from the business along with their spouses. Thus when Mayer's eldest daughter, Schonche, wed, neither she nor her husband were employed by the firm, but when his eldest son, Amschel, married, his wife, Eva Hanau, was promptly given a job. The name was what mattered.

By 1811 the Elector had become almost impossible to handle. Although in the early months of the year he agreed to invest a final £100,000 in British consols making the sum total £550,000, he suddenly became hysterical at the thought that he did not have a single piece of paper to prove that his money had been handled as he had instructed. For three and a half years he had been demanding certificates, a perfectly normal request, yet he was always fobbed off with excuses.

Buderus tried to divert his attention with a barrage of letters, some alarming, some reassuring, but the Elector refused to be placated. As a result Nathan Rothschild decided that at long last the moment had come to indulge his patron. A receipt for £189,500 was sent out of England to James Rothschild in Holland who forwarded it to the Elector. It was, in fact, the first purchase of British securities that had been made.

The Elector's money had been engaged in high adventure. Nathan had spotted a great opportunity in 1810, the year that George III was put in a strait-jacket. Times were hard for although the population numbered less than twenty million, the British Treasury had been obliged ever since 1805 to raise annual taxes to the staggering sum of £100,000,000.†

Although the Government increased its army and navy, poured out subsidies to foreign powers who would resist Napoleon, sent its merchant ships scouring the world for new markets, during the winter of 1810–11 the blockade began to bite, bringing about the worst economic crisis in British history. With the Baltic closed, with

---

†In 1815 the amount exceeded £176,000,000.

North America hostile and glutted, with only licensed goods reaching the European continent, the outlook was misty with peril.

Nathan Rothschild had become a naturalized Englishman in 1809, and the following year had established his own bank, N. M. Rothschild & Sons. His keen eyes saw that Napoleon was trying to destroy British credit by lowering the exchange rate. And this meant that gold bullion would continue to rise in value. For months he scoured the market and in the middle of 1810 learned that the East India Company had £800,000 worth of gold to sell. 'I went to the sale and bought it all,' he recounted years later. 'I knew the Duke of Wellington must have it. The Government sent for me and said it must have the gold. I sold the gold to them, but they did not know how to get it to the Duke in Portugal. I understood all that and sent it through France.'[9]

This sums up laconically one of the most brilliant and cunning financial operations ever conceived. Nathan knew that Britain was so short of hard currency that for the past two years she had not been able to scrape up enough to even satisfy the needs of Wellington's army in Portugal and Spain. Indeed, she was obliged to instruct the Duke to issue drafts on British Treasury bills. As no one wanted paper money the buyers – a mob of Maltese and Sicilian financiers – insisted on massive discounts which cut the Duke's resources by a quarter and frequently made it impossible for him to pay the troops. 'If you cannot supply us with money,' Wellington wrote angrily to Liverpool in 1810, 'you ought to withdraw us. We are reduced to the greatest distress.'[10]

As the drafts were sent back to London passing through the hands of a long chain of speculators, Nathan Rothschild frequently bought them up very cheaply. He therefore was acutely aware of Wellington's distress; and when he heard that the East India Company had gold to sell he bought it up, using the Elector's half-a-million pounds, and borrowing the rest himself. But why, if the British Government needed the bullion so badly, was Rothschild allowed to have it? 'How can you expect us to buy specie here with the exchange thirty per cent against us, and guineas selling for twenty-four shillings?' a Treasury official, William Huskisson, had asked querulously in 1809;[11] and no doubt asked again in 1810. While British civil servants waited for the price to drop Nathan Rothschild paid what was asked; and when the civil servants realized that the price was not going to drop, he sold it to them for a very large profit.

This was not all. Once the gold belonged to His Majesty's Government, Nathan offered to take charge himself of its delivery to the Duke of Wellington in Spain. Mr John Herries, a Treasury official who had been appointed Commissary-in-Chief in 1811, was only too pleased to relegate responsibility to someone else. Recently more than one vessel carrying specie had been sunk en route.

Nathan had a far more ingenious plan than shipping gold by sea.

First, he asked his father to send his young brother, nineteen-year-old James, to Paris, as he needed a reliable collaborator in enemy territory. Although it was not easy for a German to secure permission to reside in the French capital, in 1811 the Grand Duke von Dalberg pulled the right strings in return for Rothschild favours. The previous year Napoleon had married the eighteen-year-old Archduchess Marie Louise of Austria; the bride had produced the desired son and heir and the Grand Duke von Dalberg longed to attend the official celebrations in Paris. The cost of equipage and clothes, however, deemed necessary for the Prince-Primate of Frankfurt was so high that the Grand Duke could not manage it. That was where Mayer Amschel stepped in. He offered to advance the money, and in return von Dalberg not only supplied James with a passport, but arranged permission for Carl and Salomon to move about France as well.

Nathan's scheme for despatching money to Wellington was comparable to burglary in broad daylight. The second of the Rothschild combined operations, it cleverly exploited the fact that Napoleon had slightly relaxed his blockade in order to alleviate the hardship of the French consumer. Certain British goods were allowed to enter the country under licence; consequently at Gravelines, near Dunkirk, a railed-off enclosure was set up where 'legal smuggling' was permitted. Although most of the wares were manufactured articles, English gold and silver were allowed entry as part of the Emperor's policy to drain away Britain's reserves. 'A Frankfurter,' wrote the French Minister of Finance, M. Molliens, to Napoleon in March 1811, 'who . . . goes by the name of Rothschild is principally occupied in bringing British bullion from the coast to Paris.'

James Rothschild did not let the matter rest here. He talked a great deal, putting it about that Britain was planning drastic moves to stop the injurious loss of gold. 'He states that he has just received letters from London dated the 20th of this month,' Molliens continued, 'according to which the English intend, in order to check the export of gold and silver coins, to raise the value of the crown from five to five and a half shillings, and the value of the guinea from twenty-one to thirty shillings. . . . I sincerely hope that the Frankfurt Rothschild is well-informed on these matters, and that the Ministers in London will be sufficiently foolish to act in this way.'[12]

So the French Government allowed the Rothschilds to establish an artery of gold, running the length and breadth of France, to the heart of enemy resistance: Wellington's headquarters in Spain. And all the while Molliens prided himself that England's loss of the precious metal was helping the Bank of France consolidate its own position. In Paris James traded his mixture of British guineas, Portuguese gold ounces and French *napoléons d'or*, for bills of exchange on Spanish, Sicilian and Maltese banks. The notes were

The young James Rothschild was instrumental in his brother Nathan's scheme for providing Wellington's armies in Spain with gold bullion.

handed to Carl while Salomon flitted between Toulouse and Saint-Jean-de-Luz making sure that the transit points were diffuse enough not to arouse French suspicions nor to disturb the British exchange rate. Carl then disappeared into the Pyrenees, eventually emerging with the Duke of Wellington's receipts in his hand.

Even old Mayer Amschel and his eldest son, Amschel, were fully employed. They remained in Frankfurt with their ears close to the ground, despatching couriers to London and Paris with the latest news. Mayer was in a unique position to unearth the most secret secrets, for he was on the closest terms with the princely family of Thurn and Taxis who ran the Central European postal service. The Rothschilds had lent considerable sums of money to the Prince, the hereditary postmaster, who lived at Frankfurt. Consequently the Prince was not at all averse to giving instructions that certain letters should be steamed open, and a *précis* of the contents sent to old Mayer, who passed on the intelligence to his sons.

A few months after this joint Rothschild venture which Nathan later described as 'the best business I have ever done', Mayer Amschel drew up a new will. Once again he emphasized that the Rothschild name was what mattered, and that the business was to be placed exclusively in the hands of his sons.

'. . . my daughters, sons-in-law and their heirs having no part whatsoever in the existing firm M. A. Rothschild und Söhne . . . nor the right to examine the said business, its books, papers, inventory etc. . . . I shall never forgive my children if they should against my parental will take it upon themselves to disturb my sons in the peaceful possession of their business.' He went on to state that anyone who upset the family harmony would be limited to the legal minimum of estate valued far below its real worth. With the will completed, on 19 September 1812 he died in the arms of Gutle, well satisfied that he had founded a dynasty.

The sons often lamented that their father had not lived another two years to witness Napoleon's abdication. Yet the very month of Mayer Amschel's death marked the beginning of the end for the Corsican adventurer. That summer Napoleon had begun his invasion of Russia to compel the Tsar Alexander I to respect the blockade against the British. Twelve days before Mayer Amschel drew his last breath the great battle of Borodino was fought with enormous casualties on both sides. The Russian army retreated, compelling the Grand Army to continue its march to Moscow.

The world soon heard that Moscow was burning; and that this was not the prelude to a Russian surrender but to a French retreat. That October the Grand Army was struggling back to Western Europe in freezing temperatures and chaotic conditions. The wounded froze to death, the survivors starved to death. There was no question of buying food, as the gold wagons had been looted, captured or blown to bits. The French Paymaster General had set out on the campaign with seventy-eight clerks and fifty-five cart-loads of cash drawn by four horses apiece. He had been able to rescue only one cart which contained two millions of gold. 'My staff', he reported, 'no longer exist; they have all perished from cold and hunger. Some of them whose hands and feet have been frozen have been left at Vilna. All the account books have been taken by the enemy. Nobody thinks of anything except saving his own skin, and it is quite impossible to stem the panic . . .' 'The baggage taken is enormous,' wrote Sir Robert Wilson, the British general attached to Russian headquarters at the same time, 'and its value immense. One wagon was full of gold and silver ingots. Another military chest had two hundred thousand pounds in specie. . .'[13]

As armies did not know how to function without wagons of hard cash, a massive defeat was the quickest way to drain a state treasury. The Duke of Wellington exulted in the disintegration of the French army, and began preparations to lead his men through France to the Low Countries; but he informed London that he could not move until he had an adequate supply of gold.

The British Treasury called a conference and John Herries asked the brilliant Nathan Rothschild to put up a scheme. Once again this astonishing man, whose name was still being mis-spelled by the

British Treasury, stepped into the breach. He travelled to Holland, and in collaboration with his four brothers, whom he summoned to meet him, bought up at an extremely advantageous rate of exchange millions of French gold pieces which Napoleon had coined for continental use. He then shipped the bullion from the Dutch port, Helvoetsluys, to Wellington's headquarters in Spain, enabling the Duke to move through France using the local coinage which, eliminating the need for exchange bureaux, gave him vastly increased purchasing power.

Everything entrusted to Nathan had been brilliantly executed. Now not only John Herries but Vansittart, the chancellor of the Exchequer, reposed complete confidence in him. The two men asked him to handle the huge subsidy payments to Britain's continental allies. Between 1812 and 1814 the British Treasury paid out the staggering sum of £30,000,000 to the continent; over half this amount was handled by Nathan, and handled so deftly, swiftly, noiselessly, that the exchange rate did not suffer the slightest dent. 'The only perceptible commotion', commented one historian, 'was the abacuses clicking in the counting houses.' It was far from a single operation; Nathan's conception of the first great clearing house in history was original, and the means of achieving it both subtle and complicated. John Herries, who could claim Nathan as his own prodigy, basked in the sunshine of the Rothschild success. In 1822 he wrote to a friend.

It was entrusted to me by their Lordships [the Treasury] to affect the application of this very large sum in the discharge of foreign subsidies … by an arrangement entirely new which consisted principally in providing the Specie required for these services thro' a single and confidential agency …. The details of the arrangement embraced every mode by which foreign currencies could be obtained for British money or Credit; such as the purchase of Specie in all the markets of the world; the conversion of Bullion into coin at our own and at foreign mints; the coining of foreign money in England and the purchase of bills of remittance in such manner as to conceal that they were for a Public Account; the negotiation of British paper on the continent at a long date to avoid pressure upon the exchange etc. etc. …[14]

Nathan's commission may have reached £1,000,000, yet he was thought to have earned it. The fact that he managed to transfer the English subsidies without depressing the exchange rate was regarded as straight wizardry. Up till now any government advancing money faced the prospect of losing as much as a third of it. But Nathan had brothers. James in Paris and Amschel, Salomon and Carl in Frankfurt, worked so quickly and harmoniously that the transfers were carried out with no unfavourable effects, saving the Prince Regent's Government hundreds of thousands of pounds.

Nathan and James also joined forces to finance the return of a

Bourbon prince to the throne of France. Ever since 1807 the future Louis XVIII had been living in Hartwell in Buckinghamshire. The Prince appealed to the English King, the English King appealed to the Treasury; and the Treasury as usual consulted Nathan Rothschild. Together Nathan and James raised £200,000; the future Louis XVIII entered Paris on 3 May 1814.

Ten months later a spectacular array of princes and diplomats assembled in Vienna to settle the peace of Europe. The music and *politesse* came to an abrupt halt, however, when the incredible news burst on the world – in England Nathan was the first to hear of it – that Napoleon Bonaparte had escaped from Elba and landed on French soil. Louis XVIII and his court fled from Paris to Ghent in Belgium, and in March 1815 Bonaparte again took up his abode in the Tuileries. The British Treasury, of course, was plunged into feverish activity, pledging huge subsidy payments to the Continental powers for the overthrow of the resilient adventurer.

Nathan Rothschild had always understood the value of news and for some years had operated a private courier system. As his agents in Dover, he employed Messrs Nathan, Rice and Co., a firm well equipped with light vessels ready to sail at a moment's notice with Rothschild despatches. At Calais, another agent, James Levereau, (the courier who brought to New Court, Nathan's house in London, the first news of Napoleon's escape from Elba), was similarly provided. On both sides special 'post boys' were employed to carry letters to their destination. In addition, Nathan offered rewards on a fixed tariff basis to the captains of ordinary packets and the guards of the stagecoaches if they specially exerted themselves on his behalf.

Soon not only Dover and Calais, but Ostend, Ghent, Brussels and Amsterdam swarmed with Rothschild agents judged necessary by Nathan to assist him in the task of implementing the British Government's vast banking commitments. Nathan's job, assigned to him by John Herries, was to supply cash to Louis XVIII and his exiled court, which he did through Ostend and Ghent; to transmit subsidy payments to Russia and Prussia, which he did through Ostend and Amsterdam; to supply coin to Wellington's army, now in Belgium, which he did through Ostend and Brussels.

The Battle of Waterloo was fought on Sunday 18 June 1815. A dozen different accounts have been given as to how Nathan Rothschild received the news, and what he did with it, and not one is accurate. Many writers talk about carrier pigeons, and some even claim that Nathan followed Wellington onto the battlefield and stayed there until he was satisfied which way the struggle was going. Almost all biographers accept the fact that instead of imparting the news of the Waterloo victory, he pretended that all was lost in order to depress the market and make a fortune for himself. Even the version given by Leopold de Rothschild at a public dinner in 1903 was incorrect.

The Battle of Waterloo was fought on Sunday, 18 June 1815, and Nathan Rothschild was one of the very first men in England to know about the British victory through his highly efficient courier system.

He spoke of the 'Dutch' Gazette being brought to England by a trusted Rothschild captain who stumbled upon it accidentally; and told how Nathan hurried to inform Lord Liverpool who refused to believe the news.

This was nearer the truth but still inaccurate. First of all, the Gazette was published in Brussels not Amsterdam; secondly the captain did not bring the news sheet to England by 'chance'; thirdly Nathan did not call on Lord Liverpool. Throughout Sunday 18 June, the day of the battle, a number of Gazettes were issued, some regular editions, some 'Gazettes Extraordinary', all of them carrying bulletins on the fighting signed by the Secretary of State, Baron de Capellen. Altogether four editions were issued on Sunday; and at 3 am on Monday a fifth edition came out, announcing that the wounded Prince of Orange had been brought in, and referring to the 'victory of yesterday' as having been 'bloody but brilliant'. In reply to Leo de Rothschild's inaccuracies, a scholar wrote in the London *Graphic* of 15 April 1903,

that an extra Gazette Extraordinary had been issued briefly announcing the great victory. This 'special extra' was out before 3 a.m. No doubt while still wet from the printing press – say at 2 a.m. – a copy was carried post haste by one of the Rothschild couriers, or relays of couriers to Ostend. There it would have arrived about 10 o'clock in the morning. The local agent would have at once shipped himself on board one of the Rothschild boats, and by evening he would have been on British soil travelling fleetly to London on post horses supplied by the Dover agency. Hence the Gazette might well have been in Nathan's hands before breakfast in the morning of Tuesday the 20th; or some forty hours before Wellington's official despatches reached Downing Street.

This is precisely what happened, according to a Rothschild relation, Lady Colyer Fergusson, who wrote a letter to the *Daily Telegraph* on 9 November 1962.

My grandfather, Benjamin Cohen, went with Nathan Rothschild to see Lord Castlereagh ... to tell him that the Battle of Waterloo had been won. When they arrived the butler refused to admit them and all remonstrances were met with the same answer. 'His Lordship is sleeping and is not to be disturbed.'

Eventually, Lord Castlereagh woke up, but when he relayed the news to his Foreign Office officials the latter viewed it with scepticism as they had just learned of the English defeat at Quatre Bras on the previous day. Nathan Rothschild took his leave with no further ado and went straight to the Stock Exchange where he bought large quantities of British bonds. This fact is recorded in the London *Courier* of 20 June with the laconic statement: 'Rothschild has made great purchases of stock.'

Now what about Lord Liverpool? Apparently on Tuesday 21 June, the day after Rothschild had seen Castlereagh, an independent Belgian agent in quest of glory and a suitable reward, had called at 10 Downing Street. Here is the account given by the London *Courier*, which came out in the evening of the twenty-first.

The following is said to have been brought by a gentleman who states that a great battle was fought on the day before: that he was on Monday at Ghent opposite the hotel of Louis XVIII when, at 1 p.m., an officer arrived covered with dust: and as the King receives every despatch, he instantly entered the hotel with the officer who forthwith congratulated His Majesty on the great victory just gained. 'We have taken all the heavy artillery,' he explained, 'and a great decisive victory is ours.' There was immediately the greatest joy among the officers assembled. The King embraced the officer with transport. The officer then said that the battle of Sunday had been general along the whole line and had continued for nine hours – that a great number of prisoners had been taken, the French retreating with the greatest confusion leaving all their heavy artillery behind. The gentleman instantly left Ghent, and reached Ostend in the evening of Monday. The Nymph packet was then underway; without waiting a moment he embarked to be the first bearer of the good news ...

He was not the first, but the second; and apparently Lord Liverpool could not understand the man's bad English and sent for his secretary, Mr Croker, to disentangle the story. Croker, who was a regular contributor to the *Courier*, passed the information on to the editor. And when Mr Jennings many years later, came to edit the Croker papers, he took it upon himself to describe the informant erroneously as 'a Rothschild agent'. Hence the confusion as to whether Nathan went to Castlereagh or to Liverpool, and on what day, and with what information.

The *Courier* was not on the streets until late in the evening on the twenty-first. Meanwhile Lord and Lady Willoughby de Eresby were dining with their friend, Thomas Raikes, who wrote in his *Journal* that he found the company 'breathless, impatient for news of the battle'. 'I felt little alarm,' he adds, 'as I had heard that Rothschild was purchasing stocks largely and that the funds had risen two per cent.'[15]

Raikes was anticipating events. On Friday 16 June consols were quoted at $69\frac{1}{16}$ where they remained until the twentieth when Nathan Rothschild began to buy. Wednesday 21 June they had moved up to 70; three days later they were traded at $71\frac{1}{2}$.

So much for the stories of Nathan depressing the market and making a fortune. The truth was that he already had his fortune. But who promoted the fantastic tale of his attending the Waterloo battle? Apparently this story was invented many years later, after Nathan's death, by a scurrilous French journalist, Georges Mathieu-Dairnvaell, who deliberately compiled it to show the lengths to which Nathan's money greed would drive him. Dairnvaell submitted the unpublished version to James Rothschild in Paris, demanding a large sum of money for its suppression. James refused, and the report appeared in a pamphlet entitled *Histoire édifiante et curieuse de Rothschild I.* James issued a public statement, denying that Nathan had been anywhere near Waterloo and revealing the author's attempts to blackmail him.

Sometime before Waterloo the Elector of Hesse-Cassel had moved back into Wilhelmshöhe Castle, and was now busy reviving the institutions and reimposing the customs of pre-war days. He even insisted that his soldiers re-grow their pigtails. Every penny that he had entrusted to the Rothschilds was returned with interest reckoned at the rate paid by British consols, the safe stock in which his fortune had *not* been invested. As he had often despaired of ever seeing his money again he was overjoyed to receive such a large sum and he rewarded Buderus, who now was a very rich man, by showering him with honours. He had raised him to the nobility by giving him the title, Baron Buderus von Carlhausen; he now made him a Privy Councillor and appointed him his representative to the Frankfurt Diet, an assembly which had been created by the Vienna Congress and to which all the German states adhered.

The relations between the Elector and the Rothschilds were equally cordial, although now their positions were reversed, and it was William who took the trouble to keep in touch. Although the Elector remained the most affluent prince in Europe he no longer was a power, for the Rothschilds had created new standards of wealth. Years later Nathan said that during the period between his arrival in England and the end of the Napoleonic wars, he increased his original stake 2,500 times. This was not literally true for he made the bulk of the fortune by speculating with the Elector's half-a-million pounds. But speaking mathematically, if his original stake was £20,000 this gave the Rothschilds, who operated as one family and one partnership, £50,000,000. Not only were they the richest bankers in Europe, but they had invented *haute finance*, a new force destined to mould the capitalism of the nineteenth century.

Adelheid von Rothschild, Carl' wife, painted at the beginning of their sojourn in Naples.

NEW COURT in 1819.

Chapter III

Five Brothers in Five Capitals

(1815–25)

'*T*HE ROTHSCHILDS REALLY DO CONSTITUTE A SPECIAL *species plantarum* . . .' wrote Friedrich von Gentz, secretary to the great Austrian Chancellor, Prince Metternich, in 1818.

They are vulgar, ignorant Jews, outwardly presentable, in their trade the sheerest Emperialists, without the remotest inkling of any higher relationship. But they are endowed with a remarkable instinct which causes them always to choose the right, and of the two rights the better. Their enormous wealth (they are the richest people in Europe) is entirely the result of this instinct, which the public are wont to call luck ...[1]

Nevertheless the brothers still had to fight to consolidate their position in the post-war world. As banker-in-chief to the British Government, the brilliant thirty-eight-year-old Nathan of London, fountain-head of the family fortune, was the most firmly entrenched; next came twenty-three-year-old James of Paris who had the confidence of the newly enthroned French King. But the three Rothschilds in Frankfurt – Amschel, Salomon and Carl – enjoyed no comparable prestige because of the deeply engrained anti-Semitism of Central Europe.

As the three Rothschild banks constituted one firm, and the partners shared profits and losses, Nathan had determined that his brothers should acquire the same elevated position as himself. It was clear that their future lay in the great imperial city of Vienna; and the key to Vienna was held by Prince Metternich, the most influential statesman in Europe. Although Metternich was adventurous in the pursuit of women, when it came to politics he was deeply conservative. He believed that the upheaval provoked first by the French Revolution, then by Napoleonic conquest, had unbalanced the masses who needed the discipline of the old order. Equality, he insisted, was not what men wanted; fraternity was a sham; society must have its betters, otherwise its inferiors would spend their time cutting each other's throats.

Alexander I of Russia played into Metternich's hands by proposing a Holy Alliance that would guarantee the sovereignty of any monarch who adhered to Christian principles: and Metternich cleverly identified the Holy Alliance with maintenance of the *status quo*. At the Congress of Vienna he supported a new German confederation, with a diet at Frankfurt, composed of small autonomous states, so weak that they would be compelled to rely on Austria.

The Rothschild brothers followed Metternich's moves with close

Top New Court in 1819. Nathan and his family lived above the bank at first, then moved to Stamford Hill and finally to 107 Piccadilly. *Bottom* The Hôtel de Laborde, later renamed the Hôtel Fouché at 19 Rue Laffitte, James' residence in Paris, had formerly been the town palace of Napoleon's police commissioner.

attention and in 1815 Nathan advised Amschel and Salomon to ask Vienna for some form of 'recognition' for their 'services'. He was referring, of course, to the British subsidies which he had paid to Austria through the Rothschild bank in Frankfurt. Amschel and Salomon had converted the pounds sterling into Austrian currency so quietly and quickly that they had managed to maintain the full value of the money, by preventing a fall in the exchange rate.

Nathan's timing was faultless for the Austrian Government was so much in need of loans that it had no wish to offend a powerful group of bankers. Consequently the Minister of Finance, Count Stadion, sent Salomon's letter to the Emperor recommending that 'Your Majesty will graciously confer on the two brothers of this firm, resident here, the German hereditary title of nobility. . .' All that Stadion was requesting was a simple 'von' as a prefix; but Privy Councillor Baron von Lederer was indignant that such an honour be granted to a firm doing business in its own interests. 'Your Majesty should make a gift to each of the two brothers Rothschild of a gold snuff box bearing Your Majesty's monogram in diamonds. . .' Finally it was left to Prince Metternich to decide; and the Prince, prompted by his secretary and economic adviser, Friedrich von Gentz, a Jew himself, plumped for the 'von'.

Subsequently the Frankfurt Rothschilds were asked to present an appropriate coat-of-arms. In preparing the design Salomon overlooked the fact that there was mention only of two brothers and asked that a separate patent of nobility should be prepared for each of the five brothers. When the design reached the College of Heralds it had the effect of high explosive. The aged aristocrats who dealt with title deeds could scarcely believe their eyes. Never had such a preposterous, presumptuous, aggressive, overbearing proposal been submitted in the long history of heraldry. In the first quarter was an eagle (reference: Imperial Austrian coat-of-arms); in the second quarter a leopard (reference: English royal coat-of-arms); in the third quarter a lion (reference: Hessian coat-of-arms); in the fourth quarter, an arm bearing five arrows (reference: unity of five brothers). In the centre, on one side, was a greyhound, symbol of loyalty; on the other a stork, symbol of piety. The crest was a coronet surmounted by the lion of Hesse. And all this for a mere 'von'.

Outraged, the College pointed out:

They ask for a coronet, a centre shield supporters, the Leopard of England, and the Lion of Hesse. According to the rules of heraldry, the gentry are entitled only to a helmet; their suggestion is entirely inadmissible since otherwise there would be nothing to distinguish the higher ranks, as coronets, supporters, and centre shield are proper only to the nobility. Moreover, no government will grant the emblems of other governments as nobility is conferred for services to one's prince and one's countries; the lion is a symbol of courage only, which does not apply to the Petitioners.[2]

Prince Metternich, 'the key to Central Europe'.

The design returned from the College of Heralds was stripped of all its splendour; no coronet, no lion, no stork, no greyhound. In two quarters an arm, not with five but four arrows; in the other two quarters a half eagle each, which somehow became united to form a full eagle on top. But the Rothschilds were in no position to demur; and this became their family coat-of-arms in March 1817.

If Metternich was the key to Central Europe, Friedrich von Gentz was the key to Metternich. This astonishing man, an Austrian Jew by birth, a one-time member of the Prussian civil service, knew how to twist the Prince, his master, round his little finger. Gentz had infinite charm. He loved fine clothes and balls and beautiful women. A clever talker, a facile propagandist, he was the original public relations man of the early nineteenth century. He could promote anybody and everybody; he could institute a trend, inaugurate a fashion, popularize an aphorism. Gentz had made his reputation as secretary to the Congress of Vienna, an appointment later cited by Disraeli as evidence of the lasting hold of the Jews on the fortunes of mankind.

Friedrich von Gentz, 'the key to Metternich'.

Now Gentz was Metternich's secretary and, more important still, his financial adviser. Although Gentz pretended to have a wide knowledge of money his chief interest in this commodity was the accumulation of it for himself. He made it widely known that he not only was willing to accept bribes but would be affronted if they were not forthcoming. In his diary he refers to them as 'good news' or 'pleasant financial dealings'. The payments were essential to him as he wished to satisfy the exacting demands of his middle-aged mistress, Fanny Essler, the famous dancer.

The Rothschilds concentrated on Friedrich von Gentz. When he visited Frankfurt before and after the Congress of Aachen in 1818, he placed himself in daily communication with the family; and after a number of 'pleasant dealings' promised to use his influence with Metternich to alleviate the lot of the Frankfurt Jews who, since the fall of Napoleon, had been subject to many of the old forms of oppression.

But this was not all that the Rothschilds wanted from Metternich. The truth was that the brothers had been hurt and indignant to find themselves excluded from the great French loan of 1817, raised to enable France to indemnify the victorious allies. Rothschild money had been in pressing demand throughout the war; but now that peace had come, the old-established, orthodox bankers seemed to be elbowing the *parvenus* out of the way.

At least that is how the Rothschilds saw it. The idea of floating a loan of such vast proportions as 1,000,000,000 francs had originated with the famous French banker, Gabriel-Julien Ouvrard, who had financed Napoleon's Hundred Days and then switched his allegiance to Louis XVIII.

Ouvrard invited Alexander Baring of London, and Baring's brother-in-law, Labouchere, the head of Hope and Co. of Amsterdam, to join him in raising the money but under no circumstances would he allow his hated rival, the ebullient, aggressive and unforgiveably successful James Rothschild, to participate. James protested angrily and Baring did his best to change Ouvrard's mind but the latter remained adamant. He could afford to do so as the French Foreign Secretary, the Duc de Richelieu, disliked the Rothschilds whom he referred to as 'upstarts' and 'coin-changers'. Indeed, he infuriated the brothers by pronouncing that: 'There are six great powers in Europe; England, France, Russia, Austria, Prussia and the Baring Brothers.'

The first instalment of the Ouvrard-Baring combine was put on the market early in 1817 and consisted of a 350,000,000 franc, five per cent loan offered at 53. The bankers were greatly relieved to find that within a few days it was subscribed in full. They did not realize, of course, that most of it had been scooped up by the Rothschilds who decided that as they were barred from participation they would have to make a profit in other ways.

By the time that the Aachen Congress took place in 1818 two instalments of the loan had been issued. Although the Great Powers had declared that they would keep their armies in France until every penny of the indemnity had been paid, the financial burden of the occupation was proving far heavier than they had imagined. They finally decided that it would be better to accept a cut-price settlement of 24,000,000 francs (£1,000,000) and to withdraw the troops than to insist on the full amount which might require months of negotiation and result in spiralling costs.

Salomon and Carl Rothschild were present at the Congress and once again tried to participate in the third instalment of the loan. But the distinguished company scarcely seemed to notice them. Lady Castlereagh gave parties of unbelievable boredom; Metternich and Gentz flirted with the prettiest diplomatic wives; the Duc de Richelieu cantered in the Park; Nesselrode played cards; and Carl Rothschild paraded his bride, the beautiful Adelaide Herz, a member of Germany's most illustrious Jewish family, around the great conference hall but no one turned to look. Salomon meanwhile paced up and down his hotel bedroom wondering what he could do to stamp the Rothschild presence on the blasé assembly. The Civil Service was unsympathetic, merely pointing out that as Ouvrard and Baring and Hope had succeeded with their instalments of the year before there was no point in making a change; indeed, were not the bonds rising on the Paris Bourse at this very moment?

Throughout October the Rothschild brothers were neglected. But on 5 November something startling began to happen. The French *rentes*, the loan of 1817, were slipping. They fell from 74 to 73 and then to 71; from 71 to 69 and finally to 68. A near panic set in, for almost every diplomat present had speculated in the shares – on margin.

Friedrich von Gentz caught the glimmer of a smile on Salomon Rothschild's face, and suddenly realized what was happening. The Rothschilds controlled the great French loan, and as a warning they had beared the market. Ouvrard called a hurried meeting with his fellow bankers. As they had promised to float the new instalment at 70 and could not go back on their word, they would be forced to issue the shares at an enormous loss, for the market had slipped to 65. However, Alexander Baring had an inspired solution. At a second meeting attended by Prince Metternich of Austria, Prince Hardenberg of Germany and the Duc de Richelieu of France, he told the company that he was prepared to carry out his pledges; but that dealings on margin by private individuals were permissible only on a rising market. The investors, therefore, would have to pay up fully. The statesmen looked askance for none of them had the necessary cash. Prince Metternich spluttered indignantly but finally saved the situation by suggesting that the old arrangement be declared null and void and a new agreement be drawn up, favourable to bankers and investors alike. And Baring and Hope and Ouvrard gave a sigh of relief.

However, when the third instalment was issued no one made the mistake of excluding the Rothschilds. Not only had the brothers reaped high profits by buying up the 1817 loan as members of the general public, but they had forced the Concert of Europe to recognize their financial supremacy. Ouvrard could rage, Hope could enveigh, Baring could protest; but the Rothschilds had arrived. 'Fortresses so long besieged that they had almost appeared impregnable suddenly surrendered without resistance, with hardly a blow, unconditionally. The whole battered front gave way, wilted and collapsed. The conquering five, with flags flying and drums rolling – the strangest host in all history – marched on to victory...'[3] And of the five, the leader was Nathan Mayer Rothschild.

Spendthrift, Regency England served as a background for many bizarre figures, but none stranger than the post-war Croesus. Short and stocky with a huge girth, and an india-rubber face fringed by red hair out of which stared bulging blue eyes, he looked like a circus clown and was not much better educated. Although he had become a British subject he still had not mastered the language and spoke a queer mixture of English broken by Yiddish slang. However, when occasion demanded, he could swear like a trooper. Nathan was not a generous man and resented the advances made toward him by charitable organizations in search of funds. On the rare instances when he was over-persuaded to subscribe, he invariably regretted it. He would storm about the office like an excited schoolboy. 'You make out the cheque,' he would shout to one of his clerks. 'I have made a f . . . fool of myself.'[4]

Nathan spent half his day as a banker and the other half speculating in stocks and bonds. He always stood under the same pillar on the floor of the Royal Exchange, well aware that he was a centre of attraction. Other brokers watched every gesture, hoping for a clue that would lead them to a hidden store of treasure. But Nathan's joy was to tease and trick his competitors, so he often assumed an utterly blank expression.

Eyes are usually called the windows of the soul. But in Rothschild's case you would conclude that the windows are false ones, or that there was no soul to look out of them. There comes not one pencil of light from the interior, neither is there any gleam of that which comes from without reflected in any direction. The whole puts you in mind of an empty skin, and you wonder why it stands upright without at least something in it. By and by another figure comes up to it. It then steps two paces aside, and the most inquisitive glance that you ever saw, and a glance more inquisitive than you would have thought of, is drawn out of the fixed and leaden eyes, as if one were drawing a sword from a scabbard ...[5]

The only person that Nathan trusted unreservedly was his good-looking wife, Hannah. This lady bore him four sons and three daughters, the last of whom was born in 1820. They lived modestly and, as the family grew, uncomfortably, in St Swithin's Lane in the City where Nathan had moved in 1810. Their house was known as New Court because it had been rebuilt after the Great Fire of 1666. The ground floor housed the bank, the upper storeys the family. The house had a 'cantilever cornice, a covered colonnade on the south side with steps up to the front door, a brick parapet, cock-loft, garrets and flats; within there were marble chimney pieces, kitchen, scullery, warehouse and counting-houses'.[6] Nathan's rent was £175 a year.

The Rothschilds' social life revolved around Hannah's many brothers and sisters, the Cohens, who by their marriages had welded together the most prominent Jewish families in England. One of her sisters had become the wife of Moses Montefiore, merchant and broker, another sister the wife of Moses' brother; a sister and brother had married a brother and sister of Moses Samuel, banker and broker; another brother a niece of Abraham Goldsmith.

The Cohens were devout Jews, and Judith Cohen tells how Admiral Sir Sidney Smith called unexpectedly and was surprised to find the family seated in chairs that scarcely cleared the ground. When he asked 'the reason for our being seated so low I replied "this is the anniversary of the destruction of Jerusalem which is kept by conforming Jews as a day of mourning and humiliation. . ."'[7] In order to please her orthodox family, Hannah managed to persuade Nathan to serve with Salomon Cohen as Warden of the Great Synagogue. Although Nathan refused to donate any money he managed to bring the three Ashkenaz synagogues in the City together and co-ordinated their work for the relief of the poor.

Nathan, with his short, stout figure and his protruding lower lip, was a favourite subject of the London caricaturists. 'A Pillar of the Exchange' shows him standing beside his favourite column in the Royal Exchange.

While Nathan did not seek the company of those outside his family, many distinguished people sought his. The Duke of Wellington was a frequent visitor; and so was Prince Talleyrand, France's ambassador to the Court of St James, who delighted Hannah with his courtly manners, and amused the children with the statuary he fashioned from bread lumps. Another diplomatic friend was the Prussian ambassador, Count Wilhem von Humboldt. 'Yesterday Rothschild dined with me,' the latter wrote to his brother, Alexander, the famous naturalist. 'He is quite crude and uneducated but he has a great deal of natural intelligence. He scored beautifully off Major Martins who was being furiously sentimental about the horrors of war and the large number who had been killed. "Well," said Rothschild, "if they had not all died, Major, you presumably would still be a drummer." '8

Gradually Nathan acquired a reputation for bluntness that even the Iron Duke could not surpass. Once a lady was rash enough to express the hope that Nathan's children were not fond of money and business to the exclusion of more important things. 'I am *sure* you would not wish that,' she said. 'I am *sure* I should wish that,' he retorted hotly. 'I wish them to give mind, soul, heart and body – everything to business. . . . It requires a great deal of boldness and a great deal of caution to make a large fortune and, when you have got it, you require ten times as much wit to keep it.'9

Once when a foreign prince called on Nathan in his office he not only found him blunt but rude. After curtly offering his visitor a seat, the banker turned his attention back on his private papers. The caller was offended. 'Did you hear, sir, who I am?' asked the prince, slapping his card on Nathan's desk. The banker gazed at it a moment. 'Take two chairs then.'

It was a very different thing when Nathan himself was slighted. Apparently the Bank of England once annoyed him by refusing to discount a bill drawn upon him by his brother Amschel of Frankfurt. One of the directors informed the Rothschild messenger that they 'discounted only their own bills, and not those of private persons.' 'Private persons!' exclaimed Nathan when the fact was reported to him. 'I will make those gentlemen feel what sort of private persons we are!'

A few days later Nathan walked over to the bank, drew a £5 note out of his satchel and asked for gold. The clerk counted out five sovereigns looking at the great Rothschild in astonishment. Nathan put the money in his briefcase and drew out a second note; then a third, and a fourth, and a fifth. It took him seven hours to change £21,000; but as he had nine clerks doing the same thing, by the end of the day the Bank had lost £210,000 from its gold reserves. The next day Nathan and his small battalion reappeared. 'These gentlemen refuse to take my bills, so I will not keep theirs,' he explained to the restless customers who could not find any tellers free to help them. 'And I hold notes enough to keep them occupied for two months.' Two months! Eleven million pounds of gold! The directors held a hurried meeting and agreed to send Nathan an abject apology. In future Rothschild bills would be accepted by the Bank of England as readily as their own.[10]

Nathan's power not only sprang from his riches but his immense vitality. As early as 1817 the Prussian ambassador was reporting to Berlin that Rothschild was 'easily the most enterprising business man in the country. He is, moreover, a man upon whom one can rely and with whom the Government here does considerable business. He is also . . . honest and intelligent.'[11] The director of the Prussian Treasury who was visiting London confirmed this opinion adding that Rothschild had 'an incredible influence upon all financial affairs here in London. It is widely stated . . . that he entirely regulates the rate of exchange in the City. His power as a banker is enormous.'[12]

As a result of these assessments Nathan was asked to raise a loan for the Prussian Government of £5,000,000 – the first state loan entrusted to him. He secured it at an average price of 72, a 'splendid piece of business', as the stock rose to 100. A succession of loans followed; £12,000,000 at three per cent for the British Government in 1819; £2,000,000 in 1821 and £2,500,000 in 1822 for the Neapolitan Government; £3,500,000 for Russia in 1822; £1,500,000 for Portugal in 1823, £3,500,000 for Austria in 1824.[13] Nathan's banking methods made history, for he persuaded the English public to subscribe to foreign loans by the novel practice of arranging that the dividends should be paid in pounds sterling.

In 1824 a frenzy of speculation built up in England reminiscent of the South Sea Bubble of the century before. With Latin America shaking off the authority of Spain, promoters stressed the rich rewards of investing in the newly independent states and the public rushed to buy. Although almost every bank in the City floated the issues, Nathan Rothschild was too involved that year with the formation of the Alliance Insurance Company to take much part. He launched the new firm in conjunction with his brother-in-law, Moses Montefiore at the instigation of another brother-in-law, Benjamin Gompertz.

Although Gompertz was a Fellow of the Royal Society, he could not get a job as an insurance actuary because of the prevailing notion that arson had a peculiar charm for the Hebrew; and this inspired Nathan with the idea of forming his own company. The Alliance was a success from the outset and before long was the largest insurance firm in Britain. Needless to say, Gompertz was the actuary.

Nathan was fortunate to have been so preoccupied for by the end of 1825 over three thousand firms had declared bankruptcy. There were rumours that even the Bank of England might have to shut its doors but Nathan and James stepped into the breach and arranged an emergency transfer of gold from France.

A caricature inspired by the founding of the Alliance Assurance Company by Nathan Rothschild and Moses Montefiore in 1824.

Meanwhile Nathan had been directing the fortunes of his brother, James, in Paris and his three brothers, Amschel, Salomon and Carl, who, when the Napoleonic wars came to an end, began to work together once more in the Frankfurt bank. Nathan argued in favour of one of them moving to Vienna. After all, Prince Metternich not only directed the Habsburg Empire which controlled Central Europe, but had imposed his creed of absolutism on a great portion of western Europe. None of the three brothers, however, was eager to leave home for snobbish, anti-Semitic, protocol-ridden Vienna.

The fact that a Rothschild finally settled in the Danubian capital happened by chance. In the summer of 1819 crowds marched through Frankfurt shouting against the Jews with the age-old cry, 'Hepp! Hepp!' They chalked slogans on all the houses and broke the windows of the Rothschild bank. The trouble had arisen because many of the German states, after ridding themselves of Napoleon's overlordship, were appalled to find themselves once again under the yoke of Austria. A wave of nationalism swept through the German Confederation, whose headquarters were in Frankfurt. Bankers were regarded as the enemy as they supported Metternich's reactionary ideas; and as most bankers were Jewish the protests threatened to turn into pogroms.

Jewish families felt that the city was on the verge of a massacre and hid trembling in their cellars. James Rothschild wrote from

61

Paris to his eldest brother, Amschel, urging him to shut the bank and to move to France. The Austrian minister in Frankfurt, Herr Handel, heard the rumour and wrote post-haste to Prince Metternich. 'The great and rich House of Rothschild is supposed to be not entirely adverse to the idea of leaving here. . . . The question suggests itself whether it would not be to our interest . . . to induce the House to emigrate to Vienna.'[14]

Prince Metternich was deeply annoyed by the demonstrations, as he felt that they were a slap at his policy; 'revolutionary anti-Semitics', he called them. As a way of showing disapproval he gave Nathan Rothschild the position of Austrian consul in London and informed the Austrian Legation in Frankfurt that if the Rothschilds decided to leave their native city they would be welcome in Vienna.† Then he asked Salomon Rothschild to draw up a plan by which 55,000,000 gulden – about £5,000,000 – could be raised for the Austrian State.

Once again Nathan master-minded the move, and Salomon produced the unusual suggestion of a lottery designed to attract the general public. Metternich gave the proposal his blessing and Salomon carried the idea through with true Rothschild *finesse*. The first issue consisted of 20,000,000 gulden and people hurried to subscribe under the impression that it represented the total sum. In the scramble the price was forced up; then came the second instalment of 35,000,000 gulden. By this time investors felt that they were on to a sure thing, and needed no persuasion to buy. But as they did so, the first issue declined alarmingly because of profit-taking by the sophisticated few.

This was bad enough, but when the terms of the loan were published the affair degenerated into a scandal. Salomon was to be repaid 114,000,000 gulden in return for the 55,000,000 gulden he had advanced. 'A shameful Jewish ramp . . .'; 'a moment of frivolity'; 'an immoral transaction', cried the press. 'The loan is one of the most wicked things that have been done at the expense of our pockets and that is saying a good deal,' declared an outraged speculator. Many people whispered that the Minister of Finance, Count Stadion, had been bribed along with dozens of minor officials. There was little doubt that Gentz had received 'delightful news' on a really epoch-making scale; but Prince Metternich had a reputation for honesty and as he had approved the terms he stood firmly at Salomon's side. Fortunately, the first lottery issue recovered and the bonds of both instalments rose to new heights which quickly dispersed the ill-feeling.

The lottery took so much of Salomon's time that he settled in Vienna and opened a branch of the Rothschild bank. Although he enjoyed Metternich's favour, the position of Jews was far from

---

†James became Austrian consul-general in Paris a year later in 1822.

enviable in the Habsburg Empire. They could not own land, nor become judges, civil servants, lawyers, teachers or army officers. They could not marry unless they paid a poll tax, and were forced to report regularly to the 'Jewish Office'. Although 'foreign Jews' were given permits for limited periods only, an exception was made in the case of Salomon.

Nevertheless the law refusing Jews permission to buy houses was not relaxed, and Salomon took his revenge by booking every room in the Hotel Römischer Kaiser, the most luxurious hotel in the capital. He not only infuriated the King of Wurttemberg, a frequent visitor, who now was refused admittance, but annoyed the great composer, Beethoven, who would no longer give his recitals in the hotel's splendid concert hall. Salomon was quite unmoved by the complaints, and lived in great luxury with his wife, Caroline Stern, the daughter of a rich Frankfurt merchant, and his two children Amschel and Betty.

Salomon had the same corpulent body, the same round face and reddish hair as his brothers. Yet of the five sons he was the most likeable. He had none of Nathan's rudeness or James' moodiness; he was, in fact, generous, smiling and amiable; and within a few years the Frankfurt banker, Moritz Bethmann, was writing from Vienna: 'Salomon has won the affections of the people here, partly through

Salomon, Mayer Amschel Rothschild's second son and the founder of the Austrian branch, was perhaps the most generous and amiable of the five brothers.

The Rothschild coat-of-arms, as it was finally granted in 1822, with the eagles, crests and lions rampant which had been denied in 1817.

his general modesty and partly through his readiness to be obliging.'

Prince Metternich was also obliging. As Austria was chronically in debt and as Salomon's lottery loan had proved to be a huge success, Secretary Gentz urged the Chancellor to make a really spectacular gesture toward the House of Rothschild, something that would keep the indispensible bankers firmly in tow for years to come. Accordingly, in 1822, Metternich asked the Emperor to confer baronies on the five brothers. The Habsburg College of Heralds had no option now but to restore the eagles and crests and lions rampant. And this time the hand clutched not four but five arrows.

Nathan however put the imperial communication announcing the honour into a desk drawer and forgot about it. He rightly sensed that the British would not be impressed by a German Jew who had taken the trouble to become a naturalized Englishman yet insisted on sporting a foreign title. He thanked Metternich profusely but remained plain Mr Rothschild.

Salomon, on the other hand, not only emerged in full baronial splendour but soon was advising the daughter of the Emperor Francis, the Archduchess Marie Louise, on her private financial affairs. Marie Louise had been blatantly unfaithful to her fallen spouse, Napoleon Bonaparte. She made no attempt to visit him in exile; indeed, at the Congress of Vienna, Metternich, who had arranged her marriage with Napoleon, treated her as the helpless victim of despotism, and gave her as compensation the dukedoms of Parma, Piacenza and Guastalla.

The great Chancellor also provided the Archduchess with consolation in the form of a dashing young general, Count Albert von Neipperg, who had been wounded in the war and wore a black eye-patch. Marie Louise produced two children, one in 1819. As Napoleon was still alive, in far away St Helena, the birth of the little bastards was kept secret. However, when in 1821 he finally obliged her by dying, Marie Louise married her Count. The Austrian Emperor gave the children titles and a name that cleverly resembled that of their father: Neipperg came from Neu-berg, 'new mountain', so they were called the Counts of Montenuovo, the Italian equivalent.

Salomon was summoned to give the newly created Counts a fitting inheritance. He consulted Nathan and came up with an ingenious suggestion. Marie Louise was to declare that she had spent a large amount of her private fortune on the public buildings in Parma; then she could be reimbursed by the Parma Treasury. The money would be converted by the Rothschild bank into bonds, and sold to different people in different countries. Metternich extended to the Archduchess the guarantee 'that Your Majesty cannot do better than act in accordance with Rothschild's suggestion'. Apparently the Archduchess had the same idea for she put herself in Salomon's hands, ensuring a handsome heritage for her children.

Meanwhile Carl's turn had come as well. The second youngest of the five brothers, Carl was thirty-three in 1821. Three years earlier Friedrich von Gentz had described him as 'wanting in intelligence', as he was slow and ponderous and expressed himself falteringly. Because of his lack of confidence he had been employed for years as the family courier, making more journeys between Frankfurt and Cassel with messages for the Elector and Buderus than the rest of the brothers put together. Yet in 1821 Amschel and Salomon sent Carl to Naples to deal with a revolution and a military occupation, on the principle that even an ineffective Rothschild was better than no Rothschild at all.

The revolt that had broken out in Naples was an extension of the trouble that had started in Germany. The people demanded a constitution and seventy-year-old Ferdinand I, trembling with fear, at once collapsed and promised them everything they wanted. Ferdinand was the son of a Spanish king, from whom he had inherited the Kingdom of the Two Sicilies, and the husband of Maria Theresa's daughter, Maria Carolina, who had befriended Nelson's Lady Hamilton. Ferdinand's son had married the sister of Francis II, the reigning Austro-Hungarian Emperor.

Despite the close relationship between Ferdinand and the Habsburg sovereign Metternich was furious that the aged King had knuckled under to the insurgents, for he regarded the mildest form of liberalism as the thin edge of the wedge. He called a conference at Lailbach in Austria, which was attended by Alexander of Russia and Frederick William of Prussia. 'It is a matter of indifference,' he told the Tsar, 'whether the word be Buonaparte or the sovereignty of the people; they are both equally dangerous, and must therefore both be resisted. The Neapolitan revolt, and everything connected with it, must be completely stamped out, or else the Powers themselves will be destroyed.'[15]

Poor old Ferdinand of Naples was also summoned to the conference and immediately renounced all the pledges he had made to his people, agreeing that the only way to handle the situation was for Austrian troops to occupy his kingdom. But who would pay for the invasion? The Austrian Treasury was empty as usual. Prince Metternich invited Salomon Rothschild to Lailbach but the latter excused himself on the grounds that his lottery loans needed daily attention. Instead, he sent Carl who became known as 'un petit frère Rothschild'. Carl arrived with a plan concocted by Nathan and James suggesting that a loan should be raised in Naples which would defray the cost of the occupying army. This happy suggestion delighted the Lailbach congress and set the Austrian army in motion.

Nevertheless when the troops crossed the Po nerves were tense in Vienna; and when news came that in the north a rising had broken out in Alessandria, and that Piedmont might follow, Count Stadion, the Austrian Minister of Finance, completely lost his head. 'The situation is terrifying,' he wrote to Metternich. 'Never, not even in the darkest hours of the revolutionary wars, has an event produced such an effect on the Vienna Bourse than the news from Italy. . . . The whole of the population is rushing to get rid of our public securities. . . . Our credit is on the eve of vanishing completely. . . . This is the first step of our destruction. . . .'[16]

Even Metternich and Gentz were so upset that they could not eat their dinner; but the Prince recovered himself and insisted that 'it was impossible for us to take any other action. . . . I hope that one or two hard blows will decide the issue. . . .'

His wishes were granted for the Austrian army entered Naples on 24 March 1821, after a bloodless, thirteen-day march. Alessandria and Piedmont quietened down, and the eruption in Lombardy was forestalled. Carl von Rothschild accompanied King Ferdinand from Florence to Naples and breathed new spirit into him. The timid slow-witted Carl was blossoming into a man of decision. When an Italian money syndicate in Naples claimed that it could raise a loan far more effectively and cheaply than *le petit frère Rothschild*, Carl went to the Austrian general in command of the occupying army, and emerged as sole floater of the loan. The issue was a huge success. '. . . If only peace lasts for a little while,' Carl wrote to Prince Metternich, 'the loan will soon be fully subscribed, and it will not be necessary to ask for guarantees in respect of the balance, as in that case all State securities will rise in value, and the Neapolitans will follow suit. . .'[17]

Naples in the 1820s. Carl von Rothschild and his young wife, Adelheid, found it a congenial place and entertained distinguished guests in their palace on the Vesuvian shore.

Carl, flushed with triumph, found Naples a most congenial place; and Metternich, delighted by the success of 'the newest Rothschild' begged Salomon to urge him to remain. Adelheid, Carl's beautiful wife, settled the question by finding a wonderful palace on the Vesuvian shore which she persuaded Carl to buy. Here the young couple lived with their two children, entertaining the most distinguished society of the day. Among their royal guests was Leopold of Saxe-Coburg, Queen Victoria's favourite uncle, who later became King of the Belgians.

Soon the Rothschild bank opened by Carl was regarded as an Italian institution, for Rothschild money was flowing through all the states of Italy. It drained the marshes of Tuscany, fertilized the kingdom of Sardinia, and revitalized the Papal States. In 1832 when Carl visited the Vatican the Pope departed from custom and held out his hand. 'Rothschild has just kissed the Pope's hand,' reported a contemporary, 'and at his departure expressed his satisfaction with the successor of St Peter in the most gracious terms. . . . Others must bend down to the Holy Father's toe, but Rothschild is given a finger.'

Nathan watched the progress of his brothers in Central Europe with satisfaction. The chronic insolvency of Metternich's Government coupled with the chronic greed of Metternich's secretary – Gentz – enabled all three Rothschilds to dig themselves into entrenched positions by the early 1820s. Even the eldest brother, Amschel, who remained in Frankfurt and ran the patriarchal bank, benefited from the dazzling successes of Salomon and Carl. 'Most Gracious Prince! Most Gracious Prince and Lord!', he wrote to Prince Metternich, when the latter was passing through Frankfurt. 'I hope your Highness will not consider it as a presumption if I make so bold as to ask Your Highness to do me the gracious favour of taking soup with me this noon. Such a favour would mark an epoch in my life; but I would not have ventured this bold request if my brother in Vienna had not assured me that Your Highness did not entirely refuse to grant me this gracious favour . . .'[18]

Although Frankfurt society was impressed when Prince Metternich, accompanied by his mistress, Princess Lieven, accepted Amschel's invitation, the Rothschild influence already was considerable. 'Since arriving here,' wrote the Bremen Burgomaster in 1821, 'I have found to my great astonishment that people like the the Bethmanns, Gontards, Brentanos, eat and drink with prominent Jews, invite them to their houses and are invited back, and, when I expressed my surprise, I was told that, as no financial transaction of any importance could be carried through without the cooperation of these people, they had to be treated as friends and it was not desirable to fall out with them. . .'[19]

Amschel was the most religious of all the brothers and the only one of the five who was thin. He refused to touch anything but Kosher food and looked more like a rabbi than a banker.

Above, left Carl, '*le petit frère Rothschild*'.
Right Amschel, the eldest of Mayer Amschel's five sons, was by the mid-1820s the only one remaining in Frankfurt.

A man of thoroughly Oriental physiognomy [wrote one of his friends], with old Hebrew ways and manners. His hat is pushed back onto his neck … his coat is open …. From a kind of superstition he still keeps his office in the house; he feels that luck might desert him if he left the house. There he sits like a padishah among his clerks, on a raised platform, his secretaries at his feet and his clerks and agents bustling about …. No one is ever allowed to speak privately to him about business; everything is discussed openly in his office, as in the old Chinese Courts …[20]

Yet Amschel proved himself a skilful banker, eventually becoming treasurer to the German Confederation at Frankfurt which, as Prussia became increasingly dominating, was tantamout to serving as Prussian Minister of Finance. Amschel's bank on the Fahrgasse gave birth to railways, roads and factories. He was a compulsive worker and even had a desk in his bedroom.

Although he could have lived anywhere he liked, he refused to leave Frankfurt, feeling homesick away from the scenes of his childhood. Even the jack-booted young men who strode through the streets crying 'Hepp! Hepp!' failed to unnerve him. Once when an anti-Jewish crowd demonstrated outside his house he appeared on the balcony and said: 'There are forty million Germans. I have about as many florins. I will start by throwing each of you one.' He emptied a bag of silver and the youths laughed and cupped their hands, then turned and went home.

As the traditionalist of the family, it was fitting that Amschel should inherit his father's obligations. He never allowed the bonds to loosen between himself and the family of Hesse-Cassel, nor with Buderus von Carlhausen, the Elector's financial adviser who had directed so much business to the Rothschilds. Both of these men died within a few months of each other, Buderus in 1820, and the Elector William the following year. 'I will not win this battle,' the latter had observed with his usual correct appreciation of the situation.

Now Amschel maintained a link with William's son and heir, William X, the only difference being that the money flowed the other way, as Amschel financed the Prince. Often as the eldest Rothschild strode through the streets of Frankfurt in his caftan, onlookers would see him disappearing into His Serene Highness' courtyard, on his way to luncheon. 'The Hesses', a contemporary wrote in astonishment, 'take their midday meal *en famille* with their business friend.'

Although Amschel had moved to a large house in the middle of Frankfurt, his widowed mother, Gutle, seventy-two in 1825, and increasingly superstitious, refused to leave the ghetto for fear of bringing her children bad luck. She still lived in the House of the Green Shield, and from all over Europe sons and grandchildren came regularly to pay their respects. Gutle was uneducated and her hands were rough; but she understood the role played by her sons. Once, when one of her neighbours was fearful that war might break out between two German states, Gutle replied firmly: 'Nonsense. My boys won't give them the money.'

Gutle Rothschild in old age. She refused to leave the Judengasse for fear of bringing her children bad luck.

Chapter IV

Uneasy Times

(1825–36)

*T*HE ROTHSCHILDS WERE NOT LOVED BY EVERYONE. IF they made the best omelettes, they broke the most eggs, and by the middle of the 1820s their enemies ranged all the way from conservative bankers to liberal intellectuals, both of whom inveighed against the parvenus but for different reasons; the first for introducing change, the second for resisting it.

The intellectuals were the most dangerous for they fought with weapons of ridicule, and delighted in inventing a grotesque contrast between the immaculate Prince Metternich and his imaginary bodyguard of 'ghetto thugs'. Every generation must have its villains and to the young rebels on the Continent, clamouring for parliamentary government, this Prince who had patched up Europe in favour of the *ancien régime*, who had restored legitimist rulers whenever possible, represented the darkest forces of reaction. He was architect of the 'Unholy Alliance' while the Rothschilds, whose money underpinned his system, carried pitchforks and wore tails. Left-wing cartoonists gloried in depicting 'the prince of reaction' and the 'king of coin' co-operating to extinguish the freedom of Europe. One cartoon showed a gentleman with marked Semitic features, attired in a seedy caftan and an expensive lace shirt front, standing in a chariot fashioned of a strong box and drawn by the two-headed Imperial Austrian eagle, careering over Europe. In another, entitled *'Die Generalpümpe'* Rothschild, obese and coarse, stood knee-deep in a pool of gold, and with both arms acting as suction levers poured the world's wealth into the pockets of monarchs.

Nathan laughed at the cartoons and pinned them on his wall, for in London the Rothschild reputation stood high enough to withstand assault, particularly as the English did not take Metternich seriously. 'A society hero and nothing else,' pronounced Nathan's friend, the Duke of Wellington. 'An opportunist pure and simple,' declared Castlereagh, although at times he found Metternich's machinations praiseworthy. What could be more natural than the attempt of an aristocratic prince, German by birth, French by culture, to introduce a European system of checks and balances designed to preserve peace; particularly as the make-shift Austrian Empire which he served could only survive in a peaceful world?

Whereas Nathan remained indifferent to the attacks on the family, James and Salomon took the criticism to heart. Press articles not only cast aspersions on their politics but on their past, asking embarrassing questions about the sources of their wealth, and hinting at un-

Die Generalpumpe.

'*Die Generalpümpe*', an anonymous German caricature of the House of Rothschild referring to events about 1840. The figure's navel, consisting of a *louis d'or* is marked: '*Erd Achse*', or axis of the earth.

savoury reasons for their favour in high places. Even the famous Rothschild courier service became the subject of a scorching indictment.

Ever since Waterloo the brothers had concentrated on assembling the best network of intelligence agents on the continent, and organizing the fastest means of transmitting the intelligence from one point to another. All the branches had carrier pigeons trained to fly to the various capitals as occasion demanded; but now Rothschild 'stations' were set up on the main European highways to provide fresh horses and carriages for the Rothschild messengers, dressed conspicuously in the blue and yellow family livery. At Calais and Dunkirk boats and skippers in the exclusive pay of the family crossed the Channel in all weather.

As the Rothschild courier service was more efficient than any other, governments began to take advantage of it; and as the secret perusal of other people's correspondence was an accepted custom of the time, the Rothschilds did not shrink from it. Sometimes they gleaned intelligence of financial advantage but they had to move

71

warily as wily statesmen liked nothing better than to infiltrate letters into the mail containing false information designed to confuse and mislead the enemy. Thus the courier service became a factor in affairs of state and the brothers a frequent target of furious abuse. On one occasion Salomon was accused of delaying the post from Constantinople for two days outside Vienna in order to gain time 'to rig the market, and to make some hundreds for the Chancellor, Zichy and the rest of the pack of thieves, with the German fortress caretaker, Rothschild, the King of the Jews and the Jew of Kings at their head.'[1]

This was the sort of vicious broadside that James and Salomon most deplored. However, by the middle of 1824 the brothers were embroiled in undertakings which took their minds from their troubles. First of all, in July of that year, James married Salomon's nineteen-year-old daughter, Betty. The new Baroness was an immediate success. Installed on the Rue Laffitte in the magnificent Hôtel de Laborde, once the home of Napoleon's Police Commissioner (and later renamed the Hôtel Fouché), she was soon giving the most elegant parties in Paris. The Royal family took the bride under their wing, while poets and artists sang her praises. Ingres immortalized her in a portrait; Heinrich Heine dedicated a poem to her entitled 'The Angel'.

James' honeymoon, however, was only a minor distraction for in 1824 he was preoccupied with the biggest operation yet undertaken by the brothers, a plan to convert the French national debt from five per cent to three per cent. Just as Salomon was banker-in-chief to the Austrian Empire, James was banker-in-chief to Louis XVIII, whose reactionary Government fitted into the Metternich 'system'. After all, Rothschild money had helped to place the Bourbon King on his throne. Louis was not a prepossessing figure. Lame and bloated, 'an invalid of time not war', he presented a pitiful contrast to the great Bonaparte who had led his armies into almost every capital in Europe. Yet he did his best to play a role both regal and royal, placing such exaggerated insistence on ceremony that once, when he fell down, he refused to be helped up except by the Captain of the Guard. His Charter of 1814 had made concessions but stopped short of true parliamentary government; the ministers could be overthrown by the Chambers, only the ninety thousand richest citizens could vote, and only the ten thousand very richest were eligible as deputies.

Louis's chief minister, M. de Villèle, put the proposition of the loan conversion to Nathan Rothschild in 1823, suggesting that the Rothschild banks should form a consortium in collaboration with Barings of London and the famous financier, Jacques Laffitte, of Paris. The benefit of the conversion as far as the French Government was concerned was obvious: a saving of two per cent in interest payments would net the state a million francs a year. But how could the

Betty de Rothschild at the time of her marriage to her uncle James in 1824.

French rentiers be persuaded to exchange bonds worth five per cent per annum for bonds worth only three per cent? Two temptations must be placed in their way: the old bonds must rise to irresistible heights; the new bonds must threaten to follow. To achieve these results the bankers would have to raise at least £150,000,000; not only would plenty of cash be needed to buy up the old bonds, but bulling the market was always a costly operation. Nathan agreed to undertake the scheme, but for a breathtaking profit; nothing less than the full two per cent saved by the Government in the first year after conversion.

One of the conditions of the deal was that M. de Villèle would seek the consent of the French Chambre des Députés. The minister was so confident of his success, however, that he begged the bankers to begin work at once. Together, the various consortia bought up thousands of francs of old bonds, and drove up the price from 92 to 106. But when Villèle went to the Lower Chamber he was astonished at the outcry. The deputies did not seem to care what price the old bonds had reached; the idea that they were being asked to take two per cent less in interest struck them as an outrageous impertinence. They accused the Government of manipulation, exploitation and dishonesty, personally charging Villèle with robbing the country to enrich the bankers. Poor old Louis XVIII was so upset that he did not dare to show himself on the streets. Nevertheless, the Lower Chamber finally passed Villèle's bill; but to everyone's astonishment the Peers, led by the Vicomte de Châteaubriand, who hated both Louis XVIII and his chief minister, threw the bill out.

The consternation among the bankers can be imagined. All the more, as Jacques Laffitte, one of the most influential members of the consortium, suddenly discovered that the Rothschilds for some days past had been selling their five-per-cent bonds in secret. As the rest of the group was trying to bull the market they did not take a kindly view of this private bear operation. A less private manoeuvre was directed by the banker Ouvrard. He successfully drove down the shares, making a profit of millions as they fell. Baring and Laffitte panicked, and got rid of their holdings with severe losses, while the Rothschild group, minus the Rothschilds, barely scrambled out alive.

A year later Villèle managed to get his bill through both chambers and returned to the charge. James and Nathan agreed to have another try, but this time they were careful to safeguard themselves. The scheme was a total failure, only eight per cent of the bond holders cashing in old certificates for the new three-per-cent bonds.

The Liberal peers seized the opportunity to mount a new attack on the Rothschilds depicting the conversion scheme as a brutal attempt to rob the poor. James and Salomon did everything in their power to improve their public image; but whereas some newspaper owners and journalists bent to the agreeable pressure of Rothschild gifts and hospitality, there were always new writers and new papers to continue the attack. At this point the indefatigable Friedrich von Gentz came forward with a suggestion. For a consideration – rather a handsome consideration – he would write a biographical account of the House of Rothschild which would go a long way to silence the family detractors. Salomon eagerly agreed to collaborate and Gentz set to work. He was successful beyond expectation as he managed to persuade the editors of the famous Brockhaus encyclopaedia to insert his article in a condensed form, in the edition of 1827.

For nearly a century this work was accepted as the authentic history of the family. The theme, of course, was the triumph of sheer goodness, a simple tale for simple people. Every trace of Rothschild ingenuity was eliminated for the highlights not only dimmed but extinguished. For instance, Buderus, the key figure of the drama, the middle man who diverted the Elector's money into Rothschild hands, was relegated to the land of limbo. He did not exist. And as he did not exist it was only logical that there should be no mention of Nathan's successful speculation with the Elector's funds; no mention of running gold to Wellington's armies, or paying subsidies for the British Government; or bearing the French loan to force Europe to recognize Rothschild power.

Credit for the family fortune belonged entirely to the virtuous behaviour of Father Mayer Amschel who was depicted as a banker, not as a petty trader. Mayer was friend and confidant of the Elector who, when he was forced to flee from the French, entrusted all his worldly goods to him. Mayer hid the millions of money in his ghetto cellar and when, eventually, the French police arrived to search the House of the Green Shield, managed to divert the attention of the marauders by sacrificing his own hard-earned cash. At the end of the war he returned William of Hesse's treasure intact and the grateful Prince made him a rich man. It was the reward of virtue told with gushing admiration. '. . . It must never be overlooked,' wrote Gentz, 'that in addition to the reasonableness of their terms, the punctuality of their services, the simplicity and clarity of their methods and the intelligence with which they are carried through, it is the personal moral character of the five brothers that has the greatest influence upon the success of their relationship . . .'

All this was perfectly true but of course there was no mention that the Rothschilds, in partnership with Carl Buderus, had gambled with the Elector's money without the Elector's knowledge or permission. Despite the fact that all the money had been returned to William, plus interest and appreciation, the irregularity would not help the brothers to establish themselves as the world's most scrupulous bankers. So Gentz decided to eliminate it; and the elimination necessitated the suppression of a whole string of events, such as Nathan's huge purchase of gold which led to his introduction to John Herries and his work for the British Government.

Gentz was amazingly smug. He would not even admit that the Rothschilds had been lucky. 'In particular instances good or adverse fortune may indeed determine a man's destiny in life,' he wrote, 'though even then not exclusively. But enduring success, like persistent illfortune, is always, and to a far greater extent than is commonly supposed, the fruit of personal merit or personal inefficiency or wrong-doing.'

Gentz' moralizing was greatly appreciated by the family. Indeed, when he died, Salomon wrote sadly to James:

He was a friend whose like I shall certainly never meet again. He cost me something frightful – you have no idea how much. He would just simply write down on a scrap of paper what he required and the amount would be handed to him without further ado. Yet now he is gone I can see how valuable he was to us. Gladly would I give three times as much to have him back.[2]

According to the enemies of the family Gentz' *Biographical Account* provided the Rothschilds with a halo which bore a marked resemblance to a life-saver. This of course was greatly exaggerated for in life all is apt to be well that ends well; and the Elector, who apparently remained permanently in the dark about the way his investments had been handled, was so surprised and delighted to receive back even more money than he had parted with, that he had nothing but praise for the Rothschilds. Although the article gained the brothers a short respite from attack by wrapping them in the impregnable respectability of dullness, it did not prevent them from making another dashing foray – and another costly miscalculation – which again rocked their empire.

This time, as before, the trouble started in Paris. Louis XVIII died in the summer of 1824 and was succeeded by his brother, Charles X, a handsome, white-haired gentleman of sixty-seven, whose stormy youth had given way to an obtuse old age. As Austrian consul-general, James de Rothschild saw the new King crowned at Rheims, little realizing that Charles would go into the history books as the last sovereign to be annointed in the ancient city. James was well pleased with the turn of events, for Charles retained M. de Villèle as his chief minister, and Villèle retained James as his banker-in-chief.

However, the government soon found itself facing the normal dilemma of governments: rising prices, unemployment, popular discontent. In October 1827 Castellane noted in his diary, 'M. de Villèle has as many supporters . . . as the plague would have if it awarded government pensions.' So the King finally dismissed Villèle, appointing instead an even more reactionary chief minister, M. de Polignac, son of Marie Antoinette's old favourite.

Needless to say conditions did not improve. The King and Polignac were accused of being indifferent to the plight of the people, of interesting themselves in the rebuilding of the Bastille and the abolition of the metric system instead of providing food. Charles X was plotting with Polignac, but for very different reasons. He was drawing up a new and ultra-Royalist Cabinet. When the list was published Charles announced a general election hoping that the voters (restricted to ninety thousand people) would nominate a Chamber that reflected the conservative views of the new ministry. Instead, the voters returned the old Chamber, a loud slap in the face for the King.

Now the rumours came fast and thick: the Government was planning a show-down; the King was about to sign an order declaring Paris under martial law; Polignac was mobilizing troops to prevent the Chamber from meeting. No one was more agitated by the news than James de Rothschild as he had just acquired a contract for a large French loan. The new issue had been taken over at an extremely high figure, and if there was any truth in the gossip, riots were bound to occur, perhaps even a revolution, perhaps even a war. In the circumstances what would become of French credit and the expensive new bonds? From London, Nathan Rothschild reported that the energetic Ouvrard was unloading French securities at panic prices and on a truly impressive scale. He advised James to try and stop the downward trend by bulling the market; but first, of course, James must discover the truth.

James could not believe that Ouvrard, who had done his best to ruin the government conversion scheme by bearing the market, had inside information denied to him, Royal banker, government confidant, blue-eyed boy of the Bourbons. M. de Polignac restored James's confidence. He assured him that Ouvrard was making a fool of himself. Talk of a *coup d'état* was tittle-tattle. If the government took any dramatic steps James de Rothschild would be the first to know. He could return home and have a good night's sleep.

This was on the evening of 24 July. The next morning Charles x signed the famous Polignac decree, dissolving the newly elected Chamber, restricting the suffrage and gagging the Press.

Left A state of siege was declared in Paris on 28 July 1830. Meeting of the deputies – Laffitte, Casimir Périer, Lobau, Gérard, Mauguin and the Duc de Raguse.

Opposite Baroness Betty, James' wife, by Ingres. One of the most renowned hostesses of her day, she not only entertained Napoleon III, and Empress Eugénie but writers and poets such as Georges Sand, Balzac and Heine whose poem, 'The Angel', was inspired by her.

Overleaf Nathan and his family, by W. A. Hobday. The painting hangs today in the entrance hall of New Court.

Paris took up the challenge and overnight barricades sprang up on every street. The house of banker Jacques Laffitte, the man who had taken umbrage at James de Rothschild's behaviour during the conversion scheme – was the meeting place for the rebels. Bloody encounters took place between insurgents and military and two thousand people were killed. Old inhabitants said that it was 1789 all over again. Pandemonium reigned on the Bourse with *rentes* falling thirty points in a day. The King and his ministers, surprised and terrified by the storm they had let loose, fled from the capital. Yet before he shook the Paris dust from his feet the insensitive Charles X was not averse to asking a favour of James de Rothschild, the man he had almost brought tumbling down with him. With complete *sang froid* he stopped at James's country house, on the outskirts of the Bois de Boulogne, and asked him for a loan – which James of course gave to him.

Suddenly banker Jacques Laffitte produced a saviour in the form of Louis-Philippe, Duke of Orleans, and a cousin of Charles X. He had all the right credentials, including his famous father, Philippe-Égalité, of the first Revolution. When Louis-Philippe rode among the people he was acclaimed with enthusiasm. The July Revolution was over almost as soon as it had begun, and France had a new sovereign, a Citizen King. Jacques Laffitte was rewarded, (over-rewarded some thought), with the office of Chief Minister and Minister of Finance.

This was only one of the bitter pills that the Rothschilds had to swallow. Their holdings had dropped by 17,000,000 gulden and for a few weeks people whispered that the family was facing bankruptcy. The Rothschild courier service, however, had proved its worth, literally, in gold. Long before the news was received by the all powerful Metternich in Austria, or by Queen Victoria's ministers in London, or by King Frederick William's Government in Prussia, the yellow-and-blue-capped messengers had brought the Rothschild brothers an account of the fateful happenings. All over Europe bourses slumped and government securities fell to new lows. But the advance information had allowed Nathan and Salomon to sell before the bottom was reached; and later more information instructed them to buy back in time to recoup their huge losses with a resurgence of confidence that sent the shares rocketing again. No one was more impressed by the Rothschild intelligence service than the former French ambassador to the Court of St James, Prince Talleyrand. 'The English Ministry,' he had once written from London to Paris, 'is always informed of everything by the Rothschilds ten to twelve hours before the despatches of Lord Stuart [the British ambassador] in Paris arrive: and this is necessarily so because the vessels used by the Rothschild couriers belong to the House; they take no passengers and sail in all weathers.'[3]

Although James de Rothschild no longer enjoyed the confidence

The Salon Rouge at Château Lafite, with red damask upholstery and the portraits of the five brothers on the walls; it also contains a table brought from Ferrières, on which Bismarck dictated to Jules Favre the terms of the Treaty of Frankfurt.

of the government because of the hostility of Jacques Laffitte, he worked furiously to maintain peace between Austria and France. The Rothschild banks could survive a minor revolution: but would the virus spread across Europe as it had done forty years earlier? And would Metternich decide that the best way to cure the disease was to declare war on the French King, explaining to the world that he was 'cutting out the cancer'?

Prolonged disturbances of any kind were bad for banking profits but a war could be ruinous: so James organized his own counter-espionage group. He instructed every Rothschild agent in France to keep his ear close to the ground and to winkle out the secrets of the revolutionary emigrés who were conspiring to stir up trouble abroad. Although a full-scale revolt broke out in Brussels in the summer, leading to the separation of Holland and Belgium, the trouble did not spread beyond the borders of these countries. Indeed, James managed to scotch intrigues that might have resulted in major uprisings in Germany and Spain.

James' activities commended him to the new King. Although Louis-Philippe had appointed Jacques Laffitte his Finance Minister, the truth was that the King ceased to be a liberal as soon as he had seized the throne. Laffitte's radical recommendations annoyed and frightened him, whereas James de Rothschild's advice to 'restrain his followers' struck a sympathetic chord. Furthermore Laffitte's pre-occupation with government business induced him to neglect his own affairs, causing people to question his general competence. Indeed, in London, Nathan Rothschild spoke disparagingly of the man 'who imagined that he could save the finances of France but was unable to preserve his own fortune'.

The King finally acted on James' advice to appoint banker Casimir Périer – a staunch friend of the House of Rothschild – as Minister of Finance in Laffitte's place. In order to soften the blow, Louis-Philippe renamed the Rue d'Artois, where the fallen Minister had his office, the Rue Laffitte. Ironically enough, Messieurs de Rothschild Frères had quarters on the same street. 'I ask forgiveness of God and the world for my share in the revolution,' said Laffitte as he retired from power and took his place in the ranks of the Opposition.

Meanwhile the July Revolution continued to provoke repercussions, and Austria and France, as champions respectively of conservative and radical forces, glared at each other with increasing ill-will. In the spring of 1831 uprisings in Italy forced the Duke of Modena to flee from his capital, and Marie Louise to abandon Parma. In Bologna the population threw off the papal yoke.

Metternich responded to the cries for help by sending an army across the Po. Although Louis-Philippe had no desire to find himself embroiled in the struggle, one of his minions in the Foreign Office composed an ultimatum to Prince Metternich. 'Yesterday,' James wrote to Salomon, 'the note was drafted which is to be sent to

Casimir Périer, a great friend of James de Rothschild, was made Minister of Finance by King Louis – Philippe, in place of Jacques Laffitte.

CASIMIR PÉRIER.

Austria. It contained the phrase "évacuez immédiatement Boulogna" [sic] . . . . I shall see that this is left out.' It was, and the temperature dropped.

Throughout the months of crisis James soothed both sides, sending letters to Salomon specially designed for Prince Metternich, whom he referred to as 'Uncle'. He indulged in profuse flattery and even went to the length of describing Louis-Philippe as a secret Royalist.

If Uncle wants peace, and convinces our Government that he does, we shall have peace; and he will certainly have a firmer control over affairs here than he had in Polignac's time. For neither the Ministry nor the Chamber are, as had been supposed, ultra liberal: indeed their views have been modified so much that they are more inclined to Royalism.... You can see a proof of this in the way they deal with their Spanish revolutionaries; there are no more clubs or popular gatherings. Each day we have new laws for maintaining peace; there are no posters or tub-thumpers; the revolutionary papers are being suppressed ...

And in another letter, not intended for Uncle's eyes; 'Do try to find out the position, for even though we are not carrying out any transactions in *rentes* we have a holding of 900,000 [18,000,000 francs worth]: if peace is preserved they will be worth 75, while in the case of war they will drop to 45. . .'[4]

By 1832 everyone could breathe again: peace had been preserved, and Government securities were rising in all the capitals in Europe. At this point a cholera epidemic broke out in Vienna. Salomon was panic stricken and, although Metternich remained in the capital, fled to Paris. Nathan and James raised their eyebrows, but stifled their disapproval, for Salomon was the most highly strung of the four brothers and apt to fly off the handle at any serious criticism. He had always been neurotic about disease and on this occasion the epidemic pursued him to Paris, and before long thirty-two thousand people were dead, among them Casimir Périer, who had insisted on visiting the hospitals.

The Rothschilds mourned the friend whom they had put into power and who, in turn, had helped them to win the confidence of the new King. Louis-Philippe not only gave Messieurs de Rothschild Frères a virtual monopoly of all state loans but delighted James by awarding him the Grand Cross of the Legion of Honour.

Although James had a genius for survival, he deferred to Nathan as the greatest banker in Europe. Banking was still in such a rudimentary state that even bankers seemed to be baffled by it. Yet to Nathan nothing appeared mysterious. He long ago had grasped the interplay of finance and economics, the effect of political news on the stock exchange, the quickest way of bearing or bulling a market. He understood how the balance of trade affected gold reserves, and how gold reserves affected the rate of exchange. Many of the financial books written during his day quote his views as definitive:

... As Mr. Rothschild puts it the balance of payments as to those countries with which you trade is really and truly the only guide for the rate of
exchange. If the balance of payments be against you, the exchanges are
against you. *Vice versa*....Mr. Rothschild states it as a matter of fact,
within his own experience, that there is a surplus of articles exported from
this country above those imported, in consequence of which there is a
regular payment of gold to this country from the whole world. 'I purchase,' says he, 'regularly week by week, from £80,000 to £100,000
worth of bills, which are drawn for goods shipped from Liverpool, Manchester, Newcastle, and other places and I send them to the continent to
my houses. My houses purchase against them bills upon this country,
which are drawn for wines, wool, and other commodities. But if there be
not a sufficient supply of bills abroad on this country we are obliged to get
gold from Paris, Hamburg, and elsewhere.' In this way there is, in point
of fact, in the ordinary course of things, a regular payment of gold to this
country from the whole world, which shows, that the bills drawn abroad
are not equal to those drawn at home; and that 'the bills drawn upon the
Royal Exchange must bring gold from all parts of the World'.[5]

Nathan had a prodigious memory. He not only helped to regulate
the English exchange rate day by day, but could keep in mind the
fluctuating rates through Europe and their relations to one another,
which frequently enabled him to make lightning forays on the Stock
Exchange and to reap lightning rewards. Visitors to London who
wandered through the narrow streets of the City occasionally
caught a glimpse of an extraordinary figure standing in a courtyard
surrounded by a crowd of people.

He was a very common looking person [wrote an American tourist],
with heavy features, flabby pendant lips and projecting fish eyes. His
figure which was stout, awkward and ungainly, was enveloped in the
loose folds of an ample surtout. Yet there was something commanding
in his air and manner, and the deferential respect which seemed voluntarily
rendered to him showed that he was no ordinary person. 'Who is that?'
was the natural question. 'The King of the Jews' was the reply. The persons
crowding around him were presenting bills of exchange. He would glance
for a moment at a paper, return it, and with an affirmatory nod, turn to the
next individual pressing for an audience. Two well looking young men,
with somewhat of an air of dandyism, stood beside him making a memo-
randum to assist in the recollections of bargains regulating the whole
Continental Exchanges of the day. Even without this assistance he is said
to be able to call to mind every bargain he has made. Of these he may now
be esteemed the King.[6]

To many people the figure of Nathan Rothschild was even more
awesome on the floor of the Stock Exchange, hands always thrust
in pockets, hat .pulled over eyes, dressed in the funeral black of
ghetto days. Indeed, in 1833, a publicity seeker caused an uproar
when he usurped the great Rothschild's favourite pillar and refused
to give ground.

A strong sensation was created in the Royal Exchange on Tuesday, [reported the *Observer*] in consequence of Mr. N. M. Rothschild, the eminent capitalist, being prevented from taking his usual station, with his back leaning against one of the pillars of the building at the south-east corner of the Royal Exchange. A Mr. Rose, of Trinity Square, placed himself in this spot just as Mr. Rothschild entered the 'Change to conduct his transactions in the Foreign Exchanges. In vain did Mr. Rothschild courteously remonstrate with the intruder – in vain did the Exchange porters exert themselves – Mr. Rose would not stir from the pillar, and Mr. Rothschild was ultimately compelled to retreat to the benches in the rear. Mr. Rothschild . . . was so excited by being displaced that it was some time before he could compose himself and do business. We believe that sometime ago a similar attempt was made to oust Mr. Rothschild from his pillar.[7]

Had Mr Rose taken a bet? Whatever the explanation, the scene was never repeated.

Nathan received a steady stream of eminent foreign visitors at his office at New Court. He was such a celebrity that everyone wanted to meet him. The Prince of Puckler-Muskau, who was touring England in 1826, was determined to call upon the 'true lion', 'the sovereign' as he called him.

I found him, [he wrote] in a poor, obscure-looking place (his residence is in another part of the town) and making my way with some difficulty through the little courtyard, blocked up by a waggon laden with bars of silver, I was introduced into the presence of the Grand Ally of the Holy Alliance. I found the Russian consul in the act of paying his court. He is an acute, clever man, perfect in the part he has to play and uniting the due respect with a becoming air of dignity.

This was the more difficult because the very original aristocrat of the City did not stand much on ceremony. On presenting my letter of credit, he said ironically, that we were lucky people who could afford to travel about so, and take our pleasure; while he, poor man, had such a heavy burden to bear. He then broke out into bitter complaints that every poor devil who came to England had something or other to ask of them. 'Yesterday,' said he, 'here was a Russian begging of me' (an episode which threw a bitter-sweet expression over the consul's face); 'and,' added he, 'the Germans here don't give me a moment's peace.' Now it was my turn to put a good face upon the matter.

After this the conversation took a political turn, and we both of course agreed that Europe could not subsist without him; – he modestly declined our compliment, and said, smiling, 'Oh no, you are only jesting – I am but a servant, whom people are pleased with because he manages their affairs well, and to whom they let some crumbs fall as an acknowledgment.'

All this said in a language quite peculiar to himself, half English, half German – the English part with a broad German accent, but with the imposing confidence of a man who feels such trifles to be beneath his attention. This truly original language struck me as very characteristic of a man who is unquestionably a person of genius, and of a certain sort of greatness of character.[8]

Some months later the Prince was invited to the Rothschilds' house at Stamford Hill for dinner. Here he found two or three directors of the East India Company and Nathan's large family. Nathan was 'amusing and talkative' and the Prince was highly diverted to hear him explaining the pictures around his dining-room, all of which were portraits of the sovereigns of Europe presented through their ministers, and to hear him talk of the originals, not only as his good friends but his equals. The Prince was impressed by the family's pride in their Jewish ancestry and religion; but of course this was true of all Rothschilds everywhere. Not only was the family faithful to its past, but it never lost an opportunity to use its influence for the betterment of its co-religionists. When Carl lent money to the Pope he made it a condition that His Holiness should work for the abolition of the Roman ghetto; and in 1829 Nathan presented a petition to the House of Commons asking Parliament to abolish the disabili-

Nathan, 'the great humming top spinning a loan', etching by A. Crowquill, 1829.

The Great Humming Top Spinning a loan!!!

Rothschild

ties of the Jews. In Frankfurt Amschel had scored a great victory in 1823 when he had been instrumental in enacting a law permitting marriages between Christians and Jews. 'This scandalous law,' the seventy-four-year-old Goethe had fulminated, 'will undermine all family sense of morality, intimately associated with religion as it is. . . . How can a Jewess be prevented from becoming principal Lady of the Bedchamber? Foreigners are bound to think that bribery has been at work to make such a law possible. I expect that the all-powerful Rothschilds are behind it.'

Despite the long hours that Nathan worked he was devoted to his wife and seven children; finally, a short time before the Prince of Puckler-Muskau called at New Court, he succumbed to the entreaties of his over-crowded family and moved them into a large house at 107 Piccadilly. Unlike other rich men Nathan's pleasure was making money not spending it, and he was annoyed to find himself a target for every art dealer in London. As he was completely indifferent to the furnishings, his wife undertook the responsibility; but occasionally, to please a friend who recommended this artist, or that, he bought a picture. 'Give me any one you like,' he would instruct the painter, 'as long as it does not cost over £30.' His attitude toward music was much the same. When Hannah invited the well-

The long-standing Rothschild connection with the Duke of Wellington provoked the caricature 'An Untoward Event or a Tory Triumph', by 'Shortshanks', an attack on the Wellington administration, 1828.

known composer, Spohr, to give a concert, Nathan congratulated the performer, then jingled the coins in his pocket, saying: 'This is my music.'

Nathan was subjected to a steady stream of people asking him the secret of his riches. Sometimes he replied brusquely: 'Selling enough of anything.' Othertimes he moralized: 'Stick to one business, young man; stick to your brewery, and you may be the great brewer of London. Be a brewer and a banker and a merchant and a manufacturer and you will soon be in the *Gazette*.' But Nathan also believed that luck played a part for he once told his friend, Thomas Buxton: 'I have seen many very clever men who had not shoes to their feet. I never act with them. Their advice sounds very well, but fate is against them. They cannot get on themselves; if they cannot do good to themselves, how can they do good to me?'[9]

On the whole Nathan was a contented man but every now and then the begging letters, the threats, the adulation, the constant pressures because of his money, seemed to disgust him, and then he talked in a cynical vein. 'Sometimes to amuse myself,' he told Buxton, 'I give a beggar a guinea. He thinks I have made a mistake and, for fear I should find it out, off he runs as hard as he can. I advise you to give a beggar a guinea sometimes. It is very amusing.'

Although Nathan did not gladly sit through the interminably long services at the synagogue he considered himself a practising Jew. The notion that any of his children could marry outside the faith shocked him. In 1832 his beautiful seventeen-year-old daughter, Hannah, went to Paris to stay with Aunt Betty and Uncle James. They gave a ball and during the evening Prince Edmond de Clary, the twenty-one-year-old son of a famous Austrian family, fell madly in love with her. He asked his friend Prince Esterhazy, a former ambassador to London, to approach Nathan Rothschild and to press his suit. Esterhazy obliged, but his eloquence had no effect. 'I will never allow my daughter to marry a Christian,' Nathan said flatly: and immediately sent a message to Hannah to return home at once.

Normally Nathan left all problems to do with the children to his wife, for domestic affairs bored him. Although he complained about the long hours he worked, he was only really happy at the bank. Not only was he master of his craft but he knew that he had few equals; and as all five Rothschild banks in five countries were branches of the same firm, he master-minded every financial deal made by his brothers.

The German banker, Moritz von Bethmann, believed that the main reason for the Rothschilds' success was 'the harmony between the brothers'.

None of them [he wrote] ever thinks of finding fault with another. None of them adversely criticizes any of the others' business dealings, even when the results do not come up to expectations. . .[10]

However, occasionally it was expedient for the brothers to pretend that they did not see eye to eye. In 1834 Nathan decided that he must acquire the quick-silver mine at Almeida in Spain. As there were only two such deposits in Europe, and he already owned the mine at Idria in Austria, control of the Spanish mine would give him a monopoly. In order to effect the purchase Nathan had to establish friendly relations with the liberal-minded Queen Regent, Maria Christina. He did this by lending her £600,000. Unfortunately Prince Metternich was financing the Queen's opponents, the Absolutist Party led by the pretender, Don Carlos, and was furious at what he considered 'an outrageous deception'.

As Metternich's policies dominated Austria, Prussia and the King-dom of the Two Sicilies, where three of the brothers resided, and influenced the Bourbon King of France, where the fourth brother lived, it is not surprising that the Rothschilds were anxious to retain his good will. Salomon tried to mend matters by explaining to Metternich, rather ingeniously, that Nathan's wife, Hannah, 'a liberal-minded Cohen', had prevailed upon her husband to advance the money against his better instincts.

This explanation apparently did not satisfy Metternich and Salomon wrote an even more grovelling letter, referring to Nathan as 'a child in politics'. 'Nathan Mayer Rothschild is not particularly bright,' he confided. 'He is exceedingly competent in his office but, apart from that, between you and ourselves, he can hardly spell his own name.'[11] This ludicrous apology appeased Metternich who forgot and forgave, while Nathan added several more millions to his brothers' balance sheets.

In June 1836 Nathan's son and heir, twenty-eight-year-old Lionel, married his cousin Charlotte, only daughter of Carl von Rothschild of Naples. The wedding took place in Frankfurt to please eighty-three-year-old Gutle who still lived in the House of the Green Shield in the ghetto. The fact of a Rothschild marrying a Rothschild had become normal procedure; indeed, of the twelve marriages con-tracted by the sons of the five brothers, nine were with Rothschild women. It was not only that the young men were brought up to think of good matches in terms of dowries, but the number of attractive Jewesses with the same sophisticated tastes as themselves was limited, that is, outside the family.

Frankfurt was accustomed to splendour. For centuries it had witnessed the crowning of the Holy Roman Emperors, and since 1815 had been the seat of the German Confederation. Yet the general public seemed much more excited by the world-famous Rothschilds, who flowed in for the wedding from the four corners of Europe, than by royalty. The English contingent was flanked by innumer-able Cohens and Montefiores, Sterns and Goldsmiths and Gom-pertzes. In the middle of the group was the slightly incongruous

A Jewish wedding in the Judengasse in Frankfurt. Lionel's wedding to his cousin Charlotte, in June 1836, was followed a few weeks later by his father's death.

figure of the celebrated Rossini who once upon a time had instructed Nathan's daughter, Hannah, how to play her pure gold harp – a gift from her father. Crowds lined the streets to see the expensive equipages, the high-stepping horses, the silks and satins, the rustle and bustle. Many houses flew the flags of England and Naples, while the Judengasse was resplendent with floral decorations.

Fifty-nine year old Nathan had a carbuncle on his neck and on the day of the wedding was hot and flushed. At the feast he shivered, and finally took to his bed. That was the middle of June: and by the middle of July he was no better, still running a high temperature. His wife sent a courier racing to England to bring the celebrated physician, Benjamin Travers, to his side. Although the poison had spread through Nathan's system, sometimes causing delirium, much of the time his mind was lucid, enabling him to do a great deal of moralizing. He begged his sons to keep the business property intact, and not to participate in any risky ventures. The world, he said, would try to make money out of them so they must be all the more careful; and above all, they must hold together in unity.

There was a good deal of praying, of course. Ten minutes before his death a rabbi gave him the confessional and he began to read: 'I acknowledge unto thee, Lord my God and God of my fathers, that both my cure and my death are in thy hands. May it be thy will. . .' Then he stopped and put the book aside. 'It is not necessary that I should pray so much, for believe me, according to my convictions I have not sinned. . .'

Meanwhile throughout July persistent rumours of Nathan Rothschild's illness had depressed the London stock-market. 'The dangerous state in which Mr. Rothschild remains,' commented a correspondent of *The Times* in 'City Intelligence', on 2 August 1836, 'by the accounts from Frankfurt has again today had its effect upon Spanish and Portuguese securities and a further depression of $1\frac{1}{2}$ per cent has taken place in them . . . it seems generally expected that the firm would call in all the loans advanced upon these securities by Mr. Rothschild and hence the anxiety of all the borrowers to dispose of their stock. . .'

On the day of Nathan's death, 28 July, carrier pigeons were released to fly to Rothschild houses all over Europe to prevent unnecessary losses. Apparently only one pigeon reached the English coast and was inadvertently shot by a farmer who was puzzled by the message the bird was carrying: '*Il est mort*.' On 27 July *The Times* had scoffed at the notion that there was anything 'seriously wrong' with the banker; and a week later, on 2 August was emphatically denying that the great man had departed from this world. 'Some of the morning papers give a report of the death of Mr. Nathan Rothschild. We have made inquiry and we learn that there is no truth in such a report. . .'

The body reached London by boat; and the funeral procession took place on 8 August with Lord Mayor, sheriffs, aldermen, ambassadors and ministers following the coffin. *The Times*, at last on firm ground, declared:

The death of Nathan Mayer Rothschild is one of the most important events for the City, and perhaps for Europe, which has occurred for a very long time. His financial transactions have pervaded the whole of the Continent, and . . . influenced money business of every description. No operations on an equally large scale existed in Europe previous to his time . . . . Mr. Rothschild, like the rest of his brothers, held a patent of nobility with the title of Baron, but he never assumed it and was more justly proud of that name under which he had acquired a distinction which no title could convey . . . [4 August 1836]

'The Shadow of a Great Man', a caricature of Nathan Rothschild, published in the month following his death and showing him standing by his favourite pillar at the Exchange; in his hand he is holding four keys for his four brothers.

Funeral jewel of Hannah Rothschild, Nathan's widow; it is inscribed: 'N. M. Rothschild, Esq. ob. 28 July 1836'.

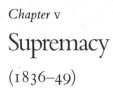

Chapter v

Supremacy

(1836–49)

*I*N JANUARY 1838 BENJAMIN DISRAELI, A NEWLY ELECTED member of Parliament, attended a concert in London crowded with important people including the Duke of Wellington. 'But', he wrote to his future bride, Mrs Wyndham Lewis, 'the most picturesque group was the Rothschilds, the widow [Lionel's mother] still in mourning, two sons, some sisters and, above all, the young bride or rather wife from Frankfurt, universally admired, tall, graceful, dark and clear, a robe of yellow silk, a hat and feathers, with a sort of Sevigné beneath magnificent pearls; quite a Murillo.'[1]

The widowed Mrs Nathan had just moved into Gunnersbury Park, the elegant country house buried deep in the countryside of Acton, yet only eight miles from Hyde Park Corner, which her husband had bought a few months before his death for £20,000. The residence had once belonged to George II's daughter, Princess Amelia, a sister of William of Hesse's much neglected wife. As it was much too large, Mrs Nathan asked Lionel and his wife to share it with her, and to take over the running of the place.

Lionel was very different from his pugnacious outspoken father, who had lived for work and prided himself on his disdain for Society. A quiet person with a puckish sense of humour he was a conformist not a rebel, a retiring man with occasional flashes of wit and a strong streak of snobbishness. In 1836 he applied to the British sovereign for permission for his brothers and himself to style themselves 'Baron', the honour bestowed upon them by the Austrian Emperor in 1822, which Nathan had so grandly ignored. A few months later Queen Victoria mounted the throne, and as her relations – George IV and his brothers – had borrowed large sums of money from the Elector of Hesse, through the services of Nathan Rothschild, she undoubtedly was well acquainted with the family name and pleased to grant the request. She gave her consent in 1838.

Lionel's desire to use the barony was understandable. But twelve years later, when his mother died, he did something quite unexpected. He laid her to rest in a grave beside her husband: and at one fell swoop embellished both parents with the titles that they had disdained to use when alive. On his mother's tomb he placed the following inscription:

Baroness Hannah de Rothschild
Relict of the late Baron
Nathan Mayer de Rothschild

Lionel de Rothschild as a young man.

Above Gunnersbury House, near London, once the summer residence of Princess Amelia, daughter of George II, was bought by Nathan Rothschild in 1835; but he never lived there and his son Lionel inherited the property.

Left Lionel de Rothschild's wife, Charlotte, with four of her children: Leonora, Evelina, Nathaniel, and Alfred.

It is not strange that the Rothschilds, richer than any family before them, said to worth an aggregate of £200,000,000 should have had magic for young Mr Disraeli who had no sense about money and was always running into debt. He struck up a friendship with Lionel which became one of the deep attachments of his life. Always present at Rothschild weddings, funerals and receptions, he frequently alluded to the family in the flowery language so natural to him. 'A delightful fête at Gunnersbury – Madame de Rothschild mère. . . . A beautiful park and a villa worthy of an Italian Prince . . . military bands, and beautiful grounds, temples and illuminated walks . . . all the world of grandeur present. . . . I got well waited on by our friend Amy, who brought me some capital turtle, which otherwise I should have missed. . .'[2]

Lionel lavished a great deal of time and money on Gunnersbury and as the years progressed the lakes and follies were linked by exquisite paths, and flowerbeds in the form of baskets rimmed with heliotropes. In one corner was a spectacular Japanese garden complete with stone bridges, rivulets, bamboo seats, palms and temples. 'Marvellous,' said the Mikado's ambassador on his first visit to England. 'We have nothing like it in Japan.'

Mrs Nathan's delight in Lionel's innovations was interrupted when her twenty-two-year-old daughter, Hannah, walked into her bedroom and told her that she wanted to marry Mr Henry Fitzroy. The young man was tall, attractive, a brother of the Earl of Southampton, a Deputy Lieutenant for the County of Northampton, and a prospective member of Parliament. But he was not a Jew. Therefore the idea was preposterous. Terrible scenes ensued, but Mrs Nathan held the trump cards. Nathan Rothschild had been so angry when the Prince de Clary had asked for Hannah's hand that he had added a clause to his will that his daughters would be disinherited if they married without the consent of their mother or brothers.

Nevertheless Hannah was so deeply in love that Mrs Nathan finally compromised. Fitzroy must go abroad for six months; if, at the end of the time, Hannah was still determined to marry him, the family would reconsider the matter.

Hannah not only remained doggedly fixed in purpose but according to her brother, Nathaniel, began to pine away. At last Mrs Nathan relented and the marriage took place at St George's, Hanover Square, on 29 April 1839. However, the only member of the family to attend the ceremony was Nathaniel who thought it a sorry affair to see Hannah in a simple morning dress instead of traditional satin. Even worse, instead of wedding presents, she received from her cousins letters of withering contempt.

The morning of the wedding Lionel left the house for New Court bidding his sister a cold 'good day'. Mrs Nathan also left the house but came back, tears streaming down her face. Calling Hannah to her, she said that she had decided to accompany her to the church. It would not do to ride in a splendid Rothschild coach, so a common 'four-wheeler' was hailed in the street. The carriage clattered along Piccadilly, through Berkeley Square, across Bond Street, finally arriving at the side entrance of St George's. Fitzroy was on the pavement waiting for her. He opened the carriage door and helped her out, while Mrs Nathan slightly rose in her seat and made a friendly gesture. Then she turned away. A few minutes later Hannah was standing between her brother, Nathaniel, and Henry Fitzroy, while the sound of the four-wheeler carrying Mrs Nathan home faded into the grey morning air. Hannah's marriage was happy but the family never forgave her for abandoning the faith of her forefathers. Indeed, years later, when her poor little son, Arthur, fell from his pony and after months of paralysis died tragically, the cousins interpreted it as 'the punishment of God'.

The young Disraeli; an engraving after a painting by A. E. Chalon.

The Rothschild daughters, however, were a secondary consideration in Nathan's last will and testament. Echoing the same theme as his father before him, he exhorted his sons to eschew all quarrels, remarking that it was a matter of complete indifference to him whether one had £50,000 more than another. And most important of all, as the five Rothschild banks were to remain a single unit, the sons were always to defer to the superior wisdom of their four uncles, and never to embark on business ventures without their approval.

The four 'uncles' had all moved into palaces where they entertained the grandest people of the day, a natural consequence of the power each had acquired through Nathan's direction. Amschel was secretary of the German Confederation at Frankfurt and financier of Prussia; Carl was overlord of the Italian peninsula; Salomon the mainstay of the Habsburg Empire and the Holy Alliance.

Yet James was Nathan's rightful successor. The mantle dropped naturally upon his shoulders and no one questioned the inheritance. He not only outshone all his brothers in brains, energy and splendour, but Paris provided the perfect setting for the *haute finance* of the new, engine-driven era. Although London was the world's chief money market, and although England was far more advanced industrially than any other nation, Louis-Philippe, the Citizen King of France, turned Paris into a banker's paradise.

Marx and Tocqueville, the two most intelligent sociological observers of the day, hit upon the same phrase to describe the July Monarchy. It was a 'joint stock company', an 'industrial combine, run for the profit of the shareholders'. The shareholders, of course, were a few hundred thousand people 'with a paw in the trough of power'. No one had ever envisaged such an era of speculation and corruption; and James de Rothschild moved complacently at the centre. The French socialist, Alexandre Weill, wrote bitterly:

There is but one power in Europe and that is Rothschild. His satellites are a dozen other banking firms; his soldiers, his squires, all respectable men of business and merchants; and his sword is speculation. Rothschild is a consequence that was bound to appear; and if it had not been a Rothschild, it would have been someone else. He is, however, by no means an accidental consequence, but a primary consequence, called into existence by the principles which have guided the European States since 1813. Rothschild had need of the States to become a Rothschild, while the States on their side required Rothschild. Now, however, he no longer needs the State, but the State still has want of him.[3]

There was no doubt that King Louis-Philippe relied on the Baron. He was genuinely grateful for James's stupendous and successful efforts in quieting Metternich, but he was also eager that James should invest – and increase – his private fortune. He gave him a monopoly of Government loans, and a cascade of contracts and concessions. Then he invited him to handle his private investments with the tacit understanding that the funds would multiply with remarkable rapidity. Even Prince Metternich, who had done Salomon plenty of favours in return for services rendered, appeared to be dismayed by the flamboyant alliance between monarch and plutocrat.

The House of Rothschild [he said] plays a much bigger role in France than any foreign government, with the possible exception of England. There are, of course, reasons for it, which to me naturally appear neither good nor morally gratifying. Money is the great motive force in France, and corruption which is in practice the most important factor in our modern system of representative Government – it is quite openly reckoned with.[4]

Heinrich Heine, the German poet, whose ancestors once upon a time had lived in the Frankfurt ghetto with the Rothschilds, watched with fascination.

A few hundred years ago [he wrote] a King would quite simply have pulled M. Rothschild's teeth out by way of inducing him to consent to a loan. Ah! well, the native ethic of the Middle Ages has happily been carried downstream by the Revolution and now Rothschild the Baron and Knight of the Order of Isabella can calmly go for a walk in the Tuileries whenever he is so disposed without fearing that the hard pressed monarch will touch a single one of his teeth.[5]

Heine was a frequent guest at James' house, and when the latter moved a few doors away into a new house on the Rue Laffitte he wrote that 'the palace . . . unites everything which the spirit of the 16th century could conceive and the 19th and the money of the 19th century could pay for. . . . It is the Versailles of a financial potentate. . .' Benjamin Disraeli, who also attended a ball, marvelled at the 'unrivalled palace with a great retinue of servants, and liveries more gorgeous than the Tuileries, and pineapples plentiful as blackberries. . .'[6] The beautiful Baroness Betty was such an

An *habitué* and close friend of the Rothschilds, the poet Heinrich Heine; a drawing by E. Mandel after a painting by F. Kugler.

accomplished hostess that invitations to Rothschild parties were as eagerly sought as royal summonses. The guests were carefully chosen, the men for their names and positions, the women for their elegance and beauty.

James was a good-natured, ebullient character, described by Disraeli as 'a happy mixture of the French dandy and the orange boy'. Although he liked to see the aristocracy gliding through his house he was even more proud of his friendship with artists and writers such as Rossini, Georges Sand, Honoré de Balzac. These people could tease James with impunity. When Eugène Delacroix, the painter, went into ecstasies over his face and asked him if he would pose as a beggar as he had 'exactly the right, hungry expression', James roared with laughter and assented. The following morning, dressed in rags, the Baron rang the bell of Delacroix's studio. A young artist who was serving as the painter's assistant was so moved by the visitor's pitiful appearance that he slipped him a franc. The next day a liveried servant brought the kind young man a letter: 'Dear Sir, You will find enclosed the capital which you gave me at the door to M. Delacroix's studio, with the interest and compound interest on it – a sum of ten thousand francs. You can cash the cheque at any bank whenever you like. James de Rothschild.'

James' fortune was now estimated at something between £40,000,000 and £50,000,000, a fact which so overawed people that they fawned over him. It afforded Heine infinite amusement.

I like best to visit the Baron in his office [he wrote] where, as a philosopher, I can observe how people bow and scrape before him. It is a contortion of the spine which the finest acrobat would find difficult to imitate. I saw men double up as if they had touched a Voltaic battery when they approached the Baron. Many are overcome with awe at the door of his office, as Moses once was on Mount Horeb, when he discovered that he was on holy ground. Moses took off his shoes and I am quite certain that a lot of these financial agents would do the same if they did not fear that the smell of their feet would be unpleasant to him.

On another occasion Heine was even more caustic.

I went to see M. de Rothschild, and saw a gold-laced lackey bringing the baronial chamber pot along the corridor. Some speculator from the Bourse, who was passing reverently lifted his hat to the impressive vessel. . . . I have committed the name of the man to memory. I am quite sure that he will become a millionaire in the course of time.[7]

Yet it was not easy to be a Croesus. No matter how generously James and Betty gave to charity – and their donations were extensive – no matter how warm their hospitality, there were always those who delighted in recounting anecdotes to show how mean they were. For instance, when James refused to commission Horace Vernet to paint his portrait on the ground that the artist was asking too much money, Vernet sent him a message saying that he was painting

him *gratis*. In his famous picture *On the Way to Smala* Vernet depicts a Jew, torn between fear and avarice, making way with a box of gold under his arm: and the features are those of the Baron.

Honoré de Balzac borrowed money from James almost as soon as he met him but was one of the few people who repaid the debt without slandering the lender. Instead, he dedicated a charming

Detail of Horace Vernet's *On the Way to Smala*; the fleeing Jew is supposed to represent James de Rothschild.

story to him entitled *Roueries d'un créancier*. Georges Sand, on the other hand delighted in telling how she accosted the Baron at a charity bazaar and asked him to buy a bottle of scent for five thousand francs. 'What would I do with scent?' chaffed the banker. 'But if you give me *your* autograph, I'll sell it and we'll split the proceeds.' Georges Sand complied. On a piece of paper she wrote: 'Receipt for two thousand francs for the poor oppressed Poles. Georges Sand.' Baron James paid up. Heine who was standing near him put his arm around the Baron's shoulder. 'For a great sorrow it is always difficult to find words.'[8]

James never allowed his glamorous social life to interfere with business. Together with Salomon he plunged his money into railways; and by the 1840s the two brothers were recognized as the railway tycoons of the continent. Nathan had been the first to advise the family to invest in the new form of transport. He himself had missed the chance to make a fortune in England, for despite the fact that the locomotive had sprung into being under his very nose, he had misjudged its marvellous future. Its precursor was Robert Fulton's steamboat, the *Clermont*, which chugged down the Hudson in 1807. In England a coal miner by the name of George Stephenson began to dream of an engine that would drive a land machine, not a boat; something that would run on iron rails and haul coal from his mine. He was allowed to experiment and in the 1820s a track was opened from Stockton to Darlington to carry coal from the Durham mines.

At first many people, including Nathan, derided the notion that anything so constricted as a locomotive could replace the flexibility of nature's horse. No doubt the scepticism stemmed from a psychological foreboding that an age of movement would destroy the security of the few. 'Railways will only encourage the lower classes to move about needlessly,' remarked the Duke of Wellington. Nicholas Wood, on the other hand, who was regarded as a 'railway expert', felt that Wellington was much too optimistic about the locomotive. 'I should not dream of telling everyone that the ridiculous expectation, or rather prophecies, of the enthusiastic speculators could possibly be realized, and that we shall see steam-coaches travelling at a speed of 12, 16, 18 or 20 miles an hour. Nobody could do more harm . . . than by spreading abroad this kind of nonsense.'[9]

For some time the speed of trains was paralyzed by the fact that a law required a postillion to ride in front of the locomotive to warn people of the approaching monster. But in 1830, when the Liverpool-Manchester railway was opened, all doubts about the future of the locomotive came to an end. In 1837 Charles Greville had his first ride on a train.

The first sensation is a slight degree of nervousness and a feeling of being run away with, but a sense of security soon supervenes, and the velocity is delightful. Town after town, one park and château after another are left behind with the rapid variety of a moving panorama . . . it certainly renders all other travelling . . . tedious by comparison.[10]

However, Flaubert, the great French novelist, refused to be impressed and complained of the *ennui* of speed. 'After five minutes I bay with boredom. They think it's a lost dog shut in the carriage. It isn't though, it's M. Flaubert groaning.'

By the 1830s dozens of private companies had sprung into being, and Nathan Rothschild sadly realized that he had listened to the wrong voices. As it was too late for him to acquire a worthwhile holding in England he wrote to his brothers in Austria, Germany and France pointing out that the Continent was virgin soil, and that in his opinion railways were bound to reap vast profits.

Salomon in Vienna was particularly receptive as he already had been approached by Professor Riepel of the Viennese Polytechnic Institute, who had worked many years in the Vitkowitz iron-works in Silesia. Riepel wanted to build a railway to transport minerals from the mines of Galicia to Vienna, a distance of 60 miles. After receiving Nathan's letter Salomon sent the Professor to England to write a report for him.

Nothing much happened for five years, but in 1835 Salomon applied to the Emperor Ferdinand of Austria for a concession to build a railway that would carry Galician salt and Silesian coal to Vienna. The newspapers got wind of the request and a storm of protest followed. Dozens of experts wrote articles claiming that the human respiratory system would not stand a speed of fifteen miles an hour; that travellers would have to be accompanied by doctors to prevent them from spurting blood from nose, mouth and ears; that they would be suffocated passing through tunnels more than sixty metres long; and if they survived these hazards they would undoubtedly be driven mad by the noise of passing trains. A few medical journals were even more horrific: men might commit suicide, women lapse into sexual orgies.

Fortunately Prince Metternich was in favour of granting Baron von Rothschild the concession; and the Emperor Ferdinand obediently signed the necessary document. 'Hail to the Monarch', Salomon wrote, 'who has most graciously deigned to take this decision in the interests of the welfare of his people!'

Salomon did not have a clear run. The banking house, Sina, soon received a licence to build a southern track from the Adriatic Sea to Vienna. Salomon countered by sending the Emperor a progress report of the Rothschild track – known as the Vienna-Bochnia line – which ended:

The most obedient and loyal servant of Your Majesty feels that he may venture in all humility most respectfully to request Your Majesty that you may be graciously pleased to permit that the Vienna Bochnia railway shall be allowed to bear the auspicious name of 'Kaiser Ferdinand Nordbahn'.[11]

Not only the Emperor, but Prince Metternich, allowed his name to be associated with the railway; and the twelve thousand shares, two thirds of which were held by Salomon himself, rocketed. Sina struck back angrily by accusing the Rothschild engineers of technical faults; and Salomon countered by instructing Professor Riepel to answer 'this insult with the contempt it deserves'.

On 7 July 1839, when the continent's first major railway was opened, the shares tripled. Salomon had greatly increased his fortune, and now was eager to ensure himself a tiny piece of immortality. In the waiting room of the resplendent Vienna station he placed a life-sized statue of himself in Carrara marble, as a gift from the Emperor Ferdinand Northern Railway Company to its founder Salomon Rothschild.

Salomon, of course, was not the only Rothschild to promote railways. Amschel in Frankfurt financed hundreds of miles of track in Prussia, while Carl loaned thousands to the Pope who believed that if he could knit the Papal states together with a steam engine, he might stave off revolution. James built his own railways, opening a line between Paris and Saint-Germain in 1837, and another between Paris and Versailles in 1839.

The Rothschilds were among the first to promote railways in France and Austria. In 1837 James' line between Paris and Saint-Germain was opened.

The following year he petitioned for a gigantic concession to be known as the Chemin de Fer du Nord which would connect the capital with the industrial north. He won the contract by giving free shares to everyone of importance from ministers to journalists. This prompted an attack from Ludvig Borne, a German Jew whose family had shared the vicissitudes of the ghetto with the Rothschilds. He asked:

> Would it not be a great blessing for the world if all the kings were dismissed and the Rothschilds put on the throne? Think of the advantages. The new dynasty would never contract a loan, as it would know better than anybody how dear such things are, and on this account alone the burden of their subjects would be alleviated by several millions a year. The bribing, both active and passive, of ministers would have to cease; why should they be bribed any longer, or what would there be to bribe them with? All that sort of thing would be ancient history, and morality would be greatly promoted . . .[12]

Three weeks after the opening of the first section of the Rothschild track in 1846, an engine rounded a bend too quickly and carriages careered down a bank killing thirty-seven people. The general outcry gave birth to an anti-semitic pamphlet, *The History of Rothschild I, King of the Jews*, which was stuffed into thousands of letter boxes. However an anonymous friend came to James's support by issuing a counter-pamphlet entitled *Reply by Rothschild I, King of the Jews, to Satan the Last, King of the Slanderers*.

James de Rothschild was not the only person to win a railway contract. The French Government gave its concessions to half a dozen combines in order to create healthy competition. Although it was not easy to raise the vast sums of money deemed necessary, everyone believed that railway licence was a licence to print money. 'The Departments that have got railways', James wrote to Count Apponyi, 'want to keep them in order to make as much profit as possible. Those that have not got them hope and wish to have them in the near future.'

With such competition, it is not surprising that the public began to speculate wildly in railway shares. Baron James refused to look upon gambling as harmful. 'As long as they are preoccupied with making money', he remarked drily, 'their minds will be kept away from plots against the Government.' In November 1845 Charles Greville wrote in his diary that 'speculation has reached its height. . . . Half the fine ladies have been dabbling in stocks, and the most unlikely have not been able to refrain from gambling in shares, even I myself (though in a very small degree) for the warning voice of the Governor of the Bank has never been out of my ears.'[13] Despite prophecies of a fearful retribution the market remained buoyant.

Meanwhile James' preoccupations were not only financial. Throughout 1840 it looked as though France might declare war on

Austria, and once again he felt obliged to flit from side to side with olive branches. In those days it was not the fashion to condemn capitalists as war-mongers; indeed, banker James and his brothers were derided by many nationalists as 'peace-mongers'. People spoke contemptuously of them as valuing profit more than honour. 'It is in the nature of things,' observed a rising young Prussian politician, Otto von Bismarck, 'that the house of Rothschild should do everything to prevent war. . .'

Bismarck's point was proved when Prince Metternich persuaded Russia and England to join with him in sending an ultimatum to France's protégé, Mehemet Ali Pasha of Egypt, demanding his withdrawal from northern Syria. Louis-Philippe's chief minister, M. Thiers, was outraged that France had not been consulted and pressed the Cabinet to avenge the nation's honour by declaring war.

All branches of the Rothschild family in all five countries went into action to prevent hostilities. They soothed ministers, cajoled editors, talked pacifism at every social gathering. So much so that Baron James was attacked by the French press for his outrageous lack of bellicosity. 'With what right,' thundered Thiers's newspaper, *Le Constitutionnel*, 'and under what pretext, does this King of Finance intermeddle with our affairs? What concern of his are the decisions which France will take? Is he the author of our honour? Are his money interests to be allowed to outweigh our national interests?' 'If I desire peace,' James snapped back, 'I desire it honourably, not only for France but for the whole of Europe. . .'[14]

Each Rothschild gathered intelligence which he passed on to the other by the famous courier service. On 22 August Lionel thanked James for a letter:

as we were distinctly uneasy. Consols opened at $89\frac{3}{8}$, it is said that the owners of carrier pigeons were buying; they closed at $89\frac{1}{8}$. . . . Everyone is of the opinion that Mehemet Ali, if he does not completely give way, will at any rate, make fresh proposals. Bülow and all the others are dining with us tomorrow, and we mean to go to Windsor and try to see King Leopold. [Leopold of Belgium was in a key position; Louis-Philippe of France was his father-in-law, Victoria of England his niece.] If there is anything of interest to report we shall send you a courier tomorrow night . . .[15]

In October the situation had worsened and Charles Greville wrote in his diary: 'Everything looking black these last two days, funds falling and general alarm. . .' But James Rothschild's influence with the King was paramount; and at the crucial moment Louis-Philippe exploited a difference in the cabinet and overruled Thiers.

James was not the only brother to work feverishly for peace. In Vienna Salomon kept a close watch on Metternich for fear that the Prince might grow impatient and make a move. He did everything to soothe him, even inventing charming remarks supposedly made by the French King about Metternich's sagacity and wit which he inserted into letters that he knew would be intercepted. And when peace finally was assured he went to Paris and had a little celebration with James.

One of Salomon's most important allies in Vienna was the vivacious Countess Melanie Zichy-Ferraris, who once upon a time had borrowed money from Salomon, and who now became Prince Metternich's third wife. Salomon paid her so much attention and loaded her with such wonderful gifts that she fell into the habit of referring to him in front of the Emperor as 'our Salomon'. The brothers joined the assault, Carl von Rothschild sending Melanie scarves from Naples, James de Rothschild frocks from Paris, and Lionel de Rothschild plant cuttings from London.

Salomon's motives were not only prompted by a wish to preserve peace. He was determined to circumvent the ridiculous Habsburg regulation that forbade Jews from buying property. Although he had taken over the whole of the Hotel Römischer Kaiser, he remained a hotel guest while his brothers were landed proprietors.

The desire to own land became such an obsession that he embarked on a long siege, content to force his way step by step. He gave immense sums to charities, erected and equipped a hospital and subsidized the municipal water supply. This won him full citizenship, which meant that he could *buy* the hotel in which he lived, if he so wished. But Salomon had higher aims. After years of leasing he finally was allowed to purchase the huge iron and steel works of Vitkowitz, in Silesia. Then he set about improving the lot of the workers. Soon the Governor of Silesia was reporting that Salomon's philanthropies were 'a blessing and a model for the whole country'.

Melanie's influence with her husband, and Metternich's influence with the Emperor, finally proved decisive. In 1843 the ban against Jews was removed and Salomon became the largest landed proprietor in the Empire with vast estates in Moravia and Silesia and finally in far-away Prussia, all of them complete with castles, moats, waterfalls, and the inevitable swans and peacocks. As Salomon's first two initials 'S.M.' happened to be the same as the abbreviation for *Sein Majestät* people began to bracket 'King Salomon' with the Emperor. The title suited Salomon for by this time he really was a king, the Railway King of Central Europe.

No matter to what heights the brothers rose, nor how grandly they lived, old Gutle, ninety-years-old in 1843, refused to abandon the House of the Green Shield in the Frankfurt ghetto, for fear that it might bring ill-luck to the family. By the 1840s she had almost become an ancient monument, part of the Grand Tour undertaken by fashionable young men of the day. She received distinguished guests from all over Europe in her tiny parlour, and still pointed proudly to the bridal wreath under glass. When the aristocratic diarist, Charles Greville, visited Frankfurt he drove to Jew Street.

We had the good luck [he wrote] to see the old mother of the Roths-childs, and a curious contrast she presented. The house she inhabits appears not a bit better than any of the others; it is the same dark and decayed mansion. In this narrow gloomy street, and before this wretched tene-ment, a smart caleche was standing, fitted up with blue silk, and a footman in blue livery was at the door. Presently the door opened, and the old woman was seen descending a dark, narrow staircase, supported by her granddaughter, the Baroness Charles [Carl] Rothschild [formerly Adelaide Herz] whose carriage was also in waiting at the end of the street.

Two footmen and some maids were in attendance to help the old lady into the carriage, and a number of the inhabitants collected opposite to see her get in. A more curious and striking contrast I never saw than the dress of the ladies, both the old and young one, and their equipages and liveries, with the dilapidated locality in which the old woman persists in remaining. The family allow her £4,000 a year, and they say she never in her life has been out of Frankfurt, and never inhabited any other house than this, in which she resolved to die.[17]

Gutle was weary of life and when a doctor, thinking to please her told her that undoubtedly she would reach a hundred she remarked acidly: 'Why should God take me at a hundred when he can have me at eighty-seven?' Then she added gently: 'You must understand I don't want pills to make me younger, but to make me older.'

Everything – even railway flotations and stock-exchange speculation – gave way to the revolution of 1848. Ever since the end of the Napoleonic wars Prince Metternich had managed to maintain the status quo in a Europe which still smouldered with the 'liberty and equality' of the French Revolution. By juggling first with one country then another, by dividing, coercing, and threatening, he had reinforced monarchies, strengthened governments, and pre-vented violent change. Although in moments of depression he referred to his system as a 'mouldering structure', the revolution that broke out in Sicily in 1848 caught him by surprise. The Vienna Bourse sensed trouble and reacted violently. Salomon von Roths-child visited Metternich on 23 January and the Prince upbraided him for not controlling the money market. 'Politically,' he said to Salomon, 'things are going well but the Bourse is in a bad way; I am doing my duty but you are not doing yours. If the devil fetches me, he will fetch you too; I am looking hell in the face; you are sleeping instead of fighting; your fate is therefore sealed.' Salomon apologized passionately and agreed to buy heavily on the morrow. '. . . You may count on me!' 'I judge by actions,' snapped Prince Metternich. 'You may buy tomorrow, but I shall not know why you did not buy yesterday. If it was in order to buy more cheaply I have no occasion to be grateful to you.'[18]

The revolution in Sicily spread to Naples. Carl von Rothschild, however, was clever enough to persuade the liberal Government to make immediate concession and the danger receded. The Grand

Duke of Tuscany and the King of Piedmont were also threatened but they followed the example of Naples, and managed to restore peace. But by February the fire had spread to inflammable France and overnight a gigantic conflagration had begun.

Everywhere people were inveighing against arbitrary rule by kings, demanding parliamentary government, elections, a franchise reaching the masses. In Paris once again barricades were erected in all the main streets. And when the seventy-four-year-old Louis-Philippe learned, in the best tradition of French kings, that the National Guard had gone over to the enemy, he fled, and the rebels declared a republic.

For safety, James sent his wife and daughter to his nephew Lionel's house in England. While the ladies were crossing the channel one way, Lionel was travelling in the opposite direction as he felt it his duty to stand by his uncle during the dangerous days ahead.

James had been ordered to appear before the Prefect of Police, M. Caussidière, who accused him of smuggling bullion out of the country in dung carts. 'Sir,' replied James, 'I am believed to be buried in gold, whereas, in point of fact, I have nothing but paper. My wealth and capital consist of securities which at this moment are of no value. I have no intention of going bankrupt, and if I must die I shall resign myself, but I would regard flight as cowardly. I have written to my family to send me cash as I must meet my obligations. Tomorrow I shall introduce my nephew to you, who has just come from London for this purpose.'[19]

Although the mob had destroyed the royal residence at Neuilly, and now was plundering the Tuileries and the Palais-Royal, throwing furniture into the streets and burning it, the Prefect of Police assured James that he had nothing to fear from the people of Paris. The following day Baron James did as he had promised and brought his nephew Lionel to the Préfecture. They delighted M. Caussidière by donating fifty thousand francs for policemen 'wounded in the course of duty'. The Préfecture responded by stationing an armed guard in front of James' house. Unfortunately it was too late to protect the Baron's beautiful villa in the Bois de Boulogne which had already been partially burned and looted.

Messieurs de Rothschild Frères were facing hard times. Just as in 1830, the House of Rothschild was saddled with an immense number of undertakings which could result in staggering losses. For instance, James had put up 82,000,000 francs as the first instalment of a government loan of 250,000,000 and it was not certain that the money would be recovered. Furthermore the bank's enormous holding of railway shares had dropped to an all-time low. And now, to add insult to injury, the new Minister of the Interior, M. Ledru-Rollin, was demanding 250,000 francs from James, telling him flatly that unless he complied, his offices on the Rue Laffitte would be razed

July 1848 in Paris: the mob burning the Throne at the foot of the Bastille column.

to the ground. James paid, but the blackmail continued. A few days later the minister demanded another 500,000 francs. Again James paid.

Meanwhile the revolution had spread to Central Europe and both Salomon in Vienna and Amschel in Frankfurt were living through frightening days. Early in March street fighting broke out in Vienna, the Emperor Ferdinand panicked and asked Metternich for his resignation. The latter borrowed money from his friend, Salomon von Rothschild, then left the capital dressed as an old woman. Rumours spread that he had taken refuge in Frankfurt at the house of the Austrian general, Count Nobil. Thousands of people collected outside the latter's house shouting: 'Pereat Metternich!' The general came to the window, announced that the Prince was not staying with him, then emerged from the house, climbed into his carriage and drove to the house of Amschel von Rothschild, who was holding a reception. A few days later another mob demanded 'equal citizenship' and smashed the window of Prussia's consul-general, who happened to be Amschel von Rothschild.

Caricature of Amschel von Rothschild complaining about barricades before his house in Frankfurt, 18 September 1848.

Nº XXVI

Baron von Rotschirm: Was geht vor in mein Haus?
Barriekatenmacher: Jetzt geht's los Herr Baron, jetzt werd gleich gethalt, aber das Eigenthum is heilig;
Baron: Was geht los? geht Jhr mir los! Eigenthum heilig? Tod? Wie heist? Mein Eigenthum is mir schon lang heilig, das braucht Jhr mir nitt an mein Thur zu schreibe, Tod? Wenn die Preusse komme seid Jhr all tod!!!

Riots in Vienna during the 1848 Revolution. Salomon's house in the Renngasse was occupied while he hid in a friend's house in the suburbs.

Things went from bad to worse. King Frederick William IV finally did the fashionable thing and abandoned his capital. Crowds prowled the streets of Baden and Frankfurt, while insurrectionists gained control of Budapest and announced the secession of Hungary. Salomon von Rothschild hoped to weather the storm despite Metternich's prediction that 'if the devil fetches me, he will fetch you too'. But when the mob got out of hand in October, and murdered the War Minister, Count Latour, hanging him naked to a lamp post, Salomon felt quite sick and decided to leave. That same night crowds ransacked the Windischgraetz Palace and occupied Salomon's house in the Renngasse. They climbed on to the roof and shot at the Grenadiers stationed inside an arsenal. The whole of Vienna became caught up in a frenzy of panic and excitement.

The Emperor Ferdinand and his court fled to Olmutz, and Salomon hid in a friend's house in the suburbs. Meanwhile the Baron's secretary, Herr Goldschmidt, who had taken his own family to the safety of Krems, returned to the capital to try to help his master. As he could not get back into the city without disguising himself, he dressed as a milkman. Surprisingly he found the Rothschild office intact. He packed up his books and papers and transferred them to the National Bank. This was on 10 October 1848. By this time Baron Salomon had left for Frankfurt where he joined his brother Amschel. He never again set foot in Vienna.

Despite the mounting dangers James sat tight in Paris. The new French government was unable to maintain order and street fighting flared up every few days. James was fortunate enough, however, to attach himself to the right man. He made friends with Eugène Cavaignac, the energetic War Minister, who soon became the virtual dictator of France. Cavaignac found James' advice useful, and for short while the latter enjoyed the same position of confidence that he had held under Bourbons and Orleans.

This drew from the Left a genuine paean of praise. 'You are a wonder, sir,' wrote the editor of the ultra-radical *Tocsin des Travailleurs*:

> In spite of legal majority Louis Philippe has fallen, Guizot has disappeared, the constitutional monarchy and parliamentary methods have gone by the board; you, however, are unmoved! . . .
>
> Although your House felt the first violence of the shock in Paris, although the effects of revolution pursue you from Naples to Vienna and Berlin, you remain unmoved in the face of a movement that has affected the whole of Europe. Wealth fades away, glory is humbled, and dominion is broken, but the Jew, the monarch of our time, has held his throne, but that is not all. You might have fled from this country where in the language of your Bible, the mountains skip about like rams. You remain, announcing that your power is independent of the ancient dynasties, and you courageously extend your hand to the young republic. Undismayed, you adhere to France.
>
> . . . You are more than a statesman, you are the symbol of credit. Is it not time that the bank, that powerful instrument of the middle classes, should assist in the fulfilment of the peoples' destinies? . . . Does that not appeal to you? Confess that it would be a worthy occasion if one day the French Republic should offer you a place in the Pantheon![20]

Yet as far as James was concerned, the sky was far from blue. Louis Napoleon, the nephew of the great Bonaparte, had hurried from London to Paris to 'place himself under the flag of the great Republic'. Gradually more and more adherents were backing his cause. As all Rothschilds had been bitter enemies of Napoleon Bonaparte they did not favour a new Napoleonic era. Yet by November 1848 there was a widespread belief that another big revolution was in the offing. 'Fear and unrest', reported the German chargé d'affaires to Berlin 'are general; business and economic interests are suffering acutely. The slump in securities has assumed alarming proportions, and yesterday there was actually a rumour to the effect that the House of Rothschild was going into liquidation.'[21]

Things were not as bad as people said: but Baron James was dismayed on 10 December to learn that Louis Napoleon, and not his friend General Cavaignac, had been elected President of the French Republic.

The only two great monarchies in Europe which emerged unscathed from the events of 1848 were the British and the Russian. London became the refuge for thousands of *émigrés* including the brilliant Prince Metternich, while St Petersburg made itself the new centre of reaction. The handsome, tight-lipped, authoritarian Emperor, Nicholas I, sent troops to Hungary and finally restored the

Prince Louis Napoleon, later Napoleon III, taking the oath of office as President of the French Republic in 1848.

Habsburg Empire to its Habsburg owner. He encouraged his uncle, Frederick William IV of Prussia, to return to Berlin; and when the question arose of uniting the scattered German states, eager for liberal constitutions, under the Prussian sceptre, Russia's scowl prevented poor Frederick William from accepting the offer. Instead, he remarked that he was not ready 'to pick up a crown from the gutter'.

By 1849 Europe was quiet once more; and the ninety-six-year-old Gutle in Frankfurt had the satisfaction of knowing that the House of Rothschild, whose foundation stone had been laid by her husband, had been built so solidly that it had weathered another storm.

The old lady died peacefully before the year was over. Her frail body was taken from the House of the Green Shield and carried to the great Frankfurt synagogue where Rothschilds from many lands gathered to pay their respects. But the new decade that was approaching would bring dangers for the House that was barely half a century old.

Chapter VI

The Challenge

(1849–68)

‘*I* HAD HEARD A GREAT DEAL ABOUT THE FAMOUS PLACE that the Rothschilds were building,’ wrote an American tourist who visited London in 1864, ‘and I sallied forth on this particular morning for the purpose of seeing it.’

The mansion was rising at 148 Piccadilly next door to the Duke of Wellington’s Apsley House; and its owner was Baron Lionel de Rothschild, head of the London bank. The tourist was shown over the half-finished structure by the master-builder and afterwards stood on the side-walk gazing at the work with admiration.

> . . . I noticed a gentleman a few feet from me watching the building, [he continued] He was a fat, portly old fellow, with a good humoured face in spite of his haughty look, and I thought from his appearance he might be a contractor for the work, so I determined to accost him and gain what information I could . . . . He was very kind in telling me much that was of interest. At last I said abruptly.
> ‘I suppose you have seen Rothschild, sir?’
> ‘Which one?’ he asked.
> ‘The old cock,’ I replied.
> ‘I see the old cock every day,’ he answered giving me a strange glance.
> ‘By George,’ I went on, ‘I should like to have a look at him! People say he is a gay old chap, and lives high. I wish I had him in my power – I’d not let him get away until he had shelled out a pile of money.’
> The old gentleman burst out into a laugh. ‘Baron Rothschild had to work for his money and deserves to enjoy it,’ he said at length, when he had got over his merriment.
> ‘May be so,’ I remarked; ‘but I reckon he did a heap of squeezing to get it.’
> The old man’s face flushed.
> ‘I have never heard the honesty of the House called into question,’ he said stiffly.
> ‘Didn’t you? Well to tell the truth neither have I. But I wouldn’t be surprised if I’m right after all.’ The old man’s face grew as black as a thundercloud, and he bit his lip without speaking.
> ‘People tell me,’ I continued, not heeding this, for I thought it natural that the old fellow should be annoyed at anything said against his employers, ‘people tell me the Rothschilds have made two fortunes. Now, as most people only make one, I feel somewhat interested to learn the manner in which this was done. Can you tell me sir?’
> ‘Certainly sir. People do say the House of Rothschild made one fortune by being careful to mind their own business and the other by letting that of others alone. Good morning sir.’

Top A watercolour of the great hall at Mentmore Towers, with the huge lanterns from the Doge’s barge in Venice. ‘I do not believe’, said Lady Eastlake, ‘that the Medicis were ever so lodged at the height of their glory.’ *Bottom* The Meet at Mentmore, with Mayer Amschel’s daughter, Hannah, in a carriage in the foreground.

Overleaf Nathaniel, Lionel, Mayer and Anthony de Rothschild following hounds in the Vale of Aylesbury, by Sir Francis Grant, *c.* 1855.

Hyde Park Corner, showing Apsley House, the Duke of Wellington's mansion and, next to it, no. 148 Piccadilly, Lionel de Rothschild's house.

Opposite The Salon Bleu at Ferrières, with boxed ceilings painted with the five arrows in blue and gold, and Delacroix' portrait of Baron James on the wall.

When the tourist had recovered from the shock of this pungent observation, he strolled over to a good-looking young man who was watching the construction and asked if he knew the gentleman to whom he had just been talking.

'Baron Rothschild,' came the reply.

There was a poignant silence, after which the American regained his composure and said: 'He's a crusty old chap. . . . He's as cross as a bear. . . . Do you know Baron Rothschild?' 'I have an appointment to wait upon him today.' 'Then I wish you'd say to him that I did not know to whom I was talking this morning or I would not have said as much; and that he need not have been so huffish about it.'

The young man gave his promise and when he departed the American stopped a workman and asked the name of the receding figure.

'That is one of the younger Rothschilds. . .'[1]

The portly, huffy gentleman with the ready wit – Baron Lionel – was the most celebrated banker in Europe, partly because London was the world's money centre, partly because the cooperation between the five Rothschild establishments, coupled with cash resources, gave them advantages against which other financiers could not compete, partly because Nathan had passed on to his eldest son all that he had learned. For some years he had given Lionel complete responsibility. For instance, when Britain abolished slavery in 1833 the Government had borrowed £20,000,000 from the Rothschild bank with which to recompense the slave owners; and Nathan had placed Lionel in charge of the funding operation.

From that time onwards Lionel spoke with authority, and when his father died three years later, he stepped easily into the position of Senior Partner, assisted by his three brothers, Mayer, Anthony and Nathaniel. In 1839 he floated a massive loan for the United States. In 1845 he helped his uncle James to finance the French Northern Railway; in 1846 he formed the British Relief Association Fund at New Court to aid victims of the Irish famine; and the following year joined with Barings to raise another £8,000,000 for the Irish Famine Loan, this time waiving his commission. In 1854 he floated £16,000,000 to finance the Crimean War. Indeed during the forty-three years that he was head of the bank, Rothschilds raised over £1,000,000,000 in foreign loans. Prussia, Russia, Portugal, Greece, Holland, Belgium, France, Hungary, Egypt, Turkey, the United States, Brazil, New Zealand, all came to New Court for money.[2]

Unlike the swashbuckling Nathan, the new generation did not despise charity. All the sons had inherited from their devout mother strong feelings for race and religion, and were glad to serve as benefactors and protectors. If a rabbi married he was sure to receive a gift from the family, while the London synagogues celebrated their feast days bedecked in flowers 'with the compliments of N.M. Rothschild & Sons'. Lionel was meticulous in observing the various ceremonies. On the morning of the Feast of Tabernacles he personally hammered palm leaves onto the walls of New Court. The office was closed on Saturdays, and like his father and uncles before him, he frequently used Yiddish as a code. Once when fighting was taking place in South Africa and Lionel got wind of a truce he wired: 'Mr Sholem is expected soon.' *Sholem* was the Jewish word for peace.

At the end of the 1830s Mrs Nathan began to complain that her sons were pasty-faced from spending so much time indoors. Furthermore they were putting on weight. Excercise was what they needed; and as Mrs Nathan was not a woman to do things by halves, she decided that the boys must ride to hounds. Without more ado she bought a few fields and a cottage near Aylesbury, in Benjamin Disraeli's 'beloved, beechy Bucks', thus launching the Rothschild invasion of the Chilterns.

All the brothers found hunting an irresistible pastime, particularly Lionel who set up his own kennels at Hastoe in the wood above Tring. In those days the Aylesbury Vale was a wild, rough country which had scarcely been hunted over. The fields were almost entirely destitute of gates, there were no bridges over the brooks and not a draining tile between Tring and Bicester. New Court, only forty miles away, was another world.

In the early 1850s Mayer and Anthony bought adjoining estates near Aylesbury; but whereas Anthony was content with a modest farm house at Aston Clinton, Mayer acquired seven hundred acres and built a fantastic house, Mentmore Towers, which created a sensation not only in Buckinghamshire, but throughout England.

Mentmore was the child of the Great Exhibition of 1851, which was dominated by the epoch-making Crystal Palace, that miracle of glass and iron designed by Joseph Paxton. As soon as Baron Mayer saw the stupendous, fairy-like structure, he got in touch with 'the new Christopher Wren' and asked if he would build him a palace. Baron James of Paris soon followed suit. On a trip to England he met Paxton at Mayer's house and was shown the plans for Mentmore. He was ecstatic and longed to see a replica erected on his own vast estate, twenty-five miles east of Paris which he had bought in the 1820s. 'Build me a Mentmore,' he commanded Paxton, 'only twice as big.' Paxton did as he was bid and the result was Ferrières which today is owned by Baron Guy de Rothschild.

Lord Crewe called Mentmore 'an amazing creation', while Lady Eastlake wrote: 'I do not believe that the Medicis were ever so lodged at the height of their glory.' The massive square towers and pinnacles, the glass roof over the gigantic hall, and the sheets of plate glass through which one could see the Chilterns, were startling innovations; so was the hot-water heating, the artificial ventilation and the parquet floors.

Most of the furniture came from France, some of it bearing the cypher of Marie Antoinette; there was also a priceless collection of French tapestries, Limoges enamels, Sèvres porcelain. Italy was represented by *objets d'art* from the Doge's Palace at Venice and spectacular gilt lanterns from the Doge's barge, while Belgium contributed a black and white marble chimney piece that had been taken from Rubens' house in Antwerp. In order to protect himself from criticisms of *parvenu* vulgarity' Baron Mayer was fond of saying that it was cheaper to buy French antiques than to go to Sir Blundell Maples' new department store on the Tottenham Court Road. Nevertheless guests were astonished to find priceless French commodes, one end sliced off to lie flush with the wall, covering the wash basins in their bedrooms.

Baron Mayer's ostentation, however, did not upset the local population. Indeed, he and Anthony were the most popular squires in the country, for they not only used their money to embellish their houses but kept their farm labourers employed all winter which was not the general practice in the 1850s. Although this was the age of inevitability, 'the rich man in his castle, the poor man at the gate', a state of affairs believed to be ordained by no less a being than the

Almighty, no beggar was ever turned away hungry from a Rothschild house. Indeed all Rothschilds of the new generation had a strong sense of duty. Their public spirit combined with the millions of money sometimes produced startling results. For instance when Baron Anthony's daughter, Constance, approached her sixteenth birthday and her father asked her what she would like to have for a birthday present, 'I boldly answered "an infants' school". My request was granted and I was allowed to lay the first stone of the new building.' It was not everyone's father who could humour a daughter with such *panache*.

All Rothschilds liked horses; and although Anthony told his bride, a Montefiore, 'you will perceive, my dear Louise, that all the family are complete slaves to business,' the brothers managed to hunt stags with the 'Baron's Staghounds' (Baron Mayer was the Master) every Monday and Thursday, and frequently found time to go fox-hunting on Tuesday, but not on Saturday which was the Sabbath. Lionel's kennels had been moved to Mentmore some years before the house was built and the Rothschilds financed the pack. Lionel was the only unlucky brother. He often hunted on Tuesday and Thursday but invariably had to forgo the Monday sport in order to attend the bank. He complained that he was 'badly used' but managed to make up for his disappointment by rising at dawn and 'turning out a deer' before catching the London express from Tring Station.

A shadow fell over this agreeable existence when Nathaniel, the soft-hearted brother who had helped his sister, Hannah, to marry Mr Fitzroy had a terrible fall. He was left half-paralysed, a permanent cripple. Nathaniel, however, was a man of great character, and soon set about reorganizing his life. He loved France and in 1851 moved to Paris where he settled down to become a collector and connoisseur of the arts. In 1853 he bought vineyards near Bordeaux which became known as Mouton Rothschild and where he lived for several months each year.

Not long after he had taken up his new residence, the organizers of an exhibition scheduled to open in Paris in 1855, with the hope of rivalling the Great Exhibition of London, decided to display France's most celebrated red wines. As there were over two thousand separate wine growers, a committee was set up to select sixty of the best clarets. Mouton was placed first in the second *cru*. Nathaniel was highly indignant at the classification, particularly as Lafite, a vineyard owned by a Dutchman M. Vanlerberghe, running adjacent to his own, was placed first in the first *cru*, a distinction which it retains to this day. He tried to get the rating altered and when he failed dismissed the matter with contempt, insisting that the decision had been purely arbitrary. As a result someone paraphrased Rohan's ditty *Roi ne peux, Prince ne veux*, with the following lines:

> *Premier ne puis,*
> *Second ne daigne,*
> *Mouton suis.*

Baron Mayer was the second of the four brothers to give up hunting but for very different reasons. Increasingly his interests became concentrated on the turf. He set up a stud farm at Crafton, near Mentmore, and had the joy of breeding a number of great horses. In the course of his racing career he won the Derby, the Oaks, the St Leger, the Cesarewitch, the Goodwood Cup twice, the Thousand Guineas three times. When the crowd spoke of 'Baron Rothschild' they did not refer to the man who ran the bank but the man who ran the horses.

The banking Baron – Lionel – grumbled about working too hard, yet he gave a great deal of time to causes dear to his heart, the chief of which was a long battle with the Mother of Parliaments. Benjamin Disraeli persuaded him to throw down the gauntlet. Although in his infancy, Disraeli had been baptized a Christian, he resented the fact that although Jews could stand for Parliament, they could not take their seats if elected, for the simple reason they had to make a statutory declaration 'on the true faith of a Christian'. Lionel not only was the most prominent Jew in England, Disraeli argued, but he had the necessary money and prestige to win what was bound to to be a bitter and protracted fight. At first Lionel refused. He was a shy man who hated making speeches, and the idea of becoming a controversial figure appalled him.

But in the end Disraeli's persuasiveness overcame his friend's diffidence, and Lionel fired the opening salvo in 1847 when he mounted the hustings as Liberal candidate for the City of London. 'My opponents say that I cannot take my seat,' he told the voters. 'That is rather my affair than theirs. I have taken the best advice. I feel assured that as your representative, as the representative of the most wealthy, the most important, the most intelligent constituency in the world, I shall not be refused admission to Parliament on account of any form of words.'[3]

Lionel was only half right. Although, when he was elected, the House of Commons passed a bill permitting him to take his seat, the House of Lords rose in revolt. To drop the word 'Christian' was the thin end of the wedge. The Duke of Cambridge could not consent to admit Jews as long as the British Government was to remain 'Christian'. The Earl of Winchelsea declared the bill to be an insult to the honour and glory of God. The Bishop of Oxford maintained that sitting in Parliament was not a right but a trust, and warned that Jews were an alien race, secretly conniving with other nations. Lord Ellenborough was the most passionate of all. He spoke to his fellow peers in 1848, when the French revolution had swept Louis-Philippe from his throne, when the Prussian King had fled from Berlin and the Hungarians had broken away from the Habsburg Empire. 'After the warnings of Providence in the shape of famine and distress,' cried Ellenborough, 'nations convulsed on every side, how can this country hope to escape such contamination except by heavenly aid?' He went on to warn their lordships not to offend the Heavenly Father 'by abandoning the exclusively Christian character of this Legislature'.[4] Their Lordships responded warmly, and the Commons Bill eliminating the restrictions against Jews was defeated.

This was the beginning of a siege that lasted eleven years. Six times Lionel was elected by the City of London. Six times he marched to the Table demanding to be sworn by the tenets of his faith. Ten times the Liberals introduced a Bill revising the Oath of Abjuration. Ten times Benjamin Disraeli who, as a baptized Jew, did not suffer from the disability clause, crossed his own party, the Conservatives, and spoke in favour of the Liberal revision. The Jewish race, argued Disraeli, were men who acknowledged the same God and admitted the same revelations; if they did not believe all that Christians did, Christians believed all that they did.

The seventh time, in 1858, the Lords relented, consenting to a Bill which allowed each House to modify the oath for its own members. On 26 July Lionel became a Member of Parliament. Although for over a decade he had spent huge sums of money electioneering, although he had stirred emotions from one end of the Empire to the other, although his long-suffering wife complained wearily, 'for eleven years we had the M.P. question screaming in every corner of the house', at last he had established his principle. Now the portals of the Commons swung open and he took his seat, but much to every-one's surprise he remained silent. Indeed, during the decade that he sat as a member of Parliament he never made a single speech.

After a long and tedious struggle to get into Parliament, Lionel de Rothschild was finally introduced in the House of Commons on 26 July 1858. A painting by Henry Barraud.

While the English Rothschilds made money almost effortlessly in their land of milk and honey, warmed by a political climate so stable as to be the envy of Europe, the French Rothschilds had no alternative but to continue along the same windswept path that they had been travelling for forty years, continuously harrassed by the storm of change. The fact that Baron James, confidant of the deposed King Louis-Philippe, had survived the revolution and managed to scrape up a polite acquaintance with the new President of the Republic, Louis Napoleon, nephew of the great Napoleon, whom the Rothschild family had fought so bitterly, was remarkable enough. Yet it had cost James a fortune. Not only had he been left with millions of francs worth of French bonds which had plummeted to new lows, but he had been forced to dig deep in his pocket to protect life and property. And now, at the end of 1849, he suffered an even worse blow when he learned that his bitterest enemy, Achille Fould, whose banking firm, Fould and Oppenheim, had backed Louis Napoleon's bid for power, had been appointed Minister of Finance.

Achille and James had opposed each other not only as bankers but as railway entrepreneurs. In the 1830s the two men had built tracks from Versailles to Paris on opposite sides of the Seine, prompting Heinrich Heine to refer to them as the 'Chief Rabbis of the Rive Gauche and the Rive Droite'. Soon the rivals were vying with one another for a plum concession: permission to build the Northern Railway. James triumphed and assigned the task to his brilliant protégé, Émile Pereire, who could be relied upon to outwit all newcomers.

The Pereires were Portuguese Jews who had emigrated to France in the early part of the century. The fact that Émile was a convinced Socialist who contributed articles to *Le Temps* and the *Journal des Débats* did not disturb James who believed that the views of his assistant would modify in proportion to the money he accumulated. By 1845, when the main track of the Chemin de Fer du Nord was completed, Émile was a rich man; yet he not only clung stubbornly to his convictions but watched closely for an opportunity to put his ideas into practice.

He reached a dramatic decision in the autumn of 1849 when the President of the Republic, Louis Napoleon, accompanied by Baron James and himself, attended the opening of the Saint-Quentin Station. The President was acclaimed by the crowds with cries of '*Vive l'Empereur*'. Émile Pereire was impressed. If Louis Napoleon had such a firm hold on the affections of his people, Achille Fould, the new Minister of Finance, and not James de Rothschild, would dominate the second half of the century. A few weeks later Émile deserted his patron and joined Fould. Baron James was so stunned that he refused to believe it. He gave instructions that Émile's desk was not to be removed for '*le petit Pereire reviendra*'.

But Pereire did not return. Instead he gave Achille Fould a novel

Above The financier Achille Fould, described by Heine as 'the Chief Rabbi of the Rive Gauche', as opposed to his rival, Baron James de Rothschild, 'the Chief Rabbi of the Rive Droite'.

Below The brothers Isaac and Émile Pereire, founders of the Crédit Mobilier, the rival to James' Messieurs de Rothschild Frères.

MM. Isaac et Émile Péreire, fondateurs de la société de Crédit mobilier.

123

idea: the conception of a popular bank to be known as the Crédit Mobilier, into which all the small savings of France would flow. Not only would this semi-socialist institution break the grip of private bankers by enabling the government to raise loans directly from the public, but it would allow the Minister of Finance to direct money into the areas where it was most needed.

This last argument was enough to convince Fould, for France lagged far behind England in industrial development and Louis Napoleon was determined to quicken the pace. His resolve had been strengthened by London's Great Exhibition where, in the acid words of Karl Marx, 'wonders far surpassing the Egyptian pyramids, Roman aqueducts and Gothic cathedrals' were on display. Although France had a larger population than any other European country, and enjoyed huge agricultural resources, she only had 2000 miles of railway as compared to England's 6600 miles. Indeed, Britain was producing 57 million tons of coal compared to Germany's 6 million and France's $4\frac{1}{2}$ million; $2\frac{1}{2}$ million tons of iron, compared to the USA's $\frac{1}{2}$ million, France's 400,000 and Germany's 250,000. Half the world's tonnage of ocean-going shipping was British; and among the amazing inventions displayed at the Exhibition were locomotives and textile machines and Applegarth's vertical printing press which turned out 10,000 sheets of the *Illustrated London News* in an hour.

While the formation of the Crédit Mobilier was being discussed in secret, James de Rothschild was fighting to maintain his position with every weapon that came to hand. He knew that he could never gain the confidence of Prince Louis Napoleon, if only because the Rothschild family had risen to fame and power by its implacable opposition to Napoleon I. Secretly James hoped that Louis Napoleon would be replaced as President of the Republic. The only man capable of ousting him was General Changarnier who controlled the military forces of the capital, the National Guard.

The general was a Rothschild man in a literal sense as he was madly in love with James' wife, Baroness Betty. He did not try to conceal his infatuation, and although the world is supposed to love a lover, apparently he was so indiscreet that he became a figure of fun. 'The feelings of popular resentment from which the General is suffering just now,' the Austrian ambassador reported to Vienna, 'is largely attributable to his intimate relations with the Rothschild family, arising out of a *sentiment de coeur* for Madame James de Rothschild. The Prince, whom Changarnier has on several occasions provoked by holding reviews of the troops without even advising him previously, learnt that the said lady was present at one of them in a magnificent equipage, and that the gallant general saluted her before the whole army of Paris.'[5]

As the prestige of the love-sick general declined, that of Louis Napoleon rose. By January 1851 the Prince felt strong enough to dismiss Changarnier. The National Assembly protested hotly but

General Changarnier whose infatuation for Baroness Betty was a well-known fact in Paris society, was dismissed in January 1851 and later arrested by Louis Napoleon.

the Prince retaliated a few months later by dismissing that body as well. 'Your Constitution and your National Assembly are detestable,' he told the people of France. 'I liberate you from them.' Now he was a dictator, and in the next months deported or arrested 27,000 people, among them Changarnier. 'The arrest of the General has brought sorrow into the home of the Rothschilds,' reported the Austrian ambassador, 'but it must be admitted that Baron James is bearing the blow with great resignation.'[6] A plebiscite of the French people declared overwhelmingly in favour of a restoration of the monarchy; and in November 1852 Louis Napoleon became the Emperor Napoleon III.

That same month Pereire's new bank, the Crédit Mobilier, sprang into being. Achille Fould had found no difficulty in winning the Emperor's approval. That the State should make itself independent of the anti-Napoleonic, pro-Orleanist Rothschilds, and raise its loans through *souscriptions nationales* was bound to interest the sovereign. Furthermore Napoleon saw the venture as an institution that would befriend the common man. Oddly enough the semi-socialist conception appealed to many leading capitalists, but for very different reasons. They envisaged an opportunity to use the huge flow of shareholders' money on the Stock Exchange.

The Crédit Mobilier's twelve thousand shares, at 500 francs each, were introduced on the Bourse at 1,100 francs; and four days later they had risen to 1,600. The list of founder shareholders was imposing. Not only did it include such eminent bankers as Barings of London, Torlonia of Rome, Heine of Hamburg, Oppenheim and Laffitte of France, but millionaire socialites such as the Duc de Galliera and the Duchess of Leuchtenberg, a daughter of Tsar Nicholas I of Russia. As Minister of Finance, the name of Achille Fould was not on the list; but his brother, Benoît, owned a quarter of the shares. Another large block was owned by Émile Pereire and his brother, Isaac. But the most surprising of the large shareholders was Napoleon III's half-brother, the Duc de Morny. It was considered astonishing that this gentleman had managed to reconcile his Government position as Président du Corps Legislatif, with the commercial post Director of the Crédit Mobilier.

Baron James Rothschild had no faith in the new organization. He did not believe that a bank based partly on credit, partly on speculation, and which had the right to purchase and grant loans on the security of its own shares could remain solvent. James' opinions were dismissed, however, as wholly biased.

Meanwhile the launching of the new company had provoked an unexpected wave of speculation, which this time penetrated to the working man. By encouraging butcher, baker and candle-stick maker to put their savings into the new venture the government was, in fact, introducing the public to the exciting pastime of gambling. Money, we are told, 'became the God, speculation the Creed, the

Right Crowds gathering in the courtyard of the Ministry of Finance for news of stock-market quotations of the Crédit Mobilier shares.

The young Eugénie de Montijo was a protegée of James and Betty de Rothschild before she married Napoleon III.

Bourse the Temple, the quotation list the Bible, the bankers the Priests, the brokers the Believers, the investors the Martyrs'. The daily newspapers featured stock-market quotations in leading positions, while James de Rothschild alone grumbled that it was impossible for everyone to become rich. When in due course the market fell those who lost their savings blamed the Duc de Morny, but he had made so much money that he did not mind becoming a scapegoat.

Baron James continued to fight a rearguard action to retain some shred of his former influence. His wife still gave the best parties in Paris, and from 1850 onwards a beautiful Spanish girl in her twenties, Eugénie de Montijo, the daughter of a Scotswoman and an Andalusian grandee, was a frequent guest. At first no one could understand why the Rothschilds made such a fuss of Eugénie. They were aware, of course, that Napoleon III had tried to seduce her but as the Emperor had an eye for the ladies this was not a singular event. Then came rumours that Napoleon was thinking of marrying Eugénie. Government circles hotly denied the stories; the Emperor would wed a princess of royal birth. Sophisticated Paris decided that Napoleon was playing a devious game in order to conclude an alliance worthy of his position.

The speculation came to an end in January 1853 when the Emperor gave a ball at the Tuileries. Baron James accompanied Eugénie while his son Alphonse escorted his mother. The gentlemen took the two ladies to the exclusive Marshal's Chamber. Eugénie had just seated herself on a sofa in the middle of the room when Madame Drouyn de Lhuys, the wife of the Foreign Minister, whispered to her that the settee was reserved for wives of ministers. Eugénie rose, her face flushed with embarrassment. The scene was observed, however, by no less a person than Napoleon himself who hurried up to Eugénie, offered her his arm, and led her to the room set apart for members of the Imperial family. Eleven days later Napoleon announced to the world that he had chosen Eugénie, 'the woman I love and honour', for his wife.

A ball at the Elysée Palace, with Napoleon III standing on the left, in the background.

Although James was still excluded from the Emperor's council chamber he confided to Betty that he had half a foot in the Emperor's bedroom. Yet even now life did not proceed smoothly. The Austrian ambassador, Count Hübner, was long on pedigree and short of money, and therefore resentful of the Austrian consul-general, no other than James de Rothschild. 'In other countries,' Hübner observed contemptuously, 'where everything has not yet been levelled by sixty years of revolution, as it has here in France, there are still, thank God, separate classes; but here money is everything, and in the sentiments of the nation the Rothschilds and the Foulds have the precedence of the Montmorencys and the Rohans.'[7] Hübner's disobliging comments were repeated to James who remarked that it was a pity that the Habsburgs had not sent to Paris a grand seigneur instead of 'a puffed-up little man'.

When Hübner learned of this remark he was so incensed that he decided to back Fould and the Pereires in every move they made against the Rothschilds. He even indulged in petty warfare on his own account. When an invitation from the Emperor for the betrothal ceremony in Notre-Dame arrived for James, sent care of the Austrian Embassy, it was not forwarded. On the great day everyone was present except the Rothschilds. Eugénie discovered what had happened and complained to Napoleon. At the court ball in March the Emperor walked past Hübner without so much as a bow, and shook James by the hand. But unfortunately this incident did not signify a change of heart on the part of Napoleon III, and only served to increase Hübner's hatred of the Rothschilds.

While Baron James was fighting Achille Fould and his new financial colossus in Paris, his brothers were exerting the maximum pressure on the governments of Europe to alleviate the condition of the Jews. Carl of Naples extracted promises from the Pope in return for loans, while Amschel of Frankfurt applied pressure on Prussia to lift the restrictions on German Jewry reimposed after the defeat of Napoleon I. Salomon in Vienna, however, was far too busy breaking through anti-Jewish barriers on his own account to give much time to his co-religionists, and in 1853 Austria suddenly passed a law which once again barred Jews from acquiring property. Although Salomon was exempted by special statute, the family rose in arms. Under James' leadership they formed a financial syndicate and drove down the price of Austrian bonds on all the European exchanges. The Austrian ambassador in Paris reported to Vienna that Baron James was 'beside himself' and advised his Government 'to soothe the children of Israel'. The Government responded and the new law was repealed.

Although the victory had been achieved by James' strategy, Amschel was convinced that the Lord had answered his prayers. As the most orthodox of Gutle's five sons, and the least intelligent

(Gentz had described him as actually 'possessing a very weak intelligence'), Amschel relied on his brothers to tell him what to do and on Jehovah to see that it was done well. Nevertheless, he occupied a geographically strategic position as Frankfurt was the most important city in northern Europe, lying mid-way between Paris and Vienna, a natural distributing point for Germany west of the Danube and the small countries contiguous to it. 'Every great operation originating in London, Paris and Vienna reached the investors in those markets through Amschel's hands, and the Frankfurt Bourse, as the outlet of the Rothschild world consortium attained an importance it had never had before.'[8]

Furthermore, as no one knew the actual distribution of power within the family circle, Amschel enjoyed a prestige fantastically out of proportion with his ability. For instance, the North German Confederation, the forerunner of the German Empire, kept its funds on deposit with him, and when it needed a loan for the Imperial Navy, the Federal Council, which sat in Frankfurt, quite naturally turned to him.

Like all Rothschilds, however, Amschel had an eye for a coming man, and when, in 1851, Prussia appointed Otto von Bismarck its representative to the Frankfurt Diet, Amschel lost no time in extending him an invitation to dinner. He asked him so many weeks in advance, to make sure of his acceptance, that Bismarck replied puckishly that he would come if he were still alive. ' "Why shouldn't he be alive?" the famous Jew asked in puzzled tones, "why should he die? The man is young and strong! . . ." '

I like the Baron though, [Bismarck continued in a letter to his wife] because he is a real old Jew pedlar and does not pretend to be anything else; he is strictly orthodox and refuses to touch anything but kosher food at his dinners. 'Take thome bread for the deer,' he said to his servant as he went out to show me his garden, in which he keeps tame deer. 'Thith plant,' he said to me, 'cotht me two thouthand gulden – on my honour it cotht me two thouthand gulden cash. You can have it for a thouthand; or if you like it ath a prethent, the thervent will bring it to your houthe. God knoweth I like you, you're a find handthome fellow.' He is such a short little thin person . . . childless, a poor man in his palace.[9]

Amschel not only was religious but extravagantly generous, giving huge sums to charities, supporting whole hospitals on his own, such as the Frankfurt Jewish Hospital. Yet, ironically, the Almighty had singled him out, the most religious of the five brothers, for punishment. He was the only one to be denied that most precious of the Rothschild commodities: sons. For years he had prayed that God would relent. 'I have never seen any man so distressed, beat his breast so much and implore the mercy of heaven as Baron Rothschild on the long day [Day of Atonement] in the synagogue,' wrote a contemporary. 'He often faints from the strain of interminable prayer, and strong smelling plants from his garden are then brought and put under his nose to bring him around. In earlier years he inflicted severe mortification on himself in order to prevail upon heaven to grant him a child, but it turned out to be in vain.'[10]

Amschel's joyless life was brightened by his superb garden which was filled with rare blooms from all over the world; and by his decision in 1850 to adopt one of his nephews as a son, Mayer Carl, offspring of his brother Carl of Naples. The Prussians were eager to keep on the right side of the banking Baron and advised the King, Frederick William IV, to appoint young Mayer Carl Court Banker to the Prussian kingdom, and to give him the Order of the Red Eagle, Third Class. The mistake His Majesty's advisers made, however, was to transform the Red Eagle, Third Class, into a Jewish Eagle. Normally the medal had a base in the shape of a cross: but now it appeared as an oval. Apparently Prussian courtiers felt that a Jew should not be allowed to wear anything that suggested a crucifix.

The young man, soon to be head of the Frankfurt House, graciously accepted the decoration, then put it in a drawer and never wore it. After three years the Prussian Government took umbrage and ordered Bismarck to send them a detailed report on Mayer Carl's medal-wearing habits, with particular reference to the Red Eagle.

Bismarck replied:

In accordance with the Royal Command of the 27th instant I have the honour dutifully to inform you that I have not seen Court Banker Mayer Carl von Rothschild wearing such a decoration, since he does not go to big functions, and when he does wear orders, prefers to wear the Greek Order of the Redeemer or the Spanish Order of Isabella the Catholic. On the occasion of the official reception which I myself gave . . . which he would have to attend in uniform, he excused himself on the grounds of ill-health, it being painful to him to wear the Red Eagle decoration for non-Christians, as he would have to do on that occasion. I draw similar inference from the fact that whenever he comes to dine with me, he merely wears the ribbon of the Order in his buttonhole . . .[11]

Prussia never de-segregated its eagles and the Rothschilds never forgot. Even though Berlin became one of the great cities of Europe after 1870, even though the Hohenzollern Emperor, William II, pressed the family to establish a branch of the bank in his capital, the Rothschilds refused. As things turned out, it saved the family from large financial losses, but it was not shrewdness that prompted the decision, only reluctance bred of a long memory.

Meanwhile the battle between the Crédit Mobilier and Baron James de Rothschild was reaching its climax, not only in Paris where Achille Fould had moved from the Ministry of Finance to the Ministry of State, but in Carl von Rothschild's Sardinia and Salomon von Rothschild's Austria. Pereire made an attempt to lure Sardinia away from the family by offering loans on cut-rate terms. James sent his son, Alphonse, to forestall the move. Alphonse succeeded but it cost him a great deal of money.

The directors of the Crédit Mobilier merely shrugged their shoulders for they had far more important plans in the offing. Meanwhile in 1854 the Crimean War broke out. Russia had attacked Turkey the previous year, and Britain was determined to prevent her from over-running the country and dominating the Dardanelles. Napoleon III joined England as the Tsar persisted in treating him as a *parvenu* and had insulted him by addressing him as '*Sire et bon ami*' instead of the customary '*Mon frère*'.

Although 'peace on earth' was a basic Rothschild principle, conducive to high profits, for the first time no branch of the family found itself on an opposing side. Austria tried to remain neutral but gave the allies her blessing: even Prussia, despite the close relationship between her King and the Tsar, refused to throw in her lot with Russia. If war was inevitable the Crimean War was an ideal conflict for the Rothschilds, as Nicholas I's anti-Semitic policies lent a moral tone to the cause. Amschel and Lionel underwrote the British war loan of £16,000,000 while James took a large part of France's war loan of 750,000,000 francs. Rothschild unity was not lost on Bismarck. 'The attitude a Government brings to bear upon the Jewish problems . . . profoundly affects the House . . .', he reported to the Prussian Government. '. . . There are occasions when other than purely business considerations determine the policy of the family . . .'[12]

Yet business – at least the business of the Crédit Mobilier – fared not at all badly as a result of the Crimean War. As usual, the Austrian Government was desperately short of cash; despite its neutrality it had to keep its army at the ready, and this cost money. Count Hübner, always eager to do a bad turn to the Rothschilds, whispered in the ear of Émile Pereire that the Austrian State Railways might come up for sale. All the railways in the Habsburg monarchy, except for the Rothschilds' Nordbahn and a railway line in the south, which belonged to the rival Sina, were owned by the state.

Pereire immediately got in touch with the bitterest of the Rothschild enemies – the Barons Sina, Eskeles and Pereira – and formed a company. Other directors were the ubiquitous Duc de Morny, Adolphe Fould, son of the minister, and the two Pereires. The object of the company was to assist the Crédit Mobilier in gaining control of the Austrian lines; and on 1 January 1855 the latter managed to buy a large chunk of the railways at a price nearly a quarter lower than the actual cost of construction. This was a great shock to the Rothschilds who had been trying for years to increase their railway ownership and who now feared that the Nordbahn might slip from their fingers.

As the battle raged with increasing fierceness, and the concentrated strength of the family was needed more urgently than at any time since the hey-day of Napoleon Bonaparte, three of the four brothers died, all in the year 1855: first Carl of Naples, then Salomon of Vienna, and finally Amschel of Frankfurt. Only death could stalk the family through the boardrooms of Europe and for much of the year business was suspended while cantors wailed their burial rites and women hooded their mirrors in order to conceal even from themselves grief that might be interpreted as a protest against God's will. The financial world watched with avid attention: was Rothschild supremacy coming to an end because the brothers insisted upon displaying the same sense of unity in dying as in living?

Certainly the Crédit Mobilier looked unbeatable. Not only had it snatched away the Austrian railways, not only had it replaced the Rothschilds as France's financial arm and gained control of over half the nation's issuing business, but now it was making record profits in a partnership with the Préfet de la Seine, Baron Eugène Haussmann. The Emperor had given Haussmann the gigantic task of 'transforming' Paris. He was to clear away the higgledy-piggledy streets and slum dwellings and to produce a network of boulevards and parks and squares that would free the monuments of the past – the Louvre, the Hôtel de Ville, Notre-Dame and many others. Paris was to be made 'a capital worthy of France'; and a capital in which insurrection would be a problem. A city with straight avenues would not favour ambushes; furthermore troops could march abreast to reach a trouble spot in record time.

During the next decade over twelve thousand houses were pulled down in the department of the Seine alone; and as the Government indemnified the owners, speculators made a fortune. 'There are people who specialize in buying, building and establishing a commercial house in the district which they consider should soon disappear . . .', wrote a contemporary observer. '. . . A coffee house keeper . . . has been demolished three times thanks to careful calculations. He had progressed from one indemnity to another until he recently managed to build an enormous and marvellous café – which he hopes to see demolished before he dies . . .'[13]

The Crédit Mobilier lent Baron Haussmann large sums of money at reasonable rates; in return the directors always seemed to know where the next demolitions would occur. Madame Haussmann innocently observed that the Baron himself no sooner purchased a house than he had to hand it over to the Government to make way for a new road.

In 1856 when the Crédit Mobilier published its accounts for the preceding year the public learned that the company had made a profit of £28,000,000 on a capital of £60,000,000. It paid the amazing dividend of forty-seven per cent. Whatever James de Rothschild might say, the directors appeared to have the patent for a formula that eventually would put every type of bank out of business.

While persistent rumours swept the Bourse that Messieurs de Rothschild Frères was facing hard times the Rothschild chief accountant, a man called Carpentier, ran off with 30,000,000 francs (about £1,200,000). For many months he had been appropriating neatly stacked bundles of share certificates and selling them in small amounts on the stock exchange. In the autumn of 1856 he had taken a few days leave and never returned. By the time the theft was discovered, however, the culprit had sailed the Atlantic in a specially chartered liner and disappeared into the anonymity of the United States. Baron James de Rothschild made a public statement saying that he, personally, would absorb the loss. There was no more talk of insolvency. Only one family in Europe could make such a grandiose gesture.

Meanwhile the Crédit Mobilier had received its first setback. At the end of 1855 the directors, encouraged by their take-over of the Austrian railways, decided to establish a Crédit Mobilier in Vienna. But when they applied to the Habsburg ministers they were told that a 'people's bank', very much like their own, was about to spring into being. It boasted the greatest families in the Empire: Fürstenbergs, Schwarzenbergs and Auerspergs. Even its name was very similar to the Crédit Mobilier, for it would be known as Kreditanstalt. And it was organized and led by Salomon von Rothschild's fifty-two-year-old son, Anselm.

As a youth Anselm had been regarded as a trifle wild. His refusal to take life seriously and his tendency to gamble at cards had so worried his father that Salomon had curtailed his stay at Berlin University and sent him to Paris to serve as an apprentice to his uncle (and brother-in-law) James. But Paris was scarcely a place for prodigals and the family heaved a sign of relief when the austere, childless, deeply religious Uncle Amschel offered his nephew a partnership in the Frankfurt Bank.

Oddly enough Amschel was not a stern task master and allowed his nephew all the latitude he desired. Not unnaturally the latter frequently stayed out until the small hours of the morning, invariably driving home in a two-horse cab and invariably giving his driver a handsome tip. Once Baron Salomon happened to hire the cab that Anselm normally used. When he paid the fare the driver stared incredulously at the money in his palm. 'What's the matter?' asked Salomon. 'Isn't it correct?' 'Yes sir. But your son usually gives me four times as much.' 'Indeed,' said Salomon, 'but you see he has a wealthy father and I have not.'

Anselm's wild oats were short lived for when he was only twenty-three he married Lionel de Rothschild's sister, Charlotte, and settled down to an exemplary existence in the exacting confines of Frankfurt society, where he remained for nearly thirty years. According to Constance de Rothschild who married Lord Battersea, he was a man of imagination and wit; according to his son, Ferdinand, a man who

loved sport and whist and amusing talk but took 'only a feeble interest in his children'. No doubt Frankfurt was something of a penance, for when Salomon died in July 1855, and Anselm was summoned to Vienna to take his place, his whole personality seemed to change. Suddenly he was smiling and animated and frantically busy. He made trips to London and Paris in a flurry of activity, and travelled regularly between Frankfurt and Vienna.

All became clear on 12 December 1855 when he invited subscriptions for shares in his great Austrian enterprise. People queued all night to buy, and by evening over 644,000,000 florins had been offered for the 15,000,000 florins worth of shares for sale. 'Everyone believed that the golden age of cheap credit had come,' remarked a contemporary, 'and everyone flocked to be among the first to receive the blessings . . .' The public was not mistaken; within a week the shares had risen from 17 to 34.

The unassuming, middle-aged, forgotten Anselm, who had spent the major part of his life in the shadow of his father's and uncle's fame, had proved himself a true blue Rothschild by stepping forward and successfully bearding the giant; and in 1857, almost as a suitable commemoration for the family deliverance, a Rothschild once again married a Rothschild. Lionel's daughter, Leonora, one of the most beautiful girls in England, wed James' eldest son, Alphonse, the crown prince of French finance. The wedding took

Marriage of Anselm von Rothschild to his cousin Charlotte, 11 September 1826; on the left are Carl and Salomon von Rothschild; on the right, Nathan, Lionel, Hannah and Louise. A watercolour by Richard Dighton.

MARRIAGE CEREMONIAL OF THE BARON ALPHONSE DE ROTHSCHILD AND MISS LEONORA ROTHSCHILD: THE BRIDEGROOM BREAKING THE WINE-CUP
(SEE NEXT PAGE.)

place at Gunnersbury Park. The bride had 'lovely . . . liquid almond-shaped eyes, the sweet complexion of a tea rose'. Benjamin Disraeli gave the toast. 'Under this roof,' he said, 'are the heads of the name and family of Rothschild – a name famous in every capital of Europe and every division of the globe – a family not more regarded for its riches than esteemed for its honour, integrity and public spirit.'[14]

Soon the four cousins were working together as smoothly as the brothers before them: Alphonse of Paris,† Anselm of Vienna, Lionel of London, Mayer Carl of Frankfurt. To call them cousins, of course, was something of an understatement for the plethora of Rothschild intermarriages had produced a jungle of double and triple relationships. Anselm, for instance, was married to Lionel's sister Charlotte, so he was not only Lionel's cousin but his brother-in-law, and as Alphonse's mother was Anselm's sister, the two were uncle and nephew as well as cousins. And as Mayer Carl was married to Lionel's sister Louisa he not only was Lionel's cousin but his brother-in-law; and of course this also made Mayer Carl Anselm's brother-in-law as well as his cousin.

Together the third generation not only attacked the Crédit Mobilier on the bourses of Europe but mounted an assault on the Habsburg railway business. Early in 1856 they offered the Austrian Minister of Finance £10,000,000 for the Lombard-Venetian railway; and later more millions for the Austrian Southern Railway. Then not only came the threat of war, but war that might be fought over the Rothschilds' newly acquired property. The great Sardinian Finance Minister, Cavour, was determined to achieve the independence of the northern Italian states from Austria, and eventually to bring about Italian unification. He was said to have paid large sums of money to the famous courtesan, the Comtesse de Castiglione, to persuade her lover, Napoleon III, that it was in France's interest to support Italy. Apparently she succeeded for in 1858, when Cavour visited Paris, he made a secret treaty with the French Emperor who promised to assist him if Austria tried to prevent the secession of the northern Italian States by force.

James was appalled at the prospect of war between France and Austria. Repeatedly he sought audiences with Napoleon III who alarmed him by his evasiveness. Although Napoleon had once upon a time declared: 'The Empire is peace', he now explained: 'I want peace but one can be carried away by the force of circumstances.' James went about Paris prophesying darkly in his bad French 'Entendez-fous, bas de baix, bas d'Embire.'

The war broke out in April 1859 and ended three months later with the defeat of the Austrian armies at Magenta and Solferino. Tuscany, Parma and Modena won their independence and France annexed Nice and Savoy. The hated Count Hübner was recalled to

Marriage ceremony of Leonora and Alphonse de Rothschild at Gunnersbury House, 4 March 1857. From *The Illustrated London News.*

†Alphonse's two brothers, Gustave and Edmond, were partners in the bank, as were the brothers of Lionel in England.

Vienna and Prince Richard Metternich sent to Paris in his stead.

Although the Crédit Mobilier had financed Napoleon's war effort, by 1860 their shares had fallen from 1600 to 800. Then came a scandal involving one of the company directors, Jules Mires, who was arrested for fraud. Although Fould was forced to resign it was only a temporary reprimand for he was reappointed a year later.

But Fould now regarded the Pereire brothers with a cold and critical eye. The Crédit Mobilier was clearly over-extended and badly managed, for every year its profits shrank. Fould advised Napoleon III that the French Government no longer could rely on the bank to provide it with loans, and advised him to patch up the quarrel with the Rothschilds. As a result, on 17 February 1862, the Emperor, accompanied by Fould, and a party which included the French Minister for Foreign Affairs and the British and Austrian ambassadors, visited Baron James' estate at Ferrières. Joseph Paxton, who had designed the house, had not lived up to his promise as 'a new Christopher Wren', and some people thought Ferrières heavy and ugly. No one, however, could fault the wonderful estate with its parks, lakes and greenhouses, its riding school and sheep farm, its bakery and Dutch dairy.

When the Imperial train arrived at Ferrières station Baron James and his four sons, Alphonse, Gustave, Salomon and Edmond, were waiting to greet the Emperor. A green carpet embroidered with Bonaparte bees ran from the train to a waiting carriage. Napoleon III stepped out wearing hunting dress. He was escorted to the Rothschild coach and four, which was attended by lackeys in new dark blue, gold-braided liveries. When the party approached the château the Imperial standard was hoisted on the flag mast of the four towers. The Emperor planted a young cedar in the garden, then sat down to a memorable luncheon eaten off Sèvres china. In the afternoon over a thousand head of game were shot.

That night a choir from the Paris opera sang a song specially composed by Rossini: and when the Emperor finally departed he rode back to his train along several miles of road flanked by torches. Despite all these civilities the rapprochement was only skin-deep and Baron James continued to allude to the Emperor as 'this third-class Napoleon'.

Even modest Lionel caught the fever of grandeur. Although he had lived all his life at 107 Piccadilly, and Gunnersbury Park, he now began to acquire new properties on a breathtaking scale. In 1864 he started building 148 Piccadilly, the edifice that the American tourist had found so enthralling. When it was finished, it was one of the most pretentious houses in London. An imposing marble staircase led to the ballroom on the first floor, which had huge windows overlooking the Park, hung with silk curtains embroidered for no particular reason with river goddesses.

Opposite, top James' château at Ferrières. *Bottom* Napoleon III planting a tree in the grounds of Ferrières. Despite the lavish entertainment which included a concert of music specially composed by Rossini and 1,231 head of game killed in one afternoon, the visit did not bring about the hoped-for rapprochement between the Emperor and the financier.

Above A German caricature of Napoleon III and James de Rothschild hunting at Ferrières during the Emperor's visit on 17 February 1862.

VISITE DE FERRIÈRES. — L'Empereur plantant l'arbre commémoratif de sa visite au château.

The marble and gold and scarlet, sumptuous, ornate, overpowering, included some wild and wonderful extravaganzas: a silver table service by Garrard weighing nearly ten thousand ounces and an apple green Sèvres china service painted by Le Bel. Every chair, a wit remarked, offered gilt-edged security.

Occasionally, very occasionally, instead of moving into a palace, a Rothschild moved out of a palace. Adolph von Rothschild of Naples was a case in point. The drive for Italian unification continued, and in 1861 the Kingdom of the Two Sicilies (of which Naples was one) was snuffed out by Garibaldi. The King and Queen fled to Paris and Adolph, who had succeeded his father Carl as head of the bank, pulled down the shutters and followed the Royal family into exile. The Italian branch never was reopened which meant that the Rothschild banks now numbered four.

More rarely still did the Rothschilds produce a black sheep. In 1864 Baron James' third son, the brilliantly clever Salomon, dropped dead. The boy had become a compulsive gambler which had caused his father great anxiety, as anyone with the Rothschild name was given unlimited financial credit. Apparently Salomon died of a heart attack which fascinated the Goncourt brothers. 'Cabarrus, Rothschild's doctor,' one of them wrote, 'told Saint-Victor that the young Rothschild who died the other day really died of the excitement of gambling on the Stock Exchange. Imagine it; a Rothschild dead of a paroxysm over money.'

However, if the Goncourt brothers had known the details of a previous heart attack suffered by Salomon they would have been even more enthralled. Three years earlier Salomon had 'dropped dead'. He had been placed in a coffin and, according to Jewish custom, carried into every room in the house. One of the pall bearers had stumbled, the coffin had crashed into a door and – Salomon had woken up! Not for another three years was he well and truly buried.

Baron James towards the end of his life. His famous prophecy 'no peace, no Empire' came true two years after his death, when Napoleon III capitulated to the Prussians at Sedan and abdicated.

Meanwhile the Crédit Mobilier, the tiger that had threatened the very existence of Messieurs de Rothschild Frères, had fallen into a moribund state. In 1864 it was forced to raise huge loans for the Emperor Napoleon III in his attempt to place the Archduke Maximilian on the throne of Mexico. The ill-fated venture had involved the company in heavy losses; furthermore it was becoming plain that the 'novel' methods of the Pereire brothers were often nothing more than rash speculation. Now individuals were taking the company to court for 'unfair practices'. 'I shall do everything to support them because the Empire is deeply indebted to them,' Napoleon said. 'But I cannot afford to impede the course of justice.'[15]

This was the final slight. The company's luck had turned, its unfortunate investments had caught up with it. It began paying dividends out of capital: and in 1866 showed a loss of 8,000,000 francs. The shares dropped to 350.

One of Baron James' last great acquisitions was the château and vineyards of Lafite, in the Médoc region near Bordeaux.

Now everyone recognized that the battle between the two great combines had ended with the Rothschilds as victors. In October 1867 the shares fell to 140 and the Crédit Mobilier went into liquidation. The Pereire brothers returned to private life and Achille Fould resigned his ministry for the last time. A few months later he died.

Baron James seemed in the best of health and, at the urging of his sons, Alphonse and Gustave, even bought a new estate – a vineyard in the Médoc adjoining his cousin's property. As this vineyard was none other than the famous Château Lafite which had been rated first in the first *cru*, as compared to Nathaniel Rothschild's vineyard, Mouton, first in the second *cru*, the atmosphere between the cousins was distinctly cool; but, of course, that was the fun of the purchase.

Unfortunately James did not live long enough to enjoy his claret. A few months later, in 1868, at the age of seventy-six, he followed Achille Fould to the grave. Some people were shocked by the fact that the awesome Baron was made of the same flesh as his rival, and half Paris took part in the funeral. Crowned heads all over Europe sent representatives, and even the President of the United States, who had never clapped eyes on James, telegraphed his condolences.

James was buried in the cemetery at Père-Lachaise; and according to his wishes, the resting place of the man whose splendour had dazzled Paris was marked by a tombstone enscribed with nothing but the letter 'R'.

Chapter VII

Victorian High Noon

(1860–80)

People of the Period.—BARON LIONEL DE ROTHSCHILD.
(THE MODERN CRŒSUS.)

Caricature of Lionel de Rothschild, 'the modern Croesus', from *The Period*, 1870. Queen Victoria, William I of Prussia, the Pope, Napoleon III and others are seen paying homage to Lionel, seated on a throne made of money-bags.

Opposite Leonora de Rothschild. The eldest daughter of Lionel, she married her French cousin Alphonse in 1857. She had, an admirer wrote, 'lovely ... liquid, almond-shaped eyes, the sweet complexion of a tea-rose'.

WHEN THE QUEEN'S PRIME MINISTER, MR GLADSTONE, suggested that Her Majesty might like to bestow a peerage on the great banker, Lionel de Rothschild, Victoria was deeply shocked. '*To make a Jew a peer*,' she replied, 'is a step she *could not* consent to. It would be ill-taken and would do the Government great harm.'

Even Lord Granville, whose opinion she greatly valued, could make no impression. 'The notion of a Jew peer is startling,' he admitted. '*Rothschild le premier Baron Juif* does not sound as well as *Montmorency le premier Baron Chrétien* but he represents a class whose influence is great by their wealth, their intelligence, their literary connections.' He added that it would be wise 'to attach the financial interest in the City of London to the Crown instead of running the risk of driving it into the extremist camp'.[1]

Mr Gladstone bravely returned to the fray arguing that 'if his religion were to operate permanently as a bar . . . it would revive by prerogative the disability which formerly existed by statute . . .' But Her Majesty remained adamant. She could not think, she said, that one 'who owed his wealth to contracts with Foreign Governments for Loans', or to 'successful speculations on the Stock Exchange' could 'fairly claim a British peerage'.[2] Thus the Victorian maxim was emphasized that whereas the best people spent money they did not make it.

This was one of the places where the Prince of Wales parted company from his mother. The landed gentry were rich and dull, whereas the new financiers and industrialists not only were creating the world of tomorrow but, like magicians, had the dazzling ability to produce millions by a wave of the hand – on the floor of the Stock Exchange. No one enjoyed luxury more than the Prince, yet compared to many of his subjects he was not a rich man. Even when he married Alexandra of Denmark in 1863 and moved into Marlborough House, his allowance was fixed by Parliament at a beggarly £100,000 a year. He complained bitterly that this sum was not large enough to provide a Court and to pay for his entertaining, clothes and travel. Certainly he was not well off by the standards of the day; from land alone the Duke of Buccleuch derived a yearly income of £217,000, the Duke of Devonshire £181,000, the Duke of Northumberland £176,000, the Earl of Derby £161,000.

Yet none of these men had the same fascination for Albert Edward as the Rothschilds. His mother might sniff at 'trade' but the new

breed of millionaire enjoyed power as well as riches and was far better company than most members of the landed gentry.

The Prince had made friends with Lionel's sons during his brief sojourn at Cambridge. The brothers were the third generation of Rothschilds to live in England, but the first generation to receive an English education. The conditions were not entirely satisfactory as Oxford and Cambridge would not award degrees to undergraduates who did not declare allegiance to the Liturgy of the Church of England. But whereas Oxford demanded the pledge before accepting a student Cambridge was willing to take the assurance at any time before matriculation, even the last day of the last term, which meant that Jews could get an education, if not become Bachelors of Arts.

In 1861 twenty-one year old Nathaniel, known as 'Natty', was in his final year at the University when Albert Edward, Prince of

Opposite 'Build me a Mentmore,' said Baron James to the architect Joseph Paxton, 'only twice as big.' The result was Ferrières, in the Brie district, near Paris. It caused Wilhelm I of Prussia to comment: 'Kings couldn't afford this. It could only belong to a Rothschild.'

Lionel's two eldest sons, Nathaniel ('Natty') and the sybaritic Alfred.

Wales, was transferred from Christ Church, Oxford to Trinity College, Cambridge, for the usual, fleeting, royal stint. At first Queen Victoria insisted that the Prince live four miles out of town, in Madingley Hall, much to the young man's disgust. The Master of Trinity, however, finally persuaded Her Majesty that the heir to the throne should be allowed rooms in college for 'occasional use'. Hereafter the Prince rode into town each morning on horseback: and soon had made friends with the two undergraduates most closely connected with riding to hounds: Charles Carrington who hunted the Drag and Nathaniel Rothschild who paid for it.

Soon the Prince numbered among his close friends not only Natty but Natty's brothers, Alfred and Leo; not only their father Lionel but their uncles Mayer and Anthony; not only French cousin Alphonse but Austrian cousin Ferdinand. Other Jews followed, the Hirshes, the Beits, the Sassoons and the Cassels, but in the Prince's youth none enjoyed the same relationship as the Rothschilds. And as His Royal Highness lived far above his means, the Rothschilds were accused of paying his debts. No doubt the banking Barons helped to invest his money, and no doubt, if and when the investments failed to come up to scratch, they made up the difference from their own pockets; but this is speculation for no one knows what transactions took place. However in 1876 a pamphlet appeared entitled *Edward VII* containing a vicious parody both on Shakespeare and the Prince. Should the Prince confide in his mother, the formidable Victoria, and ask her to pay his debts?

> Tell all or not tell all that is the question
> Whether it is better of the Jews to borrow
> To take the cash of base-born, low-bred men
> Who out of necessities would make
> A ladder up to peerages, who claim
> My notice, 'cause I take their ill-gained coin
> Who whine for invitations to my house
> As though the cad who sells the gold deserv'd
> More notice than the ones who sell you hats,
> Or build you coats, or fashion you your boots;
> Nay, not so much, for these are honest men –
> Whether 'tis better their demands to suffer
> Or make clean breast of it; declare my debt
> And pay off all the Jewish herd in full
> With money that now fills the royal purse;
> Methinks I will.

Although there was far less prejudice against the Jews in England than on the Continent, such broadsides were plentiful in the high noon of Victoria's reign. But as the Rothschilds were indispensable to the Prince's pleasure, a relentless pursuit, he refused to allow the attacks to disconcert him. When he went to Paris he liked nothing better than to be entertained by Alphonse or Gustave, sons of the late

The unruffable head of the French branch, Baron Alphonse, and his English wife, Leonora, *above*, were described as 'the most lavish entertainers of their day'.

Baron James, who now ran the bank. Alphonse was married to the English Leonora and both had a happy knack of producing a guest list with just the right mixture of grandeur and allure.

Alphonse and Leonora stood at the centre of the French world of power and fashion. Alphonse was a frail, delicately boned little man who tried to make up for his under-sized body by a pair of magnificent side whiskers. Apparently his temperament was more British than French, for he prided himself on never allowing anything to ruffle his composure. Even on the occasion of a splendid pheasant drive at Ferrières, when one of his guests managed to shoot him in the face, he maintained an icy calm. The accident finally resulted in the Baron's losing an eye, yet he never revealed the name of the unhappy delinquent.

Leonora was greatly admired by the French despite the fact that she clung stubbornly to her English ways. She taught her French chef to make treacle pudding and always served afternoon tea : and when she made her will she stipulated that her body should be sent back to Buckinghamshire for burial. She entertained her English visitors in true English fashion. Frances, Countess of Warwick (at the time Lady Brooke) tells of a visit to Ferrières in the early 1880s, describing the Alphonses as 'the most lavish entertainers of their day'. Certainly no one could have taken more trouble on this occasion, for Leonora asked her brother Natty (the future Lord Rothschild) to send her a draft of stag-hounds from the pack at Tring for the week-end. Apparently there was no difficulty in shipping them across the channel, and when the Brookes arrived they found that an English *chasse* had been arranged in their honour.

The rendez-vous in the morning, near the Chateau, was a very pretty sight, [wrote Lady Brooke]. The men wore red coats made in England while the Hunt servants were in green and gold. There was also a sprinkling of officers in full uniform, swords and all, from the neighbouring garrison at Melun. Baroness Alphonse, who hunted sometimes in England, and myself, were the only ladies in the saddle. The rest of the party, in chars-a-banc and victorias, drove with the *chasse* to different places in the vast woods where 'obstacles' – a kind of hurdle covered with bushes – had been put up in the grass rides, to give the spectators a chance of seeing us leap them. They called out 'Houp-la' in admiring tones, as if we had been performing in a circus.

Alphonse was not only sociable but extremely good-natured. Only once was he known to lose his temper. When he was travelling by his own railway – the Chemin de Fer du Nord – to Bruges to dine with King Leopold, suddenly his train veered to a siding where it remained for two hours until another, very special train roared past. Baron Alphonse missed his dinner engagement and furiously demanded an explanation. The mystery was solved when his valet admitted sheepishly that he had forgotten to pack the Baron's evening clothes and had sent it after him by special courier who, unlike the Baron himself, had taken full advantage of the Rothschild name.

Unlike his father James, Alphonse had received an education suitable for a financial crown prince. He had worked in the family banks in London, Frankfurt and Vienna, and even travelled to America to study New World methods. He was a skilful banker and a perfect gentleman, courteous, sophisticated and dazzlingly rich. His house was filled with treasures collected by his father; indeed, many of the pictures had been purchased from Napoleon's uncle, Cardinal Fesch; one of the finest acquisitions was a Vermeer, *The Astronomer*.

Alphonse sometimes entertained the Prince of Wales at Ferrières, sometimes in his enormous town house at the corner of the Rue Saint-Florentin, overlooking the Place de la Concorde, originally the home of the famous Prince Talleyrand. James de Rothschild had purchased the house from Talleyrand's niece, the Duchess of Dino, in 1838, a few weeks after the statesman's death, and eventually presented it to Alphonse.

Politically Alphonse was one of the best informed men in France. Apart from the network of Rothschild agents who reported to him regularly, he had access to everyone from Napoleon III to Otto von Bismarck: from the Empress Eugénie to the courtesan, La Castiglione, a mistress whom Alphonse apparently shared both with his brother, Gustave, and with the Emperor. Bismarck frequently stayed

A *trompe l'oeil* portrait of the Comtesse de Castiglione. After a remarkable career as a courtesan in Paris, La Castiglione became a recluse and for the last thirty years of her life went out only at night, heavily veiled so that no one would see her fading beauty.

at Ferrières when he was ambassador to Paris in 1862 and 1863; and when he visited France in 1865, as Prime Minister of Prussia, he again spent the weekend with the Rothschilds. On this occasion he hoped that Napoleon would ask him to dine on Saturday night.

'On the day the big shoot took place at Ferrières', wrote the Rothschild agent, 'C. deB.', 'M. de Bismarck said he would not dine. He was expecting an invitation from Napoleon. When this invitation did not arrive he asked permission to remain at Ferrières.'[4]

Now that Bismarck had become minister-president it was obvious that his overriding ambition was to make Prussia the dominant force on the continent. He fired an opening salvo in 1864 when he snatched Schleswig and Holstein from Denmark. And now, in 1865, rumours were rife that the next test of strength would come with the Habsburgs. The fact that Austria had been weakened by her defeat at the hands of Italy and France was grist to the Prussian mill. Alphonse who, like his father, was deeply opposed to war had a clear grasp of the situation and did everything in his power to make Austria see the futility of clashing with Bismarck. 'Prussia is not a country with an army,' he said, quoting the French military attaché in Berlin, 'but an army with a country.'

Alphonse's cousin, Anselm of Vienna, who had been so effective in forestalling the Crédit Mobilier in Austria, joined Alphonse in urging the Habsburgs to be wary of being coerced into war. Although Austria no longer was the great power it had been when Anselm's father, Salomon, had worked hand in glove with the famous Prince Metternich, it was still a vast empire and still part of the European concert. If anyone could influence the Government it was Anselm for he had become part and parcel of the Austrian way of life. His name was inscribed in the Golden Book of the capital and in 1861 he had been made a member of the Imperial House of Lords. Although occasionally clubs black-balled him because he was a Jew, he knew how to hit back. Indeed, when the Casino Club near Vienna refused him membership he bought a small sewage disposal unit from the adjoining village and installed it within sight and smell of his tormentors. The Club instantly tried to right the situation by despatching a membership card. He refused to remove his sanitary unit, however, and returned the card deliciously scented with the best French perfume.

During the crucial year of 1865 only a family wedding could induce Alphonse and Anselm to absent themselves from their banks. On this occasion Anselm's son, Ferdinand, married Lionel's daughter, Evelina. Evelina, of course, was a sister of Alphonse's wife, Leonora – and just to muddle the reader still further Anselm's wife, Charlotte, was a sister of Lionel – so the clan gathered in London in full force.

Disraeli once again proposed the toast to the bride in his flowery way. The reception took place at Lionel's newly built house at 148

Piccadilly and the Christian bridesmaids boasted the most illustrious names in the land. The bride's father could not resist teasing Disraeli who, unlike the Rothschilds, was a baptised Jew. 'Ben,' Lionel called out in front of all the guests, 'there are so many Christians present that our *chazan* wants to know whether he should just read the prayers or sing them as in the synagogue.' 'Oh! please let them sing it,' Dizzy replied. 'I like to hear old-fashioned tunes.'

When Anselm and Alphonse returned to their respective countries they continued to apply pressure on Austria to exercise some cunning in dealing with Prussia. But the Government refused to heed their warnings. In the old days the House of Rothschild prevented war merely by withholding its money; but now nations plunged into hostilities without a penny, relying on victory to enable them to establish new credit. Alphonse was particularly angry with Prince Richard Metternich, the son of the famous statesman and Austrian ambassador to France, who insisted that the Habsburg armies would 'wipe the floor' with Prussia. 'The army from the War Minister down to the junior subaltern does not doubt that Austria will be victorious,' he declared pompously, as though such opinions were conclusive evidence.

Alphonse finally decided to draw attention to Austria's recklessness by raising a storm in a tea cup. He instructed his bank to return a cheque of Prince Metternich's for the trifling sum of 5000 francs with the statement that he had not even this small amount standing to his account. The story swept Paris and Princess Pauline Metternich was so furious that she said in future she would treat the Rothschilds as tradesmen, not gentlemen. That same evening the Rothschilds gave a fancy-dress ball at which the Metternichs were conspicuous by their absence. A few days later the Austro-Prussian War broke out which ended seven weeks later in Austria's total surrender.

Europe was shocked, but the gloom did not put a stop to the whirl of social life that characterized the Second Empire. 'Gaiety is now setting in heavily,' wrote an English journalist in Paris in 1868. 'Everything indicates a prolonged and severe season.'

Baron Alphonse was convinced that Prussia would not delay much longer before seeking its climactic confrontation with France: and he was one of the few men who doubted France's capacity to resist. His information on Bismarck's intentions came from two impeccable sources: his friend and fellow banker, Herr Bleichröder in Berlin and La Païva, the most notorious courtesan in Paris. La Païva's value sprang from the fact that she happened to be the mistress of the fabulously rich German, Count Henkel von Donnersmarck, a personal friend both of Bleichröder and Otto von Bismarck.

The astonishing adventuress had begun life in the Moscow ghetto, and at seventeen had married a tailor. She had made her way to Paris where she found a rich protector; and in due course managed to

marry a Portuguese aristocrat, the Marquis de Païva-Arauje. Her ambitions were not fulfilled, however, until she ensnared Count Donnersmarck, whose fortune came from Silesian coal, and who gave her 3,000,000 francs a year to spend. She built herself a huge house on the Champs-Élysées which is today the Travellers Club. It was completed in 1866 and its extravagances, even in an age of ostentation, created a sensation. The lavatories were made of onyx and the bathroom taps and keyholes studded in jewels. 'When I visit your *hôtel*,' Baron Rothschild told La Païva, 'mine seems like a hovel to me.'

Because of Count Donnersmarck's aggressive Prussianism, people said that La Païva's house was a hot-bed of espionage. Baron Alphonse made a point of keeping in touch with the Count and in the spring of 1870, when the latter abruptly quit Paris with his mistress, Alphonse predicted that a diplomatic war would follow. He was right, for a few weeks later an Imperial messenger summoned him to attend the Emperor Napoleon at Saint-Cloud.

Napoleon III told Alphonse that Prussia was trying to foist a Hohenzollern on the Spanish throne; that France could never consent to such an impertinence and if Prussia persisted he, the Emperor, would have no alternative but to declare war. He therefore hoped that England would put a restraining hand on Bismarck: and since

La Païva's bed, in her astounding *hôtel particulier*, was made of solid, sculpted mahogany, weighing one and a half tons.

150

England happened to be without a Foreign Minister (Lord Clarendon had died and Lord Granville had not yet been appointed) he wished to make use of Rothschild channels to convey his views.

The family, of course, had been engaged in manoeuvres such as these for decades. So Baron Alphonse sent a cypher message from the Rue Laffitte to New Court which was decoded by cousin Nathaniel and taken to Mr Gladstone's residence at Carlton House Terrace. The old man was about to leave for Windsor for an audience with the Queen. Gladstone pondered; but the answer was no. The Spanish people, he said, were not adverse to a German prince, therefore Britain was in no position to interfere.

No one foresaw the fall of France. Indeed crowned heads and statesmen alike believed that at long last Bismarck had taken on an impossible task. Although the Prussians withdrew their Hohen-zollern candidate, friction between Prussia and France had reached such a pitch that Napoleon III rose to Bismarck's bait and used the famous Ems telegram as an excuse to declare war. 'The odds are fearfully against us,' wrote the Prussian Crown Princess to her mother, Queen Victoria, '. . . our existence is at stake.' The French were cock-a-hoop. While the people cried: 'à Berlin', the Minister of War declared that the French army was ready to the last button. 'We enter the war', the Prime Minister told a packed audience, 'with a light heart.'

Baron Alphonse was not so sanguine. He packed his wife and children off to England to stay with Leonora's father, Baron Lionel. Here, throughout the month of August, poor Leonora read of one Prussian victory after another. On 2 September, barely six weeks after the start of hostilities, the French suffered a crushing defeat at Sedan. Constance de Rothschild wrote in her diary that when she entered the breakfast room she was struck by the dismay on the faces of her Uncle Lionel and Aunt, while Leonora's eyes were red with tears.

A fourth person, Mr. Bauer, looking gloomy and dark, stood at the table with a telegram in his hand. These were the words of the dispatch: 'The Emperor [Napoleon] has surrendered himself to the King [of Prussia] and the army of forty thousand men has capitulated.' Poor Laurie [Leonora] felt humiliated like a French woman. Then came the fear of revolution. She was dark crimson with excitement and her voice trembled so that she could hardly speak. After a few moments her children came screaming and shouting into the room. They were allowed to make a fearful noise as no one seemed to mind them. In the midst of their childish voices came the muttered doubts and fears concerning the Empire . . .[5]

The Empire had fallen. Twenty-four hours earlier France had declared itself a republic. The new Government expected reasonable armistice terms and was astonished to learn that Prussia's demands were as rapacious as though the culpable Emperor were still on the throne. The conditions were refused and the Prussian High Com-

After a four-month siege Paris capitulated to the Prussians early in 1871. The photograph shows the Prussians troops in the Place de la Concorde.

mand decided to invest Paris and starve it into submission. Bismarck recalled his agreeable visits to Ferrières in such glowing terms that the Prussian King and Field-Marshal von Moltke decided to make the château their headquarters. King William moved into the private apartments of Alphonse but insisted on setting up his iron camp bed. Bismarck contented himself with the suite once used by Baron James while Moltke occupied the rooms of Baroness Betty. The King brought his own cooks and the estate was forced to supply fruit, vegetables and flowers. Over three thousand men and twelve hundred horses were quartered in the park.

Although guns could be heard in the distance, the weather was warm and sunny and Ferrières seemed to epitomize the delights of peace – and money. Swans glided lazily across the lakes; the green houses were bursting with grapes and orchids; the coverts filled with game, the stables stocked with thoroughbreds. 'Kings couldn't afford this,' William of Prussia is said to have remarked. 'It could only belong to a Rothschild.'

In those far away days kings behaved like gentlemen, and William made it clear to the General Staff that looting was strictly *verboten*. According to the Rothschild steward, left in charge of Ferrières, the King also restrained Bismarck from indulging his passion for shooting. The steward's reports to his master, still preserved at the château, must be treated with reservation as the author is greatly concerned to paint a flattering picture of himself. After refusing to serve wine from the Rothschild cellars to the self-invited guests he was summoned by Bismarck who rebuked him for his churlishness, and asked him if he knew what 'a truss of straw' was. The steward looked puzzled and Bismarck explained that it was an object on which obstinate stewards were laid with the backsides uppermost. Apparently this threat was sufficient to make the wine flow, but the steward let his master know that the Germans actually had threatened to beat him.

Meanwhile the *haut-monde* of Paris took their minds off France's unexpected military collapse by making jokes about the invaders. In December the Prussians shot down a balloon containing a letter to the Countess de Moustier with the following sentence: 'Rothschild told me yesterday that Bismarck was not satisfied with his pheasants at Ferrières, but had threatened to beat his steward because the pheasants did not fly about filled with truffles.'[6]

Bismarck was furious when the story was relayed to him, for the truth was that despite the King's prohibition he had been sneaking in a bit of shooting on the side. 'What will they do to me?' he asked in mock terror. 'They won't arrest me, for then they won't have anyone to arrange peace.'

The peace terms were not signed until Paris had been under siege for nearly five months and the population close to starvation. Meanwhile the King and Bismarck had moved to Versailles where they were joined by Herr Bleichröder, the Berlin banker who, until the war had broken out, had represented Rothschild interests in the Prussian capital, and none other than La Païva's millionaire lover, Count von Donnersmarck.

M. Thiers and M. Favre, spokesmen for the new Republic, travelled to Versailles to ask for peace terms. They were received by Bismarck and his financial advisers who told the Frenchmen that Prussia not only intended to annex Alsace and Lorraine but demanded an indemnity of 6,000,000,000 francs. 'Quite impossible!' M. Thiers exlaimed. 'Why if you began to count from the time of Jesus Christ and went on until today you could not finish counting out such a sum.' 'That is why I sent for Bleichröder,' replied Bismarck, 'who begins to count from a much older date than Jesus Christ.'[7]

The Frenchmen were in no mood to laugh at Bismarck's quips. It was impossible, they said, to commit their Government without taking expert financial advice themselves, and they begged leave to summon M. Alphonse de Rothschild.

Bismarck's face darkened when he heard the name of the man who had linked his name with the jokes about pheasants flying with bellies full of truffles. He said angrily that the negotiators were procrastinating: that the patience of the King was exhausted: that he himself was not willing to continue talks which the other side deliberately was trying to break down. 'It is exceedingly accommodating of me to take all this trouble,' Bismarck stormed. 'Our conditions are an ultimatum – they must either be accepted or refused. I am not going to discuss the matter further.' Then he added petulantly. 'Bring an interpreter tomorrow – I shan't speak French in future.'

Meanwhile Thiers had summoned Baron Alphonse by telegram.

Bismarck, who had been a friend of Amschel von Rothschild in Frankfurt, occupied Ferrières during the Prussian invasion of France.

He arrived at 7.30 the following evening. Bismarck was extremely rude to him, not only because of the Ferrières incident but because 'he refused to speak German and behaved as though he were a "full-blooded" Frenchman'. Bismarck reminded him, in his most offensive manner, that his father and uncles had been brought up in Frankfurt, and that Salomon had been a friend of Prussia. He then upbraided him because he had not settled the method of payment with Bleichröder and Donnersmarck during the first hour of his arrival.

The final agreement was reached the following morning: it specified that the war indemnity would be 5,000,000,000 not 6,000,000,000 francs, and that all the great money merchants of Europe would serve as guarantors. Three days after the signing of the peace Bismarck told an assembled company at Versailles how churlishly the Rothschilds' steward had behaved to him; and then referred slightingly to the Rothschilds, pointing out scornfully that Alphonse's grandfather had been 'Court Jew' to the Elector of Hesse and 'private Jew' to many other families.

In the middle of March the revolutionary Commune was established in Paris. The Tuileries were burned, but although much looting and bloodshed took place, the Rothschild house emerged unscathed. Order was restored by the end of May and slowly Government and people settled down to a new era. Baron Alphonse

Barricades in front of Alphonse de Rothschild's house at the corner of the Place de la Concorde and the Rue Saint-Florentin, during the Paris Commune of 1871.

and his cousins handled France's war indemnity so efficiently that the huge sum was paid off in 1875, two years earlier than anticipated, freeing France of German troops.

Thus the French Rothschilds not only survived but prospered; once again they emerged from an upheaval financially intact: once again they had the confidence of the new Government of France.

Although the 1870s began with the sound of cannon-fire, it was a good decade for the family. Indeed 1871 was known in England as 'the Baron's year', not because of any startling financial coups, but because Lionel's brother, Mayer, won the Thousand Guineas, the Derby, the Oaks, and the St Leger, all in the same season. The prize money totalled £25,000, regarded as a huge sum.

Although Mayer was the Member of Parliament for Hythe, he copied Lionel in never making a speech, and people said that he preferred the faces of horses to those of his fellow MPs. No doubt this was true as he gave more time to his racing stable at Newmarket than to the House of Commons, and Disraeli once referred to him as 'a man with a stable mind'. He spent a fortune improving his breed until the Rothschild colours – blue jackets and yellow caps – were seen on every race-course in England.

In 1872 Mayer was convinced that he had yet another Derby winner in a horse named Laburnum, and advised his constituents 'to follow the Baron'. His horse, however, failed to live up to his expectations; and the Baron was so chagrined at having misled the electorate that he refused to stand again for Parliament. However he consoled himself the following year by buying a charming hunting box at Ascott, near Leighton Buzzard, within view of Mentmore Towers.

That same year, 1873, Mayer's brother, Lionel, head of the bank, who had hunted in the Aylesbury Vale for years but had never owned anything but a small hunting box suddenly began to acquire land in such profusion that he left everyone breathless. A decade earlier he had moved into his vast mansion at 148 Piccadilly, but throughout his life had remained faithful to his country house, Gunnersbury Park at Acton. Now he had a longing for glorious Buckinghamshire, and gratified it by purchasing a fourteen hundred acre estate, Halton, near Aylesbury. A year later he struck again, this time acquiring Tring Park, with four thousand acres of farmland and a lovely seventeenth-century manor house designed by Sir Christopher Wren. The ceilings were profusely decorated with 'NGs' for the house had been presented to Nell Gwynn by her lover Charles II. Some people thought that the crotchety old Lionel was an odd person to take possession of a lush establishment where once upon a time an orange seller from Drury Lane had held a high-spirited court, nevertheless the Baron was immensely pleased with his new estate.

Yet it was not a British Rothschild who set Buckinghamshire agog.

Mayer Amschel, fourth son of Nathan Rothschild, was known as the sporting member of the family. A caricature by 'Ape' in *Vanity Fair*, celebrating his Derby victory in 1871.

It was Anselm's son, Ferdinand of Vienna, who trumped Lionel's aces by erecting a French château six miles from Aylesbury, the like of which nobody had ever seen before – at least in the middle of the placid English countryside.

Ferdinand's wife, Evelina, a daughter of Lionel, had died only eighteen months after their wedding in 1865. The twenty-six year old widower was distraught and gave hundreds of pounds to charity in her memory. While his father-in-law financed the Evelina de Rothschild School in Jerusalem, he founded the Evelina de Rothschild Hospital for Sick Children in London. He had taken British nationality at the time of his wedding, and although he never married again spent his life in England, becoming a great patron of the arts and, later, a Trustee of the British Museum. He also represented Aylesbury as a Member of Parliament and sat on the first Buckinghamshire County Council.

Ferdinand's interest in pictures had begun as a child. 'Long before I was born,' he wrote, 'my father had acquired a collection of Dutch pictures in Holland. Day after Day I would reverently study them, learning under my mother's tuition, to distinguish a Teniers from an Ostade or a Wouvermans from a Both.' As he grew older, however, Ferdinand became increasingly critical of Anselm's artistic judgement, particularly his passion for snuff boxes. 'My father might have formed a matchless collection as he lived in a country where for years old works of art were deemed worthless. But his taste was limited to a small range as he cared for minute articles only . . .'[8]

Ferdinand's most poignant experience came when he visited St Petersburg in 1867. Princess Golytsin's wonderful collection came up for sale and a French friend told Ferdinand that he could have first refusal on anything he fancied. 'He begged me not to tarry as a gang of foreign dealers – "*la bande noire*" as they were called – were lying in wait like a pack of wolves.' But Ferdinand was in deep mourning for his wife and 'not in the mood to take advantage of the opportunity'; so he bought only two or three *objets*, one of them a large topaz cup for his bereaved father-in-law, Uncle Lionel. However 'Uncle Lionel disdained it and put it aside as he possessed one of the same kind, only more important and finer still. . . . My only consolation for the idiocy of my behaviour was . . . the boundless rage of the "bande noire" at having lost the cup . . .'[9]

In 1874 Anselm died charging his seven children, like so many Rothschilds before him, 'to live constantly in perfect harmony' and 'never to become unmindful of the family tradition'. The bulk of the estate went to the two eldest sons, Albert and Nathaniel, who lived in Vienna. No one knows exactly what Ferdinand received but contemporary accounts talk of £2,000,000.

Ferdinand was a tall, spare, restless man with a feeling for adventure. Out hunting one day in the Vale of Aylesbury, he took a fancy

Waddesdon Manor, designed by the French architect, Gabriel-Hippolyte Destailleur, was built between 1874 and 1889. It is made of Bath stone which was transported up the hill by

a specially constructed steam tramway
and teams of Percheron horses
imported from Normandy.

to a desolate, windswept hill, a misshapen cone commanding a fine view of the valley and decided that this was the place on which he would implant a house. He bought the hill and seven hundred acres of land from the Duke of Marlborough, and work began in 1874. First, a piece of the hill to be sliced off, like the top of a soft-boiled egg; then a railway line fourteen miles long had to be built to bring the huge masses of Bath stone on to the site.

At the same time hundreds of workmen strove to transform the bleak countryside into a mellow park, complete with gardens and fountains. This required the transplanting of trees on a truly heroic scale, particularly as Baron Ferdinand had a liking for oaks, beeches and conifers. No less than sixteen horses were required to pull each one of these trees along the road; and every journey necessitat taking down the telegraph poles along the route.

Ferdinand adored the engineering dramas as it was just as enthralling to see what hazards the industrial age could overcome as to imagine the final results. Whereas in France Baron James had employed an English architect to build Ferrières, Ferdinand imported a French architect, M. Destailleur, to build Waddesdon. Furthermore, the Frenchman was instructed to incorporate in his plans the best features of four châteaux.

Waddesdon Manor took nearly seven years to complete, the first house party being given there in 1881. Guests were amazed to find the two towers of the Château de Maintenon; the chimneys of Chambord; the dormer windows of Anet; two versions of the staircase of Blois. Most of the furniture came from France where it once had been in the possession of the royal family, and priceless *objets d'art* included Savonnerie carpets, Beauvais tapestries, Sèvres porcelain. The enormous manor consisted of seventy rooms and, as a journalist put it, was 'an absolutely stunning circumvention of cosiness'.

While Waddesdon was being built, Mentmore Towers, the first great Rothschild house in Buckinghamshire, passed from father to daughter. The originator, Mayer de Rothschild, Lionel's brother, died in 1874, followed shortly afterwards by his wife. Their only child Hannah inherited not only the house but also £2,000,000 in cash, making her the greatest heiress in the land. Four years later, in 1878, Hannah married Lord Rosebery who was widely regarded (quite rightly as things turned out) as a future Prime Minister.

As the twenty-seven-year-old bride was not beautiful and rather plump, Rosebery was believed to be marrying her for her money, and soon dozens of anecdotes, all invented, swirled around the couple. For instance, Rosebery was said to have written to a friend: 'I am leaving tonight. Hannah and the heavy baggage will follow later.' These ungallant stories have been relayed from one writer to another and there is not a word of truth in them. In fact, Rosebery was devoted to Hannah and overjoyed when she accepted him.

The Comtesse de Castiglione, a renowned Florentine beauty, numbered among her lovers Napoleon III and the brothers Alphonse and Gustave de Rothschild.

Right Mayer Amschel's daughter Hannah married the Earl of Rosebery in 1878 but died tragically twelve years after the marriage, at the age of thirty-nine.

Opposite The Astronomer, by Vermeer, was bought by Baron James from Napoleon III's uncle, Cardinal Fesch in 1863. It is still in the family today.

One line to say that I am really engaged and very happy in my engagement [he wrote to a friend, Mrs Duncan, on 10 January 1878]. The awful deed was done at 4.25 pm on Jan. 3. May I never go through such another ordeal.

You do not know my future wife. She is very simple, very unspoilt, very clever, very warm-hearted and very shy. This description is for your private eye. I never knew such a beautiful character . . .[10]

When Hannah died twelve years after the marriage Rosebery was heart-broken and remained inconsolable throughout the years. The racing world had acclaimed the union, not because of the alliance between two houses, but between two studs; the Crafton and the Durdans. They were right in thinking it an important event for eventually Lord Rosebery won the Derby.

Hannah was the third female Rothschild of the English branch to wed a Christian. Her cousins Annie and Constance, daughters of Anthony, had married Eliot Yorke, son of Lord Hardwicke, and Cyril Flower, the future Lord Battersea. Both girls retained the Jewish faith and managed to secure parental consent. But although Hannah also clung to her religion the prominence of the bridegroom attracted a glare of publicity and prompted some members of the family to make a muted public protest by refusing to attend the ceremony. Disraeli however played his usual role as a Rothschild master of ceremonies and gave away the bride, while the Prince of Wales made up for the omissions in the guest list. The English girls had started something. On the continent two of the seven daughters of Mayer Carl, who had left Italy to take over the Frankfurt bank, followed their example and during the 1870s and early eighties became the brides of Christian aristocrats: the Duc de Gramont and the Prince de Wagram.

Although Lionel competed in the property field, he never allowed this absorbing pastime to obscure a good business deal. Indeed, in 1875, four years before his death, the venerable Baron pulled off the greatest financial coup of his life and at the same time made history. It started at dinner at the Rothschild house at 148 Piccadilly. Prime Minister Disraeli made it a habit to sup with his old friend on Sunday nights. At the end of the meal a footman brought the Baron a telegram from one of the foreign agents, announcing that the Khedive of Egypt, a notorious spendthrift who was drowning in debt, had decided to sell off a large block of his shares in the Suez Canal. The Khedive had offered them to the French Government but the latter was haggling over the price; two syndicates were competing but neither had agreed to pay the price he was asking. Disraeli had known for some time that 176,000 out of a total of 700,000 shares might come on the market. More than once he had expressed fears that the French Government might snap them up in order to gain control of what he termed 'a vital British interest'. 'We must buy them', he exclaimed to his host, and the Baron despatched a telegram enquiring what price was being asked.

Two days later Disraeli tackled his Cabinet. The Prime Minister's secretary, Monty Corry, has left a colourful version of what happened. He tells how he waited outside the Cabinet room; how Disraeli poked out his head and uttered the single word 'yes'; and how he sped to New Court and told Baron Rothschild that he needed £4,000,000. 'When?' asked Lionel who was sitting at his desk eating muscatel grapes. 'Tomorrow.' The Baron spat out a seed. 'What is your security?' 'The British Government.' 'You shall have it.'

'. . . It is just settled, you have it, Madam,' Disraeli wrote jubilantly to Queen Victoria on 24 November. '. . . Four million sterling and almost immediately. There was only one firm that could do it – Rothschilds. They behaved admirably: advanced the money at a low rate, and the entire interest of the Khedive is now yours, Madam . . .'[11]

The House of Commons was not as ecstatic as Disraeli about the financial arrangements. The Rothschilds had provided £2,000,000 on 1 December, £1,000,000 on 16 December and £1,000,000 on 5 January. They had charged two and a half per cent commission which came to £100,000. This sounded reasonable enough but as Parliament repaid the money on 20 February the Opposition pointed out that the average rate of interest worked out at thirteen per cent. Baron Lionel justified the amount, however, on the grounds that only he could have raised the money swiftly and secretly enough to avoid upsetting the exchange rate. As these sleight-of-hand

THE LION'S SHARE.
"Gare à qui la touche!"

A *Punch* cartoon showing Disraeli handing over £4,000,000 advanced by Rothschilds to the Khedive of Egypt, in exchange for a large block of shares in the Suez Canal.

operations had been invented by the Rothschilds most people were satisfied with the explanation. As time passed the £100,000 seemed a bagatelle, for the purchase turned out to be one of the best investments ever made by the Government. In 1898 the market value of the shares was £24 million; in 1914 £40 million; in 1935 £95 million. And for nearly twenty-five years earnings were at a rate of fifty-six per cent on the original investment.

In the 1870s, the last decade of the magnificent English brothers, the Rothschild family seemed to stand at the apex of their financial power.

Not only were they railway magnates but they controlled large quantities of mercury, copper, nitrates. They financed Cecil Rhodes' diamond dominion in South Africa, acquiring a large block of shares in De Beers; and in 1883, through the French Rothschilds, they lent the Tsar of Russia money in return for a petroleum concession in Baku that was so large that it made them the chief competitors of Rockefeller's Standard Oil. Of course in those days oil was not important, being used mainly as a substitute for candles. But in 1911 they sold the B'nito Petroleum Company to the Royal Dutch Shell Combine for a handsome profit although not as handsome as it would have been twenty years later.

Nevertheless, the empire that Baron Lionel and his two brothers passed on to the new generation was a formidable institution still underpinned by the famous Rothschild solidarity. The unity was present even in death, for although this time the three English brothers did not leave the world in the same year, they departed in the same decade: Mayer in 1874, Anthony in 1876, Lionel in 1879.

Chapter VIII
Magnificent Brothers
(1880–1901)

'WHENEVER I WANT TO KNOW AN HISTORICAL FACT,' SAID Disraeli, 'I always ask Natty.' Dark, bearded, forty-year-old Nathaniel Mayer headed the new triumvirate of English brothers who ushered in the 1880s. Although Natty lacked the soaring intelligence of his rough, unsociable grandfather he had a strong personality and the authoritative air of a man who is not accustomed to being contradicted.

It was fitting that this Rothschild, whose self-confidence seemed to symbolize the impregnability of Victorian England, should have become the first Jewish peer. The sparkling personality of Queen Victoria's dear departed and much mourned Prime Minister, Mr Disraeli, had modified the Royal view about Jews and peerages: and when Mr Gladstone gave another gentle prod Her Majesty assented. In 1885 Nathaniel Mayer placed his hand on the Old Testament and repeated the oath, head covered, then took his seat in the House of Lords.

Jews all over the world were thrilled at what they regarded as a triumph over prejudice, a step toward social equality. Yet when on-lookers saw the portly frame of Lord Rothschild emerging from his brougham at New Court, social equality was not the first phrase that sprang to mind. 'King of the Jews' seemed more apt a description. Indeed, a story went the rounds that a Polish Jewish immigrant, who was spending the Day of Atonement at an East End synagogue, sud-denly heard someone whisper: 'The Lord has come!' He prostrated himself before the Messiah: then saw the famous top hat of Lord Rothschild.

Natty shared the Partners' Room at New Court with his two brothers, blond, aesthetic Alfred and gentle, sports-loving Leo. But only the most important people in the land were ushered into the triple presence for here callers were expected to relax and chat and have a glass of wine. Lesser mortals were shown into an ante-room and sometimes terrorized by a visit from Lord Rothschild himself, always watch in hand.

By the 1880s the Rothschilds had become an institution and people looked upon their idiosyncrasies as an integral part of the Victorian landscape. Richer than any family before them, they were famous for their huge, over-furnished houses glowering in red damask and silk against an intimidating background of heavily carved mahogany. They were also famous for living in clusters. Not only did they rub shoulders in the Vale of Aylesbury, but in London

Natty, the first Lord Rothschild, by 'Lib' in *Vanity Fair*. 'Those who know him well appreciate him, but he requires to be very well known to be appreciated, for his manner is always uncertain and rarely caressing.'

they reconstructed a fairy tale version of the Frankfurt ghetto. They owned four houses on Piccadilly, another three 'a diamond's throw away'. Natty lived at 148 Piccadilly, Hannah Rosebery at 107, Ferdinand at 143, his sister, Alice, at 142. Around the corner Anthony's widow, Louise, lived at 19 Grosvenor Gate, Leo at 5 Hamilton Place and Alfred at 1 Seamore Place.

Rothschilds were also famous for employing the best cooks and serving the best wine; for their adherence to the Jewish faith; their race-horses; their mania for collecting *objets d'art*; and their clannishness when it came to marriage. Sons-in-law who did not bear the Rothschild name were still excluded from the Partners' Rooms of the family banks.

It was thought that Natty had done the right thing by marrying Emma Louise, daughter of Frankfurt's Mayer Carl. Not only was Emma Louise the product of two Rothschilds but so was Natty himself, son of Lionel of London and Charlotte of Naples. The relationships were all nicely confused with Emma Louise's mother a sister of Natty's father, and Emma Louise's father a brother of Natty's mother.

Alfred and Leo, Natty's younger brothers, were more original. Alfred declined to marry at all, remaining throughout his life England's most eligible bachelor, while Leo found himself a beautiful Italian Jewess, Maria Perugia, a sister of Mrs Arthur Sassoon. The wedding took place in 1881 with the Prince of Wales fighting his way through a blizzard to reach the Central Synagogue on Great Portland Street. Apparently it was the first time that a member of the Royal family had attended a Jewish service and the Prince not only signed the register but afterwards asked to be shown one of the Scrolls of the Law, used for reading lessons, complete with ornamental appurtenances. Of course Mr Disraeli was present at the reception. He had not missed a Rothschild wedding for years. But perhaps on this occasion he had some premonition that his death was not far off, for he wrote a nostalgic letter to Leo, indelicate, some people thought, because he referred to the probable consequences of the union by declaring: 'In my opinion there cannot be too many Rothschilds.'

The first Lord Rothschild lived at 148 Piccadilly and Tring Park, both of which he had inherited from his father. At weekends he entertained important people, and occasionally the children of his friends. 'We have a very interesting party here,' wrote the twenty-one-year-old Winston Churchill to his mother from Tring in 1896. 'Mr. and Mrs. Asquith – Mr. Balfour, the Recorder and Mr. Underdown who has great railway interests in Cuba, several ladies – ugly and dull – Hubert Howard and myself. Lord Rothschild is in excellent spirits and very interesting and full of information. Altogether, as you may imagine, I appreciate meeting such clever people and listening to their conversation very much indeed . . .'[1]

Natty was brusque and humourless and did not suffer fools gladly. He never hesitated to contradict anyone whom he thought was talking nonsense, and some people bracketed him with Lord Randolph Churchill and Sir Michael Hicks-Beach as one of the three rudest men in England. He had an explosive temper and, although he was immensely generous, resented guests who 'took advantage' of

THE GRAPHIC

AN ILLUSTRATED WEEKLY NEWSPAPER

No. 583.—Vol. XXIII.
Reg.d at Central Post Office as a Newspaper]
SATURDAY, JANUARY 29, 1881
WITH EXTRA SUPPLEMENT [
PRICE SIXPENCE
Or by Post Sixpence Halfpenny

THE MARRIAGE OF MR. LEOPOLD DE ROTHSCHILD AND MDLLE. MARIE PERUGIA IN THE CENTRAL SYNAGOGUE, GREAT PORTLAND STREET.

Marriage of Leopold de Rothschild and Maria Perugia, 19 January 1881.

him. When Lady Figall, for instance, plucked one of his famous musk roses without asking, he upbraided her in front of the entire dinner table. Although he tried to make amends by placing an enormous bouquet of roses in her carriage when she left, she did not return to Tring in a hurry. But perhaps she was not asked.

Natty's bluntness was always to the point. When people suggested that he must have a secret formula for making money he invariably replied: 'Yes. By selling too soon.' This was no idle rejoinder, for extreme caution was the guide-line of his life. Occasionally he reminded people of his grandfather's observation that although it took a great deal of wit to make money it took twice as much to keep it.

Lord Rothschild not only kept it but increased it by the simple expedient of reducing the bank's activity to a near standstill. He did not search for new business, only safe investments. Frank Harris, the writer, tells how he ran into Lord Rothschild in a restaurant, dining with his university friend, Sir Charles Dilke. Harris had just come from Lord Revelstoke, the head of Barings, who had held his guests spell-bound by recounting how his bank had netted a cool million pounds by floating Guinness Breweries as a limited liability company. Harris repeated the story and asked Lord Rothschild what he thought of such a tremendous deal. 'The Guinness promotion was offered to us first but we refused it,' the latter replied. 'That must cause you some regret,' exclaimed Harris. '. . . Even Rothschilds must think a million worth putting into their pockets.' 'I don't look at it that way,' retorted Lord Rothschild. 'I go to the bank every morning and when I say "no" I return home at night without a worry. But when I say "yes" it's like putting your finger into a machine – the whirring wheels may drag your whole body in after the finger.'[2]

Lord Rothschild's point was duly emphasized when ugly rumours began to sweep the City that Barings had over-extended itself in promoting the Argentine 'boom'. Lord Revelstoke had flung restraint to the winds and, without consulting his partners, had pledged millions of the firm's money to mushroom developments.

His final investment was £10,000,000 for a port, which money he hoped to raise by public subscription. But the bonds were not sold and in November 1890 Lidderdale, the Governor of the Bank of England, was informed that Baring's had reached the end of its resources. Lord Goshen, who visited the Bank on 10 November, wrote in his diary that he found Lidderdale 'in a dreadful state of anxiety'. Four days later a broker burst into the Governor's room unannounced. 'Can't you do something or say something to relieve people's minds: they have made up their minds that something awful is up and they are talking of the very highest names,' – he leaned forward, his eyes staring, '*the very highest.*'[3]

The public was oblivious to the crisis, and hummed the catchy tune from Gilbert and Sullivan's *Iolanthe*:

> . . . *The shares were a penny*
> *And ever so many*
> *Were taken by Rothschild and Baring.*

On this occasion the names of Rothschild and Baring were bracketed together behind closed doors in a very different context. The Chancellor of the the Exchequer sent for the Governor of the Bank of England and the two men finally decided to pass the hat around the City. The key figure was Lord Rothschild, as other bankers would follow his lead. Would Rothschild rescue Baring? Or did the family memory stretch back to the days after Waterloo when Baring had prevented Rothschild from taking part in the great French loan?

Natty may not have forgotten, but he forgave. He headed an emergency committee to raise the necessary money and not only donated £500,000 himself but, through his cousins in Paris, persuaded the Bank of France to put up £3,000,000. Gold from Russia, a payment from the Bank of England, subscriptions from a dozen merchant banks, and the total amount came to £17,000,000, enough to prevent a crisis. 'When you thank the Bank of England,' said the Governor, a few weeks later, 'it is very important to bear in mind the willing and cheerful aid that we have received from others, in the first place from Lord Rothschild, whose influence with the Bank of France was of such assistance to us . . . [in rendering] . . . the aid we were enabled to give.'[4]

The very fact that Natty was renowned for his caution meant that on the comparatively rare occasions when his firm launched an enterprise the issue was apt to be over-subscribed. Indeed, in 1889, when Rothschilds offered the public shares in Burma Ruby Mines there was such a crowd in St Swithin's Lane that His Lordship's carriage could not enter. His driver and footman got out, and tried to clear a path for His Lordship on foot but the crush was so great there was no hope of reaching a door. Finally a ladder was lowered from the first floor and Lord Rothschild, complete with top hat and cane, climbed into the bank through a window. After that the firm lapsed into its customary inactivity.

But the first Lord Rothschild was not cautious when it came to spending money. Each year N. M. Rothschild & Sons headed the list of donors to charity, and legion were the hospitals and schools and museums that benefited. Natty's gifts were far from perfunctory. This rather aloof, awesome man had a deep sympathy for ordinary men and women. He derived pleasure from giving pleasure, and if he was looked upon as a public figure, it was because he served the public in a very direct way.

For instance, he not only presented the Metropolitan Police with a handsome cheque every Christmas but made it known that a hungry policeman could always get a four-course meal at 148 Piccadilly. Through the years hundreds of bobbies, particularly those on night duty, availed themselves of Rothschild hospitality. As a result Rothschild carriages, with their dark blue hoods and thin yellow line around the body, always were given right of way. And so was the pet goat belonging to 'Mr Alfred', who lived at Seamore Place; this disdainful animal roamed Piccadilly at will, quite indifferent to carriages and motor cars, and quite oblivious of the astonishment of passersby.

If the police benefited from Rothschild *largesse*, the employees at New Court frequently doubled their basic salaries by annual bonuses known as 'touchings'. The Partners seemed to revel in giving presents, not only at Christmas and birthdays but for silver weddings and long years of service which were recognized by the equivalent number of sovereigns. Occasionally members of the senior staff were given boxes of cigars, sent to London by the French bank. ' "What do you think of these cigars?" one of the New Court employees asked another. "Just right." "How do you mean 'just right'?" "If they were any better Paris would not have sent them; any worse and we would not have smoked them. Just right." '[5]

The three brothers sat behind three desks in the same thickly carpeted, richly ornamented office, known reverently as 'The Room'. The panelled walls were hung with ancestral portraits and framed curiosities, including a receipt for the £2,000,000 paid to Wellington's army. The upper half of the door leading into the room from executive quarters was made of glass. When a senior Rothschild employee wished to see a partner he never knocked. He just stood silently outside the door waiting to be summoned; and sometimes he waited for a long time. One head of department estimated that he spent nearly a year of his life waiting outside the door.

Despite the fact that the three brothers shared the breathtaking inner sanctum, Natty was the only *bona-fide* banker. Indeed, the brothers seemed to reflect perfectly the Rothschild muses. Natty stood for finance, Alfred for the arts, Leo for sport.

Leo had no intellectual pretensions but was famous for his kindness. He lived at 5 Hamilton Place, now a club, Les Ambassadeurs; at Gunnersbury Park, inherited from his father; at Ascott inherited from his uncle; and at Newmarket in a house which he bought himself. Like his Uncle Mayer, he had a passion for breeding and racing, and Newmarket became his spiritual home.

In 1896 his celebrated horse, St Frusquin, put him at the top of winning owners with £46,766 to his credit. But although this champion was a favourite for the Derby it was beaten by a neck by the Prince of Wales's Persimmon. Some people insisted that this was a glaring example of Leo's generosity. Whatever the explanation Mrs Leo maintained an unflagging pride in St Frusquin, commissioning Fabergé, the Russian court jeweller, to cast a model of the horse in silver, which she gave to her husband as a birthday present.

Leo's happiest moment was his election to the Jockey Club in 1891. But, ironically enough, his greatest claim to fame was not the speed of his horses but the speed of his motor cars. He was one of the first men to buy an automobile and chafed at a speed limit fixed at fourteen miles per hour; he badgered everyone in authority until he got the limit increased to twenty miles in 1902. Two years later he was instrumental in forming an Automobile Association which, when it received Edward VII's blessing in 1907, changed its name to the Royal Automobile Club.

Although 'Mr Leo' usually deferred to his elder brothers on matters of finance, at New Court he was the most loved of the Partners. A Rothschild employee, Ronald Palin, wrote:

'Mr Leo', described as 'an angel – with a revenue', dressed as the Duc de Sully for a costume ball at Devonshire House.

Like his uncle Mayer Amschel, Leopold de Rothschild was a keen sportsman. Apart from horse-racing, his great passion was motoring. He is seen *right* in one of his first cars at Gunnersbury House.

. . . he devoted himself to the welfare of the clerks, not so much as a duty or in a spirit of *noblesse oblige* as because it was his character to do so. . . . One man suffering from a chest complaint was sent by Leopold to Australia for six months; another distraught by the death of his wife, was given a trip by sea around the world.[6]

The devotion to Leopold was such that after he had been unwell the clerks gathered at the window of the bank to watch his arrival and to gauge his health. 'Ah, the darling, I think he is looking a little better today,' exclaimed one. Another contemporary composed a ditty which no one thought in the least extravagant:

> *Of men like you*
> *Earth holds but few*
> *An angel – with*
> *A revenue*

The consternation can be imagined when an attempt was made upon his life as his car turned in at New Court. A demented Jewish student ran toward him pointing a revolver. A detective employed by the firm, Charles Berg, struck the youth's hand, the bullet went wild and embedded itself in Berg's neck. Luckily the wound was not fatal. Leopold offered Berg a pension for life but the latter preferred to stay with the firm as a courier.

Although Alfred yawned at the mention of horse-flesh and combustion engines he employed both forms of energy to transport his guests from station to country house and back again. The most magnificent of all the brothers, Alfred also was the most eccentric and the least Rothschild in appearance. With his slender frame, blue eyes, fair hair and exquisite side whiskers, he was the dilettante *par excellence*. He loved music, clothes, furniture, paintings, beautiful women and, above all, luxury. He never went to the office on

Fridays; on this day an employee from the bank turned up at Sea-more Place with Mr Alfred's week-end spending money – £1000 in cash. At New Court he had a mink foot-warmer; and when his motor car met his country guests at the station it was always followed by a second car in order to eliminate the annoyance of a possible break-down.

He was regarded as the greatest expert on French eighteenth-century pictures in England; yet his eye failed him when it came to houses. He decided to emulate cousin Ferdinand and build a French château in Buckinghamshire; but whereas Ferdy's Waddesdon Manor excited wonder, Alfred's Halton House, near Wendover, created deep despair. 'An exaggerated nightmare of gorgeousness and senseless and ill-applied magnificence,' pronounced Algernon West. 'I have seldom seen anything more terribly vulgar,' wrote Eustace Balfour. 'Outside it is a combination of a French château and a gambling house. Inside it is badly planned, gaudily decorated. . . . O, but the hideousness of everything, the showiness! the sense of lavish wealth thrust up your nose! the coarse mouldings, the heavy gildings always in the wrong place, the colour of the silk hangings! Eye hath not seen nor pen can write the ghastly coarseness of the sight!'[7]

The hospitality was as lavish as the decoration – but no one complained of this. The nearest station was at Tring some miles away. In order that he should be ready to receive his guests, Mr Alfred posted men at intervals along the road who signalled ahead with lanterns as the carriage progressed. When the visitors departed their broughams were packed with hot-house flowers and fruit, and delicacies of every kind. The only complaint of the guests was that they found it difficult to sleep at night due to the heavy tread of the night watchman employed to keep an eye on their host's priceless treasures.

A story that has appeared in every book about the Rothschilds and has been attributed to each in turn was, in fact, first told by Prime Minister Asquith after a visit to Waddesdon. But it might just as easily have been Halton, for nowhere was Rothschild hospitality more thorough. It began as soon as the curtains were drawn in the morning. A powdered footman followed by an underling with a trolley would query politely:

'Tea, coffee or a peach off the wall, Sir?'

'Tea, please.'

'China tea, Indian tea, or Ceylon tea, Sir?'

'China, if you please.'

'Lemon, milk or cream, Sir?'

'Milk, please.'

'Jersey, Hereford or Shorthorn, Sir?'

Alfred gave a house-warming party in 1884 attended by the Prince of Wales and all the most fashionable people of the day.

One of Alfred de Rothschild's gold clocks, in the form of a three-wheeled carriage pushed by a Chinaman and studded with diamonds, rubies, emeralds and pearls.

Opposite, top Caricature of Alfred de Rothschild by Max Beerbohm: 'A quiet evening in Seamore Place. Doctors consulting whether Mr Alfred may, or may not, take a second praline before bed-time.'

Bottom A study in Alfred de Rothschild's house at Seamore Place; the furniture was mainly eighteenth-century French and the collection of Sèvres porcelain was particularly fine, but like his country house, Halton, it was 'an exaggerated nightmare of gorgeousness'.

'He exhibited a number of Japanese dogs,' wrote Lady Warwick, 'which had been taught to perform. Great confusion was aroused by the fact that, although the chief little dog performed, it was not according to the programme.'

Soon Halton had its own orchestra and the host an ivory baton banded by a circlet of diamonds which he used in his role as a conductor. He adored music and through the years induced such celebrities as Patti, Niccolini, Melba, Liszt and de Reszke to sing and play for him.

> In the famous white drawing-room at Seamore Place [wrote Lady Warwick], I have heard the greatest artistes in the world, who were paid royal fees to entertain a handful of his friends. Unfortunately he [Alfred] could not share in the hospitality that he lavished upon those he esteemed, for he suffered from some obscure form of dyspepsia which no doctor could cure. Many a time I have seen him sit at the head of the table, exercising all the graces of a host, while he himself took neither food nor wine.
>
> He used to ride every morning in the park, followed by his brougham. Park-keepers soon learnt how generous the millionaire was; they used to put stones on the road by which he would enter, then, when he came in sight, they would hasten to remove them – a courtesy which was invariably rewarded. He was shrewd enough to know just how the stones got there, but this childish device amused him, so he pretended ignorance.[9]

Lily Langtry, the lady in many of Alfred's 'adoration' dinners.

Alfred, of course, had a permanent box at Covent Garden but his enthusiasm was not confined to music. He took over the Gaiety Theatre when it was in financial trouble and ran it in partnership with Henry Tennant during its great years. As a result, of course, he met all the most beautiful actresses and was greatly envied by his men friends. Sometimes he arranged what he called 'adoration' dinners, inviting one particularly alluring star to dine alone with himself and three or four gentlemen. Before the evening was over he always drew his guest of honour aside, whispering: 'What shall I give you beautiful lady?', and then presented her with a charming bibelot. However, this well-established routine was almost shattered when Mrs Langtry was the chief guest. When he asked: 'And what shall I give you beautiful lady?' she picked up a priceless enamelled and bediamonded Louis XVI snuff-box, the gem of a collection lying on a table, and said calmly, 'Oh, this will do.' 'He had a weak heart,' she wrote later, 'and for a moment I thought I had stopped it. When he got his breath he promised me something much prettier and out came one of the well-known gift-boxes.'[10]

Some people thought that the aesthete went too far when he assembled ponies and dogs and hoops and produced his own circus. He bought a very long whip, adorned himself in a blue frock coat and lavender kid gloves and took over the role of ring master. However Alfred never allowed his idiosyncracies to interfere with his banking life and turned up regularly, if tardily, at New Court. He adored grandeur and towards the end of his life the ceremony with which he was conveyed from his house in Mayfair to New Court was hardly excelled by the Royal family.

> A policeman, seeing him leave, [wrote Ronald Palin] would signal to another at the end of the street and the word was passed along the route. Traffic was held up where necessary so that his progress should not be impeded and if there were an obstruction the driver would not hesitate to avoid it by passing islands on the wrong side.
> At New Court the man at the gate, warned by telephone, was on the alert to spot either partner's car as soon as it turned into St. Swithin's Lane from Cannon Street and at his whistle all the six or seven couriers on duty lined up in the courtyard. At that time a fire engine manned by two men was stationed permanently in the yard and the firemen would fall in too. When the car drove in under the archway the firemen sprang to attention and saluted, and the couriers raised their bowler hats with almost military precision and one of them stepped forward to open the car door.[11]

Nevertheless Mr Alfred's erratic working hours caused the staff uneasy moments. He usually arrived at New Court at 2 pm, lunched between 3.30 and 4 pm, and when his brothers departed at 5 o'clock curled up on the leather covered sofa and took a nap. As the staff could not leave until all the letters were signed, and as the letters required the signature of a partner, and as the only partner was asleep, the problem seemed insoluble until an eye lit on Kelly's Dictionary, a volume weighing a good ten pounds. The book was dropped outside the door of The Room, with a force that made the dust rise from the carpet and produced the desired result.

Alfred was not only a partner at New Court but a Director of the Bank of England, an appointment he had been given in 1868 because the Governor felt it would not be a bad thing to keep in close touch with the Rothschilds. The relationship came to an abrupt end in 1889, however, over a slightly unorthodox situation. Alfred had paid a very high price for a French eighteenth-century painting after being assured by the dealer that he, too, had been forced to pay an excessive sum for it and was making only a marginal profit. A day or two later Alfred discovered that the dealer had an account with the Bank of England. He could not resist taking a peep to see what, in fact, the man had given for the painting. He was outraged when he discovered that he had been charged a price 'out of all proportion to decency!' He spread the story about London and, not surprisingly, got the sack from Threadneedle Street.

If Alfred was the most extravagant Rothschild, cousin Ferdinand of Vienna, who had become a naturalized Englishman, was the most interesting. 'He was a delicate man, all intellect,' wrote Lady Warwick, 'with unerring taste in art, and a princely conception of hospitality. I thought of him as a reincarnation of Lorenzo the Magnificent.' When Natty became a peer 'Ferdy' took his place as MP for Aylesbury; and at his astonishing Waddesdon Manor, still the marvel

of the age, entertained everyone from the Empress Frederick to the Shah of Persia. Of course he entertained in London as well; once, when he gave a ball at which both the Prince of Wales and the Crown Prince Rudolph of Austria were present he offered twelve of the lady guests dresses from Doucet in Paris. However, rich men have their idiosyncracies and when greedy Lily Langtry offended once again – this time by ordering a petticoat to go with her gown – she promptly received a bill for it with a message that Baron Ferdinand had not authorized it. Mrs Langtry claimed that the Crown Prince Rudolph chose her as a partner for the Cotillion; yet another shock was in store for her.

As the evening was warm [she wrote], and he danced with great zest, the natural consequence was that he got very hot, which caused a friend of mine, whose soubriquet was 'Mrs. Sloper' to whisper: 'Take care of your dress; there are marks on it. Make him put on his gloves.' This I proceeded to do on the first opportunity, calling attention to the finger marks around the waist in support of my request. And what do you think the young man's delicate reply was? 'C'est vous qui suez [sweats], Madame.'[12]

Like Alfred, Ferdinand spared no expense to create the right atmosphere. Once Lady Warwick arrived in a thunderstorm and was dismayed to find that the masses of red geraniums had been beaten down by the storm. She happened to arise very early next morning and looked out to see

Above Baron Ferdinand in his study at Waddesdon. On the table behind him is a miniature of Nathan Rothschild and his family, after the painting by W. A. Hobday reproduced on pages 78–9.

Opposite The Morning Room at Waddesdon Manor. The huge black lacquer secrétaire, bearing the stamps of two French cabinet-makers, I. Dubois and J. Goyer, is thought to have been made for Catherine the Great of Russia.

an army of gardeners at work, taking out the damaged plants and putting in new ones, which had been brought from the glass-houses in pots. . . . After breakfast that morning I went into the grounds, the gardens had been completely transformed![13]

Waddesdon was filled with visitors every weekend. In 1884 Ferdy's cousin, Constance, Lady Battersea, listed a dozen guests 'and last but not least H.R.H. with a youthful equerry. . . . The Christy Minstrels and a Hungarian Band performed alternately and gave great satisfaction, particularly the latter. But the house itself with all its wonders, pictures, objets d'art, and magnificent couches and satin cushions and palms and photos of crowned heads with autograph signatures, was a never ending source of pleasure. Lady Jane said it was *seraphic* . . .' But sightseeing was not exclusively an indoor sport, for Baron Ferdinand also had a zoo. 'We used to go and feed the ostriches with bread,' wrote Lady Warwick. '... He had aviaries, too, filled with lovely birds. Naturally he wished to adorn the hill on which the Manor stood, but he did it in such a fashion as to enable him to enjoy its full beauty during his life-time – to do this he transplanted full grown forest trees. As a frequent visitor I saw these trees take root though some were of enormous size when taken from their original home.'[14]

Finally Queen Victoria's curiosity could stand it no longer. That she should be almost the only member of the Royal family who had not seen the wonders of Waddesdon was too much; and in 1890 she asked Baron Ferdinand if she might pay him a visit. She was not disappointed in what she saw: only disconcerted when Lord Hartington, the future Duke of Devonshire, absent-mindedly shook her hand instead of kissing it. However, she recovered her composure after a ride through the grounds in a Bath chair pulled by a pony. 'The host was as delightful,' she wrote, 'as the place was beautiful.'

This episode broke the ice between Her Majesty and the Rothschilds. When the Queen spent a few weeks in Grasse, in the south of France, the following year she payed a visit to Ferdinand's sister, Alice, who had a marvellous house in the neighbourhood. Indeed, she took such a fancy to the garden that she scarcely allowed a day to pass without calling. Alice was so flattered that she renamed her house the Villa Victoria, and built a road for the Queen's convenience. Her cousin, Constance Battersea, was a member of Princess Louise's party and described the goings on in letters to her mother. 'As a surprise to the Queen', she wrote, 'she [Alice] has just ordered another mountain road to be levelled and widened, and this to be done in *three* days, which means, building up small walls, picking out huge stones, covering the smaller ones with macadam and *turning a stream...*'

Nevertheless Constance Battersea was filled with admiration for Alice's powers of organization. 'She is quite *wonderful*. She is on her

A gold snuff-box from Baron Ferdinand's collection at Waddesdon. It was made in 1772–3 by the French goldsmith Louis Roucel and is decorated with six Sèvres plaques painted with dogs and parrots which may have belonged to Madame de Pompadour.

legs from morning to night, walks miles up and down hill, and gives
her orders to the Inspector of Police, the Royal coachmen, her fore-
men, and workmen, in the voice, with the manner of Napoleon.'[15]

However, Alice's tyrannical nature was not confined to the workmen. The pride and joy of her life was her garden, and when she saw
the Queen walking on a newly planted flower-bed she was outraged.
'Come off at once!' she exploded. The Queen did as she was told and
henceforth referred to Alice as 'The All Powerful'. The friendship
survived and so did the nickname. 'Alice . . . reigns absolutely,'
Constance wrote in her journal. 'There is nothing constitutional
about this monarchy. No wonder the Queen has named her "The
All Powerful" . . .'[16]

Alice moved to England to look after her bachelor brother and
not only bought Eyethrope, near Waddesdon, but also took the
imposing mansion next door to Ferdinand on Piccadilly. Rothschild
Row had become a formidable enclave; but it was not until bus
conductors began to point out the houses to their passengers that the
Row was recognized as one of the sights of London. The interest of
the busmen sprang from the fact that Ferdy organized large shoots
at Waddesdon but never knew what to do with all the dead birds.
Even after generously supplying his friends there were thousands left

On 14 May 1890 Queen Victoria
spent the day at Waddesdon; she was
driven around the gardens in a Bath
chair pulled by a pony and, like
Napoleon III at Ferrières, was asked
to plant a young tree. The spade with
which she planted it is still displayed
at Waddesdon.

over. Finally he and his cousin Leo, who also had shooting parties at neighbouring Wing, concocted a plan. At Christmas every bus driver and conductor who passed the Rothschild doors in Piccadilly were given a brace of pheasants. This practice became an institution, and soon the whips of all the drivers, and the bell cords of all the conductors, were decorated with blue and amber ribbons – the Rothschild racing colours. And when, at the end of the century, Ferdy died, the drivers paid their tribute by entwining mourning streamers with the rest.

As usual politically the French Rothschilds had the thin edge of the wedge. While the English Rothschilds entertained a glittering society and pursued adventure in the hunting field, the French Rothschilds found themselves in a mounting storm of anti-Semitism which culminated in the Dreyfus Case.

Just as in Britain a triumvirate of brothers ran the French House: Alphonse, Gustave and Edmond. Although the two eldest were the most effective bankers, Edmond, fifteen years younger than Alphonse, and only thirty-five when the 1880s slid into being, was the Rothschild earmarked for posterity.

Edmond's life work lay in financing and encouraging colonies of destitute Jews to settle on the rocky soil of Palestine and in teaching them how to 'make the desert bloom'. Although a return to Zion in a political sense was not part of his original purpose, his persistence paved the way for the future state of Israel.

Edmond inherited his interest in Palestine from his father, the famous Baron James, and from his tutor the famous Albert Cohen. Palestine was part of the Turkish Empire and when the Crimean War broke out in 1853, provoked by Tsar Nicholas I who insisted that the Sultan acknowledge Russia's authority over the 'Holy Places', the Jewish community of Jerusalem was reduced to semi-starvation. This tiny enclave of a few hundred religious fanatics was almost wholly dependent on outside aid, and the war cut them off from their supporters. Baron James apologized to his eleven-year-old son, Edmond, for depriving him of his tutor and sent Albert Cohen to Jerusalem to see what could be done. On the latter's recommendation he decided not to distribute alms but to establish an institution. The result was the James Mayer de Rothschild Hospital in Jerusalem.

Young Edmond was fascinated by Cohen's Palestinian travels and as a young man contributed generously to the Rothschild charities in Jerusalem. Then came 1881 and the assassination of Tsar Alexander II of Russia. When it was discovered that the terrorists who killed the 'Tsar-Liberator' had met in the flat of a Jewish girl, Jessica Helfman, terrible pogroms broke out in all parts of Russia. The new Emperor, Alexander III, encouraged the riots as he had been indoctrinated by his anti-Semitic tutor and believed that international Jewry was involved in a plot to end the monarchical system.

Miss Alice de Rothschild, nicknamed by Queen Victoria 'The All Powerful'.

Edmond de Rothschild, Baron James' youngest son and the future 'Father of Israel', in 1863.

The following year the Tsar went one better and published his famous May Laws. Only in exceptional circumstances could a Jew leave the Pale of Settlement; no Jew could hold an administrative post, or become a lawyer, or own land; no books were to be printed in Hebrew and all Jewish schools were to be closed; no Jew could marry a Christian unless he gave up his religion; no Jew could appeal against any sentence of any court; only a small proportion of Jews could attend universities. As a result, during the six months after the publication of these laws, 225,000 destitute Jewish families left Russia for western Europe. The Emperor was delighted. 'Let them carry their poison where they will,' he said.

The Chief Rabbi of France, Zadok Kahn, was well-acquainted with the characters and incomes of the most important Jews in his community. Consequently, on 28 September 1882 he introduced to Edmond de Rothschild a Russian Rabbi, Samuel Mohilever. The latter was not an ideal advocate as he was unable to speak French and he stammered; yet he had a burning mission. He overcame his difficulties by asking permission to chant his message, which he could do without faltering, and by requesting Kahn to translate his Hebrew song. He began by reminding Edmond that the Lord had chosen another stammerer, Moses, to lead the Jews from Egypt to Israel, and explained that God had done this deliberately to show that a smooth tongue was not important; what mattered was the Voice of the Lord. Would Edmond heed this Voice and help the displaced Jews to settle in Palestine, the homeland from which they had been driven two thousand years earlier?

As Zadok Kahn had anticipated, Edmond was more than receptive. Not only had he been interested in Palestine since boyhood but as he was the most religious member of his family the prospect of resettling the Children of Israel in the land of their forefathers touched his deepest emotions. Being a Rothschild he was also cautious. Would the Jewish people, whose talents seemed to bloom in the field of usury, have the patience and persistence to earn a living by farming? The Baron was not sure and insisted on beginning with an experiment; he would pay for a dozen selected Russian-Jewish farmers to attend an agricultural school in Palestine; and if they did well he would buy land and settle them upon it.

The Baron had found his life's work. From that time until his death fifty-two years later his Jewish colonies occupied most of his time and attention, and cost him over £6,000,000. He not only formed new colonies but gave money to the sprinkling of Jews already settled in Palestine, who repeatedly faced bankruptcy.

Despite the fact that the Chief Rabbi had brought Mohilever to see the Baron, he (Kahn) was not at all sanguine about the idea of settling Jews in Palestine. The Turks were hostile: the land was barren. The fabulously wealthy Baron Hirsh favoured the Argentine; other Jews spoke of San Domingo: still others the United

States, or for that matter, even western Europe. Yet Edmond persisted in his dream of reviving Judaism, a far more elaborate idea than merely extending a helping hand to persecuted Jewry: and it could only be accomplished if the Jews had the tenacity to reclaim the once-fertile earth which the Arabs allowed to lapse into wasteland. 'I am not a philanthropist,' he explained repeatedly. 'There are many unfortunate Jews in Russia and Rumania and we shall not be able to help them. I have gone into this affair as an experiment, to see whether Jews can be settled in the land of Israel ...'[17]

For many months the Baron refused to let his name become public and was referred to as 'the Renowned Benefactor'. His original group of farmers made a success of the agricultural school and he bought them land at Ekron. They paved the way for a dozen colonies in various parts of the country.

The Baron's money drained swamps, dug wells and built houses. It founded industries ranging from scent factories to glass works, from wine cellars to bottle manufacturers. The Baron established his own administration in Palestine and his overseers dictated to the farmers exactly what crops were to be grown and where. Most of his officials were experts, some of them 'borrowed' from the great wine-growing estate, Lafite, now the property of his cousins, Alphonse and Gustave. Edmond guaranteed the harvests by buying up the produce at a fixed sum, but he soon learned that the man who holds the purse strings can expect very little but abuse. If the price was too low the immigrants complained of starvation; too high and they hired Arab labour and went abroad on a holiday.

It was impossible to keep the name of the Renowned Benefactor secret and before long everyone knew that the Jewish colonies in Palestine were the focal point of Baron Edmond de Rothschild's life. Between 1887 and 1899 the Baron made three trips to Palestine, each time on board his palatial yacht, each time accompanied by his wife, a daughter of Baron Willy von Rothschild of Frankfurt. The yacht dropped anchor at Jaffa and the couple visited the primitive farming communities, calling on people in their houses and listening to an endless flow of complaints. Quite unselfconsciously Edmond invited settlers and administrators aboard his yacht, which seemed far more of a Paradise than rocky Palestine. The ship was fitted with a splendid Kosher kitchen; one of the cabins was used as a prayer room, and all the cabin doors had mezzuzahs.†

On his first trip Edmond tried to buy the Wailing Wall with the intention of transforming the neighbourhood into a Jewish shrine. As compensation he offered to resettle the Arabs on a piece of land of their choosing. Apparently the scheme lapsed, not because of Arab indifference but because of the mysterious opposition of the Jerusalem rabbis.

†The mezzuzah is a little box holding a parchment on which is written the most famous Jewish prayer (Deuteronomy VI verses 4–9) – the prayer of deliverance when the Jewish first-born were spared in Egypt.

The rabbis had other obstructions to place in the Baron's path and in 1888 produced a crisis of the first order by declaring that 1889 must be recognized as a Sabbatical year. According to Jewish law the tilling of Jewish land is forbidden every seventh year; yet it was obvious that if labour ceased for a whole year all the effort and money that had been expended since 1882 would be wasted and the building would have to start from the beginning again.

Although Edmond remonstrated, the rabbis were adamant and for months he was locked in a fierce theological controversy. What infuriated him most of all and aroused unpleasant suspicions was the fact that Samuel Mohilever, the father of the Palestine venture, refused to take up the cudgels on Edmond's behalf. The Baron composed a letter in German with Hebrew characters which he sent to the Chief Rabbi Kahn with instructions to pass it on to Mohilever. He accused the latter of bad faith and ingratitude, then said:

Now comes the Sabbátical year. I understand and respect all religious beliefs . . . but the Sabbatical year was merely an excuse for the Ekron colonists not to work. For there are things that were permitted by the most pious rabbis who lived in the days when Palestine was a Jewish land . . . I felt that rebellion was preparing and I therefore had Rabbi Mohilever informed about it. What did this rabbi do – he who is responsible for this? He did not reply, not one word . . .

Herr Ober Rabbiner, do you know what I think? I will tell you the truth. These Ekron colonists want to take the land away from me and the houses away from me and then to scoff at me. But this will never happen. Let Rabbi Samuel know that I will send the colonists of Ekron and all their families back to him [in Russia] and then we will see what he will do with them. And besides travelling expenses I will not give them a cent. . .'[18]

In the end Edmond solved the insoluble as far as the Sabbatical year was concerned by proposing an ingenious plan. If all the Jewish land in Palestine was sold, for one year only, to people of other faiths, settlers would remain blameless in the eyes of God when they tilled the soil. The rabbis of Jerusalem inveighed fiercely against this 'fraud upon the Eternal'. But Edmond managed to enlist the allegiance of the Rabbi Isaac Elchonon, Spector of Kovno, Lithuania, famous as the greatest orthodox authority in the world. And Elchonon proclaimed that under the Baron's safeguard the soil of Zion could be worked.

Throughout the 1880s, at the same time as Edmond was building up his Palestine colonies, the virus of Jew-baiting spread to France.

Ironically Edmond's banking brothers, Alphonse and Gustave, fanned the flames by the financial measures which they took to crush their anti-Semitic opponents.

The family were the first to be attacked. The battle began in 1876 when a right-wing deputy, Bonteaux, talked about 'a financial system sucked dry by the Hebrews, especially the Rothschilds'. In 1880 he published a prospectus announcing his intention of 'grouping and transforming into a powerful lever the capital of Catholics. . .' With the blessing of Pope Leo XIII he persuaded the 'faithful' to part with their money and raised 4,000,000 francs with which he launched an anti-Jewish bank, the Union Générale.

The shares rose from 500 to 2000 francs within a few months, which encouraged Bonteaux to try and spread his wings. He allied himself with the Austrian Landerbank, a rival of the Rothschild Kreditanstalt, but apparently was not aware of the tactics that the Rothschilds employed against hostile agencies. Once again the family quietly bought up a large packet of Union Générale shares, then dumped the lot. Between 5 and 20 January 1882, quotations dropped from 3000 points to 900. Under Bonteaux's amateurish management the bank had extended itself so recklessly that it could not meet its commitments and was forced into liquidation.

The fact that thousands of Catholics had lost their savings did not help the cause of the Semites and 'the Jewish question' began to be discussed with mounting emotion. Extreme Catholics declared that the Jew was an alien who not only conspired against Christendom, but against France itself.

At this point Édouard Drumont made his entry. This gentleman, unknown to the general public, had worked for the Pereire brothers who had organized the Crédit Mobilier Bank in the hope of smashing the Rothschilds. Instead they had perished and now Drumont sought revenge on their behalf. In 1886 he published a two-volume book *La France Juive*, whose theme was the evil power of Jewish finance, with the Rothschilds as central characters. Although Drumont's former employer, Isaac Pereire, was also a Jew, the author declared that he was blameless and exceptional, a Socialist who had worked for the common man.

The book was widely read and in 1889 its author formed the National Anti-Semitic League to fight 'the clandestine and merciless conspiracy' of Jewish finance which 'jeopardizes daily the welfare, honour and security of France'. Not content with this, three years later he founded a newspaper *La Libre Parole* which began a campaign to drive Jews out of the army. As a result two Jewish officers challenged Drumont and one of his most virulent supporters, the Marquis de Mores, to duels. The Marquis killed his opponent. He was charged with foul play but was acquitted in court.

Two years later, in 1894, Captain Alfred Dreyfus was arrested, tried, and convicted of having betrayed military secrets to Germany. This stiff, reserved, thirty-six-year-old artillery officer was not liked by his colleagues: furthermore he was a Jew. Although material proof of his guilt could not be found, two of his brother officers made up for it by helpful fabrication. When Dreyfus was condemned, Drumont's newspaper explained his motives as public revenge for slights received, and the desire of his race for the ruin of France. The ceremony of Dreyfus' degradation took place on the parade ground. '*A mort! A mort les Juifs!*' the crowd shouted.

Caricature of the anti-Semitic writer Édouard Drumont by B. Moloch.

The Paris correspondent of the Vienna *Neue Freie Presse*, Theodor Herzl, was among the throng. That such a thing could happen in France was a traumatic experience for him. 'Where was heard the cry against the Jews?' he asked in anguish. '... In republican, modern, civilized France, a hundred years after the Declaration of the Rights of Man.' The shock crystallized half-formed ideas in Herzl's head; he went home and wrote *Der Judenstaat*, the first sentence of which established its aim: 'restoration of the Jewish state'.[19] Eighteen months later he organized the first Zionist Congress, composed of two hundred delegates from fifteen countries.

The Rothschilds became Herzl's primary target. If he could persuade this powerful family to back Zionism – the establishment of a Jewish state in Palestine – half his work would be accomplished. But the Rothschilds were not sympathetic. Indeed, their approach was diametrically opposed to Zionism. As a family they had demonstrated more conclusively than any other that Jews could integrate themselves in whatever country they chose to live. Baron Edmond, who had settled thousands of destitute Jews in Palestine was the only member of the family who might listen.

I had expected to find him much older [wrote Herzl]. He looks like an ageing youth, is given to quick and nervous movements, has a light brown beard just turning grey, a long nose and an unpleasantly large mouth. A red neck-tie set off his white waistcoat, which hung loosely about his lank frame .... I began: 'A colony' is a little state, a state is a big 'colony'. You desire a little state, I propose to set up a big 'colony'. And once again, as so often before, I unfolded the whole plan. He listened at times with surprise; once or twice I read admiration in his eyes.

But he does not believe in Turkish promises. And even if he did believe in them, he would not participate in the undertaking. He holds that it would be impossible to control the influx of the masses into Palestine. At the start 15,000 schnorrers [beggars] would pour in and they would have to be fed. For his part, he did not feel equal to it; perhaps I did? He could not undertake such a responsibility ... [20]

So Edmond continued to support his colonists and Herzl continued to try and win the backing of the rich and powerful for the Zionist cause. Herzl died in 1904; and years later, in 1919, the Baron admitted that Herzl had been right. 'When he explained to me his idea of convoking a Congress and starting a public agitation among Jews and non-Jews for the creation of a Jewish state I was frightened,' he told a Russian *émigré*, Isaac Naiditch. '... First of all it was difficult on account of the possible repercussions in the attitude of the Turkish government towards our efforts. Besides I thought it was harmful to the welfare of Jews all over the world, since the anti-Semitics would raise the cry that the Jews ought to be made to go to their own country.... But history has shown that it was Herzl who was right and not I...'[21]

While France resounded to threats against the Jews, snobbish,

Viennese Baron Albert dressed as a Renaissance nobleman for a costume ball. Although the youngest of Anselm's sons, he was chosen by his father to take over the bank.

implacable, anti-Semitic Austria, relaxed its restrictions – at least as far as the Rothschilds were concerned. The Habsburg court prided itself on its exclusiveness, only admitting those persons who possessed sixteen 'quarterings', which meant noble lineage on both sides of the family for generations. Now, in 1887, the Emperor Franz Joseph announced that the Rothschilds were *Hoffähig* – acceptable in the highest circles – which meant that they could attend the innumerable dry-as-dust levées, receptions and balls given by the Emperor.

In Vienna S. M. von Rothschild und Söhne was represented by Salomon's grandsons, the two brothers of Ferdy and Alice, now the richest men in Austria. As Albert, the youngest, was the only one interested in banking, his father, Anselm, appointed him his successor as head of the firm. Outwardly Albert had nothing to worry about. Not only was he banker-in-chief to a firmly entrenched government but, through the Kreditanstalt – the Rothschild subsidiary invented as a weapon against the Crédit Mobilier – held controlling interest in innumerable industries ranging from coal to railways; and when, in 1881, he converted the famous six-per-cent Gold Loan to Hungary the bank was recognized as the greatest financial force in the empire.

Yet Albert never took his luck for granted. He could not rid his memory of the revolutionary days of 1848. Barely four years old at the time, he still remembered being bundled out of his cot in the middle of the night and hurried out of Vienna, past excited mobs, to the safety of the country. When he finally built his great town house on the Prinz Eugenstrasse he constructed it in such a way that it could not be easily attacked from the street. It was surrounded by a stone wall seven feet high, on top of which was a massive iron fence measuring another eight feet. Its size and impregnability prompted wits to nickname it 'the Albert Memorial'.

His brother Nathaniel, on the other hand, constructed a far more elegant mansion in the Theresianumgasse. Nathaniel had the same flair as Ferdinand, not only collecting ornaments of great beauty, but of unusual historical interest; 'among his most prized possessions was a dagger with a rich gilt handle which had once belonged to Wallenstein and a toilet-box in a rosewood case which Napoleon I left behind in his carriage after the Battle of Waterloo'.

These young men dutifully reflected the family traditions. Although they had inherited five large estates from their father, among them castles at Schillersdorf and Beneschau, and a magnificent schloss at Enzesfeld† – each insisted on creating a house of his own. Like their English and French cousins they introduced the blue and amber racing colours to the Vienna race-course and won the Derby three times; they accumulated priceless furniture and silver and gave millions to charities, founding among other things an

---

†The Duke of Windsor took refuge here at the time of his abdication.

Im Schlosshof.

institute for the blind, an institute for deaf mutes, a general hospital, a neurological clinic, an orphanage, and a wonderful botanical garden, the Hohewarte, that became one of the sights of the capital.

Yet the Habsburg concession, bidding the Rothschilds to Court, was due neither to banking nor to philanthropy. The fact was that Albert's sister, Julie, married to a Naples Rothschild, Adolph, had become a close friend of Franz Joseph's wife, the beautiful Empress Elizabeth. Julie and Adolph lived partly in Paris and partly in a fairy-like villa at Pregny on Lake Geneva. Julie's hobby was horticulture and her conservatories were filled with a staggering array of flowers, arranged according to countries and climates.

The Empress loved Pregny and in September 1898 expressed a desire to pay another visit there. She turned the trip into an escapade, travelling incognito and refusing any special attention. After taking the waters at Nauheim she spent a night in Munich, in the room she had occupied as a girl, and then moved on to Switzerland staying at the Hotel Beau Rivage in Geneva. Although Baroness Julie offered the Empress her yacht Elizabeth declined as the fun was to be an ordinary person. Next day, accompanied by a lady in waiting, Countess Sztaray, she took a passenger steamer across Lake Geneva to the Quai du Mont-Blanc.

That evening Elizabeth and Julie dined alone in magnificent state, drinking from precious crystal glasses and eating from old Viennese china while a hidden orchestra played gentle melodies. Afterwards they strolled in the garden which, of course, was not like any other garden 'a remote, enchanted world where tame miniature porcupines from Java and exotic coloured birds decorated a private park planted with cedars of Lebanon'.

About ten o'clock the Empress departed. But first she signed the Visitor's Book which caused her a moment of acute distress. Absent-mindedly she turned the pages back and suddenly caught sight of the signature of her beloved son, the tragic Crown Prince Rudolph, who had died with his mistress in a love pact at the Mayerling hunting lodge. Tears sprang into Elizabeth's eyes and on the way home she could talk of nothing but death. When Countess Sztaray said she personally had no fear of death, Elizabeth replied: 'I fear death although I often long for it: the transition and the uncertainty make me tremble, and especially the thought of the terrible struggle which one must undergo before reaching the other side.'

The next morning the two ladies once again set out for the Quai du Mont-Blanc to take the lake steamer, but awaiting the Empress now was an Italian anarchist, Lucheni. He moved into her path, lifted his arm and plunged a dagger into her breast. She died four hours later. The remote Villa Pregny was caught in a blaze of publicity, flashed upon the front page of almost every newspaper in the world, while Baroness Julie went into history books as the last person to entertain the ill-fated Empress of Austria.

Opposite, top. Albert's palace at Prinz Eugenstrasse, dubbed the 'Albert Memorial' by some of his English cousins. The fortress-like walls protected, among other treasures, a gold ballroom and a silver dining-room.
Bottom Members of the Austrian branch of the Rothschilds at Schillersdorf, one of their four great castles.

On 10 September 1898, the day after she had dinner with Baroness Julie von Rothschild at Pregny, the Empress Elizabeth of Austria was stabbed to death by an Italian anarchist.

ASSASSINATION OF THE EMPRESS OF AUSTRIA.

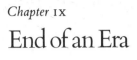

Chapter IX
End of an Era

(1898–1918)

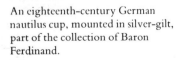

An eighteenth-century German nautilus cup, mounted in silver-gilt, part of the collection of Baron Ferdinand.

*A*S THE CENTURY DREW TO A CLOSE EVEN QUEEN VICTORIA was astonished by the luxury and extravagance of the upper class. 'I have come from my house to your palace,' she remarked to the Duchess of Sutherland. At Chatsworth the Duke and Duchess of Devonshire could put up a hundred guests and three hundred servants for the weekend. Alfred de Rothschild not only had his own orchestra and his own circus but his own private train with carriages upholstered in the blue and yellow family racing colours. Dinners were gargantuan and chefs vied with one another in concocting elaborate dishes: *gigot Rothschild*, lamb baked for twelve hours and so tender it literally melts in the mouth, made its début; an invention, the spiteful claimed, to complement the bad teeth of Barons Alphonse and Gustave.

If, as Nathan Rothschild had pointed out, it took sharper wits to keep money than to make it, it required nothing less than genius to spend it to the approval of one's contemporaries. Yet even here the Rothschilds were more successful than their rivals. No one criticized their vast houses and regiments of gardeners, their orchestras, private trains and greenhouses bursting with out-of-season delicacies, for what other landlord sent wagons around his estate each morning with 'elevenses' of coffee and rolls for his employees? Lord Rothschild produced a Beveridge Plan of his own, seventy-five years ahead of the times. He provided not only his own people but all the inhabitants in the town of Tring with free medical treatment, free nursing, free housing and old-age pensions. He obliterated unemployment in the area by the simple expedient of taking the jobless on to his own pay-roll.

Consequently when Leonora Rothschild asked innocently how people got dead leaves in their parks, and Alfred Rothschild inveighed against March because it was 'the end of the strawberry season' people smiled at such charming eccentricities. Everyone knew that the Rothschilds supported more charities, championed more causes, and subsidized more art dealers than any family in Europe.

Almost all the Rothschilds had a passion for 'collecting', a pastime that stemmed from the Frankfurt ghetto where Mayer Amschel Rothschild had scoured the markets for antique coins. His son Nathan had been too busy building the family fortune to bother with art; and although his brother James had 'artistic pretensions' someone compared the tasteless, overcrowded interior of Ferrières to 'a chest of drawers that had been knocked over'.

Rothschilds of the third generation, however, began to buy with discrimination; and by the second half of the nineteenth century the family name was synonymous with the greatest collections in Europe. Indeed a whole school of dealers sprang into being on Rothschild custom alone: these included Friedrich Spitzer, Arthur Wertheimer, the Goldschmidts, the Davises and the Duveens. Lionel de Rothschild specialized in Dutch and Flemish paintings of the seventeenth century while his brother Mayer bought Italian Renaissance furniture and Limoges enamels. In Germany Baron Willy bequeathed to the Frankfurt Staatsbibliothek a unique collection of rare books while his brother Mayer Carl gave the city a private library. Mayer's main interest, however, was silver, and he amassed such a superb collection, catalogued by Luthmer, that it was used by Rosenberg when he compiled the standard work on silver-smiths' marks. Mayer intended to give this priceless collection to Frankfurt, along with his library, but the incipient anti-Semitism of the Germans manifested itself in a device for weighing coal carts which was erected next door to his house with the deliberate aim of spoiling the beauty and cleanliness of his surroundings. As a result the silver went to his seven daughters, one of whom married the English Lord Rothschild.

The French made no such mistake. While Baron Alphonse assembled priceless enamels and goldsmithery of the late Middle Ages and the Renaissance, his brother Edmond specialized in rare engrav-ings, which went to the Louvre after his death and may be seen today in the Salle Edmond de Rothschild. In Vienna the museums received gifts from Anselm and his son Nathaniel Mayer, while in England, another of Anselm's sons, Ferdinand, the most discerning collector of all, gave the British Museum the crystals, Limoges enamels and precious wood carvings that are known as the Waddesdon Bequest, one of the most magnificent gifts ever received by the Trustees.

'Of all people I give the palm to the cultured Jew, and of all cultured Jews to the Rothschilds,' wrote an English contemporary. 'Whether it is enamel or stones, horses or carts, flowers, cigars, pictures, music or anything you like, they know all there is to know, but they are always ready to listen...' Not only to listen but to buy: as a result the entrance hall of the Bank at New Court was thronged with dealers, 'a sort of royal levée,' wrote Philip Roth, 'with the magnates of the world of art foremost among the courtiers'. The brothers would stop on their way to or from the Partners' Room. 'What have you got to show me?' was the prelude that frequently led to the exchange of thousands of pounds.

But Lord Rothschild was more than a banker and a collector. He was the leading English Jew; and as England was the leading world power he was looked upon as the lay head of world Jewry. This undefinable position meant that every vexatious problem to do with Jews anywhere was brought to his attention. For thirty-six years he

served as President of the United Synagogue, an inter-congrega-
tional organization founded by his uncle Anthony. In this capacity he
more or less dictated who should be chosen as England's Chief
Rabbi, although the candidate was supposed to be elected. His last
appointment involved such a prolonged struggle that, after getting
his own way, he remarked wearily: 'I hope I may not live to see
another Rabbinate election.' At Queen Victoria's Jubilee celebration in 1897 Cardinal Vaughan presented a loyal address on behalf
of Her Majesty's Catholic subjects; and, of course, Lord Rothschild
did the same for the Jews.

Meanwhile, so many Jews were pouring into Britain from Russia's
persecution in eastern Europe that the question of restriction was
raised in Parliament. While Edmond was giving millions to establish
Jewish colonies in Palestine, Lord Rothschild was trying to improve
conditions in the East End of London. As early as 1889 he had
offered to give £20,000 towards the construction of a communal
centre in Whitechapel Road, but the idea had been opposed by
Anglo-Jewish leaders jealous of the Rothschilds. The only solution
seemed to be to send the thousands of newcomers to America which
was crying out for more labour.

The prime mover of this scheme was Hermann Landau, a Jewish
philanthropist of eastern European origin. On one occasion Landau
returned home to find his house in Bryanston Square ringed by a
mass of humanity – Russian refugees fresh from the docks. Without
a moment's hesitation he drove to New Court where he was shown
to the Partners Room. Temporary shelter, he said, must be provided
for the arrivals until they could be transhipped across the Atlantic.
The cost would be £5000 annually for five years. Lord Rothschild
nodded. £30,000 would be placed in Landau's account the next day.
'But you have made a mistake,' said the visitor. 'I need only £25,000.'
'Do you hear that Leo?', Natty said to his younger brother. 'Landau's
having *rachmonus* [pity] on us.'

By 1902 the question of restricting immigration had become such a
burning topic that a Royal Commission on Alien Immigration was
set up, and Lord Rothschild appointed as one of the members. It was
at this point that he met the handsome Austrian journalist, Theodor
Herzl, who for nearly seven years had been trying to interest the
Rothschild family in Zionism – the establishment in Palestine of
a Jewish State, protected by law. Indeed Herzl originally had entitled
his treatise on the Jewish State *Address to the Rothschilds*, as he regarded
this family as 'the most effective force that our people have possessed
since their dispersion'. 'We shall probably model the constitution
after that of Venice but profit by her mistakes,' he wrote in his diary
on 7 June 1895. 'If the Rothschilds join with us, the first *doge* is to be a
Rothschild. . . ' Yet Herzl's conception of a state, to which all loyal
Jews pledged allegiance, was the antithesis of Rothschild thinking.

The family had based its existence on adherence to the countries of their adoption, and had no wish to repair *en masse* to Palestine.

Herzl, however, could not understand any sentiments that differed from his own. In June 1895 he headed a paragraph in his diary 'To the Rothschild Family Council':

> You older men will stand by with advice as to finances, banking, railroads, and politics, and will enter our diplomatic service. Your sons, and I hope you will have as many of them as possible, will play their part in the army, diplomatic corps etc. according to their capacities – and govern provinces, etc. We will reward your daughters with our best officers, finest artists, and most brilliant officials. Or marry them off in Europe, as the Americans do, and which I believe to be very useful . . . [1]

It is not surprising that Herzl's plans did not appeal to the Rothschilds. Baron Edmond was unresponsive: the Viennese Rothschilds did not reply to his letters; the London Rothschilds made no overtures despite being told by a stream of go-betweens that an interview was his most ardent desire. Not until 1902 did a meeting take place between Lord Rothschild and Herzl. One of the members of the Royal Commission on Alien Immigration invited Herzl to appear as a witness in the hope, apparently, that his enthusiasm for Zionism would lead him to testify that a good Jew could never be a good Englishman. Natty sensed this and did his best to ensure that Herzl's testimony would not prejudice Jewish immigration to Britain.

> At a quarter to one [wrote Herzl], I set out for New Court to see Rothschild . . . . Punctually at one o'clock I passed through the gate, had myself announced to the Lord of Banking Hosts, and was shown to a room that had a mercantile air. Boxes of sample merchandise in the corners etc.
> I hadn't waited longer than a minute when his Lordship came in, a good-looking, Anglo-Jewish old gentleman . . . . He has very attractive, large Jewish eyes, and he is very hard of hearing . . . . He did not believe in Zionism. (After a few introductory remarks in English we both spoke in German.) He was no Zionist. We would never obtain Palestine etc. He was an Englishman and proposed to remain one. He 'desired' that I should say this and that to the Alien Commission, and not to say this and the other. This was too much for me. I had already broken in several times with remarks. But now I began to shout him down so loudly that he held his tongue, nonplussed and astounded. [2]

However, in the end the two men parted as friends. Herzl gave testimony to the Commission that did not prejudice Jewish immigration; and although Lord Rothschild would not support Herzl's plans he mollified him by calling him 'a great man'. Leo de Rothschild invited him to a garden party, and Lady Battersea made a great fuss over him, introducing him to Edward VII's sister, Princess Louise, which delighted him.

Lord Rothschild's daily attendance before the Royal Commission, his stubborn and heated championship of the Jewish immigrant as a valuable addition to Britain, made a deep impression. Frequently he

A watercolour by Eugène Lami of Barons Alphonse and Gustave with their families at 23 Avenue de Marigny. On the facing wall is Rembrandt's *Portrait of Oopjen Coppit* which, together with its pendant, the *Portrait of Maerten Soolmans*, is still owned by the family.

himself cross-examined hostile witnesses in order to mitigate the harm they might have done; and occasionally questioned friendly witnesses to emphasize helpful points that they had been too nervous to remember. The report of the Commission, in 1903, admitted that the 'alien immigrant' was law-abiding, hard-working, thrifty and industrious. The only charge against him was 'overcrowding' which was not his fault. Yet this was the basis on which the Alien Immigration Act of 1905 was passed. Although it broke one of England's most cherished traditions, an open door for the persecuted, the bill probably would have been far more stringent if it had not been for Lord Rothschild's efforts.

The effectiveness of this unsmiling autocrat lay in his total lack of imagination. The Establishment measured dependability by an absence of levity; and during the first decade of the new century Lord Rothschild was looked upon as the financial oracle of the Tory party. Although he had followed the family tradition and sat in Parliament for twenty years as a Liberal MP his politics could not be described as anything but reactionary. Indeed the advent of a Liberal Government in 1906 filled no one with more anxiety than Nathaniel Rothschild, an anxiety which seemed to be justified when, in 1908, the Welsh radical, Lloyd George, was appointed Chancellor of the Exchequer.

From the pinnacle of the House of Lords Rothschild inveighed against the irresponsible ideas of Britain's new reformers. In 1909 Lloyd George was obliged to raise an extra £16,000,000 to pay for the implementation of the Old Age Pensions Act and for the Navy's eight new Dreadnoughts; and he chose to do it by a 'Tax-the-Rich' budget. Landowners felt they were witnessing the beginning of socialism, and that socialism was 'the end of everything'. Mr Arthur Balfour declared that you cannot 'abolish property by abolishing riches' and Lord Rosebery said that the measures were 'not a Budget but a revolution'. In the City a group headed by Lord Rothschild protested against the valuation of property by 'irresponsible tribunals' such as those which had 'cost one Stuart his head and another his throne'. Lloyd George counter-attacked fiercely.

In all these things I think we are having too much Lord Rothschild. We are not to have temperance reform in this country. Why not? Because Lord Rothschild has sent a circular to the peers to say so. We must have more dreadnoughts. Why? Because Lord Rothschild said so at a meeting in the City. We must not pay for them when we have them. Why? Because Lord Rothschild said so at another meeting. You must not have estate duties and a super-tax. Why? Because Lord Rothschild signed a protest on behalf of the bankers to say he would not stand it. You must not have a tax on reversions. Why? Because Lord Rothschild, as Chairman of an Insurance Company, has said that it would not do. You must not have a tax on undeveloped land. Why? Because Lord Rothschild is Chairman of an Industrial Dwellings Company. You ought not to have old age pensions. Why? Because Lord Rothschild was a member of a committee

that said it could not be done. Now, really, I should like to know, is Lord Rothschild the dictator of this country? Are we really to have all the ways of reform, financial and social, blocked simply by a notice-board, 'No thoroughfare. By order of Nathaniel Rothschild?'[3]

Despite the fact that Lord Rothschild was singled out for attack many members of the new Liberal Government were every bit as conservative as the great banker. The Prime Minister, Mr Asquith, was deeply opposed to granting women the vote, and the more militant the suffragettes became the more stubborn grew the opposition. Mr Asquith did not think 'our legislation' would be more 'respected' or 'our social and domestic life' more 'enriched' if women had the vote, while Lord Curzon pronounced bluntly: 'It would make Britain a laughing stock among nations.' Lord Rothschild, of course, felt he must pronounce on this matter as well as the budget, and put forward a view that was original if nothing more. 'If by any chance,' he told a City Conservative meeting, 'this ill-fated measure should become law, the electors of the City of London would be mainly charwomen, who would probably send to Parliament members who were not qualified to represent the interests of the finance and commerce of this great empire.'

Frequently Lord Rothschild's scepticism stood him in good stead. When the world's greatest passenger ship, the *Titanic*, was launched in 1911, the giant Rothschild firm, the Alliance Assurance Company, refused to insure it. People whispered that Lord Rothschild was losing his flair, for the premium was enormous and the risk negligible. However, when the ship went down on her maiden voyage in April 1912, with a loss of fifteen hundred lives, the same people marvelled at Rothschild's sagacity. Had he had a premonition? Nothing so fancy. Lord Rothschild explained, quite simply, that it had seemed 'too big to float'.

The genes are famous for playing tricks, and Lord Rothschild's heir, Lionel Walter, followed the family pattern only in one respect: he had a passion for collecting. But even here he deviated, for his interest centred not on works of art but on insects. As a child he collected butterflies, as a boy fleas, and as a youth a startling variety of animals from giant tortoises to cassowaries. On one occasion he eclipsed the splendour of Mr Alfred's goat by driving a team of zebras down Piccadilly; and when he went up to Cambridge as an undergraduate he took a flock of kiwis with him. Professor Albert Newton, the foremost authority on natural history, directed his taste for research, and when he left the university in 1889 he had a collection of 300,000 types of beetles.

Collecting is an expensive hobby; and Lord Rothschild was appalled by the amount of money which his son managed to spend. Nevertheless he provided two cottages at the edge of the park for the specimens, unknowingly laying the foundations of the Tring

Some members of the Rothschild family, from a collection of miniatures and photographs at New Court: *from left to right and top to bottom* Lionel, Hannah, Evelyn Achille, Louise, Mrs Leopold, Adele, Hannah again and Bettina.

Lionel Walter, second Lord Rothschild, with his team of zebras. A considerable authority on natural history, he is said to have made one good speech in his first year in Parliament as an M.P. for the Aylesbury Division – on the subject of undersized fish.

Zoological Museum which one day would consist of a building and annexe spread over three acres of ground.

Young Walter was a bitter disappointment to his father. Adored by his mother, a Rothschild from Frankfurt, he was looked upon as a delicate child and not allowed to go to school. Under a regime of 'unrestricted coddling' he grew into a handsome man of six foot three with a constitution of iron; yet at the same time he developed a pathological shyness. He conversed with his eyes on the floor, sometimes talking in a choking whisper, sometimes in a bellow.

Lord Rothschild, however, was accustomed to having his own way; and as a result ignored his son's handicaps and persisted in trying to mould him into his own image. Walter was made to serve as an officer in the Royal Buckinghamshire Yeomanry, later sat as a Justice of the Peace, entered the firm of N. M. Rothschild & Sons, and became a Member of Parliament.

Yet the museum remained uppermost in his mind. Although only twenty-four years old, he selected two men as his curators, Ernst Hartert and Karl Jordan, who proved to be exceptionally brilliant scientists. He continued to add to his collection and whenever he could escape from the bank hurried to Tring and spent the evening in the laboratory. It was quite apparent, wrote his niece Miriam Rothschild, that his talent for finance 'lay in one direction only – that of spending and this he achieved at a speed and on a scale that left his entourage breathless'. Nevertheless his father refused to face facts and continued to demand his presence at New Court. Gradually Walter developed the cunning of a truant schoolboy, often pretending that his attendance was required by the House of Commons but sneaking off to the Natural History Museum, or escaping with his butterfly net and pill-boxes into the fields.

He was always in trouble; sometimes over income tax demands, sometimes over chorus girls, more often simply because of his father's annoyance. Once Lord Rothschild found the door to the bank blocked by a pair of bear cubs attended by an inarticulate keeper who appeared to be asking for 'Mr Walter'.

The biggest scrape, which finally resulted in the severance of Walter's ties with the hated bank, occurred in 1908. Walter was desperately short of money for his museum and finally hit upon the happy idea of raising £200,000 on his father's life. He did not realize, however, that insurance companies like to spread their risks; and one of the firms invited to participate was none other than the Allied Insurance Company of which Lord Rothschild was chairman. When the latter asked, as was his wont, to see a résumé of new business for the week, he was stunned to find his own name at the top of the list. His son Walter, after fifteen uneasy years at New Court, at last found himself free to spend all his time at his beloved museum. There were other repercussions. Although Lord Natty settled a very large sum of money on Walter he disinherited him in favour of his second son Charles, a clever, moody man, also a scientist by inclination but who worked full time in the bank to please his father.

Meanwhile in France another Rothschild had embraced another branch of science. Baron Henri, a grandson of Lord Rothschild's uncle Nathaniel, who had moved to France in the 1850s after a hunting accident, was four years younger than Walter. He attended medical school and became a general practitioner in the 1890s; like all Rothschilds he took a short cut by building himself a hospital, and like all Rothschilds had a number of diversions, one of which was motor racing.

Indeed, Baron Henri had much more in common with Lord Rothschild's nephew Lionel, (one of Leo's sons) than with scientist Walter, for Lionel had inherited a passion for motor cars from his father and frequently toured the Continent. In the 1900s rich young men like Lionel and Henri never travelled without their mechanics, as all journeys were highly precarious. Windscreens and starters were inventions of the future: and although engines were capable of doing eighty, even ninety, miles an hour neither roads nor chassis were built for such speed. Springing was non-existent and tyres were pumped rock hard to enable them to hold the course.

In 1907 Baron Henri boasted that he could travel the six hundred miles from Paris to Monte-Carlo in faster time than his cousin Lionel. The latter accepted the challenge and, accompanied by his mechanic, Harper, and a friend named Montgomery, turned

Baron Henri de Rothschild, doctor, playwright and inventor, during a crocodile hunt in the British Sudan.

the bonnet of his Mercedes '60' south. The hazards of motoring became only too apparent as the journey progressed.

As we thumped and thundered along [wrote Harper], edging towards the ninety mark, I became aware that Mr. Montgomery's knees, which were just touching my back, were twitching and shaking out of tune with the car. Leaning towards the right, and putting my shoulder under the dash to keep out of the wind, I glanced over my left shoulder at our passenger. I was amazed to see that his mouth was wide open, and all that could be seen of his face – because of goggles, helmet and scarf – had a bluish tinge to it. I swung my left arm over, touched the owner, Mr. Lionel, on the knee and pointed to his companion at the same time giving the slow down sign. We came to a halt very quickly, and for some seconds our passenger gulped and gasped for breath. At some moment he had opened his mouth as we were speeding, the wind had caught him in the throat, and he had been unable to close his mouth again. An unpleasant experience, but one from which he soon recovered. I remember Mr. Lionel calmly recommending that he really should keep his mouth closed, as if being half chocked was an every day matter of little importance . . . [4]

The five Rothschild banks had become four with the demise of the Naples branch in 1861; and now, in 1901, the year that Edward VII came to the throne, the four became three with the closing of the patriarchal company, the forerunner of all other Rothschild enterprises, the Frankfurt bank. In this city the Rothschild role had been steadily diminishing for half a century: a lack of incentive, people said, for the River Main seemed to place a curse on the family, denying them the most important of all incentives – sons. Old Amschel had died childless in 1855. He had been succeeded by two nephews from the Naples branch: Mayer Carl, who had presided over the bank for thirty-one years and sired seven daughters, and then his brother, Baron Willy, father of three daughters, who took over the firm in 1886 and ran it until his death in 1901.

Three months later the following notice was circulated:

It is our sad duty to inform you that in consequence of the decease of Baron Wilhelm Karl von Rothschild, the Banking House of M. A. von Rothschild und Söhne will go into liquidation. The liquidators are:
1 The Right Hon. Nathaniel Mayer, Lord Rothschild, London.
2 Baron Edmond de Rothschild, Paris.

Before deciding to shut the bank the family had held hurried councils, but no one in London, Paris or Vienna wanted to move to Frankfurt which, by the turn of the century, had become a Prussian backwater. Soon stories were circulating that Kaiser William II was determined to persuade the family to open a bank in Berlin, but by 1901 tension between Germany and the two Western powers, Britain and France, was mounting, and nothing was done.

This was particularly disappointing to Alfred of London, who took a passionate interest in foreign affairs and for years had been trying to bring about an accord between England and Germany. Some people said that his allegiance had been captured by his honorary post as Austrian consul-general, a sinecure which had passed from Nathan to Lionel and from Lionel to himself. There may have been a modicum of truth in this as Alfred was more aware than most people of the sharp rivalry between Austria and Russia in the Balkans. He was well briefed on the Pan-Slav movement which animated Russian imperialism, and he often argued that Russia's predatory nature was more likely to spark off a world war than German militarism.

At the end of the 1890s, when the European powers were busy wringing concessions from China, Russia moved into Manchuria and refused to move out. Joseph Chamberlain, the Colonial Secretary, regarded Russian expansion as a serious threat to the British Empire. 'Both in China and elsewhere,' he wrote in 1889, 'it is to our interest that Germany should throw herself across the path of Russia. An alliance between Germany and Russia . . . is the one thing we have to dread. . .'

Joseph Chamberlain and Alfred de Rothschild saw eye to eye. England no longer could continue her role of Splendid Isolation. She must find allies on the Continent. If she could not work out an agreement with Germany, a member of the Triple Alliance, she must turn to France, a member of the Dual Alliance. Mr Alfred arranged cosy dinners at his house in Seamore Place to which he invited Chamberlain and Baron von Eckardstein, a secretary to the German Embassy, who was acting for Count Hadzfeldt, the ailing German ambassador. Eckardstein had married a daughter of Sir Blundell Maple, the department store magnate, and was more English than the English. He was fervently in favour of an Anglo-German agreement and throughout 1900 did everything in his power to promote it. Meanwhile, Alfred, who loathed Russia, partly because of her foreign policy and partly because of her persecution of the Jews, used his influence in the City to refuse the Tsarist regime the loans it was always seeking.

I remember once, in the spring of 1900, I was lunching with Alfred Rothschild, in New Court, his City office, when the Russian agent, Rothstein, was suddenly announced [wrote Eckardstein]. The servant had hardly said the name Rothstein when Alfred Rothschild cried out excitedly 'I won't see this *chuzpe ponem*.' [Yiddish for 'impudent fellow']

The servant was sent to say that he couldn't see Herr Rothstein, but brought back a message that Mr. Rothstein had come to London on behalf of Count Witte about a most important business matter with the Rothschild firm, and that he had to deliver a personal letter from the Russian Minister of Finance. Whereupon my mild and aimable friend, Alfred, flew into a regular passion. He sent for his secretary, and told him to say to Mr. Rothstein in so many words that he wouldn't see him even if he brought twenty personal letters from the Tsar of Russia.[5]

Apparently even this was not enough to discourage Mr Rothstein who, of course, had tried both Lord Rothschild and Mr Leo but had been told that they were at Epsom Downs. He therefore borrowed a newspaper and said he would wait until he could catch Mr Alfred on the way out. But Mr Alfred was equal to such emergencies. He gave orders to his coachman to pick him up in Cannon Street, and led Eckardstein down the back stairs, through the basement and out the service entrance. The next day Lord Rothschild received Mr Rothstein; but Alfred scored a moral victory, for it transpired that Rothstein had no letter from Count Witte, and only wanted to discuss the possibility of a new loan which he did not get.

Talks between Chamberlain and Eckardstein were proceeding satisfactorily when, in 1901, Queen Victoria died and Kaiser William II appeared at Windsor to sit at his grandmother's death bed. He kept himself well briefed on the current political situation and when he learned from Baron von Eckardstein of Chamberlain's proposal for an Anglo-German agreement, he wired ecstatically to his Chancellor; 'So "they come" it seems. This is what we have waited for.'

But the Kaiser's enthusiasm was premature. Count von Bülow, influenced by the sinister Foreign Office *éminence grise*, Baron Holstein, managed to drown the offer in cold water. Although Eckardstein warned the German Embassy that if England did not reach an understanding with Germany she was bound to turn to France, the officials refused to believe it. 'The threatened understanding with Russia and France is a patent fraud,' Holstein wrote to the senior diplomat in the Kaiser's suite. 'Time is on our side . . . a rational agreement with England . . . will only come within reach when England feels the pinch more acutely than she does to-day. . .'

Meanwhile the German press was encouraged to inveigh against the British Expeditionary Force in South Africa and to ridicule the Royal family. In 1902, Alfred de Rothschild wrote a letter to his friend, Eckardstein, which he hoped would be passed on to Chancellor von Bülow.

People here would have been glad to hear that the caricatures of our Royal Family, which were sold in the streets of Germany, had been confiscated by the police. In a word, of recent years Germany's policy toward England has been a kind of 'pin-prick' policy, and, although a pin is not a very impressive instrument, repeated pricks may cause a wound, and, since I hope and pray with my whole heart that no serious wound may result, I am venturing to address these lines to you in the hope that you will clearly explain to Count Bülow how difficult it is my position in this matter has become with regard to the British Government since I have done everything possible over such a long period of years, and that I feel now that you do not fully appreciate the great advantage of a genuine understanding with England . . . [6]

Alfred's efforts came to naught; and three years later Britain signed her famous entente with France.

No one lamented more acutely the system of alliances that threw Austria into the opposite camp from Britain and France than Baron Albert von Rothschild of Vienna. A brother of Ferdinand and Alice of Waddesdon, and a son-in-law of Baron Alphonse of Paris, he deplored the widening breach, so inimical to family traditions. Yet Albert refused to allow anything to interfere with his role as the perfect Rothschild; he ran the bank, entered his horses in the Derby, bought the first automobile seen on the streets of the capital, held musical *soirées*, collected works of art, entertained the nobility at huge shooting weekends; and even found time to climb the Matterhorn, a distinctly un-Rothschild pastime. Two of his five sons were unbalanced; George was sent to a lunatic asylum, Oskar committed suicide. Of the three remaining, only one was interested in finance. When Albert died, three years before the outbreak of the World War, he left the direction of the bank to Baron Louis, his third son.

In France as well as Austria the family was giving way to a new generation. Baron Alphonse had gone to his grave in 1905 when his heir, Édouard, was thirty-seven years of age, while his brother Gustave died the same year as Viennese Albert, in 1911, and was succeeded by his thirty-one year old son, Robert. In England, Ferdinand had died in 1898 and although his successor at Waddesdon, his sister Alice, scarcely represented a new generation she installed a very new régime. Whereas Ferdy had adored his week-end parties with their flow of guests and entertainments, Miss Alice, the 'All Powerful', drew the curtains to protect the brocade, forbade smoking except in the smoking-room and reverted to the forbiddingly formal luncheons and dinners so dear to the Victorian heart.

Of course in London the three magnificent brothers continued to entertain on the same luxurious scale throughout the Edwardian era although, like the new King himself, they were now elderly men with the ailing indigestions of the very rich.

Yet of all the Rothschilds of this period Baron Edmond of Paris remains the most fascinating. 'It is doubtful,' wrote the great Jewish statesman, Ben Gurion, in 1951, 'whether throughout the entire period of close on two thousand years which the Jews have spent in exile, any person is to be found who equals or who can compare with the remarkable figure of Baron Edmond de Rothschild, builder of the Jewish Settlement in the Homeland...'[7]

Edmond continued to pour money into Palestine – more than all the rest of the Jews in all the rest of the world put together – in an effort to make his colonies self-sufficient. There were many people who jeered at him for 'building on sand' and who prophesied that the rocky, waterless soil could never be reclaimed. Baron Maurice de Hirsch, for instance, bought huge tracts of land in the Argentine, lush and fertile, where he settled hundreds of refugees. He urged Edmond to follow suit but the latter clung to his dream of restoring

Baron Edmond de Rothschild exercised dictatorial control over his administration of funds to buy and cultivate land in Palestine during the early days of Zionism.

Israel; the same dream that dazzled Herzl, but to be accomplished quietly, stealthily, not by shouting from the roof-tops.

Yet the Baron was a dictator who expected the colonists to obey him unquestioningly. When he paid his third visit to Palestine in 1899 he was deeply depressed by the endless quarrels and complaints. Two years later the Jewish Community sent a delegation to Paris to talk frankly to the 'renowned benefactor'. '... If you wish to save the Yishuv [the Jewish settlement] first take your hands from it,' said the spokesman, 'and . . . for once permit the colonists to have the possibility of correcting for themselves whatever needs correcting . . .' But Baron Edmond snapped back furiously: 'I created the Yishuv, I alone. Therefore no men, neither colonists nor organizations, have the right to interfere in my plans . . .'[8]

Edmond not only continued to exercise dictatorial control throughout his administration but bought land and set up colonies at strategic points in Judea, Samaria and Galilee; strongholds, he explained, if in the future the country should be threatened: strongholds that proved their worth half a century later.

However as far as Zionism was concerned a new figure was arising. Herzl died in 1904 and gradually his place was taken by the Russian Jew, Chaim Weizmann, destined to be the first President of the State of Israel, who settled in Manchester and exerted his almost magical influence on the leaders of Anglo-Jewry. A consummately skilful diplomat, Weizmann was more tactful than Herzl and soon established links with the 'Father of the Yishuv'.

When I first met the Baron Edmond [he wrote, referring to their encounter in 1913], he was a man in his sixties, very much alert, something of a dandy, but full of experience and *sagesse*. Everything about him was in exquisite taste, his clothes, his home – or rather his homes – his furniture and his paintings, and there still clung to him the aura of the bon vivant which he had once been. In manner he could be both gracious and brutal; and this was the reflex of his split personality; for on the one hand he was conscious of his power and arrogant in the possession of it; on the other hand he was rather frightened by it, and this gave him a touch of furtiveness.[9]

The Baron told Mr Weizmann that he would contribute money for a Hebrew University in Palestine. 'The news was unexpected, for we still thought of the Baron as the rich autocrat interested exclusively in the philanthropic aspects of the Jewish problems, and disdainful of political Zionism. We were quite mistaken, but through no fault of ours, for the Baron was not a man to explain himself. In part he would not, for that went against his dictatorial temperament, in part he could not, for I doubt whether he really understood himself.'[10]

As the years passed Edmond moved closer to the Zionist organizers: and in 1914 Weizmann was delighted to learn that he had decided to visit Palestine once again to note the progress that had been made. He had not seen his colonies for nearly fifteen years. Once more he and his wife embarked on the huge steam yacht and dropped anchor at Jaffa.

Edmond could scarcely believe his eyes. Tel Aviv had become a city and his miserable windswept colonies had been transformed into lush gardens – miles of orange groves, and vineyards; forests of young trees; olives and apples and cherries; artesian wells gushing water.

This time Edmond's journey was likened to 'a prince returning to his people'. He travelled through Lower Galilee, and visited Petach Tikvah, Mikveh Israel, Rishon-le-Zion, Rehoboth, Ekron, Nachlath Yehuda, Ness Ziona. Everywhere he received such a stupendous welcome that he often was close to tears. Worn out by emotion, when colonists from Rosh Pinah begged him to honour their colony with his presence, he shook his head. 'I am old and weak,' he said. 'Soon my son James will come to you and he will speak to you in Hebrew.' Baron Edmond could not know that however old he felt he was to live another twenty years; and that James was destined to

When Baron Edmond revisited Palestine in 1914, after an absence of nearly fifteen years, he was given a rapturous welcome.

serve in the British Army that would conquer and occupy Palestine. However, James did as his father promised; he visited Rosh Pinah and spoke to the inhabitants in Hebrew. And Edmond finally embraced the cause of Zionism. When he returned to Paris he told Weizmann: 'Without me Zionism would not have succeeded, but without Zionism my work would have been struck to death.'[11]

Whatever historians write now about the inevitability of the First World War, the outbreak came as a shock to the mass of people everywhere. In 1914 relations between Britain and Germany were better than they had been for two decades. Indeed, at the beginning of the year Lloyd George, the Chancellor of the Exchequer, had observed jauntily 'never has the sky been more perfectly blue'. Then came the Sarajevo murder and the flame that set Europe alight. Like royalty, the Rothschilds were forced to abjure family solidarity and to give their loyalty to the countries of their adoption.

In England, Lloyd George, not long before had alluded indirectly to Lord Rothschild as 'a Philistine' adding rather indecently, 'not all of whom are uncircumcized'. But now the Chancellor was eager to make peace with his political enemy. He sent for the banker to discuss what measures should be adopted to keep the currency steady. He tells us that he awaited his visitor with some trepidation, as he was keenly aware that he had made more than one reference 'not of the kind to which the great House of Rothschild had hitherto been subjected'. 'Lord Rothschild,' said Lloyd George as he shook hands, 'we have had some political unpleasantness. . .' Natty brushed the attempted apology aside with his famous curtness. 'No time to bring up such things. What can I do to help?' 'I told him,' wrote Lloyd George 'He undertook to do it at once. It was done.'

All Rothschilds, in all three countries, served in whatever way they could. James de Rothschild, one of Baron Edmond's sons, managed to enlist successively in three armies: the French, the Canadian and finally the British. In Austria Baron Albert's son, Eugene, had a leg shattered on the Russian front, while in England Leo learned that his son, Evelyn, had been killed fighting the Turks in Palestine. In Paris the doctor of medicine, forty-two-year-old Baron Henri designed and built ambulances and took them to the front; and in London seventy-two-year-old Alfred learned that the allies were short of pit props for the trenches, and offered the glorious trees at Halton. 'I am not an expert,' he wrote to the Prime Minister on 28 February 1917, 'as regards what sort of timber would be suitable for pit props, but I cannot help thinking that, as there are so many pine trees in my woods at Halton, some of them at least would be suitable for the purpose. May I ask you very kindly to send down your expert who would very easily be able to report fully on the subject, and I should indeed be proud if my offer should lead to any practical result.'[12] It did and many trees were carried away.

All three of the magnificent English brothers died during the four years of war. The eccentric Lionel Walter became the second Lord Rothschild in the spring of 1915. He came under Weizmann's spell and embraced the Zionist cause with fervour, to the anger of most of his relations who were bitterly opposed to the concept. One Rothschild, no one knows which, defined a Zionist as 'an American Jew who gives an English Jew money to get a Polish Jew to Palestine'. Perhaps Walter's most implacable antagonist was Leo's widow, his Aunt Maria. Indeed when Mrs Leo's son, Evelyn, was killed in Palestine, she wrote to the Zionist Organization forbidding anyone 'to make a case of it'; in other words, to dramatize her son as giving his life for the liberation of Palestine. The recipients were amazed as the idea had not occurred to them.

When the allies drove the Turks onto the defensive throughout the Middle East and established themselves in Palestine, Britain's Foreign Secretary, Mr Arthur Balfour, responded to the pressure of the Zionists and issued a statement of intent: and he chose to address his famous Declaration not to the Chief Rabbi, nor to Weizmann, but to the second Lord Rothschild. The name still carried a magic of its own.

Foreign Office
November 2, 1917.

Dear Lord Rothschild,

    I have much pleasure in conveying to you, on behalf of his Majesty's Government, the following declaration of sympathy with Jewish Zionist aspirations which has been submitted to, and approved by, the Cabinet:

    'His Majesty's Government view with favour the establishment in Palestine of a national home for the Jewish people and will use their best endeavours to facilitate the achievement of this object, it being clearly understood that nothing shall be done which may prejudice the civil and existing religious rights of existing non-Jewish communities in Palestine, or the rights and political status enjoyed by Jews in any other country.'

    I should be grateful if you would bring this declaration to the knowledge of the Zionist Federation.

Yours sincerely,
Arthur Balfour

Shortly after the letter was published Walter Rothschild decided that he had endured the public gaze long enough. He was a scientist, not a politician; he refused to sit on any more committees, to attend any more meetings, and returned to Tring Park where once again he immersed himself in his birds and beetles and fleas. It was ironic that the first Lord Rothschild's heir – a man so determinedly unpolitical – should stumble into the history books because of his brief incursion into the Zionist struggle. However, one of Dr Weizmann's colleagues, Nahum Sokolow, explained that the Balfour Declaration had been 'sent to the Lord and not the Jewish people because they had no address, whereas the Lord had a very fine one'.

Chapter x

The Years Between

(1918–39)

Baron Louis, the tall, slim, blond head of the Viennese bank was not only an accomplished polo player and huntsman, but a scholar as well.

*W*HEN THE SMOKE CLEARED FROM THE BATTLEFIELD IN 1918, wrote a contemporary, 'nothing was the same, not even the Rothschilds'. Nothing but the legendary cohesion. The first thing that the victorious French and English Rothschilds did was to put the Austrian Rothschilds on their feet again. The Viennese bank, S. M. Rothschild und Söhne, was not run by Rothschild partners, as were the banks of London and Paris, but by a single Rothschild who handed on the sceptre as he saw fit. As two of Baron Albert's sons, Alphonse and Eugene, had impressed their father with their ability to keep themselves fully occupied as gentlemen of leisure, he had given control to his third son, Louis. This tall, slim, blond Rothschild, 'the image of an Anglo-Saxon aristocrat for all his synagogue-going', was thirty-four years old when the war ended. Like his two brothers he had served in the Austrian army and was lucky to be alive: yet the financial chaos that greeted him was far from heartening.

Before the war the Austrian branch had been the greatest bank in the Habsburg Empire, a force to be reckoned with throughout central Europe. But shortly after the turn of the century, the news of German naval rearmament caused Lord Rothschild to ponder deeply as to what would happen to the Rothschild firm as a whole if hostilities broke out. Because of the system of alliances, it was clear that Austria would be on one side, France and England on the other. And as someone would have to lose, Rothschilds could not win: that is, unless the family reorganized the banks as three separate entities.

Fortunately that is exactly what Lord Rothschild did in 1908, for eleven years later the Treaty of Versailles stripped the Austrian fatherland of thousands of square miles, and turned the monarchy into a republic. The new state was only a shadow of its former self; before 1918 Vienna had been the capital of a country of fifty-three million people; now the population had shrunk to seven million. Needless to say, the Austrian krone (and the German mark) reacted violently and began a long steady descent. Baron Louis bought state securities by the million in an attempt to steady the market, but his rivals felt no such loyalty to the newly demarcated state. Herr Castiglione, Louis's principal antagonist, sold the currencies short and made a fortune.

People began to whisper that the Austrian Rothschilds were finished and predicted that soon their palaces and treasures would

come under the hammer. However, the Germanic currencies were not the only ones to plummet: suddenly the French franc caught the infection, and began a downward lunge, with a see-saw effect on pound and dollar. None of it made much sense. 'In a manner entirely unintelligible to a layman endowed with ordinary common sense,' wrote Count Corti, 'even the most experienced financiers in Germany and Austria, speculated on a fall in the currency [of France] the most powerful of the victorious states. . . . A similar fate was prophesied for the franc as for the mark and the krone.'

Once again Herr Castiglione plunged into the fray. French francs were thrown on the market in breathtaking quantities and he sold them short on an equally breathtaking scale. Then the unexpected happened. Overnight the franc righted itself, and with startling speed began to soar. The experts were amazed and poor Castiglione lost so much money that he was put out of business. What had happened? The same old story: the French Rothschilds had formed a secret combine, this time with J. P. Morgan of New York, who realized that if France was allowed to slide into an economic slump, everyone, including America, would suffer.

At a prearranged signal Rothschilds and Morgans boosted the franc, which inevitably caused a fall in sterling; but as they were calling the moves, they coined money on the downward turns as well as the upward swings. Of course they shared the secret with the Austrian Rothschilds, telling them to the very day when the franc would rise. As a result the Vienna house made such enormous profits that they almost recouped the losses of the war. Once again Baron Louis sent out invitations to a ball in his palace on the Prinz Eugenstrasse; once again he organized shooting parties in Bohemia and sported the finest string of polo ponies in Austria.

The French Rothschilds benefited as well, and one by one members of the family began to take up the threads of their life in Paris. Alphonse's heir, Baron Édouard opened his huge house at 2 Rue Saint-Florentin off the Place de la Concorde, while Gustave's son, Baron Robert, brought his young family back to the even larger house at 23 Avenue de Marigny. Baron Edmond, seventy-five years old in 1920, began to receive callers again at 41 Rue du Faubourg Saint-Honoré; while Baron Henri, a few doors away entertained in a house, almost as large as the Élysée Palace, now known as the Cercle Interallié. He also lived at La Muette, newly built, which later became the seat of the organization for European Economic Cooperation, originally founded in 1948 to administer Marshal Aid.

Baron Robert de Rothschild, son of Baron Gustave, ran the French bank with his cousin Édouard.

Barons Édouard and Robert ran the bank, but they ran it in a very different way from their grandfather James, and their fathers Alphonse and Gustave. Very rich, very quiet, very passive, they showed more interest in family investments than in acquiring new business. Somehow the war had taken the dynamism out of Rothschild banking. Those who had survived the terrible blood-letting were thankful to be alive, and, like plants climbing toward the sun, reached out for a very unRothschild commodity: leisure.

The means for enjoyment were not in short supply. Rothschilds not only possessed Paris houses and country houses, but in the aggregate: vineyards and racing stables, theatres, yachts, stud farms and holiday resorts. Yet they amused themselves with such circumspection that only two Rothschilds cut a public swathe in the field of pleasure. One, oddly enough, was the doctor, Baron Henri, grandson of the English Nathaniel who had moved to France after his hunting accident; the other Baron Maurice, son of the deeply religious 'Father of Israel', Baron Edmond. Henri felt that he had done his share of good works by founding the Henri and Mathilde Hospital in Paris;† by publishing papers on pasteurization and hygiene; by inventing ambulances and putting jam into tubes, like toothpaste, for the boys at the front. Now he built the Théâtre Pigalle in Paris, wrote plays under the pseudonym, André Pascal, and invited the prettiest actresses to sail around the Mediterranean in his enormous yacht, aptly named the *Eros*. Soon Henri's son, Philippe, had taken over the direction of the Pigalle, and had made history by producing the first talking-picture in France, *Lac aux Dames*.

Despite Baron Henri's success with the ladies, he ran a poor second to his cousin Maurice. This gross, rather ugly man had the sort of charm that many women found irresistible. Of course his

†This was a small hospital compared to the *Hôpital Rothschild* founded by the Baron James in 1852 and still one of the great institutions of Paris.

Above A caricature of Henri de Rothschild, dancing with one of his leading ladies, Mlle Dorziat. *Below* A caricature of the brothers Maurice and James de Rothschild, sons of Baron Edmond. The caption, referring to James, reads: '*Tout de même, il a le chic Anglais!*'.

extravagant gifts of jewellery did not harm his reputation and made him a target for the world's most accomplished adventuresses, but during the last years of his life he was protected by a comely young woman, Milly, a professional nurse who accompanied him every-where because, he explained, she shared his 'blood group'. As he was old and infirm, Milly gave him confidence; but some people said that she also was paid to give him a weekly blood transfusion as he was under the impression that the transfer increased his virility.

Yet Maurice had a serious side and for many years served in the French Parliament as Senator for the Hautes-Alpes region. He was a wonderful host, high-spirited and witty and, despite his peculiarities, immensely clever when it came to money. Several of the richest men in France consulted him regularly, and with good reason, for when he died in 1957 he left more money than any other single French Rothschild. His fortune went to his son, Edmond.

Meanwhile the English Rothschilds were down to their last millions. Ironically, of all the cousins they were the hardest hit financially. Although Great Britain emerged from the war neither scarred like France nor vanquished like Austria, the English partners were forced to dig deeper into their pockets than any of the continental relations. The deaths of the three magnificent brothers within twenty-four months of each other had torn gaping holes in the firm's reserves, as huge sums went to the Government in death duties. To make matters worse, Alfred had defied the family rule which insisted that Rothschild money ignore the female of the species and pass un-challenged to Rothschild males. When his will was read in 1917 it was learned that the bulk of his fortune, larger than Natty's or Leo's because of his bachelorhood, had been left to his natural daughter, Almina Wombwell, wife of the Earl of Carnarvon. As things transpired, the Countess made history with the money. She en-couraged her husband to back Howard Carter's archaeological expedition which, in 1922, at Thebes in the Nile Valley, uncovered the grave and treasures of Tuthankhamen.

The new generation of English Rothschilds was not greatly concerned by the diminishing standard of luxury. Like their French cousins, they were very different from their fathers. The 1920s had exploded on the scene and were in the process of sweeping away the last traces of Victorian decorum, or hypocrisy, as some called it. Girls bobbed their hair, shortened their skirts and, to be perverse, flattened their chests. Their emancipation was celebrated by the shimmy and the cocktail party. Although it was still nice to be rich, pretentiousness was out of fashion. Liveried servants had faded away with the horse and carriage and mammoth London houses soon would be as extinct as the dinosaur. The sports car had arrived with a revolutionary new era in tow: easy come, easy go, night-clubs, informality – at least after dark.

The Rothschilds were quick to sense the change and one by one their huge London houses came up for auction, or demolition. Even some of the country houses were sold. Aston Clinton where Sir Anthony had lived was turned into a country hotel, while Halton, the scene of Alfred's luxurious entertainments, was bought by the Air Force and became an officers' training centre. Gunnersbury Park, the country seat acquired in 1836 by the great Nathan, was turned into a museum and the grounds thrown open as a public park.

One by one the Piccadilly houses changed hands. Some of them became clubs, others were demolished to ease the traffic problem. Alfred's house at Seamore Place was pulled down to give Curzon Street an outlet into Park Lane, while 148 Piccadilly eventually was razed to make another entrance into Hyde Park. But all this took time, and for a while a few Rothschilds continued to hang onto a few oversized houses. Anthony moved into his father's residence at 5 Hamilton Place, and spent his weekends at Ascott near Wing. Natty's widow, the Dowager Lady Rothschild, continued to live at 148 Piccadilly and Tring Park, and Miss Alice continued to administer Waddesdon until her death in 1923. As she had no direct heirs she left the vast property to her great-nephew, Baron Edmond's elder son, James de Rothschild, who had married a charming English lady, Dorothy Pinto, in 1913, and became a naturalized Englishman in 1919.

A Frenchman by birth, an Englishman by choice and the beneficiary of a second inheritance from an Austrian relation who had taken British nationality, James – or Jimmy as he was called – seemed to be the composite Rothschild. Yet apart from the fact that he was a Croesus – when he died he left £11,000,000 – it was impossible to fit him into any existing mould. A tall, thin, rakish man, he might have been a grandee or a bookie, a librarian or an auctioneer; nothing would have seemed out of character. His absorbing passions, in fact, were horses, politics and art, in that order. His introduction to English sport had begun in 1896 when he was sent to Cambridge. Although as a boy he had been a scholar he became so enthralled with hunting and steeplechasing that when his three years were up he begged his father to allow him to remain for an extra year. Baron Edmond would agree only on condition that Jimmy won a scholastic prize. His friends were astonished to see him lock himself into his room for three months; and even more surprised when he emerged with an essay, 'Shakespeare and His Day', that won the Harness Prize. Although Jimmy finally was sent to Hamburg to study banking he still managed to preserve his links with the English equestrian world. By enduring long night journeys, wrote his widow, he contrived 'to spend his occasional free days hunting or steeple-chasing'.

In 1915 Jimmy was awarded the DCM. He raised a Jewish Battalion, served under Allenby and ended the war in Palestine. Not

James – or Jimmy, as he was called – de Rothschild: his absorbing passions were horses, politics and art, in that order.

long after the Peace Treaty he had the misfortune to lose an eye playing golf at Deauville – a mishit by the Duc de Gramont – but although his remaining eye was weak, he did not allow the incident to dampen his spirits. With his usual panache he simply transferred the monocle he always wore to his blind eye; and to his great joy found that the weak eye gathered strength.

'Waddesdon is not an inheritance, it is a career,' pronounced Lord d'Abernon when he heard that the estate had passed to Jimmy. Nevertheless the beneficiary found time to squeeze in other careers as well. For sixteen years he sat as Liberal MP for the Isle of Ely, and for thirty-seven years devoted himself enthusiastically to the Turf. He built a stud farm at Waddesdon, worked out an intricate pattern of breeding, and often bet large sums on a 'hunch', once winning £40,000.

No one thought it at all strange that the lovable Jimmy should be odd; after all he possessed a highly individual father and had spent a highly individual youth. But why should the two sons of that dutiful, magnificent, Victorian figure, the first Lord Rothschild, married to a Rothschild, oracle of the City, pillar of the State, have turned out to be cuckoos in the nest? What defiant element had crept into the breeding to transform Rothschilds bred of Rothschilds into such startlingly un-Rothschild patterns; not bankers but scientists, not doers but thinkers, not sophisticates but recluses?

The first Lord Rothschild had been so infuriated by his eldest son's ineptitude at the bank, his pursuit of chorus girls and his zoological extravagances that he had disinherited him in favour of his second son, Charles. Before he rewrote his will, however, he settled on Walter a sum which guaranteed him the life to which he was accustomed.

After Walter's brief spell in the limelight as recipient of the Balfour Declaration he had returned to his natural history museum at Tring, more convinced than ever that he had discovered the only satisfactory existence. Although the first Lord Rothschild left his house to Charles, Walter continued to live at Tring Park and 148 Piccadilly with his mother until her death in 1933.

Walter struck many people as a grotesque figure, as his bashfulness, his whispers and his inability to look people in the eye offered a strange contrast to his spectacular height and his 300 lbs. Everything about him was massive, not only his size, but the scale of his collection, the scope of his contributions. In conjunction with his two brilliant curators he produced over eight hundred scientific papers, and described several hundred species new to science. 'Few, if any, zoologists during their lifetime have had so many living creatures named after them,' wrote Walter's niece, Miriam Rothschild. 'Suddenly Rothschilds appeared among the giraffes, the zebras, the cassowaries, the mice, the fish, the birds of paradise, the silk-moths, the swallow tails, the flies and the lilies of the fields.'[1]

The *Diomedea immutabilis rothschildia*, one of the many species of birds and other animals named after the Rothschilds.

DIOMEDEA IMMUTABILIS, ROTHSCH.

Walter's collection proceeded to grow on an equally impressive scale until the museum boasted over a hundred thousand bird skins and two million sets of butterflies and moths. But the costs mounted as dizzily as the acquisitions, and in 1932 Walter Rothschild was obliged to sell his precious birds to the New York Museum of Natural History to prevent both Tring Museum and himself from going bankrupt.

This set-back did not dim his enthusiasm and he continued to search assiduously for new species. Once, by an extraordinary chance, he managed to add to his collection of tree kangaroo pelts in Park Lane. As a chauffeur opened the door of a stationary car he caught sight of a lap rug that made his pulse race. He went up to the vehicle, took a closer look, found out the owner's name, and finally bought the tree-kangaroo rug for £30.

Walter's younger brother Charles, a highly gifted but gentle, unassuming man, was senior partner in the bank. Although he was an able financier he worked at Rothschilds out of deference to his father, for his true love, like that of his brother, was science. In 1907 he had married a handsome and amusing Hungarian Jewess, Rozsika von Wertheimstein, who had produced a noisy and vibrant brood of children, three girls and a boy. Charles liked nothing better than to take the children into the fields to catch butterflies. 'Had I my way England would see little of us,' he wrote wistfully. 'What I really like is to live in a nice island or settle in Japan and Burma and be a professional bug-hunter.'[2]

As far as the children were concerned, however, England seemed to offer the carefree island life for which Mr Rothschild longed. The

Above, left Mrs Charles Rothschild and *right* her son Victor, the present Lord Rothschild.

family lived in Palace Green, in a house that is now the Rumanian Embassy, facing Kensington Gardens; and although it should have been an easy task to take the little ones out to play, the expeditions invariably degenerated into a metée of shrieks and kicks. The fact that the children were all fast runners resulted in a rapid turnover of nursery maids, until one enterprising miss solved the problem by tying them together to the surprise of passersby.

Victor and his sister Miriam, two years his elder, were the most precocious of the flock, but whereas Miriam was Mrs Rothschild's little darling, Victor was sensationally naughty. He not only carried on a running war with his sisters but plagued his nanny relentlessly. No sooner had she finished packing his suitcase than he burrowed through it, throwing everything onto the floor on the pretext of searching for something. Even at the age of six he knew how to create a stir, once walking through the drawing-room and sweeping

Miriam Rothschild at seventeen.

all the objects from the mantelpiece onto the floor. Apparently old Lord Rothschild liked the boy's spirit, for when Victor was four years old he threw a plate of spinach at his grandfather, who subsequently left him £25,000.

Frequently the intrepid Charles Rothschild took Miriam and Victor on zoological outings. Years later Victor described how, at the age of four, his father sent him into the garden 'to try and catch a very rare butterfly, a gynadromorph orange tip, that is one which is half male and half female and which, therefore, only had the orange tip on one wing. I remember being punished a few years later,' he continued, 'for going into the long grass without my galoshes on, to catch another rare butterfly. The punishment was terribly severe; I had to give the butterfly to my elder sister. She gave it back to me, beautifully mounted, as a twenty-first birthday present.'[3]

One of Charles Rothschild's specialities was fleas. He had become interested in these insects as disease spreaders while an undergraduate at Cambridge, and in 1902 the *Daily Express* had carried a headline:

'10,000 FLEAS MR. ROTHSCHILD'S HOBBY'.

Although Charles's research was limited to after-hours at the bank, weekends and holidays, it absorbed much of his thoughts. In 1908 he published a paper in conjunction with Karl Jordan entitled *Revision of the Non-Combed Eyed Siphonaptera*. 'Jordan and I are just publishing an article in the Journal of Hygiene about the fleas associated and allied to *P. Cheopis*, the plague carrier,' he wrote to a fellow entomologist. 'We have taken a lot of trouble with it and I think it is good. . . . Please criticize it fully. . . '

In 1913, after years of meticulous work mounting and labelling, he donated his flea collection to the British Museum. A year later he published a paper on the three species of *Xenopsylla* occurring on rats in India, suggesting that fleas probably were responsible for the spread of the bubonic plague. Fabian Hirst, who subsequently proved the theory, wrote that his contribution was 'the natural outcome of the purely zoological researches of Rothschild and Jordan on the systematics of Siphonaptera'.[4]

Charles was also concerned with the preservation of plants and animals and founded and financed a Society for the Promotion of Natural Reserves which received a Royal Charter in 1916. Before the outbreak of war, he spent many years working on a map of England, at the behest of the Ministry of Agriculture, marking areas for conservation. When, after the Second World War, the Attlee Government set up committees to do a similar survey, the members came up, roughly, with the same recommendations. What was remarkable about Charles Rothschild was that all his work was done outside office hours. Tragically, in 1916 he contracted sleeping sickness, then an incurable disease, which plunged him into bouts of deep depression. He consulted doctors all over Europe, spent long and lonely sojourns in the rarefied air of Switzerland, but finally, in 1923, went to his room, turned the key in the lock, and killed himself.

Charles's widow did not find her high-spirited children easy to handle; but the three daughters were less exhausting than the rebellious and brilliant boy, twelve-year-old Victor, who was sent to Harrow in the autumn. Mrs Rothschild never did things by halves and when Victor's history master reported that his grasp of the Carthaginian Wars left much to be desired she not only made him work in the holidays but worked herself. At two desks, side by side, they wrote essays on the hated subject and compared results.

Victor inherited £2,500,000 from his father, apart from 148 Piccadilly and Tring Park. The money remained in trust until October 1930 when he celebrated his twenty-first birthday. By this time he had acquired an arrogance which made him very unpopular with his contemporaries, particularly as it was based on merit. At Cambridge he had taken a triple First in English, French and Physiology, but this was not as impressive as it seemed, as it had been an Ordinary, not an Honours degree. However in 1935 he became a Prize Fellow of Trinity College, Cambridge, every bit as grand as it sounded.

One of the few people who occasionally could get the better of him was Miriam. Although higher education was still thought to be a waste of time for females, and Miriam consequently had not been encouraged to attend a university, she knew almost as much science as Victor. Not only had her father and uncle tutored her through the years, but she spent many hours doing research at Tring Museum with the celebrated Karl Jordan. She adopted her father's particular interests and in the late 1930s people frequently saw a tall, dark-haired handsome girl, striding through the streets of London on her way to a laboratory, a box of fleas under her arm.

In the best tradition of elder sisters Miriam bullied Victor about everything, even manners. Once they were lunching with a friend who had an exceptionally pretty daughter. Miriam gave her brother sternly reproving glances. Afterwards she drew him aside and hissed: 'Stop looking at her like that or she'll think you want to marry her.'

Marriage clearly was an ominous threat for Victor was very much admired by the opposite sex, not only because of his fast sports cars, his Oxford bags and his talent as a jazz pianist, but because of his dark, romantic looks and his biting tongue. Some people referred to him as a modern Lord Byron; others, more struck by the rudeness with which no one could compete, save for Winston Churchill's boy, nicknamed him 'the black Randolph'.

When Victor was twenty-one his mother begged him to enter the bank. 'It came as rather a shock,' he later recalled, 'to learn that my parents, while realizing that I was a scientist, were most anxious for me at least to try the life of a banker in the City of London. This I did but the moment was unfortunate. In 1930 there was a world recession and the City seemed dead, boring and rather painful, so after six or so months, I returned to Cambridge University to be a science don . . . where I lived in a relaxed and somewhat unworldly atmosphere.'[5] However, an explosive element was introduced in 1932 when he married Barbara Hutchinson, daughter of St John Hutchinson, KC. Barbara was clever and attractive and much preferred to cut a dash in sophisticated London than in the academic world of Cambridge. She produced two daughters and in 1936 a son, Jacob; but the marriage ended in divorce after the war.

With the march of the 1930s the Rothschilds boasted only two bankers, Leo's sons, Lionel and Anthony. Lionel had become senior partner when Charles died in 1923. At that time he was forty-one and Anthony thirty-six. Like their French cousins, the English brothers felt no urge to add to their worldly possessions, and tended to regard the financial competitiveness that was beginning to spring up as a sordid pastime. N. M. Rothschild & Sons had sufficient *réclame* to run on its own momentum; and the two partners, like all civilized men, had other interests besides business.

While Lionel's passion for motoring had become less acute – now that cars had shock absorbers the excitement was gone – and he sought the more static delight of a magnificent, 2,600-acre estate in the New Forest at Exbury, which he bought in 1919. Flanked on one side by the River Beaulieu, on the other by the Solent, he was able to indulge his new enthusiasms: fishing and sailing. Before long, however, he had acquired a new interest which threatened to eclipse the other two: breeding rhododendrons. Like all Rothschilds he became increasingly absorbed in his hobby and increasingly professional in the pursuit of it. He left his London office at 3.30 pm every Friday, in his sports car, and when he arrived at Exbury his senior gardening staff, consisting of some twenty men, would be assembled, awaiting him. He would hand each a cigar, then give his orders for the weekend's operation.

Lionel created many of his plants by effecting crosses, 1,210 in all. He named and registered 416 new varieties, and did most of the hand-pollinating himself. If he heard that there was a superior specimen of a plant in Scotland, for instance, he would not hesitate to send his chauffeur a thousand miles there and back to secure the pollen. He personally determined the position of all plants of importance, pushing his walking stick into the ground and saying: 'Plant it there.' And they planted them with such effect that at the outbreak of war in 1939 his rhododendron gardens contained a million plants and was the best in the world.

Of course he spent a fortune doing it. For ten years 150 men dug bore holes and enriched the soil. Altogether twenty-two miles of pipeline were laid ensuring a water supply of 250,000,000 gallons a day. Rothschild blacksmiths made 150 tons of metal fittings for the greenhouses, and a nearby hamlet was doubled to house the scores of under-gardeners.

Fortunately Lionel's wife, Marie-Louise Beer, a sister of Baroness Robert de Rothschild of Paris, had unlimited vitality. She not only ran Exbury House with traditional regard for food, drink and comfort, but sailed and fished with her husband in all weathers, and occasionally accompanied him on motor trips to North Africa and Greece. Exbury was covered with family trophies, stuffed fish and stags' heads, silver yachting trophies and racing prints belonging to Lionel's father Leo, and to Leo's uncle, Mayer. Also present, of course, were the inevitable masterpieces – Romneys, Reynoldses, Cuypses – that were part and parcel of all Rothschild homes.

Lionel was not bothered by changing times. He was a rich man with expensive tastes which he made no attempt to conceal, with the result that some of the employees of the bank tended to regard him as a divinity. When one of the clerks died an envelope was found inscribed: 'Pellets from a pheasant shot by Mr Lionel'. Mr Lionel drove to work every morning in an open two-seater Rolls Royce, the envy of all the young men in the building; and when he was invited to address the City Horticultural Society, composed of suburban members, he did not mince his words. 'No garden,' he said, 'however small, should contain less than two acres of rough woodland.' On another occasion, Lionel saw a box lying on the table in the Bullion Room. When he was told that it contained table mats and was a wedding present from the staff to one of the accountants, he said: 'Let's have a look.' When it was opened he was disappointed. 'Well, that's not much good. You could never have more than twelve people to dinner.'

Anthony was less exuberant than his brother, a quiet, donnish sort of man who had taken a double first at Cambridge and did not suffer fools gladly. His tastes were eclectic and over the years he built up a remarkable collection of Chinese porcelain at his home at Ascott, mainly of the Ming and K'ang Hsi Dynasties. Although he was apt to be stand-offish with his employees, he was much respected in the City where he had a reputation as 'a great gentleman'. In those days it was considered inexpressibly vulgar for a merchant bank to solicit new business, even to advertise; and to cultivate men whom one did not like for the sake of valuable contacts was nothing less than a gross breach of integrity. Anthony de Rothschild scrupulously observed the unwritten rules. 'He did not travel himself,' wrote Palin, 'and he did not sit on the boards of the numerous public companies which would have been delighted to have him. "They know where we live," he would say of potential clients, "if they want to do business with us let them come and talk to us".'[6] And when they did come, if he did not like their faces or their manners, at the end of the conversation he would bow them out with his

The Viennese bank, S. M. von Rothschild und Söhne, by R. Alt.

Overleaf A bronze fountain group by Julian Story in the grounds of Ascott House. The half-timbered house was bought in 1873 by Mayer Amschel Rothschild, together with some ninety acres of land; it was taken over the following year by his nephew Leopold who used it mainly as a hunting box and it was later used extensively by Leopold's son, Anthony.

Detail of the library at Ascott, showing a large *famille noire* jar of the K'ang Hsi period, with elaborate enamel decoration; this is part of the outstanding collection of Chinese porcelain, mainly Ming and K'ang Hsi wares, gathered at Ascott by Anthony de Rothschild.

customary old-world courtesy, but find an excuse for letting the matter drop.

The truth was that N. M. Rothschild & Sons was an autocracy ruled by feudal and dynastic lords. In the inter-war years subordinates accepted the system unquestioningly. To many men, including Palin, the family seemed to be a higher order of creation than ordinary mortals.

It was in the nature of things [he wrote] that a young male Rothschild should inherit a partnership in the family business when he attained a suitable age in the same way as he inherited material possessions and it did not enter anybody's head that any other qualifications could ever achieve the same result. When I heard in 1926 that Anthony was going to get married, I asked Hugh Miller if this was a dynastic marriage, thinking that it was perhaps an alliance 'arranged' by the family for political or business reasons. It did not occur to me that a Rothschild, particularly one who was in the firm, could marry for love like anyone else.[7]

Yet this was what Anthony had done. His fiancée was a charming French lady, Yvonne Cahen d'Anvers, but at least the match was in the best tradition as the bride came from a Jewish banking family.

Despite the advent of aggressive new rivals in the City, N. M. Rothschild & Sons remained in the front rank of merchant banks; but now, instead of being 'first of the firsts' it was merely among the firsts. Even so it retained privileges that sprang from the days of its unchallenged supremacy. Every morning at 10.30 experts from the London bullion market met in 'Mr Anthony's room' and solemnly fixed the price of gold, just as the great Nathan had done long ago only less comfortably, often standing in a courtyard. The Rothschild name still had magic, for foreigners and bankers and industrialists from all over the world continued to call at New Court to discuss loans, flotations and mergers. On more than one occasion bright-eyed Rothschild subordinates were forced to bite their lips to keep from laughing out loud. This happened when the firm was acting for Charringtons the brewers, in their merger with Hoare and Co. Lionel, who seldom if ever had entered a pub, turned to Hoare's auditor and said: 'Tell me, where are those Hoare houses? Are they in the West End or in the East End?' The accountant replied gravely: 'They are all over London, Mr Rothschild.' Apparently it was even more difficult to keep a straight face when a German industrialist described a rival as having 'how do you say? – a finger in every tart'.

The fact that Rothschilds was run on 'feudal lines' meant that the employers had obligations towards their employees; and in the 1930s many men had reason to be grateful for the protection they received, for these were the years of depression, unemployment, financial crises, and 'defaults one after another of the debtor countries'. While other firms laid off members of the staff no one at Rothschilds, no matter how insignificant his contribution, was asked to leave or to accept a reduction in salary.

Anthony de Rothschild, with his wife Yvonne, at Epsom for the Oaks; with them is Lord D'Abernon.

Although N. M. Rothschild & Sons was still an international name, writers who scrutinized the family in the late 1920s referred to their accomplishments in the past tense. Of course times had altered, and governments had stepped into the happy breach once occupied by Nathan Rothschild. But even taking the changes into consideration, it looked as though Rothschild wizardry had disappeared as silently and magically as the word implied. The historian of Anglo-Jewry, Cecil Roth, believed that the death of the three English magnificos in the Great War had marked the end of an epoch. 'When, after four years' nightmare, the darkness lifted again, all had passed away. There was no one who could take their places.' Mr R. E. Ravage declared that 'the incentives of the fathers do not spur the descendants. . . . So the lustre of the House of Rothschild is sadly dimmed, and but for the survival of its fortune the latter-day banking corporations would hardly think it worth while consulting.'

Only Count Corti reserved judgement, pointing out that although Rothschild power had declined 'it would be a mistake to believe that they have lost all influence. . . . Throughout the centuries, one factor has remained constant – the power of money: indeed the importance of this factor has increased . . . since the total population, and therefore the numbers who lack money, has expanded to an extraordinary degree.'

Corti was right, for the day of the Rothschilds was far from over. The advent of Hitler in 1933 did not at once grip the attention of the world, but it began to stir the Rothschilds from their slumbers. Oddly enough, the first English Rothschild to realize the full implications of what was happening was French-born Yvonne, wife of Anthony. By the autumn of 1933 Yvonne had become president of a society 'to aid German Jewish women and children'. She organized a fund-raising women's lunch at the Savoy Hotel on 10 December at which Lady Violet Bonham Carter was the main speaker. This was only the beginning; a few months later Yvonne persuaded the distributors of *The House of Rothschild*, starring George Arliss, to give the proceeds of the first night to her society. She collected all the great names of English Jewry and scored a financial triumph. A year later she repeated the success with an Eddie Cantor first night.

During the latter half of the 1930s, Baron Robert de Rothschild of Paris became President of an organisation for Jewish refugees, and with his beautiful wife, Nelly, one of the great hostesses of the day, embarked on an arduous programme of fund-giving and fund-raising. Meanwhile in London Miriam Rothschild had made herself responsible for a number of children who had arrived in England from Germany, while Jimmy de Rothschild imported from Frankfurt a whole orphanage consisting of two dozen boys between the ages of five and fifteen, accompanied by a warden and his wife, with two daughters and a sister-in-law. He provided a house for them in Waddesdon and sent the children to the local schools. 'They were marvellously accepted,' wrote James' widow, Dollie, many years later, 'a tribute not only to the refugees but to the village who took these children and their guardians to their hearts – no mean feat on both sides considering the feelings about Germans, refugees or not, at that time.'

Walter Rothschild died in 1937 and Victor succeeded to the title. As Lord Rothschild he became, of course, head of the family, and as head of the family he received thousands of letters begging for help. He took an active interest in the Central British Fund for German Jewry, founded by Simon Marks and Herbert Samuel, which had its headquarters at New Court. The pressures were unabating after November 1938 when a Jewish boy living in Paris, whose parents had been sent to a concentration camp, shot and killed Herr von Rath, the third secretary of the German Embassy. The Nazi Party used the occasion to incite a pogrom in which thousands of Jews were rounded up and sent to concentration camps and millions of pounds worth of Jewish property was destroyed.

On 12 November 1938, Lord Rothschild wrote a letter to *The Times* calling the attention of the British public to what was happening in Germany. Although some people warned, he said, 'that criticisms made in foreign countries of the treatment of the Jews would only increase their torments,' he had 'no fear of doing this because their torments cannot be increased except by such refinements of torture as would· create general horror in Germany itself...'[8]

The following month, however, Lord Rothschild apologized to a large gathering at the Mansion House for his optimism. The occasion was the launching of Lord Baldwin's Fund for German refugees which Victor himself had been instrumental in setting up. 'I have discovered that I was wrong. Tortures have been invented and have been inflicted, and the word medieval which has so often been used to describe what is going on is an insult to the past.' A few months later, in May 1939, Lord Rothschild put to auction at Christie's his most valuable picture – *The Braddyll Family* by Joshua Reynolds – and donated the proceeds to the Baldwin Fund.

While the English and French Rothschilds were raising money for refugees, Baron Louis of Austria was arguing with Herr Heinrich Himmler in a Viennese prison.

The Third Reich had cast its grim shadow over Austria from the moment of Hitler's accession. Those who bothered to read *Mein Kampf* knew that Hitler regarded the reunion of Germany and Austria as 'a task to be furthered with every means our lives long'. It was not surprising, therefore, to learn that German Nazis were supplying Austrian Nazis with weapons and dynamite. Soon a reign of terror had begun in which railways, power stations and government buildings were blown up, while officials were kidnapped and murdered. In July 1934, 154 members of the Viennese Nazi Party, wearing army uniforms, burst into the Federal Building and shot Chancellor Dollfuss in the throat at a range of two feet. Hitler received the news while listening to *Das Rheingold* at the annual Wagner Festival at Bayreuth. Friedelind Wagner, a granddaughter of the great composer, was sitting near him and later wrote that 'he could scarcely wipe the delight off his face'.

Despite the assassination of Dollfuss the Nazis failed in their attempt to seize power. Thirty-seven-year-old Kurt von Schuschnigg, a deputy, rallied government forces, led them into action and quickly regained control. Shortly afterwards he assumed the chancellorship but like most of the statesmen of Europe he was no match for Hitler's twists and turns, lies and promises and frenzied ravings. In May 1935 Hitler declared that Germany 'neither intends

Baron Eugene von Rothschild, younger brother of Louis, moved his family and fortune out of Austria after the Nazis began to be given important positions in the government in 1936.

nor wishes to interfere in the internal affairs of Austria, to annex Austria nor to conclude an *Anschluss*'. Yet at the same time Hitler's minister in Vienna, Herr von Papen, was writing to Berlin: 'National Socialism must and will overpower the new Austrian ideology.'

The Rothschilds were on close terms with Dr von Schuschnigg who kept them informed on his dealings with Germany. As there was no place for a leader without hope, it was inevitable that Schuschnigg should cling to the belief that he could preserve Austria's independence; and no doubt a logical consequence that he tried to do it by adopting a policy of appeasement. Although neither Baron Louis, nor his two brothers, Eugene and Alphonse, shared his optimism, they could offer no alternatives. In July 1936 Schuschnigg signed an agreement with Germany which he called a compromise but which proved to be Austria's death warrant. In secret clauses he agreed to pardon Nazi offenders and to allow Nazis to occupy important government positions.

When the Rothschilds learned of this deal they were convinced that Austria's days were numbered. Alphonse and Eugene moved their families and transferred their money to France and Switzerland. But Louis, who was a bachelor, settled down to a legal tussle in Vienna. He summoned lawyers from London and Prague and began the long complicated process of transferring Vitkowitz, the vast iron and steel works in Czechoslovakia, acquired by his grandfather, Salomon von Rothschild, from Austrian ownership to British ownership.

The legal proceedings exploited the fact that a minority shareholder, another Jewish family called von Gutmann, needed cash and wished to sell its holding. This excuse was seized upon to revise the company's corporate structure. It was not difficult to persuade the Czech Prime Minister that Austrian control of Vitkowitz could prove dangerous because of the growing Nazi Party; nor to persuade Schuschnigg that the Czech Government itched to seize an Austrian company, an event that would shatter relations with Hitler. Both agreed that the company shares should be transferred to the great British company, Allied Assurance, which happened, of course, to have been founded by Nathan Rothschild and was still controlled by the family.

Louis' brothers begged him to leave Austria while there was still time. But the cool, sophisticated, fifty-five-year-old bachelor Baron did not believe that disaster could overtake a Rothschild. Indeed Louis' celebrated company, the Kreditanstalt, had recovered from a threat that seemed almost as dangerous as Hitler. In 1930 the Kreditanstalt tottered on the verge of bankruptcy, and was forced to suspend all payments. This was because the Federal Chancellor had begged Louis to take over the BodenKreditanstalt the country's largest agricultural bank which was nearing collapse; and to extend credit to Balkan firms and governments, once part of the Austrian

The beautiful Baroness Kitty, Eugene's first wife, was to die soon after the war.

Empire, but which now were too impoverished to meet their obligations. Louis was unwise to accept for a year later his life-saving operation landed his own company in the quagmire. However the Rothschild family closed ranks and came to the rescue in a dramatic way,
for Louis had pledged the Rothschild name. Years later Baron
Guy explained: 'My family raised the sum of eight million dollars,
nearly a hundred million francs, a staggering sum at the time, so
that it could never be said, not even once in History, that a Rothschild had failed to honour his signature.'[9]

The money enabled Louis to recover his position, and once again
he controlled a network of industries throughout Central Europe. To
flee from the enemy before his business empire was irrevocably lost
would be, he decided, abject behaviour for Austria's most famous
Jew. Whatever he did, it would have to be done with panache.

In February 1938, scarcely eighteen months after Hitler's assur-
ances that he had no design on Austria, Schuschnigg was summoned to Berchtesgarten. All vestige of self-control had vanished
and the German leader was wild-eyed and hysterical. Unless Schush-
nigg appointed the Nazi leader, Seyss Inquart, to the Ministry of the
Interior, German troops would invade his country. 'Here is the draft
of the document,' cried Hitler, almost flinging the paper at him.
'There is nothing to be discussed. I will not change one single iota.
You will either sign it as it is and fulfil my demands within three days,
or I will order the march into Austria.'

When Schuschnigg returned to Austria he did as he was told and
gave Seyss Inquart the ministry. But at the same time he broadcast
to the nation saying: 'This far and no further.' In Graz a mob of
twenty thousand Nazis, infuriated by his speech, invaded the town
square, tore down the Austrian flag and raised the German swastika.
On 1 March a courier from Baron Édouard in Paris knocked on the
door of Baron Louis's chalet at Kitzbühel, where he was skiing,
begging him to leave Austria with no further delay. But although
the nonchalant Louis put away his skis, he returned to Vienna.

Meanwhile rebellion fomented by Germany had broken out in
many parts of the country and Schuschnigg announced that a
plebiscite would be held to determine Austria's future. This decision
threw Hitler into such a fury that he sent Schuschnigg an ultimatum:
unless he resigned, and appointed Seyss Inquart his successor, German troops would cross the frontier. Schuschnigg capitulated to
both these demands but in the end, at 9 pm on the evening of
11 March, the German troops came anyway and Schuschnigg was
arrested and thrown into jail.

The next morning Baron Louis, accompanied by his valet, went
to the airport to fly to Italy where he was due to play polo. But it was
too late. The S.S. were in charge of the field and confiscated his passport. 'After that', said the valet, Édouard, 'we went home and waited'.

In the evening two men with swastika arm bands knocked on the

Rothschild door. A butler appeared and told them that Baron Louis was not at home. The next day six steel helmeted soldiers called to take him away and this time the Baron received the spokesman. He would accompany the men, he said, but after luncheon which was just about to be served. The soldiers held a whispered consultation and apparently could think of no reason why the Baron should not have his lunch. After coffee and liqueurs he departed with them and when he had not returned by nightfall, the valet packed his master's toilet kit, books, bedsheets, embroidered slippers, clothes for indoors and out. But when he arrived at police headquarters with the pigskin case embossed with the Rothschild crest, he was greeted with furious laughter and told to go home.

Baron Louis scarcely turned a hair at the hardships to which he was subjected. An athlete who climbed mountains and played polo, who rode the famous Lippizaners in the Spanish Riding School and was a scratch golfer, he possessed a body that was hard and fit. Indeed, when he was told to busy himself moving sandbags in the cellar, along with a number of Communist prisoners, he found that he could work quicker and better than his companions. 'We got on rather well,' he recalled later. 'We agreed that it was the world's most classless cellar.'

However, Louis was not relegated to the basement for long. Soon he found himself at the Hotel Metropole in Vienna which had been requisitioned by the Gestapo. He was placed in a room next to his old friend, Chancellor von Schuschnigg. Now he had twenty-four guards – 'my grenadiers', he called them; and he whiled away the tedious hours by lecturing them on geology and botany. Outside, only a few streets away, his home was being looted, not by unruly mobs, but systematically by the country's new rulers. 'I myself from our apartment in the Plosslgasse,' wrote William Shirer, 'watched squads of S.S. men carting off silver, tapestries, paintings and other loot from the Rothschild palace next door.'

Baron Louis was interviewed by a man named Weber, who introduced himself as an intermediary of Hermann Goering. The Baron could have his freedom if he paid Goering £40,000 and turned over Vitkowitz to the German Reich. But, the Baron explained with exaggerated apology, Vitkowitz no longer belonged to him. A few weeks later Weber was arrested. 'Apparently internecine war had broken out in Berlin, and Goering suffered a set-back in favour of Heinrich Himmler. Himmler did not send an intermediary but travelled to Vienna and interviewed the Baron himself. He offered the prisoner a cigarette but Louis declined, his eyes searching the dreaded face of his inquisitor. Later he said indignantly: "That fellow had a sty in his eye, and was trying to hide it." '

Louis, not the Nazis, dictated his own ransom terms, in conjunction with his family. For his freedom he would assign to the Third Reich all his Austrian assets. (He knew that the Nazis would seize them anyway.) But Vitkowitz would only be surrendered after he was safely out of the country – and for £3,000,000. This also was a bluff as Louis believed that war was inevitable, in which case the iron and steel works would pass out of his possession anyway.

Apparently Himmler did not share this view, as he did his best to persuade Louis to modify his terms. He began by trying to make the room of his distinguished prisoner more comfortable. His guards carried out his order by bringing in a number of hideous objects, including an orange velvet bed-cover, an ugly Louis XV vase, and a radio with a skirt sewed around the base. 'The place looked like a Cracow bordello!' Louis reminisced.

The Baron refused to bargain over the ransom terms and a few days later he was told that Himmler had accepted his conditions. He was free to leave at once. But Louis was not a man to be ordered about, and to everyone's astonishment he announced that he would remain until the morning. Eleven pm was too late an hour to disturb his friends, he explained, as the servants would be in bed.

A few days later Louis arrived safely in Paris, and two months later, in July 1939, the Reich undertook to buy Vitkowitz for the agreed sum. But war broke out in September and the contract was never signed. However when the holocaust was over pressure was applied to Communist Czechoslovakia to honour the agreement. The Rothschilds finally were compensated to the tune of £1,000,000 which everyone agreed was better than nothing at all.

While Baron Louis was busy transferring Vitkowitz to the care of his British relations, twenty-six-year-old Lord Rothschild, was instructing Messrs Sotheby and Co. to offer for sale the contents of his grandfather's vast house at 148 Piccadilly. The house was almost a museum, packed with pictures and furniture and *objets d'art* acquired by the great Nathan's son, Lionel. As Victor was a scientist, living at Cambridge, he had no use for the house; and without the house no place for the contents. So he came to the conclusion that there was no option but to sell the lot.

The sale began on 19 April 1937 and lasted four days, while a further three days were devoted to the auction of his grandmother's wonderful silver collection which had belonged to her father, Baron Willy von Rothschild of Frankfurt. On the opening day twenty-one pictures were sold. 'In realizing £41,252 the first day's sale at 148 Piccadilly far exceeded expectations,' wrote the correspondent of *The Times*. This was because *The Courtyard* by Pieter de Hooch went for £17,500, while in 1928, only nine years earlier, a work by the same artist had fetched but £11,600. *A Maidservant Returning from Market* by Rembrandt's pupil, Nicholas Maes, which had sold in 1822 for £76 went for £1,100; an interior by Eglon van der Heer which in 1823 had fetched £430, for £800; an inn scene by Philips Wouvermans sold in 1832 for £120, for £850.

Almost all the prices were regarded as high. Frank Partridge paid a thousand pounds for a Louis XV marquetery *bureau de dame*; a rock-crystal chandelier, inscribed 'F. Rinnaldi, 1648 Milan', went for £340; a sixteenth-century Augsburg clock for £620. Duveen bid against a number of French dealers for a secrétaire by Martin Carlin, cabinet maker to Louis XVI, which he secured for £8,000; a pair of Gobelins tapestries designed by Charles le Brun went for £1,300.

The proceeds from the sale of continental silver which took place in Sotheby's auction rooms totalled £40,000 which also was considered 'eminently satisfactory'. The two rarest items were a painted ostrich egg cup mounted in silver gilt, the work of a sixteenth century Leipzig craftsman, Elias Geier, which went for £2,900; and a Strasburg crystal and gilt double cup, of the same date, which fetched £2,000. Altogether the contents of the house brought a grand total of £125,000.

That same year 148 Piccadilly was sold to a Garden Club. When a reporter asked Lord Rothschild whether he was planning to buy another house in London he replied laconically: 'I'll think about that when the forthcoming war has come and gone.'

Although it was rare for a Rothschild to dispose of a Rothschild inheritance, Victor was not entirely devoid of family characteristics. One of his most strongly developed traits was a collector's instinct. Throughout the 1930s he bought a few pictures (among them several Cézannes), a few pieces of early eighteenth-century silver, a few rare books and manuscripts, which today, in the aggregate, are valued at £2,000,000. However many of these pictures and pieces are no longer in his possession. For instance in 1951 he donated to Trinity College, Cambridge the library he had assembled which included such items as *Lyrical Ballads* by Wordsworth and Coleridge with corrections in Coleridge's hand-writing; Gibbon's annotated copy of Herodotus; and Gray's *Odes*, annotated by Horace Walpole.

Chapter XI

The Second World War

(1939–45)

ALL THREE FRENCH ROTHSCHILDS AT THE HEAD OF THE bank today were serving at the front when Germany over-ran France in the spring of 1940. The sons of Baron Robert – Alain and Élie, thirty and twenty-three years old – were taken prisoner, Alain in the hospital where he was removed after being wounded, Élie, near the Belgian frontier. Élie had gone to war on a horse and was captured along with most of his cavalry regiment, the truly Anciens 11èmes Cuirassiers. Both brothers were fortunate enough to be treated as officers, not as Jews.

Nevertheless, they raged at the inactivity imposed upon them. Élie immediately began to plot an escape from Nienburg, near Hamburg, where he was imprisoned, but his plans were detected and he was sent to Colditz for a year, then to Lübeck, an even more rigorous reprisal camp, where he finished the war. The camp, however, had one attraction; here he became united with his brother, Alain, who had tried to escape from Oflag 6, at Soest, in a laundry basket of dirty linen. He had been caught and transferred to Lübeck as a punishment.

Only in the unlikely field of matrimony was the restless, rebel-lious Élie successful in imposing his will. He wrote to his childhood sweetheart, the clever, vivacious Liliane Fould-Springer, and asked if she would marry him by proxy. Although the Fould-Springers were opposed to the idea, pointing out that it was not helpful to bear the name of Rothschild with the Gestapo swarming over France, Liliane agreed. The wedding ceremonies of bride and groom took place on different days many months apart. Élie gave his pledge at Colditz on 7 October 1941, and Liliane at Cannes on 7 April 1942.

Such circumstances would make any marriage poignant, but this one also had a Romeo and Juliet flavour, for Liliane was a great-niece of Achille Fould who had fought James de Rothschild so bitterly in the days of the Second Empire. Fould's Crédit Mobilier had threatened to smash the Rothschild financial supremacy, but in the end attacker, and not attacked, had bitten the dust.

The third Rothschild who was at the front when German armour came pouring through France was Guy, son and heir of the senior partner of Messieurs de Rothschild Frères, Baron Édouard. Édouard and his cousin Robert, both elderly gentlemen, had fled to New York in the spring of 1940. Guy served in a motorized cavalry unit which fought in Belgium and eventually retreated to Dunkirk

Élie de Rothschild's photograph from the files of Colditz Castle where he was imprisoned for a year during the war.

where it was evacuated by the British. Guy returned to France almost at once; a few months later his regiment was disbanded and although the tide was running strongly against Jews, he was singled out to carry the standard, an honour reserved for the bravest. A year later he joined his wife and father in America, but in the spring of 1943 he made his way back to London to serve Charles de Gaulle. His ship was torpedoed *en route* and he spent the night – seven hours in all – on a raft top-heavy with people and washed by every wave. At dawn the survivors were rescued by a British destroyer. When Guy reached England he spent a few days recuperating as a guest of his cousin, Miriam Rothschild, in Northamptonshire. Ashton Wold, the big house belonging to Miriam's mother, had been turned into a hospital. Miriam worked at the Ministry of Supply during the week

235

but often helped in the hospital at weekends. Here she met a handsome Hungarian-Jewish refugee who had anglicized his name to George Lane, joined the British commandoes, and been wounded in action. In 1941, after a whirlwind courtship, Miriam married him.

All Rothschilds of fighting age squeezed the maximum adventure out of the war. It was a conflict that perfectly suited the family temperament. Not only was the cause just, not only did it have a special significance for Jews, but the swiftly changing tempo, the cross currents of passionate allegiance and secret resistance offered great scope to intrepid spirits. Although, as someone pointed out, the Rothschilds were field-marshals in civilian life, a rank denied them in war, each one operated with the authority and individuality of a special agent; and in some instances that is what they were.

Dr Henri de Rothschild's two sons, both over forty in 1943, arrived in London within a few months of Guy. James, who had flown aeroplanes in the First World War joined de Gaulle's Military Liaison section, while Philippe trained in the civil affairs department. Philippe had had all sorts of hair-raising adventures. He had gone to Morocco in 1940 to escape the German occupation but had been

Guy de Rothschild with his parents, Baron and Baroness Édouard. Guy served in a motorized cavalry unit which was eventually evacuated by the British at Dunkirk and, in 1943, joined General de Gaulle's forces in London.

236

arrested by the Vichy Government. In prison he started a keep-fit campaign and a language school, his star pupil being M. Mendès-France. Finally he was released and returned to France but as he soon saw that he was heading for a concentration camp, he walked across the Pyrenees, made his way to Portugal and embarked for England. When he arrived in London he went to see M. Gaston Palewski at the Hyde Park Hotel. As he was walking through the lobby a stranger ran up to him and embraced him with deep emotion saying: 'Thank you, thank you, for helping us through the blitz and making life bearable.' Philippe was amazed. 'Who are you? What on earth are you talking about?' 'Mouton Rothschild, Baron Philippe, those lovely bottles, each one with your name on it!', the man replied and then introduced himself as Cyril Connolly.

Before long Philippe found himself billeted at the Free French Club, none other than 107 Piccadilly. This was the house bought by Nathan Rothschild in the 1820s and later occupied by Nathan's daughter Hannah, a sister of Philippe's great-grandfather. However, with the cross-channel invasion the Rothschilds again were scattered far and wide. James's wife, Claude, was smuggled into France before the landings to make contact with resistance workers imprisoned by the Germans. For her work she received the Croix de Guerre and the Légion d'Honneur. Guy was one of the first to arrive in Paris where he served as an aide to de Gaulle's Military Governor, while James was attached to a French fighting unit as an interpreter. Philippe was put in charge of the Le Havre area and, like Claude, won the Croix de Guerre and the Légion d'Honneur; these decorations were also won by Guy, Alain and Élie.

Meanwhile Lionel's eldest son, the English Edmund, was serving in the British Army. Eddie had graduated from Cambridge in the spring of 1938 and in the autumn had been sent around the world by his father as the finishing touch to the educative process. The year, of course, was overshadowed by Hitler's menacing behaviour and Eddie, a quiet, thoughtful youth with a profound sense of mission unusual in someone barely twenty-two was deeply disturbed. 'Am I Civis Britannicus or have I to give up everything I know and have and become Civis Judaeus?' he wrote in his diary after Munich, on 5 October 1939. '. . . A day of almost unceasing rain. The world seems to weep for the tormented people of Israel – or is it fancy?'[1]

When war broke out Edmund joined the Buckinghamshire Yeomanry, and served as a captain in an artillery regiment in North Africa and Italy. In 1944 Churchill authorized the formation of a Jewish Infantry Brigade and Edmund joined the field regiment as a major in command of 'P' Battery. The Brigade began as a mixture of Yorkshiremen and Jews but grew to contain Jewish refugees from almost every country in Europe and from Palestine. As Palestine was not a nation, and the British did not wish to offend Arab susceptibilities, no Palestinian flag was allowed to be displayed. However

Major Rothschild found a happy compromise. 'When we had a march past the General,' wrote Edmund, 'I arranged a dais with two flagpoles, one with the Union Jack and the other with the blue-and-white Magden David flag. The General looked very sharply at me and asked. "What is this?" I replied, "Sir, that is the P Battery Standard", and we got away with it.'[2]

After VE Day Edmund's brigade marched from Italy across the Alps, through Germany to Holland and Belgium. On the way they went through Mannheim. At the entrance to the city they passed a stone triumphal arch with the inscription '*Judenrein*' engraved on it. The city had been heavily bombed and shelled and there was scarcely a house left standing.

I was leading the column in an armoured car, [wrote Edmund]. As we entered the city, a few people came out of the rubble of their shattered house to stare at us and the word went round: 'Die Juden kommen, die Juden kommen.' More and more people came out to watch us pass and by the time we came to the centre of the city before crossing the Rhine, about two hundred people had gathered in the central square. Suddenly there was a scuffle and from out of the crowd came three or four people dressed in Belsen garb who ran toward my armoured car, where they knelt down and kissed the sign on it, the Magden David.[3]

It would have been even more dramatic if Edmund's regiment had marched through Frankfurt or Cassel, but these cities were in the American sector. Nevertheless history had its own bizarre twists, for the princely family of Hesse-Cassel, like the Rothschilds, had continued to prosper through the years and, when war broke out in 1939, were one of the richest families in Europe. Although in the days of Napoleon the Hesses and the Rothschilds had joined hands against the common aggressor, this time the two families were on opposite sides.

The head of the Hesse-Cassels, Prince Philip, was a passionate supporter of Hitler; and as he was married to Princess Mafalda, daughter of the King of Italy, he was chosen to serve as a messenger between Hitler and Mussolini. When Hitler quarrelled with the Italian dictator, poor Mafalda was thrown into a concentration camp. A deeply spiritual woman, she managed to forget her own tribulations and devoted herself to nursing and caring for her fellow sufferers. Eventually she died of starvation and maltreatment, one of the great heroines of the war.

Prince Philip survived and is still alive, living not far from Frankfurt at the palace of the Empress Frederick (Queen Victoria's eldest daughter), the Friedrichshof at Kronberg which has been turned into a hotel. Apparently the Hesse-Cassels continue to have a talent for making money, for although Prince Philip backed the wrong side and survived a holocaust, he is reputed to be the richest man in Germany, and the richest prince in Europe. This is the same claim that people made in 1800 for the Elector of Hesse-Cassel, the ancestor who unwittingly helped Mayer Rothschild to lay the foundation of his own family fortune.

Meanwhile Anthony and Lionel de Rothschild tried to keep the bank running. During the terrible air attacks on the City in 1940–41 Anthony was at his desk in New Court every day. In the evenings, accompanied by his wife, Yvonne, he had supper in the restaurant and slept in the cellar, surrounded by vaults and safe deposit boxes. The morning sun often rose on a world of chaos: street after street not only had its gaping holes, but was inundated with water from broken mains. New Court seemed to be protected by some magical hand, for soon it stood alone, a single building, looking on a sea of rubble.

Nevertheless the brothers took precautions. Early in 1940 it occurred to them that if a bomb hit New Court both the dynasty and the business might come to an end. As a result they formed Rothschild Continuations Ltd, a holding company to which the shares of the bank were transferred and which guaranteed a future for Rothschild youths. Lionel died peacefully, however, in 1942, and Anthony remained in sole charge until his own retirement fourteen years later.

The war offered not only scope but variety, and the Rothschilds took full advantage of the diversions open to them in the line of duty. This particularly applied to twenty-nine-year-old Victor, the present Lord Rothschild, who offered his services to the Ministry of War and soon found himself detailed to dismantle 'sabotage bombs'.

This occupation had one advantage. It was not overcrowded, therefore if one survived it was easy to reach the top. Furthermore there were no experts to awe the novice, as the sabotage bombs manufactured by the Germans were new and ingenious. They were camouflaged to look like a variety of harmless objects such as lumps of coal, a thermos flask containing real tea, a mackintosh, a walking stick, a coat hanger.

The bombs contained a fuse connected to a delay mechanism which sometimes operated by clockwork, sometimes by acid eating through metal. The problem was to get the fuse out of the bomb. The enemy made the operation as difficult as possible, usually by incorporating booby traps so that the removal of the fuse caused the bomb to explode; sometimes the fuse itself was booby-trapped so that it exploded when it was being examined after removal.

Many of these bombs found their way from Algeciras to Gibraltar. The Spaniards allowed the Germans to sink a vessel outside the Algeciras harbour, from which deep sea divers swam across to Gibraltar. Sometimes they tried to blow up Allied shipping, sometimes they slipped their bombs into crates of vegetables, or other articles, being sent to Britain.

There was no one to instruct Lord Rothschild in his work. Dismantling bombs, he was told, was simply a question of trial and error, and not too much error. Fortunately he proved to be a brilliant choice. 'Who else', commented a colleague, 'combined nimble, jazz-playing fingers with a first-class scientific brain?' A stout heart also was a qualification, for Victor frequently was forced to face the unpleasant consequences of failure. Once he was called upon to deal with a crate of onions that had been imported from Spain and had turned up in Northampton. 'The fuse,' he wrote, 'turned out to be a type that might be booby-trapped. On this occasion when taking the bomb to pieces I thought it desirable for there to be a record in case of accidents, and I therefore dictated through a microphone each step in the process of dismantling the bomb.'

On another occasion, after travelling to Liverpool to lecture the police on sabotage, one of the officers asked him to look at a large can of liquid eggs which had come from China but was thought to have been interfered with in Gibraltar. 'Having extracted the fuse,' wrote Victor, 'which was a seven-day clock-work type, I took the bomb and its fuse to London in my car. The fuse was suspected of being booby-trapped as a Naval Officer in Gibraltar had, a few weeks earlier, been seriously wounded when taking an identical fuse to pieces. I took the fuse to pieces in my office in London, kneeling behind a heavily padded armchair so that if it was booby-trapped, only my hands and the lower part of my arms would be damaged. All went well.'[4]

Soon Colonel Rothschild was looked upon as the nation's leading expert in dismantling; and as one step leads to another, it occurred to some fanciful brain that he was just the person to protect one of Britain's 'key points' against enemy saboteurs. The key point was Winston Churchill; the anticipated weapon, poison; the carrier, gifts of food, drink or cigars. On one occasion when the Prime Minister was walking from 10 Downing Street to the House of Commons, a French General came up to him, saluted smartly, and presented him with a Virginia ham, one of his favourite delicacies. Churchill told the secretary who was accompanying him to give it to the Downing Street cook with instructions that he would have it for breakfast. According to routine, however, the ham was sent to Rothschild to ensure that it had not been poisoned. The latter consulted the Medical Research Council who said that in the twelve hours available there was no chance of testing it for deadly bacteria. But if, on the other hand, it had been poisoned, the best way of finding out would be to feed a slice to the Medical Research Council's cat, which they were prepared to sacrifice for the sake of the Prime Minister. This was done, and when in the early hours of the morning the cat leapt out of its basket and swished its tail, Churchill was allowed to have the ham for breakfast.

The Prime Minister was not told that his food was scrutinized for poison; but officials were unable to hide the fact that his cigars were examined, for the simple reason that whenever he received this sort of gift he did not see it for days, sometimes weeks. On one occasion, when he was running out of Havana cigars, an admirer sent him a supply of ten thousand. 'But where are they?' he fumed. 'Who's whisked them away? It doesn't seem too much to ask that I should be allowed to enjoy my own cigars. . .' So he was told that Victor Rothschild, whose grandfather had entertained him as a youth, was vetting them for explosives or other lethal substances. In order to satisfy Churchill's impatience Lord Rothschild decided to rely on statistical techniques, testing one in every ten, or some such number. Apparently this fascinated Churchill who liked to speculate on the gamble, comparing it romantically to Russian roulette.

Occasionally the Rothschild team derived unexpected benefit from their protective role. At the end of the war they accompanied Churchill to Paris, supposedly to ward off attempts on his life. A distinguished industrialist presented him with twelve bottles of very old, priceless Armagnac which, as usual, were sent to Victor for examination. 'I said,' Lord Rothschild wrote many years later, 'that I could not take the responsibility of releasing the bottles to him unless a thirteenth was produced for testing. The industrialist reluctantly agreed to this and I and my colleague had a very enjoyable evening.'[5]

While in Paris Victor installed himself at 23 Avenue de Marigny, the great house set in several acres of gardens in the midst of Paris, belonging to the Robert de Rothschilds and their children, Diane, Alain, Cécile and Élie. This imposing residence, across the street from the Élysée Palace, was packed with priceless furniture and *objets d'art*. Inexplicably, it was the only Rothschild property in the capital that had not been stripped of its possessions, despite the fact that it served as German Air Force Headquarters and often was frequented by Hermann Goering, famous for his light fingers. Later, when the Rothschilds, housekeeper who remained in charge throughout the occupation was asked why the Germans had respected the property, she replied: 'Even the Germans know that Führers come and go but the Rothschilds remain forever.' The French servants, however, had taken no chances and had done everything in their power to remove temptation from the path of the invaders. They had removed the most valuable pictures and other priceless objects to a secret room, behind the book-cases, where they remained undiscovered throughout the occupation.

The house was not very comfortable in 1944 due to a shortage of fuel for heat and water. But Victor decided that as it had escaped despoliation by the Germans it would be sad to see it ransacked by the Allies, and dutifully took possession. Luckily he had some influence with the Americans as he was seconded by the United States Army to give a course on the mysteries of counter sabotage. Indeed, in 1946 he was awarded the US Bronze Star for his work. In the citation President Truman referred to him as 'one of the world's greatest experts'. 'He gave unstintingly of his time and energy,' said Truman, 'in personally training American officers as counter-sabotage specialists. He wrote and edited many technical manuals used as text books by the US Army, especially by bomb disposal engineers and counter-intelligence personnel.'[6]

During this period Victor prevented rapacious generals from taking possession of his cousins' house. He managed to hold them at bay until Baron Robert's daughters – Diane and Cécile – his sons, daughters-in-law and grand-children reinstalled themselves under the spacious family roof.

Other Rothschilds were not so fortunate. Forced to flee for their lives when the German army streamed through France in the spring of 1940, all members of the family made hasty attempts to safeguard their most valuable possessions. The task was daunting, as many Rothschilds – such as Henri, Édouard, Maurice, and Maurice's sister, Miriam, not only owned large houses in Paris – (in the Rue du Faubourg Saint-Honoré, La Muette, the Rue de Monceau, and the Rue Saint-Florentin), but equally imposing houses in the country, ranging from Robert's Château de Laversine, near Chantilly, to Édouard's palace at Ferrières; Henri's Abbaye des Vaulx de Cernay to Maurice's Armainvilliers. They placed their valuables in the homes of friends, in bank vaults, neutral embassies and museums. One of the hiding places in the south west of France was discovered by the French authorities because of 'denunciation' by an anonymous informer. The directors of the Louvre were informed and immediately took the treasures under their protection, 'for the duration'.

Yet much of it was to no avail. In the autumn of 1940 Field Marshal Keitel, Commander of the German Armed Forces, announced that Alfred Rosenberg had been appointed custodian of the arts, a polite word for looter-in-chief and that all subterfuges to protect Jewish property would be uncovered and declared null and void by the Gestapo. Keitel's declaration read as follows:

The ownership status before the war in France, prior to the declaration of war on September 1, 1939, shall be the criterion.
Ownership transfers to the French State or similar transfers completed after this date are irrelevant and legally invalid (for example Polish and Czeck libraries in Paris, *possessions of the Palais Rothschild or other ownerless Jewish possessions*). Reservations regarding search, seizure and transportation to Germany on the basis of the above reasons will not be recognized.
Reichsleiter Rosenberg and/or his deputy Reichshauptstellenleiter Ebert have received clear instructions from the Fuhrer personally governing the right of seizure; he is entitled to transport to Germany cultural goods which appear valuable to him and to safeguard them there. The Fuhrer has reserved for himself the decision as to their use.

Hitler meant business for he instructed the Gestapo to assist Rosenberg in uncovering 'hidden Jewish treasures', and Rosenberg assembled a staff of art experts to deal with the confiscated objects. When Paris was liberated one of Rosenberg's Nazi assistants told the French military authorities:

After the seizure of the most famous Jewish art collections in Paris, all abandoned dwellings of the wealthy Parisian Jews, as well as the warehouses of all shipping firms and many other art depots of emigrated Jews, which were very often camouflaged by French gentiles, were systematically searched by the special staff for pictorial art and very considerable art treasures were found in this manner. These seizures were carried out on the basis of exhaustive preliminary investigations into the address lists of the French police authorities, on the basis of Jewish handbooks, warehouses inventories and order books of French art and collection catalogues. The clearly established Jewish origin of the individual owners was proved in each case in cooperation with the French police authorities and the Sicherheitsdienst (Security Service) as well as on the basis of the political source material of the staff itself.[7]

The author of this statement swore to the following affidavit, revealing that nearly twenty per cent of the confiscated treasures came from the Rothschilds.

Reichsleiter Rosenberg's Staff   St. Georgen/Attergau
Special Staff for Pictorial Arts   Kogl 1, 14 July 1944

Ennumeration of seized works of art, according to the inventory lists received up to 13 July 1944 from 203 locations.

The most important locations [collections] are:
I.   ROTHSCHILD with 3, 978 inventory numbers
II.   KAHN with 1, 202 inventory numbers
III.   David WEILL with 1, 121 inventory numbers
IV.   Levy de VENZION with 989 inventory numbers
V.   SELIGMANN Brothers with 556 inventory numbers
The total number of objects is 21,903.

Over 137 freight cars stacked with works of art left France for Germany in the three years from 1941 to 1944. Yet once again the adage about the ill wind was proved accurate, for if the valuables had not been removed it is doubtful whether they would have survived the incoming allied armies. As it was, they were handled with great care by the German art experts.

These shipments were taken to six repositories in the Reich, unpacked and stored with attention to all conservation, air raid and fire protection measures .... A restoration workshop equipped with all technical aids was established by the special staff at one of the repositories (Buxheim) and has been occupied with the care and restoration of seized articles of artistic value .... Several hundreds of the works of art that had been neglected by their Jewish owners or had earlier been inexpertly restored were restored in this workshop and their preservation assured.[8]

In the autumn of 1944, however, no one knew what had happened to the treasures exported to Germany. That spring James Rorimer of

Overleaf It was in the theatrical, pseudo-Gothic castle of Neuschwanstein, built by Ludwig II of Bavaria that most of the Rothschild art treasures were found after the war.

the New York Metropolitan Museum of Art had been appointed Monuments, Fine Arts and Archives Officer attached to the American Seventh Army. Originally his task was to protect cultural objects in the wake of the invading forces, but after a stay of several months in Paris he became increasingly interested in 'the missing treasures' that had vanished from France to Germany. He did his own detective work, and placed his faith in Mlle Rose Valland, who had worked at the Musée du Jeu de Paume, and been present during Goering's many visits to select works of art for his private collections. Rose was certain, although she had no proof, that many of France's treasures had gone to the two castles near Füssen on the southern confines of Bavaria. One of these was Neuschwanstein, a fantastic pseudo-Gothic castle constructed by the mad King Ludwig II of Bavaria.

James Rorimer put his faith in Rose and when the American army reached Füssen in the spring of 1945 he took a jeep and drove to Ludwig's remote summer palace. 'As we approached from the north through an open valley,' he wrote, 'it looked in its mountain setting like a prototype of all story-book castles. It was a castle in the air come to life for egocentric and mad thirsters after power; a picturesque, romantic and remote setting for a gangster crowd to carry on its art looting activities.'

As the castle was built at the side of a mountain the floors were linked by almost vertical winding staircases. Works of art were stacked in every nook and cranny, most of them marked with a Paris cypher; paintings, jewellery, furniture, tapestries, books, silver, bric-a-brac, everything was there.

We were guided to a hidden, thick steel door; this one locked with two keys. Inside there were two large chests of world-famous Rothschild jewels and box upon box of jewel-encrusted metalwork . . .

In April of 1941 thirty special baggage cars of art objects, and in October of that same year twenty-three carloads more, had been brought here from France. One shipment alone of these objects back to France required 36 freight cars for 1,221 crates which contained 6,000 objects. I passed through the rooms as in a trance, hoping that the Germans had lived up to their reputation for being methodical and had photographs, catalogues and records of all these things. Without them it would take twenty years to identify the agglomeration of loot.[9]

Rorimer's hopes were realized. In one room there was a photographic laboratory in which Rosenberg's acquisitions were recorded of the 203 private collections taken from France. Their contents revealed that the bulk of Rothschild property was in the building: furniture stacked to the ceiling in specially constructed racks, tapestried fire screens, books, jewels, and paintings, among them Baron Maurice's *Three Graces* by Rubens.

The filing cabinets were so vitally important that they had to be protected.

We could take no chances on any harm coming to these irreplaceable records [wrote Rorimer]. We decided that neither the Germans nor the American guards could be permitted to enter these two rooms under any circumstances. Toward that end we nailed down the trap door in the floor, which connected with a secret escape ladder, and covered it with a heavy steel trunk. We locked the doors behind us, and as a final expedient I took one of the antique Rothschild seals – SEMPER FIDELIS – and sealed the doors with sealing wax and cord.

Gradually members of the Rothschild family filtered back to France and gradually their possessions were restored to them. As the older generation had been stripped of their nationality by the Vichy Government, and some of the properties put up to auction, lawyers wrangled for months to straighten out the legal complications. Apparently most of the people who had bought their confiscated possessions were only too willing to return them if they could get back their money. The new government agreed to reimburse, and in the end the difficulties were overcome.

The Austrian Rothschilds decided to remain in the United States. As most of Central Europe had come under Soviet rule, there was no future for private bankers in this part of the world. Eugene bought a house on Long Island where he lived with his wife, a famous beauty, the former Countess Kitty Shönborn. In 1946 she died, and after this he spent most of his time travelling.

He had a minor triumph involving no less a person than Einstein. Although Eugene had never cared for banking he was very good at figures and amused himself by studying mathematics. Indeed, like other Rothschilds he grew so professional in his hobby that he read Einstein's theories for relaxation; and one day he came across a mistake in the great man's logic. He wrote to him, and a week later received effusive thanks for having discovered a printer's error.

The fortunes of Eugene and Louis seemed to resemble a see-saw, for when one was down the other was up. Only two months before Eugene became a widower, sixty-four-year-old, dyed-in-the-wool bachelor Louis, had walked to the altar with an enchanting Austrian lady, Countess Hilda von Auersperg. Hilda soon made a home for her sophisticated bridegroom in Vermont of all places. Apparently the hills reminded Louis of the Alps, and the taciturn Vermonters, who talked in monosyllables, were a welcome contrast to prying gossip writers. Furthermore, as Louis was a scientist he enjoyed filling his house with professors from nearby Dartmouth College and discussing botany and art.

In 1947 Louis and his bride visited Austria. The Russians were still in Vienna, and the country, once again truncated, was in severe economic difficulties. News of the Rothschild visit spread and a crowd gathered outside the hotel where they were staying. Hundreds of people begged the Baron for help and he gave it to them. He turned over to the Austrian Government all the properties that originally had been seized by the Austrian Nazis but which, after much litigation, had been partially restored to him. His gift, however, had a proviso. The Government was obliged to pass a special law converting the Rothschild assets into a state-administered pension fund, the object of which was to provide each of Louis' former domestic and business employees with the same security and income as that enjoyed by retired civil servants. Then Louis returned to Vermont. He made a practice of visiting the Caribbean in the winter, and in 1955 died while swimming in Montego Bay.

Meanwhile Louis's brother, Eugene, had married an English actress, Jeanne Stewart. They lived for many years in the house on Long Island but in the 1960s returned to Europe and bought a flat in Monte-Carlo. Eugene is still alive, and will soon celebrate his ninetieth birthday.

While the Austrian Rothschilds were buying houses in America, the French Rothschilds led by seventy-seven-year-old Baron Édouard and sixty-three-year-old Baron Robert were trying to pick up the pieces and reopen the bank on the Rue Laffitte. Within a few weeks of returning to Paris in 1945 Édouard sent a trusted employee, old M. Moccand, on a tour of France to 'dig up' the securities that had vanished from the vaults, almost magically, as German armour rolled into the capital.

The trip was not easy as hundreds of bridges had been destroyed and miles of railway track pulled up by the Germans. He first went to Vercors, a grassy plateau five hundred miles south east of Paris, where bitter fighting had taken place. Part of the way, Moccand travelled by train, but where there were no tracks he thumbed rides from army lorries or took to his feet, stumbling over roads blasted by shelling. As things were still in a state of flux he slept with a gun beside him, never knowing whether he would be accosted by stragglers or confronted by members of the resistance wedded to an anarchistic life.

Finally he reached a small farmhouse on the edge of the plateau. The tenant farmer had once been employed by Messieurs de Rothschild Frères as a teller. 'It's all here,' he told Moccand warmly. 'Come and see for yourself.' Moccand followed him into a cellar where several iron chests were stored. They were stacked with important papers; 50,000,000 francs in negotiable securities, property titles, industrial records, archives. The scene was yet another variation of history. One hundred and fifty years earlier there had been another cellar with chests filled with important documents. On this occasion the Rothschilds had saved the fortune of the Elector; now others, if not in a position to save the fortune of the Rothschilds, at least were shoring up the losses of Rothschild customers, for almost all the valuables belonged to Jewish clients.

Moccand spent three weeks travelling about France. Among the people he visited was a young Parisian clerk and his wife at a seaside villa near Marseilles, who had hidden securities in an artesian well; an insurance salesman in the Dordogne and a shopkeeper in Auvergne who had concealed bank notes under planks in the floor. When Moccand had finished his preliminary visits, he bought an old truck and retraced his steps picking up the valuables. After three months he limped into Paris with cash and papers worth some millions of francs.

However, M. Moccand was not the only person engaged in retrieving the bank's treasures. Over fifty dummy accounts had been opened in provincial banks all over France to conceal the property of more Jewish clients. There were also two holding companies in Lyons and a third in Marseilles, created solely as repositories for imperilled securities. It took six months before this errant capital was rounded up and once again placed in the vaults of the Rue Laffitte. What was astonishing was the fact that not a single stock or bond withdrawn under the noses of Germany's financial *gauleiters* had been lost or misappropriated by the chain of hands through which it had passed.

No one knew what to make of the Paris Bourse on 30 June 1949. There was no reason for a slump, yet the great Royal Dutch Shell shares dipped unexpectedly. So did those of the metal combine, Rio Tinto; the giant mining corporation, Le Nickel; and the diamond trust of De Beers. Brokers were surprised, then anxious, and many hurried to sell. At the close of the day prices were lower than they had been for months.

Next morning the mystery grew less mysterious when the public read that eighty-one-year-old Baron Édouard de Rothschild had died in the morning of the previous day. The Rothschilds were heavy shareholders in all the companies that had fallen. The Baron's obituary, on the front page of the Paris papers, was accompanied by financial articles speculating on his estate, and explaining that the tax on the dead man's investments would be based on closing prices on the day of the decease. The family always mounted combined operations in time of crisis, and together had driven down the quotations. And now, while the funeral arrangements were being made, they again acted in concert, rebuying all the shares which they had sold forty-eight hours earlier.

A new generation was now in charge of the Rothschild interests in France, for Baron Édouard's two cousins, Robert who had run the bank with him before the war, and Henri the doctor-playwright, had preceeded him to the grave by a few months. The main responsibility fell on Édouard's only son, forty-year-old Baron Guy. This slim, elegant, fair-haired man was the most unRothschild looking Rothschild ever to become head of the bank. As one writer pointed out he looked more like a marquis in a sophisticated play than the grandson of the formidable Alphonse who had raised the French indemnity after the war with Prussia, or the great-grandson of James, gold-runner to Wellington's armies and founder of the Chemin de Fer du Nord.

But if Guy lacked the protruding lip and the protruding Rothschild girth, no one could accuse him of a scarcity of Rothschild energy. Everything seemed to fall on his plate at once, but he dealt with it all, quietly, quickly, effectively. He sold the great family house off the Place de la Concorde which had once belonged to Prince Talleyrand, to the only customer rich enough to buy it: the United States Government. The residence had been stripped of its furnishings by the Nazis and would have cost millions to put in order. Besides, in the uncertainties of the post-war era it was too big, even for a Rothschild. First it became Headquarters for the Marshal Plan; then Headquarters for the US Mission to NATO; and finally the home of various European regional organizations.

However, Guy held on to Ferrières, the family château built a hundred years earlier and set in nine thousand acres of farmland, nineteen miles east of Paris. This, too, had been ransacked by the Germans who not only took carpets and furniture but to everyone's puzzlement even stripped the zoo of its animals, why nobody knows to this day. Gradually the *objets d'art* unearthed by Rorimer arrived back in France and Ferrières became a huge storage vault for the entire family. First came train loads of looted Italian faïences and master paintings; then fifty-nine cases of rare books; then tapestries and silver and furniture, some of the pieces restored by craftsmen and in much better condition than when they were taken. Other works of art came from other hiding places; some from the foreign embassies who had hidden them in their cellars for the duration; others from the Louvre which had managed to disguise them by mixing them in other people's collections. As usual, the Rothschilds showed their gratitude in a princely way. Alain and Élie and their sisters said thank you by bequeathing to the Louvre several priceless works of art including Gainsborough's *Lady Alston*, while Guy and his sisters donated *The Countess Doria* by Van Dyck.

Ferrières remained shut and uninhabited for over a decade. During this period an American visitor was taken through the dismantled rooms by a caretaker. 'At first he found himself in a golden thicket of clocks. He thought he had stumbled into a clock museum until the caretaker explained that this was merely the room where the château's time pieces were stored. Next the visitor came upon a huge, glorious array of Louis XIV and XV chairs. In still another chamber there was a dazzle of tables. Finally he saw a number of objects adorably wrought out of rosewood and flowered antique Chinese porcelain. He puzzled, looked again – and understood the caretaker's smile. Here stood scores of the world's most exquisite bidets.'[10]

Houses and *objets d'art* were only a small part of Baron Guy's concern. As his father had been the biggest race-horse owner in France, and as his stables had been put up to auction in 1941, the consequences took a great deal of unravelling. Some things, of course, could not be put right. Many of Édouard's mares had been crossed with stallions belonging to Marcel Boussac, France's textile king and Rothschild's greatest rival at Longchamp.

M. Boussac ungenerously pronounced the forced unions as 'unauthorized and irregular'; yet it was vital for the Baron Guy to persuade the arbiters of the *Stud Book*, the equine *Almanach de Gotha*, to register the Rothschild colts, the progeny of these illegal matches. At first the committee refused to consider it, but after months of argument the judges relented and legitimized the issue.

Under Guy's aegis the reconstructed stables began to acquire the same prestige that his father had enjoyed. As early as 1950 he topped the list of both owners and breeders and in 1963 his champion, the four-year-old stallion, Exbury, won the Coronation Cup at Epsom and the Arc de Triomphe at Longchamps. Shortly afterwards it was sold to a syndicate for over £400,000 and for years Exbury earned its owners a steady quarter of a million a year.

While the French Rothschilds were feeling their way in the post-war world, the English Rothschilds were trying to come to grips with the austerity imposed by the hardships of peace, and exalted by a Labour Government determined, as Churchill unfairly put it, on an equality of misery. More of the Rothschild houses came on the market. Leo's house at 5 Hamilton Place became a club, Les Ambassadeurs, while Charles Rothschild's house in Kensington Palace Gardens was sold to the Rumanians for an embassy. And although Anthony, senior partner of the bank, continued to live at his country house, Ascott, near Wing, filled with treasures gathered by himself over the years, in 1949 he handed it over to the protective embrace of the National Trust.

Since the death of his cousin Lionel, in 1942, Anthony had run the bank alone. Although in 1946 he was joined by Lionel's son, Edmund, who had inherited the great estate at Exbury, the young man could not relieve him of any responsibility until he had learned the business. The war years were worrying enough for bankers; but the post-war years, with their periodical currency crises, were even more of a nightmare. The depressed 1930s seemed to belong to a world of serenity. The fact that times were changing became startlingly apparent when, in 1949, Anthony ceased to arrive in New Court in a chauffer-driven limousine and took the tube to work. Much to his surprise he found the journey far quicker than travelling by car; others copied him, causing 'a tycoons' mini-revolution'.

Many people felt that by this act alone the Rothschilds had accepted the ultimate in democratization. Yet in other ways Anthony was not prepared to compromise. A grand *seigneur*, intellectual, artistic, a man of impeccable taste, the new era with its strident voice and aggressive competition was inimical to everything in which he believed. Yet while newcomers scrambled to get business, one of the biggest development schemes of all times fell into Anthony's lap, without his so much as lifting a finger for it.

It happened because of the Rothschild name. In 1951, shortly after Winston Churchill had become Prime Minister for the second time, he received Mr Smallwood, the Premier of Newfoundland. Small-wood unfolded plans for a vast development scheme in Labrador and Newfoundland. To carry it out British capital was needed on a truly mammoth scale. 'After Mr Smallwood had left the Cabinet Room', wrote Edmund de Rothschild, 'Churchill turned to his private secretary, J. R. Colville and said: "Jock, whom do we know in the City?" ' It is one of those coincidences of destiny that Jock Colville, a life-long friend, had been that very day at New Court and he at once replied: 'Rothschilds.' ' "Good",' said Churchill and began to quote from the Lord Chancellor's song in Gilbert and Sullivan's *Iolanthe*·

> *The shares are a penny and ever so many*
> *Are taken by Rothschild and Baring,*
> *And just as a few are allotted to you*
> *You awake with a shudder despairing . . .*

The great man was a personal friend of Anthony and when the consortium of firms was formed he was delighted that N. M. Roth-schild & Sons should head it. Later he wrote to Edmund referring to the close relations between the two families and adding: 'I am very glad to feel that the connection is not broken in my old age.'

After a good many luncheons and a good many hours of talk Brinco – the British Newfoundland Corporation – came into being, backed by a consortium of twenty-nine major firms, among them the Anglo-American Corporation of South Africa, the Anglo-Newfoundland Development Company, Bowaters, English Electric, the Frobisher Mining Company and Rio Tinto.

Although Anthony laid the foundation of Brinco, he was taken ill a few years later and the project fell into Edmund's lap where it has remained ever since. Brinco's terms of reference were breath-taking: the exploratory rights to sixty thousand square miles in Newfoundland and Labrador, an area larger than England and Wales, containing enormous resources in minerals, timber and water. Altogether in the last twenty years Brinco has earmarked over £1,000,000,000 for development. The hydro-electric power scheme at Churchill Falls in Labrador is the largest private-enterprise undertaking in North America. Here, at one site, seven millions of horse power are harnessed. The underground power house covers more space than New York's Grand Central Station, and each of the eleven generators is the size of a nine storey building.

But Brinco was only a beginning. More Rothschilds and more triumphs were on the way.

A painting by Hepple of the Partners'
Room in the old building of New
Court.

Chapter XII

The Rothschilds Today: The Bankers

(1953–73)

'*T*HE TIMES NEVER MOVE WITHOUT THE ROTHSCHILDS, for the Rothschilds always move with the times,' someone observed in the 1950s, when the French Rothschilds gave up their Bentleys and began riding around Paris in chauffeur-driven Minis.

Rothschild financial supremacy, of course, was a thing of the past. No longer did the family – or any family for that matter – control the money markets of the world or regulate the rates of exchange or crown and uncrown kings. When *haute finance*, that mysterious capitalist invention, disappeared into the mists of the First World War, the Rothschild monopoly vanished with it. Even the structure of Rothschild banks had altered drastically, for although they remained private concerns, ever since 1908 they had operated as independent entities. This was convenient in war, but in time of peace the separation deprived the family of the internationalism that had once been its strength.

Then came three perilous decades with special hazards for bankers: the inflation of the 1920s, the depression of the 1930s, the violence of the 1940s. Temporarily much of Europe was overrun by Hitler, permanently much of it enslaved by Stalin. During this process the Rothschild banks shrank from three to two, although New Court and the Rue Laffitte bravely continued to sport the emblem of the five arrows.

For a while it even looked as though that very special Rothschild commodity, money, might be in short supply. Once again death duties had torn gaping holes in the pockets of the English Rothschilds, while the Austrian Rothschilds tried in vain to get adequate compensation for the vast properties seized by the Nazis and later nationalized by the Iron Curtain régimes. And although the majority of the fabulous treasures owned by the French Rothschilds trickled back to Paris, some Rothschilds, Maurice's sister, Miriam, for one, had come off badly. The valuables sent to Germany were recovered, but many pictures that she had hidden herself were lost. Apparently the place where she concealed them was ransacked by a looter who was never caught.

Yet the Rothschilds were famous for their resilience and most people were confident that when the fog of disorder lifted, the clan would play its part again as one of the rich and civilized families of Europe. Others were less sanguine, arguing that the post-war era of mass-movement, mass-production and mass-control was bound by its very nature to frown on the individualism that had made the Rothschilds famous.

No one prophesied a Rothschild renaissance. No one predicted that the family would welcome the new era and breathe vitality into it; that they would embrace the age of the common man, cosset it, enhance it, walk to the altar with it. And that this enthusiasm would recapture Rothschild power, not as a family, not as a financial giant, but as a group of individuals, each with his own particular contribution, his own particular influence.

It was befitting that the opening shots in the revival should have been fired by the London bankers, heirs of the great Nathan. The reverberations came in 1962 when New Court was turned over to a demolition gang, and in 1965 when N. M. Rothschild & Sons moved into a glossy, glassy, black marble and aluminium plated building on the same site. Apparently the Japanese were not surprised. This was the sort of thing they expected from the Rothschilds, but when their London correspondent telegraphed that the new building would consist of six storeys, Tokyo thought the figure must be a misprint for sixty. Surely the Rothschilds still did things in a big way?

If the way was not yet spectacular, the reorganization at least caught the attention of the City, for a new generation of Rothschilds had taken over the firm. Anthony had died in 1961 after an illness which for several years had kept him away from the office. Edmund, at forty-five, had taken his place as senior partner, assisted by his thirty-four-year-old brother, Leo, and Anthony's twenty-nine-year-old son, Evelyn.

The changes came slowly as English merchant banks were deeply set in their ways, hemmed in by traditions that made them unlike any other banks in the world. Herded together in what is known as 'the Square Mile', they stand on streets with wonderful names – Bishopsgate, Poultry, Cheapside, Lombard, Threadneedle, Old Jewry. Perhaps because they are within a stone's throw of one another everyone knows everyone else's business. Consequently more verbal deals, running into more millions, are done in the City than in any place in the world. This means that integrity is the merchant banker's most priceless asset, and the expression 'an Englishman's word is his bond' is quite literally true. Paradoxically, although the merchant bank is looked upon as England's most English possession, nearly all the originators were foreigners. The Rothschilds came from Frankfurt; the Barings from Bremen; the Warburgs and the Schröders from Hamburg; the Lazards from Alsace; the Brandts from St Petersburg; the Morgans from Boston.

Even in 1945 Rothschilds still had the distinction of being the private bank with the most famous name in Europe. As it was also run as a feudal hierarchy, with stern rules and traditions that had never been broken, every change created a stir. In 1960 the company accepted the first outsider as a partner – a position hitherto only open to Rothschild men – and in 1970 the bank ceased to be a partnership and was reorganized as a limited company. Both events were widely reported. Partnerships were forbidden by law, first to have more than ten, and then more than twenty partners, and ambitious young newcomers would not stay with the bank unless they felt they could reach the top. The limited company, of course, was still in Rothschild hands with a paid up capital of £10,000,000, excluding reserves, 95 per cent of which was owned by the family. The number of directors began to expand rapidly, and today there are twenty-nine, only four of whom are Rothschilds.

The modernization that took place in the 1960s included mechanization and advertising (hitherto frowned upon) and new methods of recruiting personnel. Not everyone welcomed the changes and Ronald Palin, secretary to the bank, felt that the civilized Anthony would have hated the brashness of the modern approach. Yet Anthony's son, Evelyn, seemed to disprove this theory. Although Evelyn was not quite thirty when his father died in 1961, and inherited the largest single shareholding in the bank, he not only welcomed changes but instigated many of them himself. He was the first Rothschild to press for the inclusion of non-Rothschild partners, and the most enthusiastic Rothschild in favour of demolishing New Court and erecting a new building. Indeed, although fairly inexperienced, he made himself entirely responsible for the new building. He selected the architect and worked alone with him, achieving a result that was both striking and practical.

Evelyn was devoted to the memory of his father, and longed to vindicate his conscientious overlordship during the most difficult years of the century. He was convinced that only by drastic reorganization could the bank once again leap to the forefront; yet what gave the spirit of change the velocity of a high wind was the arrival of Nathaniel Charles Jacob Rothschild, son and heir of Victor, the third Lord Rothschild.

Unlike his father, who went to Harrow and Cambridge, Jacob was educated at Eton and Oxford. A tall, gangling youth with what writers like to call 'the protruding Rothschild lip' – although no other living Rothschild has this characteristic – Jacob was brilliant, moody and aggressive: He had a deeply ingrained belief in his own intellectual superiority which did not make him an easy boy to manage. Needless to say he was not a success at Eton, and was very unhappy. He left at seventeen and did his national service with the Life Guards at Windsor. He began as a Lance Corporal and was popular with the NCOs and privates, one of whom gave an interview to the press describing him as an eccentric because he frequently claimed to be 'broke'.[1] Unfortunately he produced an unfavourable impression on his superiors, and applied three times before he was accepted in a training course for officers.

Opposite A corner of the Grand Salon in Baron and Baroness Élie de Rothschild's house in Rue Masseran, built by Brongniart in 1787–8 for Prince Masserano, ambassador of Charles IV of Spain to the Court of St James. Above the Louis XIV *cabinet-bibliothèque*, worked in the manner of Boulle, is Gainsborough's *The Marsham Children*, painted in 1787.

Overleaf Interior of the great vat-house at Château Lafite. The twenty-four vats of Bosnian oak contain an average of 150 hectolitres each.

Jacob Rothschild has been instrumental in the reorganization of N.M. Rothschild & Sons.

Not until he arrived at Christ Church, Oxford, did he come into his own. Here he made half a dozen life-long friends; and here he took first-class honours in history. The bank was his objective, but he did not want to enter the firm until he had some knowledge of money. So he took a crash course in accountancy, did a short apprenticeship with a London finance company, and another spell in New York with Morgan Stanley.

From the moment that Jacob stepped into Rothschilds he knew that he had found his *métier*, and so did his cousins. At first meeting he seemed quiet and controlled, a pleasant young man with a high forehead and a steady gaze, but beneath a deceptive air of modesty, he concealed an iron will and strong likes and dislikes which were not easy to dislodge. Yet no one was left in any doubt that the mantle of the great Nathan had fallen on Jacob's shoulders, for his incisive brain seemed automatically to understand every nuance of the market-place, and he took decisions as quickly and easily as his famous predecessor who had boasted that he was 'an off-hand man' who settled prices on the spot.

One of a pair of Louis XIV cabinets in the Hôtel Masseran. It is decorated with tortoise shell, inlaid with mother-of-pearl and ivory, and traditionally attributed to Boulle, although its style shows evidence of Dutch influence.

Jacob's immediate concern was to introduce modern techniques, for the firm had just suffered a humiliating defeat by failing to defend its client, Odhams, from a take-over bid by the Mirror group, directed by Sigmund Warburg. 'The boom years for take-over struggles had begun,' wrote a City Commentator, 'and Rothschild was publicly seen to be not as much of an adept as it ought to have been in this branch of banking practice.' Other financial writers criticized Rothschilds for tactical errors, such as advising Odhams to send its shareholders a letter raising dividends from $17\frac{1}{2}$ to $37\frac{1}{2}$ per cent and according to the *Sunday Times*, 'illustrating the records of Odhams and the Mirror with a strange selection of profit figures'. 'They failed to save Odhams from being taken over by the *Daily Mirror*,' chirped the *Sunday Telegraph*, 'though of course they can always look back with pride to having helped Disraeli get control of the Suez Canal.'

Jacob had no intention of looking back at anything. A new department of corporate finance was introduced with himself at the head, whose business was takeovers, mergers, Euro-dollar loans, in fact, all the services that modern investment bankers could devise. Jacob's ideas were positive. 'Merchant bankers must not wait for opportunities,' he told the press, 'they must create them. Conversely, clients should come to us for ideas, not only for money.'

The notion that a bank should be a Brains Trust is no longer a novel conception, but Jacob strengthened it by bringing into the firm a handful of talented contemporaries, the star of which was Rodney Leach, Balliol's cleverest classical scholar for a generation. The new group became so expert in raising Euro-dollar loans that today Warburgs, the first English bank to pioneer the field, is being given a strenuous run for its money. Although all the bank's departments have been revitalized, the corporate department has drawn the heaviest fire and kept Rothschilds continually in the public eye. During the first years of its existence it was successful in advising Showerings in its takeover of Harveys, and equally successful in defending Metropolitan Estates, England's largest property company, against a takeover by the Commercial Union. It helped the Sun Alliance Insurance Company to swallow one of its competitors, a particularly satisfying transaction as the Alliance had been founded by Nathan Rothschild. Now it was worth £100,000,000 and, gratifyingly, a loyal Rothschild client. Among the most famous takeovers was the £420,000,000 offer by Grand Metropolitan for Watneys, the largest bid in British commercial history. In this operation Rothschilds was referred to as the '*éminence grise*'. However, the part played by the firm in advising Mr Jim Slater in his triumphant bid for Isaac Wolfson's master company, Drage's, was not at all shadowy or even *grise*.

The rise of the corporate department was so meteoric that the staff, which in 1959 consisted of Jacob alone, today boasts 108 members and ten directors. And in this age of advertisement the publicity it provoked undoubtedly increased the bank's prestige. Even the orthodox business of raising loans has reached new heights – over a billion pounds in the last ten years, with such famous borrowers as Shell, Anglo-American, and Philips, the electrical giant. The British Government also became a client, for after the Conservatives came to power in 1970, Rothschilds was invited to find buyers for the Industrial Reorganization Corporation's portfolio of investments which had been built up by the Labour Government. And recently another public servant – this time the liquidator of Rolls Royce – selected Rothschilds from a dozen applicants to dispose of the profitable Rolls Royce Motors.

In 1972 another of Jacob's particular concerns, the Rothschild Investment Trust, reached new heights. Jacob took over the chairmanship in 1970 and within two years the market value of the Trust had grown from £5,000,000 to £80,000,000 while the original shares, owned by the public had more than doubled. Some of the investments were amusingly original. The Trust bought twenty per cent of Sotheby's, the famous auctioneers, and fifteen per cent of Wedd, Durlacher, the City's most successful jobbers. Jacob and his partners are not eager to acquire a controlling interest in any business, no matter how profitable; bankers, they feel, should stick to their last. 'What do we know about frozen fish?' Jacob asks blandly.

Jacob is married to Serena Dunn, who is not Jewish. She is a granddaughter of the Earl of Rosslyn and of Sir James Dunn, a Canadian financier who made a fortune of Rothschildian proportions. Her father, Philip Dunn, is a business man, who at one time found himself in the surprising position of Chairman of the *News of the World*. Serena and Jacob have three daughters and a son, Nathaniel, born in 1971.

Jacob works a twelve-hour day, complaining that he does not know how other bankers have time for pleasure, but the truth is that work is his recreation. He is doing what he likes best, and he does it superlatively well. Although he sometimes finds it difficult to hide his arrogance, stepping on people's toes and arousing needless hostility, the cleverest men in the City acknowledge his expertise and place him among the top handful of his profession. Indeed a former member of the World Bank refers to him as 'the most brilliant banker in Europe'.

Like most English Rothschilds, Jacob lives modestly. He has a London house in Little Venice, charming but unpretentious, and a house in the country at Hungerford. He plays tennis and collects early twentieth-century English paintings. His main hobby, however, smacks of a busman's holiday, for recently he bought P. D. Colnaghi, one of the oldest and most distinguished firms of art dealers in London; and a few years ago he acquired a hundred acres in Corfu, a purchase likely to provide a handsome inheritance for his son.

The Queen presenting the Queen's Cup, to Evelyn de Rothschild whose polo team, 'The Centaurs', often played against teams led by the Duke of Edinburgh and Élie de Rothschild.

If Jacob is the cleverest of the banking Rothschilds, Edmund is the most kindly, Leo the most modest, Evelyn the most diplomatic and perhaps the most generous. All three are sportsmen. Edmund and Leo like to fish and to race their yachts, while Evelyn is a crack polo player who, until several years ago, frequently led his team, 'The Centaurs', against teams captained by Prince Philip or his French cousin, Baron Élie.

As Chairman of Rothschilds Edmund's office abounds in family portraits and historical mementos. He sits behind the desk once owned by his great grandfather, Baron Lionel; and on the wall is a letter authorizing Nathan to ship gold to Wellington's army in Spain. One of the ancestral paintings looks exactly like Edmund, grey hair, grey mustache, pink cheeks, large kindly eyes. This is grandfather Leo, that 'angel with a revenue' who seems to have endowed Edmund not only with his looks but with his pride in his Jewishness.

Of all the Rothschilds Edmund is the most race-conscious. Although he does not pretend to be strictly orthodox he regularly attends the Great Synagogue where he is warden. He is on the board of many Jewish philanthropies, including the Association of Jewish Ex-Servicemen and Women of which he is president, and the Council of Christians and Jews of which he is joint treasurer. His four children have been brought up in the Jewish faith. When his eldest son, Nicholas, became a *barmitzvah* in 1964, the ceremony marking the event – the equivalent of confirmation – was conducted by the Chief Rabbi Brodie. A great many relations were present including Baron Eugene of Austria, Baron Philippe of France and Lady Rothschild of England.

Like all Rothschilds Edmund was deeply disturbed by the Six-Day War, and spent time and thought trying to find a practical solution to an insoluble problem. At the end of June 1967 he wrote a letter to *The Times* suggesting that Britain, the United States and Russia build de-salination plants capable of producing 100,000,000 gallons of water a day in Israel and Jordan, and a smaller plant in the Gaza Strip. The idea was that if the desert suddenly bloomed there would be food for all, and nothing to fight about.

Edmund de Rothschild with one of his dogs at Inchmery House, Exbury, in Hampshire.

Although he inherited his father's three thousand acre estate near Southampton, both he and Leo live in modest houses overlooking the sea. The lovely, eighteenth-century Exbury House, once upon a time occupied by the Mitford family, stands empty and forlorn, although it is neither large nor forbidding. For two months a year, when the wonderful shrubs burst into bloom, the public is allowed to wander about the grounds, and fifty thousand people take advantage of the opportunity every year. Edmund has inherited Lionel's love and knowledge of flowers and has won many horticultural prizes including the trophy presented by his father. Although he has cut the number of gardeners from sixty to thirty to make the undertaking pay, he has not dimmed its glory.

Unlike their forbears Edmund and Leo do not move in fashionable London circles or, for that matter, even in the corridors of power. Edmund entertains distinguished overseas visitors at the bank, and anyone fortunate enough to be invited to luncheon will be given delicious food and drink. But Edmund's social life takes place in the country, and the four or five days that he spends in London are given over almost entirely to official business or to one of his many charities, which range from the Freedom from Hunger Campaign to the Institute of District Nursing.

Leo is even less interested in social life. He heads the Latin-American department in the bank, serves as a Director of the Bank of England, and sits on the board of Covent Garden. His outside interests are classical music and industrial archaeology. Of the Rothschilds, he is the least publicized.

Cousin Evelyn, on the other hand, graces all the most amusing London parties. Tall, dark and handsome, he is much admired by the ladies; and, like his father, has a splendid stud farm and takes a keen interest in racing. Nevertheless at forty he is hard working and serious. Proof of the impact he has made on the City is the fact that in 1972 he was invited to become chairman of *The Economist*, Britain's most respected financial journal. He is also deputy chairman of the corporation that runs the new town of Milton Kenyes, a Government appointment.

Whereas Jacob is chairman of the executive committee which runs Rothschilds and master-minds the big financial deals, Evelyn concerns himself with the bank's overall strategy and the smooth running of the various departments. Many people regard him as the most charming of all the Rothschilds as he not only is tactful and perceptive but a man of infinite good will who takes pleasure in helping those around him. Apart from his domestic responsibilities he acts as the firm's roving ambassador. During the past ten years he has made many trips to America, Canada, Australia, the Far East and Africa, in search of new business. One of the feathers in his cap is the close relationship existing today between Rothschilds and the De Beers Anglo-American Charter Group.

Evelyn also spends a good deal of time in France, and just as Guy de Rothschild serves as a director of the English bank, so Evelyn sits on the board of directors of the Banque Rothschild. As he is half French he is the right Rothschild to throw a bridge across the Channel, and to keep the French and English cousins *au fait* with each others' plans. In 1972 N. M. Rothschild & Sons launched a new company with Evelyn as Chairman, known as the New Court Investment Trust. Its aim is to make money for itself and its clients by investing in expanding European businesses.

The most striking feature of the English and French banks is the same element that has distinguished them since their inception: the family. Despite the changes of the last ten years, male Rothschilds and only male Rothschilds still financially control both firms. In London two Rothschild brothers and two cousins work together while in Paris two Rothschild brothers and one Rothschild cousin direct the business, with three young ones as recent recruits; Guy's son, David, Alain's son, Éric, and Élie's son, twenty-six-year-old Nathaniel, the first member of the family to have graduated from Harvard Business School.

The French Rothschilds did not lag behind their English cousins but so far their reorganization has proved less fruitful than the revolution across the Channel. Unlike English bankers French bankers have an irresistible urge to control industry. Therefore when, in 1967, the French Rothschilds grouped their interests into a holding company, La Compagnie du Nord, which had been formed 130 years earlier to launch the Chemin de Fer du Nord, their most important satellites were commercial not financial. The world-famous Rothschild bank, for instance, was a small venture while Le Nickel-Penarroya was the second largest producer of nickel in the world and one of the leading producers of zinc and copper.

Baron Guy de Rothschild is Managing Director of the Compagnie du Nord; and although the latter is not a giant but a medium-sized company capitalized at about £60,000,000, its subsidiaries are both varied and far-flung with interests which stretch from New Caledonia to South America, Africa and Europe. Its mineral companies range from the famous Le Nickel to Miferna which produces iron ore in Mauretania and to the Compagnie Française des Minerais d'Uranium which produces uranium ore in France. The 'Nord' also controls real estate companies, food companies, credit companies, tourist organizations, cargo ships and a group ready to finance a tunnel under the English Channel.

However it was the reorganization of the bank Messieurs de Rothschild Frères that aroused the most interest. It was something of a feat that Baron Guy and his two cousins, Élie and Alain, had been able to reconstruct the roughly-handled firm at the end of the war. They not only put it on its feet again but attracted a recruit who was to become one of the great statesmen of France. M.

Baron Élie's son, Nathaniel, is the first of the Rothschilds to have graduated from Harvard Business School.

Pompidou joined the firm in 1956 when M. Fillon, formerly a tutor of Baron Guy, and an employee of the bank, decided to go into politics. Fillon offered to find someone to take his place, and came up with the name of Pompidou who was doing a rather dull job as a civil servant. Pompidou had remained a schoolmaster throughout the war; and in 1945 someone had recommended him to de Gaulle who had asked him to study the French educational system and to give him a report on what changes should be made.

Pompidou had an impressive academic record. He had graduated first from the École Normale Supérieure, and as a schoolmaster had prepared boys for the matriculation in Greek and Latin. He served de Gaulle as a minor civil servant and when the latter went into the wilderness in 1946 remained in his obscure job. He gladly accepted Baron Guy's offer in 1956 and rapidly rose to the position of general manager. In 1958 de Gaulle again sent for him, and he left Rothschilds' for nearly a year. However, he returned in 1959 and remained until 1962 when de Gaulle invited him to become prime minister. Fillon who had left banking for politics was temporarily eclipsed but he emerged again at Rothschilds where he is now Chairman of two companies and a director of many others.

In 1967 the bank underwent drastic alteration. Like their English cousins, the French directors said goodbye to the famous old building at 19 Rue Laffitte and pulled it down to make way for a modern, concrete, superstructure. Baron Élie's wife, Liliane, who has a brilliant flair for colour and design, was responsible for the interior which she supervised in partnership with Michel Boyer. The function of the bank also changed; instead of specializing in investment services it became a deposit bank with a drive-in counter on the ground floor. Even the name was changed to 'La Banque Rothschild'. 'A banker,' Baron Guy told reporters, 'is Mr A who borrows money from Mr B to lend to Mr C.' This, of course, was the definition of a purely commercial bank, something very different from an English bank, and very different from the role played in former days by Messieurs de Rothschild Frères. Apparently M. Pompidou was among those who advised Guy to make the change as a certain way of attracting new capital to invest in industry.

Unfortunately things did not work out as the family hoped, for the Rothschild bank found itself a small fish in a big pond. The cost of opening deposit branches in the suburbs and provincial towns was excessive, while the attempts to compete advantageously with the publicly-owned French giants was a losing battle. And the bank was not the only worry.

Far more serious was the fact that Le Nickel was in difficulty due to a world slump in the demand for nickel. Shares which had reached $54 in late 1970 were in the region of $20 as 1973 began. Inevitably Le Nord's shares suffered too, declining from $12 in 1971 to $8 in 1973.

Above Baron Élie de Rothschild, one of the partners of the Banque Rothschild, is President of the PLM, a company which builds and promotes hotels, motels and restaurants such as the new Hôtel Saint-Jacques, *below*.

However, at the first sign of trouble the Rothschilds had begun an impressive reconstruction of their many holdings. Shipping interests were pruned down, credit and real estate companies streamlined. Jimmy Goldsmith, the London financier, was brought in to reorganize the Rothschild food business, and Baron Edmond, owner of the Banque Privée in Switzerland, and a merchant bank in Paris, was invited to become a director of the Banque Rothschild. Although the future policy of the bank is still under discussion, the younger generation – Éric, Nathaniel and David – are believed to favour closer ties with the English bank, even a merger following the pattern of the last century.

Despite the publicity, not all Rothschild interests suffered and *Newsweek* reassured its readers that the family was 'hardly on the rocks'. Others predicted that the graph of the Compagnie du Nord had already started its upward swing and after a bad start the seventies would mark a triumphant advance. One of the family's most challenging and successful enterprises is the PLM. These initials were taken from two Rothschild railway companies which were merged in 1857 – the Paris–Lyons and the Lyons–Méditerranée. The dashing Baron Élie, became president of the PLM in 1956, at the age of thirty-nine (displacing a gentleman of eighty-nine) and ten years later turned it into a firm to build and promote hotels, motels and restaurants. The first PLM hotel in Paris, the Hôtel Saint-Jacques, with 812 rooms, was opened in 1972.

The Baron's wife, Liliane, was in charge of the decor and dozens of Rothschild employees were asked to spend a night there during the first month, to test beds, mirrors, hot-water taps, lavatories, food, service, in fact everything that came their way. Baron Élie himself knew exactly what he regarded as essential. 'I want my bath to run hot in two minutes flat. I don't want to hear plumbing noises. I want a good bed and pillows. I want my breakfast right away. I want good croissants. After all, we're in Paris. I want people to be polite to me and I don't want to hear their side of the story.'

The Baron got what he wanted, and as a result the Saint-Jacques is booked up several months in advance. The hotel is only one of a chain in various parts of France, and in Switzerland. There are seven PLM restaurants on the French motorways, and one in the Casino in Chamonix which was bought by PLM, in partnership with M. Ortiz Patino, several years ago. Apparently permission to renovate the Casino was difficult to secure as the building had been occupied by Napoleon III and Eugénie when they visited the resort and was classified as an historic monument.

Although Barons Alain and Élie are very different in temperament and move in very different French circles they are devoted to one another. Alain is a distinguished-looking man who heads the Jewish community in France. He prefers the conservative atmosphere

of the Faubourg Saint-Germain to fashionable society. In his spare time he sails and occasionally competes in yachting races. He is married to the former Mary Chauvin du Treuil, one of the prettiest and most amiable hostesses in Paris.

After the war the two brothers shared the house at 23 Avenue de Marigny where they had grown up as children. This was the great mansion into which Lord Rothschild had moved during the war. But in the late 1950s Baron Élie and his wife Liliane moved into a house of their own at 11 Rue Masseran. Their new residence was almost as big as 23 Marigny, but more attractive; an eighteenth-century house, previously owned by Count Étienne de Beaumont, and built by Brongniart in 1785. Liliane has impeccable taste and today the house is a brilliant mixture of Rothschild portraits and bibelots, eighteenth-century furniture, twentieth-century paintings and old world masterpieces.

The Marigny house is very different, a blaze of gilt and red damask that the English call 'Victorian' and the French '*le style Rothschild*'. Until the end of 1972, 23 Avenue de Marigny was the only Paris residence built by a Rothschild (it was built by Gustave in 1885) still occupied by a Rothschild, Baron Alain. But even this sentimental distinction has ended, for in 1972 the house was sold to the French

Page 269 The Rothschild Cameo, a Byzantine double-portrait carved in sardonyx and thought to represent the Emperor Constantine II and his wife: the cameo is dated *c.*335 but the silver-gilt filigree mount is late twelfth-century Byzantine work.

Opposite Portrait of Henry Bernstein as a boy, by Édouard Manet, from a Rochschild collection in Paris. The playwright Bernstein, a friend of the Rothschilds at the turn of the century, was the author of *Judith*, *Félix* and *La Galerie des Glaces*.

Below Rembrandt's *The Standard Bearer*, believed to be a self-portrait, is in Baron Élie's collection.

Government for £2,500,000, much to the fury of the left-wing press. 'The Gift Of Pompidou To The Rothschilds' was the headline of *Minute* on 27 October. 'The Pompidolian Republic', commented the editor, 'is a young lady who can never say "no" to a Rothschild.'

Alain de Rothschild has surprised people by reserving a piece of the garden where he will build a new house of considerable proportions. Apparently no one has embarked on such a novel course since the end of the First World War. 23 Avenue de Marigny is only a few yards from the Élysée Palace and the Government will turn it into a guest house.

As very few Rothschilds find themselves in the divorce courts, Baron Guy's separation from his wife Alix, who was adored by the family, and his re-marriage in 1957 caused something of a stir. The bride was a twenty-six-year-old divorcee whose grandmother had been a Rothschild, Countess Marie-Hélène van Zuylen, married to Count Nicolai Although the Countess was a Catholic her marriage had been annulled by the Vatican, which left her free to re-marry. It was not easy for Guy, however, who after much thought decided to withdraw as head of the religious organization of the Jewish community, a position which passed to his cousin Alain. Nevertheless Guy remained as chairman of the largest social organization in France, the French Jewish United Appeal; and their only son, Édouard, has been brought up in the Jewish faith.

Marie-Hélène is one of the most controversial figures in Paris. A woman who arouses strong likes and dislikes, the very mention of her name can plunge a dinner party into heated and prolonged argument. For this relatively drab age, her entertainments are on a grand scale. Every few years she throws open the doors of Ferrières and gives a fancy-dress ball which is attended by the 'beautiful people' the world over. Her last party took place in December 1972. Salvador Dali did the decor and the guests were asked to come in surrealist costume. Everyone was there from the Comte de Paris to Elizabeth Taylor, from Princess Grace to Gunther Sachs—the new world against a fabulous background of Old Masters.

After Guy's second marriage his eldest son, David, moved into a flat with his mother Alix. One day in 1969 there was a knock on the door, and in walked a twenty-three-year-old gunman, Joseph Stadnik, formerly of the French Foreign Legion. Joseph brandished a revolver and threatened to shoot Alix and David unless they produced £150,000 in cash. David telephoned to Guy who assured him that he would come to the flat as soon as he could collect the money.

Young David, twenty-six years old at the time, took charge of the situation, advising his mother to go to her bedroom and wait until his father arrived. Meanwhile he sat with the gunman making stilted conversation. At one point Stadnik accidentally pulled the trigger and fired a bullet into the carpet, and poor Alix, shivering behind

Baron Guy, with his second wife, Marie-Hélène, and his son David at Longchamp.

a locked door, thought that David had been murdered and came running into the room.

Eventually Baron Guy appeared with a satchel full of notes. He insisted that Stadnik count them, in order to gain time, as he had told the police who were in the process of organizing a trap. Stadnik, however, was wary and insisted that David drive him out of Paris in his (David's) car. But Guy managed to persuade the gunman to leave David behind and to take him instead.

The two men climbed into Guy's car and began making their way through Paris. Soon a police car was in front of them, another behind them, one at the side, all were disguised and Stadnik was unaware of what was happening. The traffic was halted by a red light and suddenly Stadnik's door was whipped open and he was staring down the barrel of someone else's gun. It happened so quickly that he had no time to put up a fight.

The story had an odd ending. Apparently Guy felt sorry for Stadnik who was not a criminal, merely a young man searching for 'social justice'. The culprit bemoaned the fact that he had 'ruined the Baroness' carpet' by firing a bullet into the floor. This melted Guy's heart and he gave his testimony in such a way that Joseph received a suspended sentence of five years. For once the newspapers – at least the English papers – were disapproving of the Rothschilds. 'Nobody wishes to quarrel with the humanity of the judge,' wrote the London *Evening Standard* on 28 May 1971, 'but other would-be imitators of this particular act might now be tempted to put a political gloss on crimes of this nature.' Baroness Alix, however, was delighted. 'He had read too many thrillers, that was all,' she explained to reporters.

Everyone had behaved astoundingly well. David had been brave, Guy even braver, and Alix had turned the other cheek. The result was gratifying. The gunman relinquished crime and took a steady job. Every December he sends Guy a Christmas card.

273

Chapter XIII

The Rothschilds Today: The Others

(1953–73)

WHILE THE BANKING ROTHSCHILDS REASSERTED THEM-selves in the financial world, the non-banking Rothschilds sprang into bloom in all sorts of unexpected places with the hardiness of wild flowers. During the past twenty-five years these unorthodox members of the family made names for themselves as scientists, poets, civil servants and entrepreneurs; and as they are still very much alive, the past at last has caught up with the present.

In London one Rothschild is paid to advise the Cabinet, in Paris another is often consulted by the president. In the aggregate, Roth-schilds translate Elizabethan poetry, grow superlative shrubs, direct great racing stables, produce memorable wine, create enchanting houses and probably give more to charity than any other family in the world. As all of them are competitive, they invariably collect the same things, and vie with each other in their knowledge of silver, porcelain, eighteenth-century furniture and rare books. Very agreeably for their friends, all Rothschilds remain true to the tradi-tion of 150 years by serving superb food. 'When I want to set my French cousins quarrelling among each other,' Lord Rothschild told a friend, 'all I have to do is to invite them to dinner and ask them who has the best chef.'

Needless to say, Lord Rothschild is the most provocative member of the family. He is also the cleverest, the most entertaining and, apparently, the most unfathomable, for no two people ever agree on an assessment of his character. Indeed, when Mr Heath's Government announced in October 1970 that Lord Rothschild would head a new agency known as the Central Capability Unit, journalists could not decide which was the most puzzling, the job or the man. The job was to organize a 'think-tank' which would analyze problems that departmental civil servants viewed in a partisan light. The man was a brilliant academic who shunned fashionable society and who had spent his life as a Cambridge research worker and scientific director. The *Sunday Times* published a pen portrait of him that began like this:

When asked about Victor Rothschild his friends variously describe him as a genius, an oaf, an academic recluse, a man of the world, a frustrated failure, a remnant of old Bloomsbury, a fierce perfectionist, a character out of one of Scott Fitzgerald's poorer novels, and an administrator of immense skill. They all agree, however, that the quadruple burden of his name, his race, his money and his intelligence have made him one of the most complicated personalities in contemporary life.[1]

Lord Rothschild, 'the most provocative member of the family'.

Victor's career, on the other hand, at least in outline was very uncomplicated. He had returned from the war with a Bronze Star, a George Medal, and a fiancée, Miss Teresa Mayor, a charming young Cambridge graduate who had joined the War Ministry in 1941 and been detailed to assist Lord Rothschild in some of his counter-sabotage activities. Miss Mayor was a great-niece of Beatrice Webb, and a Labour supporter; indeed, her first peace-time job was secretary to Mr Philip Noel-Baker, one of Mr Attlee's ministers.

Victor and Tess were married in 1946 and although Lord Rothschild was not a political animal, he began to look on the socialist scourge, which had so upset his grandfather, with a friendly eye. Even before the war he had taken his seat in the Lords on the Labour benches, although this was more an act of defiance than a pledge of faith. It happened because of provocation on the part of Winston Churchill. Although Churchill at that time was not a member of the Government he was indignant to learn that a Rothschild – and a grandson of the grand old man of banking at that – had taken a neutral position on the cross benches and was not prepared to defend the capitalist citadel. 'So you're on the cross benches,' he growled to Victor, 'sitting on your dividends, I suppose.' Churchill seemed to have forgotten that in the early part of the century he himself had abandoned Toryism for Radicalism, and now it was Victor's turn to take umbrage. Without further ado the latter took his seat on the Labour benches and gave an interview to *Reynolds News* on his reasons for supporting the Socialists. The reporter, however, seemed more interested in how a Rothschild lived than in what a Rothschild thought and soon Victor was denying that Rothschilds ate off gold plates or owned taps that produced pound notes. 'I do not believe,' he said, 'that people should be allowed to have a lot of money unless they have earned it. Being the son of a rich man is not good enough.'

In order to justify himself, Victor became one of the hardest working science dons in Cambridge. He specialized in the biophysics of reproduction, trying to discover what happened to the metabolism of an egg when it was joined by the sperm; how a sperm swam, where it got its energy. He used cinematography to record the behaviour of a sperm under microscope, and claims to be the only person in the world to be able to show you a moving picture of a bull's spermatazoon joining a female egg. During the years of his research Lord Rothschild was elected a Fellow of the Royal Society, awarded two Cambridge doctorates, and given honorary doctorates at Newcastle and Manchester Universities.

Apart from his scientific work, Victor became chairman of the Agricultural Research Council in 1949. In those days he championed the unfettered independence of all scientists. 'One of the features of University life that we most cherish is the pursuit of knowledge for its own sake,' he told the Council on 8 October 1951. 'The great advances in science, whether of a fundamental or of an applied nature, come in peace-time from the labours of good workers rather than from the minds of central coordinators assessing the needs of the nation. Research councils are the servants and not the masters of the scientists they subsidize, and it is a good thing to remind them of this from time to time.'

Some people were surprised in 1959 when Victor accepted a very lowly job with the Royal Dutch Shell Company as a part-time adviser on the company's vast research organization. His salary was in keeping with his humble duties and although the Shell managers were confident that they had bought a good horse, they were unaware that they had picked a Derby winner. Victor displayed such brilliant powers of analysis, not to mention skill as an organizer, that within six years he rose to the dizzy heights of research coordinator of the whole Royal Dutch Shell group which embraced more than five hundred companies. He was responsible for an annual budget of £34,000,000 and supervised a staff of seven thousand people in twenty-eight research laboratories spread over seven countries. His salary leapt to Rothschild dimensions and in 1968 he reached his final goal by becoming chairman of Shell Research; but in 1970 he also reached the company's retiring age of sixty, and subsequently fell into Mr Heath's net.

When the press learned that the Prime Minister had invited Lord Rothschild to head his Capability Unit, known as a think-tank, journalists were intrigued that a former Labour supporter had become an adviser to a Tory Government. However, almost all of them praised the appointment, and Richard Crossman congratulated Heath on 'putting a tiger into the tank'.

But the subtle Lord Rothschild does not operate as a tiger. Witty and amusing, he can charm the birds off the trees when he chooses, but when he does not choose he can be a formidable opponent with a sharp cutting edge disconcertingly concealed in a sheath of flattery. 'No one can mix extreme discourtesy with extreme courtesy so effortlessly as Lord Rothschild,' commented a friend admiringly.

But Lord Rothschild pleases far more than he displeases. He is warm-hearted and generous, a man of deep sympathies who nevertheless tells you that the head is more important than the heart. Everything about him is paradoxical; at one and the same time he is devious and outspoken, arrogant and bashful, a millionaire with a conscience who works sixteen hours a day to justify himself as a Rothschild. Apart from a Rolls-Royce brain, his most outstanding characteristic is an acute sense of humour. When the Prime Minister invited him to Chequers in 1971 to address the Cabinet for the first time, Victor was well aware that there was considerable hostility toward both himself and his organization. Although it might be tactless to refer directly to the antagonism, there would be no harm in taking a mild poke at the head of the Treasury. 'When I first

Mrs James de Rothschild is the President of Hanadiv, a trust for the promotion of education, science and culture in Israel.

arrived in Whitehall,' he told the Cabinet blandly, 'Sir Douglas Allen looked at me as though he were Lord Longford examining a piece of porn.' There is nothing that British politicians like better than being made to laugh; and with one stroke Lord Rothschild had entrenched himself and his think-tank.

The 'tank' is composed of some thirty people, three-quarters of whom are first-class academics still in their twenties. The group have made reports on subjects ranging from aircraft to regional government; from Ireland to energy; from trade unions to the nationalized industries. But nothing raised such a storm as Lord Rothschild's recommendation, in contradiction to what he had said publicly ten years earlier, that Scientific Research Councils should be controlled by the consumer, in this case mainly government departments. 'A revolutionary in Whitehall,' shrieked the *New Statesman* triumphantly, while the columns of *The Times* were inundated with correspondence from scientists all over Britain, not one of whom appeared to be in agreement with Rothschild. In the end, the usual British compromise was reached which did not satisfy anyone.

In London Lord Rothschild has a flat in the spacious house of his cousin, Mrs James de Rothschild – 'Dollie' to her friends, – a sharp-witted, enchanting woman who looks sixty and is, in fact, well over seventy. Dollie's residence is the only one of a row of houses which survived the blitz. Two of those demolished belonged to the late Lord Camrose and the late Lord Beaverbrook. 'The Rothschilds had more energetic fire-watchers,' explains one of the Camrose children. 'They simply picked up the fire bombs that fell on their roof and tossed them onto their neighbours'.'

Victor's home is in Cambridge, a large, low sprawling white brick house, with a complex of cottages and garages. It has several acres of land, a garden, a tennis court, a croquet lawn, and the most spectacular swimming pool in England, complete with sauna bath. The pool is under glass like a green-house, with a dome that can be opened or shut according to the weather. Lord Rothschild also has a holiday home in Barbados, where he spends a few weeks of every year, and a large farm, Rushbrooke, near Cambridge where he grows apples which he sells to Marks and Spencer. The children of his second marriage are the brilliant twenty-five-year-old Emma, who graduated from Oxford at the unheard of age of seventeen and then won a scholarship to the Massachusetts Institute of Technology; Victoria, twenty, and Amschel, eighteen.

Almost as clever as Victor is his sister, Miriam, two years his senior. A handsome woman with a highly original mind, Miriam Lane is one of the most entertaining conversationalists in England. Everything about her is unusual; for instance, although her son, twenty-five-year-old Charles Lane, took first-class honours in science at Cambridge, and a prize doctorate at Oxford, she is fiercely opposed to examinations, arguing that they waste the pupils' time by concentrating his mind on presentation rather than the acquisition of knowledge. Miriam's own academic career is unique. As her parents did not believe in higher education for females she did not attend a university; yet because of her contribution to science today she is an Honorary Fellow of St Hugh's College, Oxford, an Honorary D.Sc., and Professor of Biology at London University. Apparently the colleges broke all the rules in showering its distinctions on a lady so glaringly deficient in the most elementary of university degrees.

This does not mean, of course, that Miriam lacks scientific training. She acquired an impressive knowledge from her father, her uncle, and the curators of her uncle's museum at Tring. She specialized in bird parasites and in 1951, when she was having a baby, wrote a book in collaboration with Theresa Clay entitled *Fleas, Flukes and Cuckoos* which went into four editions. This was the prelude to a labour of love, the cataloguing of her father's ten thousand species of flea, which she has done over the past twenty years. The result is five impressively large, illustrated volumes.

Miriam is a rich woman, having inherited a fortune from her disinherited uncle, the second Lord Rothschild, who was forced to make ends meet on a niggardly million. She also inherited two thousand acres of farm land in Northamptonshire from her mother, and a manor house built by her father known as Ashton Wold. Apparently Charles Rothschild fell in love with the Northampton countryside when he was searching for butterflies. He was particularly struck by an empty Elizabethan house, once upon a time occupied by a farmer. He enquired to whom the property belonged and was told: 'An old crank who refuses to sell.' More enquiries and he discovered that the old crank was none other than his father, Lord Rothschild. Apparently the farm had been given to the latter in lieu of a bad debt.

Charles persuaded his father to make it over to him, and his father, in turn, persuaded him to sell the Elizabethan house because it was in a hollow and all Rothschilds believed that 'living low' was bad for the health. So Charles built a new house on a suitably high piece of ground, a rambling manor with very large and very pretty Elizabethan windows as a reminder of the abandoned property. Today Miriam Lane is transforming the manor into four or five flats for herself and her various children. The village of Ashton consists of thirty-five or forty very large thatched cottages which, although built by Charles in the 1900s were all equipped with bathrooms and electricity. Like his father he was one of the most progressive landlords in the country. Recently Miriam transferred the farm to the joint ownership of three of her four children, and hopes that they will be able to reconcile two incompatibles: keeping the cottages of Ashton tied to the farm, and making the farm pay.

Like most Rothschilds, Miriam is immensely generous. She has four children of her own, and two adopted children, the offspring of

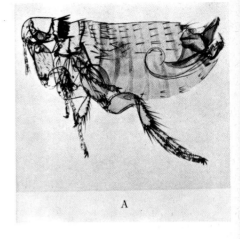

A

Diagram of a flea from Miriam Rothschild's *The Illustrated Catalogue of the Rothschild Collection of Fleas.*

a close friend who died. For the past ten years she has been living in a large, rambling house on the outskirts of Oxford where each Sunday she keeps open house. Here she provides delicious luncheons for friends, both young and old, who wander in and out as the spirit moves. Although a writer who attended one of these celebrated meals recently observed that the wine 'was not Mouton Rothschild but a plain claret', the wine was, in fact, (and always is), Château Lafite.

Miriam's houses have the usual Rothschild masterpieces hanging on the walls, but here the resemblance ends, for Miriam lives in the middle of a sea of books; books that reach from floor to ceiling, overflowing onto tables and floors where they remain in stacks. Her bedroom is partly a laboratory, complete with microscope, caged birds, sets of files, wired-in butterflies and hundreds more books. Miriam reveres the memory of her father and grandfather and, like Victor, has inherited them from a deep sense of obligation.

Like other Rothschilds she pays frequent visits to Israel, sometimes taking one or two of her children with her. At the time of the Six-Day War in 1967 her brother, Victor, organized a fund-raising dinner to which thirty of the most prominent Jewish families in Britain were invited. Although the Rothschilds insisted that individual contributions remain anonymous, the dinner guests stunned everyone, even the Israelis, by producing the staggering sum of 7,000,000 dollars.[2]

On many occasions Israel serves as a meeting ground for English and French Rothschilds. For instance, the late Baron Edmond's Trust, administered by James de Rothschild, financed Israel's first golf links, an eighteen-hole course in a hundred acres of land, laid out at a cost of £200,000. The course was near the Roman port of Caesarea on the Mediterranean coast which the current Baron Edmond is developing, and was opened jointly in 1961 by himself and his cousin, Victor. The latter managed to drive a golf ball 175 yards down the fairway with a No. 2 iron club, despite a 25 mph wind, while Edmond pursued the more cautious role of formally presenting the key to the club-house to Mr Abba Eban, the Minister of Education.

Forty-seven-year-old Baron Edmond is the richest of all the Rothschilds. A grandson of the great Edmond, and a nephew of the late James de Rothschild, the last private owner of Waddesdon, Edmond was the only son of the only Rothschild who might be described as a playboy. The reference is not wholly apt, however, as his father, Maurice, had an uncanny flair for money, a talent not usually associated with big spenders. Apparently Maurice fled from the Germans in 1940 with £250,000 of gems sewn into his satchel. He arrived in England and began to play the stock markets of London and New York, multiplying his fortune many times over.

Baron Edmond de Rothschild is the immensely energetic head of a world-wide business empire.

Maurice's wife, Naomi Halphen, also possessed business acumen. Descended from the famous Pereire family, which once upon a time challenged James de Rothschild's financial supremacy, and suffered for it, Noémi parted from Maurice shortly after the birth of Edmond in 1926 ending a marriage of seventeen years. She loved Switzerland and travelled around the Alps with her baby son and his nanny, Mlle Pfeiffer, who became her close friend and business associate. Naomi decided to develop a new resort, and commissioned two mountain guides to advise her. After a lengthy survey the men recommended two regions, Val d'Isère and Megève. She chose the latter, built a splendid hotel at the foot of the Mont d'Arbois, but was unable to continue developing the resort through lack of money. Later, however, her son Edmond proved that she had made a good choice.

Edmond was barely twenty when the Second War ended. A handsome young man with immense drive and enthusiasm he was more of an entrepreneur than a banker and decided to use his fortune to support enterprises that interested him. With true Rothschild intuition he managed to hit upon the gold spinner of the century – mass tourism. He backed the Club Méditerranée and began to build anything and everything that would service the rapidly growing tourist industry: Pan American's Intercontinental hotels, bungalow villages in Majorca, a luxury resort in Israel, housing projects in Paris, developments in Guadeloupe and Martinique, and finally chalets and ski-lifts and another superb hotel in his mother's resort, Megève. The Hôtel du Mont d'Arbois was perched five thousand feet above the village, with such innovations as a heated swimming pool under glass, and a terrace from which a helicopter could lift skiers to the mountain tops.

Baron Edmond had a showman's flair, and celebrated the opening in 1963 by inviting 120 guests from Paris and New York and flying them to Megève in specially chartered aeroplanes for a four-day skiing party. He took out an £8,000,000 insurance policy to cover guests against loss or theft of their jewels which provoked a good deal of newspaper comment and no doubt was the inspiration of his press agent.

Edmond's Paris office is situated at 45 Rue du Faubourg Saint-Honoré where he has a staff of thirty assistants. His business interests represent an empire that stretched from Europe to South America, from the Middle East to New York. The Compagnie Financière is the holding company for his French interests. Apart from tourism, he owns a private bank in Paris, more like an English merchant bank than his cousins' Banque Rothschild. He also controls the largest toy company and the largest frozen food company in France. In Switzerland he has another bank, known as the Banque Privée, and a company that promotes hotels in Geneva, Frankfurt and Hamburg, and is involved in the trailer business in Germany and Holland. In Belgium he is a director of the Banque Lambert, in South Africa of De Beers Consolidated Mines, in Holland a member of the Steering Committee of the Bilderberg Meetings, in Israel Chairman of Tri-Continental Pipelines which was founded in 1958 to link the Red Sea to the Mediterranean, but now is merely a holding company, Chairman of the Israel Corporation, and Chairman of Isrop, an investment company which controls the Israel General Bank.

His philanthropic activities are on the same gigantic scale as his business interests, and range from sitting on the board of the Hebrew University of Jerusalem, to directing the Middle East Peace Institute which he founded after the war in 1967. He has helped to create French schools in Jerusalem and Tel Aviv and donates money regularly to the Biological-Physio-Chemical Institute, founded by his grandfather, the first Baron Edmond. In France and Switzerland he sits on a dozen boards of a dozen hospitals and scientific institutes.

In 1961 Edmond married a beautiful girl, Nadine Lhôpitalier, who was a singer in a night-club. In 1963 she gave birth to a boy, Benjamin, his only son. Edmond's Paris house in the Rue de l'Élysée is as spectacular as his energy. Situated within a few yards of his office, across the street from the Élysée Palace, he has an incredible swimming pool ninety feet long built to look like a natural pond and bordered by a tropical garden all of which is under glass. As the pool is basement level, he has continued his underground world to include a magnificent gymnasium and a cinema room that seats fifty people.

As a showman Baron Edmond only has one rival in the family: the romantic, highly intelligent Baron Philippe, owner of Mouton Rothschild which he inherited from his father, Henri. Philippe fell in love with the vineyard during the First World War when, as a boy of sixteen, he was sent to Bordeaux to escape the ravages of Big Bertha. In those days the Médoc was primitive; bad roads, no electricity or running water. In 1922 Baron Henri turned over the vineyards to Philippe who, despite the fact that he was attracted to every sport that combined speed and danger, such as sailing and motor-racing, did not neglect Mouton. He opened it to the public and poured money into improvements although in those days making wine was far from profitable. But Mouton was in Philippe's blood. The serenity of this little enclave stretching along the Gironde, the beauty of sun and soil and season, combined with the skill and patience of man, gave Philippe a feeling for the grace and timelessness of existence which added a new dimension to his understanding.

In 1940, when the Germans overran France, they took possession of the two Rothschild vineyards – Mouton and neighbouring Lafite which is now owned jointly by Barons Guy, Alain, Élie and Edmond, and Jimmy de Rothschild's widow, Dollie. The French Government nationalized the property in an effort to prevent the invaders from scooping up the thousands of bottles of wine mellowing in the cellars, and exporting it to Germany as 'Jewish contraband'. As things turned out, the conquering army behaved well, for the Nazis appointed a 'wine *führer*' who took up residence in Bordeaux. The job of the official was to make sure that the cellars remained unharmed so that Goering and his colleagues could celebrate the final victory in the world's best claret. As a result, although Mouton became HQ of the German general commanding the aircraft batteries of the south-east of France, the vineyards and cellars were treated with respect. Unfortunately the same did not apply to the living rooms. One night soon after their arrival the officers got drunk and began shooting at three pastels of Philippe and his brother and sister, James and Nadine. They destroyed two of the pictures but in the middle of the hilarity the family cook walked into the room, grabbed Philippe's portrait, put it under her arm and marched out.

Next day the cook left, taking the picture with her, not to set foot in the château until Philippe's return. The portrait hangs on the wall today.

During the ten years following the Second World War, Philippe had a difficult time retaining his inheritance. With half Europe behind the Iron Curtain, the other half suffering from shock and dislocation, and the U.S.A. only interested in hard liquor, it seemed impossible to make the vineyards pay. Philippe grasped at any new idea that would give the wine publicity, one of which was to invite famous artists each year to design the labels for the bottles. In 1947 Cocteau drew a romantic impression of the harvest; in 1955 Braque produced a very messy table recalling the end of a convivial evening; in 1958 Tchelitchew did an abstract painting of a gold and crimson splash against a black background; in 1967 Henry Moore showed hands holding glasses; in 1970 Marc Chagall painted lovers in a prairie.

However, long before Moore's contribution, Mouton Rothschild had turned the corner and moved into the category of one of the world's most profitable businesses. 'If I had not been a Rothschild,' Philippe confided to a friend, 'I could never have survived the difficult times financially.' But being a Rothschild meant that the banks extended credit. And suddenly in 1955 things began to change. Overnight, it seems, the Americans began to drink wine. From that year onwards the proprietors in the Médoc have never looked back.

Today Baron Philippe not only has two vineyards – Mouton Rothschild and Mouton Baron Philippe – but in 1970 he added a third *cru*, Château Clerc-Milon. He has built up a merchant company called La Bergerie which distributes Mouton-Cadet and others. His vineyards now total about three hundred acres and are worth at least £7,000,000. But far more important than the money is the love that he has lavished on his little kingdom. He is the only Rothschild, or for that matter the only Parisian proprietor, to make the Médoc his home, living there several months each year. As the one owner who has personally directed the work of his vineyards for over fifty years he is virtually prince of Pauillac.

Very different from the revolution in American drinking habits was another spectacular change that took place in Philippe's life about the same time. The first Baroness Philippe had been arrested in Paris during the Occupation (their small daughter, Philippine, was incredibly lucky not to be picked up as well) and sent to a concentration camp where she died. In 1954 Philippe married again. His bride was a fascinating American lady, Pauline Potter of Baltimore, who might have stepped out of the pages of a Henry James novel. Yet despite her distinguished colonial ancestry she was more French than American having spent most of her childhood in Paris. When Philippe met her she was working for Hattie Carnegie as a designer. Soft-spoken, with wide-apart eyes and a seductive smile, Pauline not only was clever and humorous but had an outlook so unusual, a

Top Baron Philippe in his vineyard at Mouton, near Pauillac, in the Médoc.

Bottom Baron and Baroness Philippe in a room of the wine museum at Mouton which they established in the early 1960s. All the objects in the museum – which is housed in an ancient *chai* – are connected with the grape.

personality so different, that if the word 'enchanting' were not debased by indiscriminate usage it would be the right adjective to choose. She is an artist who does not paint, but who creates beauty, sometimes by shape and colour, sometimes by visual ideas. At night she dresses in silk shirts and knickerbockers, her hair plaited over one shoulder. In the summer she does not seek the sun but moves north to Scandinavia, Siberia, even Iceland. In 1965 she took a trip to Russia and wrote a book *The Irrational Journey*, more poetry than prose and memorable for its vivid imagery.

Pauline's marriage to Philippe marked the beginning of a distinguished partnership. For many years Philippe had written poetry; indeed one of his poems *Vendange* had inspired a three-act ballet by Darius Milhaud with décor and costumes by Dali and choreography by Serge Lifar. However, story and script lay forgotten in the drawers of the Paris Opera House for nearly twenty years. Then, in 1972, it was decided to celebrate Milhaud's eightieth birthday with a special offering. *Vendange* was rediscovered and performed in Nice in May, to the satisfaction of the author and the acclaim of the critics.

Soon after their marriage, Pauline encouraged Philippe to undertake the task of translating the Elizabethan poets, among them such metaphysical thinkers as Marvell, Donne, Crashaw and Henry Vaughan. The work was absorbing, yet so complex – at times almost impossible – that it took fifteen years; every word, every phrase, every intonation was puzzled and argued over before it was deemed ready for the public. In 1969, however, the glowing reviews justified the meticulous care. Philippe also translated two of Christopher Fry's plays, *The Lady's not for Burning* and *The Dark is Light Enough*, both of which were performed at the State Theatre in Paris. His latest achievement is a brilliant translation of Christopher Marlowe's *Dr Faustus*, which was published in 1972.

Together Philippe and Pauline redecorated the small Victorian château at Mouton, and redesigned the seventeenth-century stables, turning them into a luxurious new house with an enormous drawing-room and a library containing books in four or five languages. But the greatest of their joint enterprises was the establishment of a wine museum which must rank as one of the most original and most perfect private museums in Europe.

The idea was inspired by a wonderful group of silver ceremonial vessels that Philippe inherited from his grandmother, a daughter of Baron Carl of Frankfurt. How amusing it would be, he thought, to collect works of art connected with the grape. For the next seven or eight years Philippe and Pauline searched the world for objects that might qualify.

The result is a unique and marvellously diverse collection ranging from a Gilgamesh Cup carved 2,500 years before Christ to a vessel with black pictorial scenes done by the Greek painter Theseus; from blue and white porcelain bowls of the Ming period mounted in

Opposite Top Table set for lunch in a corner of the long drawing-room at Château Mouton. The windows look out on to the vineyards and the life-size, sixteenth century Italian horse and dummy were once used as artists' models: *Bottom* One of a set of five early sixteenth-century tapestries depicting the grape harvest, made near Strasbourg or Nederweiler and now in the wine museum at Mouton.

Overleaf Two German nautilus cups mounted in silver-gilt, in the wine museum at Mouton. The taller of the two, decorated with a horse, a siren, dolphins and sea-horses, was made at Augsburg in 1680 by the renowned goldsmith Johann Phelot; the smaller, which came originally from the collection of Lionel de Rothschild, is decorated with a kneeling figure of Atlas, masks and a siren; it was probably made in Nuremberg at the end of the sixteenth century.

Elizabethan English silver-gilt to a fragment of a fifth-dynasty bas-relief once part of a tomb at Sakkarah; from tapestries of the wine harvest made near Colmar at the end of the fifteenth century to jugs of the ninth century B.C. from Iran. Some of the most striking pieces are the high German covered cups, a French silver chalice dated 1570, a Burgundian wine vessel that van Eyck might have painted, a Chinese silver bowl of the twelfth century, an Amlash bowl of gold, embossed with the walking deer that are now extinct, a Sassanian silver and gold drinking bowl showing a king, long ribbons streaming from his crown, hunting. Modern sculpture is represented by an astonishing piece entitled *The Spirit of the Vine*, a spray of gold thread, platinum and copper covered with red enamel, executed in New York in 1957 by Richard Lippold.

When the editor of the English art magazine, *Apollo*, Mr Denys Sutton, visited Mouton, he was lyrical.

> The study of art [he wrote] has many attractions but one of the most rewarding is when . . . one has the good fortune to come across a collection which has been assembled with enthusiasm, and a fastidious sense of quality. This Museum, in fact, reveals that a collection can still be formed which is out of the ordinary and a tribute to personal taste . . . . It is perhaps significant that this Museum is situated in the Gironde and that the grape is the chosen theme. Inevitably much nonsense is talked about wine and its virtues, but, surely, it is undeniable that the ability to detect quality, so vital in the tasting of wine, holds a message applicable to the study of art . . . I like to think that spending part of one's life in a district in which *La qualité et la gloire* are sought after at all levels of society would have a tonic effect on the eye. It was certainly produced in this case a museum which will perpetuate the memory of its founders and provide endless pleasure to the visitor.[3]

Mouton Rothschild is an exciting place to visit, as everything about it bears the strange, exotic stamp of its imaginative and warm-hearted owners. The one-time stables are now part of the main house, painted white, long, low and rambling. The immense drawing-room, eighty feet in length and twenty feet in width has seven arched windows that look onto the vines that grow up to the edge of the house. At night they are flood-lit and resembled a foam-flecked sea.

Baroness Philippe is a perfectionist and the house runs fault-lessly. Guests are looked after with nineteenth-century care, their clothes packed and unpacked, washed and pressed, laid out and hung up. But apart from this routine nothing at Mouton is the same from one day to another. For instance, no two meals are ever served in the same room, and the hours of eating vary according to the whim of the hostess.

The big drawing-room is dominated by a sixteenth-century Italian life-sized wooden horse which stands at one end; and the rooms of visitors are enlivened by exotic trees which reach the ceiling. The dining-room table is a work of art in itself, with floral decora-

Silver-gilt figure of a grape-harvester with his dog from the wine museum at Mouton; it is enamelled in places and was made in Augsburg at the end of the sixteenth century.

The huge drawing-room at Mouton.
The floor is made of blue and pale
brick-red tiles and all the windows
look out on to the vineyards.

tions that no one would think of, except Pauline; one of the prettiest
effects was massed cabbage leaves, the curly kind, that looked like
bowls of feathers.

Philippe, who wanders about in the day time in tweed trousers and
velvet jacket, makes an entry at night in coloured dinner jacket and
embroidered slippers. The food is perfect but of course what fasci-
nates the visitor is the wine. At every meal guests are given three
clarets which sometimes span a hundred years. The meals always end
with a thimble-full of iced Château Yquem. From some of the
windows of Mouton it is possible to look onto the vines of the other
Rothschild establishment, the great Lafite, which is separated from
Mouton by a narrow footpath.

The interior of the little eighteenth-century house where Philippe
lived as a bachelor and which Pauline shared with him while the
stables were being re-done is a gem of Victoriana. The walls are
decorated with a riot of colourful *petit-point* samplers, and on the
floor is a needlework carpet showing Queen Victoria exchanging a
treaty of friendship and trade with Napoleon III. The guests are often
asked to guess whether or not the figures are larger than life. To
prove their point they sometimes lie down on the carpet. 'But never,
never on Queen Victoria,' notes Pauline, 'always on the Emperor.'

Today the Rothschild family consists of twenty-two males, twenty-seven females, fifteen Rothschild wives and five ex-wives, a grand total of seventy. The eldest Rothschild is Baron Eugene, formerly of Vienna, who lives in Monte-Carlo with his wife, the former actress Jeanne Stewart; the youngest is two-year-old Nathaniel, son of Jacob and Serena Rothschild, who one day will be the fifth Lord Rothschild.

If you were allowed only two adjectives to describe the Rothschilds you would stumble automatically on the paradox that distinguishes the family, for the words 'rich and energetic' do not spring to mind naturally as a pair. Generation after generation of Rothschilds have refused flatly to accept the leisured role usually welcomed by those with inherited wealth. Although the second generation of English Rothschilds built themselves enormous country houses, and at one time owned thirty thousand acres in Buckinghamshire alone, they were not interested in settling down as landed gentry. It is some measure of the family vitality that in the past forty years every one of the great Rothschild country houses in England have been sold or given to the National Trust, their former owners moving into smaller, more manageable houses in keeping with the times. Indeed, the only house built by a Rothschild and still in private hands is Mentmore Towers, the property of Hannah Rothschild's son, the present Lord Rosebery.

First and foremost the Rothschilds are a family of doers and givers. Although they are not intellectuals they have an intellectual streak that began with the children of the first Lord Rothschild, the famous Natty. Not only did Natty have two clever sons, Walter and Charles, both scientists, but Charles had a clever son and daughter, Victor and Miriam, again both scientists, and Victor had a clever son and daughter, Jacob and Emma, a banker and a journalist, and Miriam had a clever son, Charles, a boy of twenty-four who shows brilliant promise as a scientist. The other intellectual Rothschild is Philippe who, although his forbears have lived in France for 130 years, is claimed by the English Rothschilds as their own because his great-grandfather, Nathaniel, was Nathan's son and an uncle of the first Lord Rothschild. However, the French Rothschilds are able to counter with Nathalie Josso, a grand-daughter of Baron Robert de Rothschild, who at twenty-one was the youngest doctor in Paris.

Along with Rothschild riches and Rothschild vitality marches another quality, an urge to create, which displays itself not only in vineyards and gardens, racing stables and collections, but in the art of living. All Rothschilds are superlative hosts. The French cousins still live in enormous Paris houses, waited on at table by footmen in white gloves. The English Rothschilds, on the other hand, spend a great deal of money to achieve simplicity. According to the press, the labour-saving house, cottages and swimming pool built by Victor Rothschild in Cambridge in 1960 cost £100,000; and a figure twice as large was mentioned in connection with alterations

Above Baroness Alix, first wife of Baron Guy. *Below* Baroness Cécile de Rothschild, sister of Baron Guy.

carried out about the same time at Eyethrope, which stands a few miles from Waddesdon, and once upon a time was Miss Alice de Rothschild's tea pavilion. James de Rothschild's widow, Dollie, turned the folly into an exquisite eight-bedroomed house which looks onto a magnificent park of rolling green hills, lawns and leafy trees.

A few miles away lives Anthony de Rothschild's widow, Yvonne. Her son, Evelyn, occupies part of Ascott which was given to the National Trust, while his mother and grandmother – a wonderfully alert Russian lady of 95 – live in an enchanting cottage which looks like an illustration to a fairy tale. Painted white, and surrounded by roses, it is everyone's dream of life in the country.

There are no poor Rothschilds, only Rothschilds who are richer than other Rothschilds. The owner of one of the greatest private collections in the world is Guy's mother, eighty-nine-year-old Baroness Édouard, who lives on the Avenue Foch against a background of magnificent Renaissance jewellery and the superb eighteenth-century furniture and Sèvres porcelain so dear to Rothschild hearts. On her wall is the only privately-owned Vermeer in France, *The Astronomer*, bought by James in 1863 and now owned by Guy.

The French and English cousins are linked by strong ties of affection. Baroness Alix often takes trips with Victor's sister, Miriam; Baron Guy and Evelyn, Baron Edmond and Jacob are close friends. Lord Rothschild's favourite French relations are Cécile and Liliane. Cécile is in her fifties, the sister of Élie and Alain, a clever, well-read woman who has never married and lives in a flat in the Rue du Faubourg Saint-Honoré surrounded by Goyas, Renoirs, Manets and Picassos. She gives dinner parties celebrated for food, wine and conversation, and plays scratch golf, often accompanying Victor on golfing holidays.

Yet of all the Rothschild ladies on both sides of the Channel, Liliane probably plays the most indispensable role. A clever, talented person, who loves a joke, she is the family lynch-pin, assuager and healer. This is an interesting role for a woman who not only could have earned her living as a designer or decorator, but who has such a good eye for pictures, both old and new, that she might have become a leading art dealer. Instead, she has been content to play her part as a Rothschild wife. She knows more about the family history and the family possessions than any other person, and gives considerable time to biographers, art editors and photographers in quest of Rothschildiana. Her husband, Élie, runs Château Lafite, which, although it is 'first of the first', is nevertheless hotly challenged by Philippe's Mouton. When the latter's daughter was married in 1961, and hundreds of guests travelled to Bordeaux for the wedding, Liliane and Élie gave the wedding dinner in the giant cellar at Lafite, and the cousins toasted the bride in clarets from the two vineyards.

Liliane de Rothschild, Baroness Élie.
A brilliant decorator with a great
knowledge of art, she is also the
foremost authority on Rothschildiana.

Today, Rothschilds on opposite sides of the Channel are still held together by finance and business but the State of Israel has forged a new bond. At the time of the Six-Day War the French and English cousins alone contributed over $1,000,000, a gift unequalled by any other family. When Baron Alain visited Israel shortly afterwards, and went to the Wailing Wall he was so moved that he burst into tears. Baroness Alix is the World President of Youth Aliyah, which is concerned with the emigration of Jewish children to Israel. Edmund de Rothschild is treasurer of the Friends of the Hebrew University of Jerusalem. Evelyn de Rothschild is chairman of the Board of Governors of the Technion, Israel's Institute of Technology. As the country's very existence depends on its skills and inventiveness, both in peace and war, this last appointment is one of the most crucial that the Government can give. It not only calls for faultless management but the ability and determination to raise large sums of money.

However, as far as money is concerned nothing in the family rivals the donations made by the Trusts established so many years ago by the late Baron Edmond. These organizations represent an unbroken chain of support for the people of Israel over a time span of nearly a hundred years. Originally the principal Trust was known as Pica – Palestine Jewish Colonization Association – but when it became clear, after the establishment of the State of Israel, that colonization would be handled by the Government, its functions were changed. Edmond's son, James, renamed it 'Hanadiv' the Hebrew word for 'benefactor' by which his father was known throughout Palestine; and at the same time rechannelled the Trust's funds to the promotion of education, science and culture. When James died in 1957 his widow, Dollie, assumed the presidency which she still holds. For many years she has been powerfully assisted by Lord Rothschild, and recently she has enlisted the help of the latter's son, Jacob. The Trust knows no boundaries. In the 1960s it carried out James' wishes by providing money for the Knesset, the new Parliament building in Jerusalem. Today its beneficiaries range from universities, hospitals and public libraries to archaeological digs; from the board of the Weizmann Scientific Institute to the organizers of Instructional Television.

The Rothschilds have always given freely, yet of all the qualities that distinguish them – generosity, creativeness, or sheer vitality – none is more conspicuous, even today, than the cardinal principle which the founder implanted in his five sons: solidarity. If old Mayer Amschel Rothschild never tired of demonstrating the frailty of a single stick and the strength of a bundle of sticks, the lesson was well learned. All Rothschilds still accept the belief: 'A family that works together is invincible.'

Mayer Amschel Rothschild (1744–1812)
m. 1770
Gutle Schnapper (1753–1849)

- **(Schönche) Jeanette (1771–1859)**
  m. 1795*
  Benedict Moses Worms

- **Amschel Mayer (1773–1855)**
  m. 1796
  Eva Hanau (1779–1848)

- **Salomon Mayer (1774–1855)**
  m. 1800
  Caroline Stern (1782–1854)

  - **Anselm Salomon (1803–74)**
    m. 1826
    Charlotte de Rothschild (L)

    - Mayer Anselm Leon (1827–8)
    - **(Caroline) Julie (1830–1907)**
      m. 1850
      Adolph von Rothschild (F)
    - **(Hannah) Mathilde (1832–1924)**
      m. 1849
      Wilhelm Carl von Rothschild (F)
    - **(Sarau) Louise (1834–1924)**
      m. 1858*
      Baron Raymondo von Franchetti
    - **Nathaniel Mayer (1836–1905)**
    - **Ferdinand James (1839–98)**
      m. 1865
      Evelina de Rothschild (L)
    - **Salomon Albert (1844–1911)**
      m. 1876
      Bettina Caroline de Rothschild (P)

      - Albert Anselm Salomon Nimrod (1922–1938)
      - **Georg Anselm (1877–1934)**
      - **Alphonse Mayer (1878–1942)**
        m. 1911
        Clarice Sebag-Montefiore (b. 1894)
        - **Bettina Jemima (b. 1924)**
          m. 1943*
          Matthew Looram
        - **Gwendoline Charlotte Frances Joan (b. 1927)**
          m. 1948*
          Roland Henry Hoguet
      - **Louis Nathaniel (1882–1955)**
        m. 1946
        Countess Hildegard Johanna Caroline Marie Auersperg (b. 1895)
      - **Eugene Daniel (b. 1884)**
        m. 1925
        Countess Kitty Schönborn-Bucheim (nee Wolff) (1885–1946)
        m. 2nd 1952
        Jeanne Stuart
      - Charlotte Esther (b. & d. 1885)
    - **Alice Charlotte (1847–1922)**

  - **Betty (1805–86)**
    m. 1824
    James (Jacob) de Rothschild (P)

    - **Charlotte (1807–59)**
      m. 1826
      Anselm Salomon von Rothschild (V)
    - **Leonora (1837–1911)**
      m. 1857
      Mayer Alphonse de Rothschild (P)
    - **Evelina (1839–66)**
      m. 1865
      Ferdinand James von Rothschild (V)
    - **Valentine Noémi (b. 1886)**
      m. 1911*
      Sigismund, Baron Springer (b. 1875)
    - **Oscar Ruben (1888–1909)**

- **Nathan Mayer (1777–1836)**
  m. 1806
  Hannah Barent Cohen (1783–1850)

  - **Lionel (1808–79)**
    m. 1836
    Charlotte von Rothschild (F)

    - **Nathaniel Mayer (2nd Baronet, 1st Baron U.K.) (1840–1915)**
      m. 1867
      Emma Louise von Rothschild (F)

      - **Lionel Walter (3rd Baronet, 2nd Baron U.K.) (1868–1937)**
      - **Charlotte Louise Adela Evelina (1873–1947)**
        m. 1899*
        Clive Behrens (d. 1935)
      - **Nathaniel Charles (1877–1923)**
        m. 1907
        Rozsika von Wertheimstein (1870–1940)

        - **Mirian Louisa (b. 1908)**
          m. 1911*
          George Lane
          Div. 1956
        - Elizabeth Charlotte (b. 1909)
        - **Nathaniel Mayer Victor (3rd Baron U.K.) (b. 1910)**
          m. 1933
          Barbara Judith Hutchinson (b. 1911)
          m. 2nd: 1946
          Teresa Georgina Mayor (b. 1915)

          - Sarah (b. 1934)
          - **Nathaniel Charles Jacob (b. 1936)**
            m. 1961
            Serena Dunn
            - Hannah Mary (b. 1962)
            - Beth Mathilda (b. 1964)
            - Emily Magda (b. 1967)
            - Nathaniel Philip Victor James (b. 1971)
          - Miranda (b. 1940)
          - Emma Georgina (b. 1948)
          - Victoria Katherine (b. 1953)
          - Amschel Mayor James (b. 1955)
        - **Kathleen Annie Pannonica (b. 1913)**
          m. 1935*
          Jules de Köenigswarter
          Div. 1956

    - **Alfred Charles (1842–1918)**
    - **Leopold (1845–1917)**
      m. 1881
      Maria Perugia (1862–1937)

      - **Lionel Nathan (1882–1942)**
        m. 1912
        Marie-Louise Beer (b. 1892)

        - **Rosemary Leonora Ruth (b. 1913)**
          m. 1934*
          Denis Gomer Berry (b. 1911)
          m. 2nd: 1942*
          John Antony Seys (b. 1914)
          - Katherine Juliette (b. 1949)
          - Nicholas David (b. 1951)
          - Charlotte Henrietta (b. 1955)
          - David Lionel (b. 1955)
        - **Edmund Leopold (b. 1916)**
          m. 1948
          Elizabeth Edith Lentner (b. 1923)
        - **Naomi Louisa Nina (b. 1920)**
          m. 1941*
          Jean Pierre Reinach (1915–1942)
          m. 2nd 1947*
          Bertrand Goldschmidt
        - Leopold David (b. 1927)
      - **Evelyn Achille (1886–1917)**
      - **Anthony Gustav (1887–1961)**
        m. 1926
        Yvonne Lydia Louise Cahen d'Anvers (b. 1899)
        - Renée Louise Marie (b. 1927)
        - Anne Sonia (1930)
        - Evelyn Robert Adrian (1931)

  - **Anthony (1st Baronet) (1810–76)**
    m. 1840
    Louise Montefiore (1821–1910)

    - **Constance (1843–1931)**
      m. 1877
      Cyril Flower (1st Lord Battersea) (d. 1907)
    - **Annie (1844–1926)**
      m. 1873
      Hon. Eliot Yorke
    - Nathalie (b. & d. 1843)

  - **Nathaniel (1812–70)**
    m. 1842
    Charlotte de Rothschild (P)

    - **James Edouard (1844–81)**
      m. 1877
      Laura Thérèse von Rothschild (F)
    - Mayer Albert (1846–50)
    - Arthur (1851–1903)
    - **Henri James (1872–1946)**
      m. 1895
      Mathilde Weissweiler (1874–1926)

      - **James Nathaniel Charles Leopold (b. 1896)**
        m. 1923
        Claude Dupont (b. 1904)
        m. 2nd: Yvette Choquet
        - Nicole (b. 1924)
        - **Monique (b. 1925)**
          m. 1945*
          Jean-François Drach
          m. 2nd: 1950
          Georges Halphen
      - **Nadine Charlotte Thérèse (1898–1958)**
        m. 1919
        Adrien Thierry
    - **Jeanne Charlotte (1874–1929)**
      m. 1896
      David Leonino

  - **Hannah (1815–64)**
    m. 1839*
    Hon. Henry Fitzroy

  - **Mayer Amschel (1818–74)**
    m. 1850
    Juliana Cohen (1831–77)

    - **Hannah (1851–90)**
      m. 1878*
      Earl of Rosebery (1847–1929)

  - **Louise (1820–97)**
    m. 1842
    Mayer Carl von Rothschild (F)

    - **Adele Hannah Charlotte (1843–1922)**
      m. 1862
      Salomon James de Rothschild (P)
    - **Emma Louise (1844–1935)**
      m. 1867
      Nathaniel Mayer (Lord Rothschild) (L)

- **(Belche) Isabella (1781–1861)**
  m. 1802*
  Bernard Judah Sichel

The Rothschilds

Descendants of female Rothschilds who did not marry members of the Rothschild family have not been listed; the omissions are marked with an asterisk. The letters F, L, N, P, V refer to Frankfurt, London, Naples, Paris and Vienna.

Breinliche (Babette) (1784–1869)
m. 1808*
Sigmund L. Beyfus

Carl Mayer (1788–1855)
m. 1818
Adelheid Hertz (1800–53)

Julie (1780–1815)
m. 1811
Meyer Beyfus

Henrietta (1791–1866)
m. Abraham Montefiore*

James (Jacob) Mayer (1792–1868)
m. 1824
Betty von Rothschild (V)

Charlotte (1819–84)
m. 1836
Lionel de Rothschild (L)

Mayer Carl (1820–86)
m. 1842
Louise de Rothschild (L)

Adolph (1823–1900)
m. 1850
(Caroline) Julie von Rothschild (V)

Wilhelm Carl (1828–1901)
m. 1849
(Hannah) Mathilde von Rothschild (V)

Anselm Alexander (1835–54)

Charlotte (1825–99)
m. 1842
Nathaniel de Rothschild (L)

Mayer Alphonse (1827–1905)
m. 1857
Leonora de Rothschild (L)

Gustave Salomon (1829–1911)
m. 1859
Cécile Anspach (1840–1912)

Salomon James (1835–64)
m. 1862
Adele Hannah von Rothschild (F)

Edmond James (1845–1934)
m. 1877
Adelheid von Rothschild (F)

Clementine Henriette (1845–65)

Laura Thérèse (1847–1931)
m. 1871
James Édouard de Rothschild (P–L)

Hannah Louisa (1850–92)

Margaretha Alexandrine (1855–1905)
m. 1878*
Agénor, Duc de Gramont (1851–1925)

Bertha Clara (1862–1903)
m. 1882*
Alexandre, Prince de Wagram (d. 1911)

Georgine Sara (1851–69)

Adelheid (1853–1935)
m. 1877
Edmond James de Rothschild (P)

Minna Caroline (1857–1903)
m. 1878*
Max B. H. Goldschmidt (d. 1940)

Bettina Caroline (1858–92)
m. 1876
Salomon Albert von Rothschild (V)

Charlotte Beatrix (1864–1934)
m. Maurice Ephrussi

Édouard Alphonse James (1868–1949)
m. 1905
Germaine Alice Halphen (b. 1884)

Octave (b. & d. 1860)

Zoë Lucie Betty (1863–1916)
m. 1882*
Baron Leon Lambert (d. 1919)

Alice Caroline (1865–1909)

Bertha Juliette (1870–1906)
m. 1887
Sir Edward A. Sassoon, Bart.
m. Baron Emmanuel Leonino *

André (1874–?)

Robert Philippe Gustave (1880–1946)
m. 1907
Gabrielle Nelly Beer (1886–1945)

Helen Betty Louise Caroline (1863–1947)
m. Baron de Zuylen de Nyevelt (d. 1934)*

James Armand (1878–1957)
m. 1913
Dorothy Pinto (b. 1895)

Maurice Charles (1881–1957)
m. 1909
Naomi Halphen

Miriam Caroline (b. 1884)
m. 1910
Albert Max von Goldschmidt

Philippe (b. 1902)
m. 1935
Elizabeth de Chambure (d. during World War II, 1939–45)
m. 2nd: 1954
Mrs Pauline Fairfax Potter (b. 1908)

Alphonse Édouard Émile Lionel (1906–1911)

Guy Édouard Alphonse Paul (b. 1909)
m. 1937
Alix Schey de Koromla (b. 1911)
m. 2nd: 1957
Marie-Hélène, Comtesse de Nicolai (née Van Zuylen) (b. 1931)

Jacqueline Rebecca Louise (b. 1911)
m. 1930
Robert Paul Michel Calmann-Lévy (b. 1899)
m. 2nd: 1937*
Gregor Piatigorsky

Bethsabée Louise Émilie Beatrix (b. 1914)
m. 1948
Donald Bloomingdale (b. 1913)
Div. 1951

Diane Cécile Alice Juliette (b. 1907)
m. 1932
Anatole Muhlstein*
Joseph Benvenuti (b. 1898)

James Gustave Jules Alain (b. 1910)
m. 1938
Mary Chauvin du Treuil (b. 1916)

Cécile (b. 1913)

Élie (b. 1917)
m. 1942 (by proxy)
Liliane Fould-Springer (reunited 1945)

Edmond Adolphe Maurice Jules (b. 1926)
m. 1958
Mme Lina (née Georgina) Blanc
m. 2nd:
Nadine Lhopitalier

Philippine/Mathilde Camille (b. 1935)
m. 1901*
Jacques Sereys

Charles Henri (b. & d. 1937)

David René James (b. 1942)

Édouard Étienne Alphonse (b. 1957)

Béatrice Juliette Ruth (b. 1939)
m. Armand de la Baumelle*

Eric Alain Robert David (b. 1940)

Robert James (b. 1947)

Nathaniel (b. 1946)

Nelly Sabine (b. 1947)

Elizabeth Clarisse Esther Gustava (b. 1952)
m. 1970
Marc Leland

Benjamin (b. 1963)

Notes

The full title of the book and the name of the author is repeated in each chapter where subsequent references occur. The name of the publisher and date of publication are given only once, the first time that a work is mentioned.

Chapter I
THE JEW AND THE PRINCE

1 J. W. von Goethe, *Poetry and Truth*, Vol. I, London 1908, p. 129

2 M. E. Ravage, *Five Men of Frankfurt*, London 1929, p. 25.

3 A. Dietz, *Stammbuch*, quoted by Eugene Meyer in *Jews of Frankfurt*, Jewish National University Library, p. 408.

4 *Memoirs of Sir Thomas Foxwell Buxton*, edited by Charles Buxton, London 1848, p. 352.

Chapter II
THE ROTHSCHILDS AND NAPOLEON

1 *Correspondence of Napoleon I*, Vol. XIII, Paris 1865, p. 585.

2 *Ibid*, p. 588.

3 C. W. Berghoeffer, *Meyer Amschell Rothschild*, Frankfurt-on-Main 1928, p. 79.

4 *Ibid*, p. 78

5 Count Corti, *The Rise of the House of Rothschild*, London 1928, pp. 64–5.

6 Ravage, *op. cit.*, p. 85.

7 Corti, *op. cit.*, p. 95.

8 *Ibid*, p. 106

9 *Ibid*, p. 112

10 *Ibid*, p. 114.

11 *Memoirs of Sir Thomas Foxwell Buxton*, p. 333.

12 John Sherwig, *Guineas and Gunpowder*, Cambridge, Mass., 1944, p. 232.

13 John Fortescue, *History of the British Army*, Vol. VII, London 1912, p. 235.

14 M. Marion, *Histoire financière de la France depuis 1715*, Vol. IV, Paris 1914, p. 358.

15 Robert Wilson, *Private Diary*, Vol. I, London 1861, p. 226.

16 Sherwig, *op. cit.*, p. 329.

17 Thomas Raikes, *Portion of a Journal*, Vol. I, London 1912, p. 457.

Chapter III
FIVE BROTHERS IN FIVE CAPITALS

1 *Briefwechsel zwischen Friedrich Gentz und Adam Heinrich Müller*, Stuttgart 1857, p. 267

2 *Ibid*.

3 Ravage, *op. cit.*, p. 202.

4 John Reeves, *The Rothschilds*, London 1887, p. 195.

5 *Ibid*, pp. 192–3.

6 Ronald Palin, *Rothschild Relish*, London 1970, p. 13.

7 *Diaries of Sir Moses and Lady Montefiore*, Vol. II, edited by L. Loewe, London 1890, p. 3.

8 *Wilhelm and Caroline von Humboldt in Ihren Briefen*, Vol. IX. Berlin 1912, p. 320.

9 *Memoirs of Sir Thomas Foxwell Buxton*, pp. 345–6.

10 Reeves, *op. cit.*, pp. 182–5.

11 Corti, *op. cit.*, pp. 214–5.

12 *Ibid*.

13 A. Ayer, *A Century of Finance*, compiled for N. M. Rothschild & Sons and privately printed, London 1905.

14 Corti, *op. cit.*, p. 237.

15 *Ibid.*, p. 253

16 *Ibid.*, pp. 265–6.

17 *Ibid.*, p. 274.

18 *Ibid.*, p. 291

19 M. Schwenner, *Geschichte der Freien Stadt*, Vol. II, Frankfurt-on-main 1840, p. 138.

20 Ignatius Balla, *The Romance of the Rothschilds*, London 1913, pp. 246–7.

Chapter IV
UNEASY TIMES

1 Count Corti, *op. cit.*, p. 346.

2 Hormayr zu Hartenburgh, *Kaiser Franz und Metternich*, Leipzig 1848, p. 80.

3 Ravage, *op. cit.*, p. 305.

4 *Mémoires du Prince Talleyrand, Publiées par le Duc de Broglie*, Vol. III, Paris 1892, p. 456.

5 Corti, *op. cit.*, p. 433.

6 M. J. Quinn, *Trade of Banking in England*, London 1833, pp. 45–6.

7 *An American in England*, quoted in *Transactions of the Jewish Historical Society*, Vol. XIII.

8 The *Observer*, 1 December 1833.

9 Prince Puckler-Muskau, *Tour of a German Prince*, Vol. III. London 1832, pp. 62–4.

10 *Memoirs of Sir Thomas Foxwell Buxton*, pp. 343–5.

11 *Simon Moritz von Bethmann und seine Vorfahren*, Frankfurt-on-Main 1898, p. 128.

12 Count Corti, *The Reign of the House of Rothschild*, London 1928 p. 133.

Chapter V
SUPREMACY

1 W. Monypenny and G. Buckle, *Life of Benjamin Disraeli*, Vol II London 1910–20, p. 20.

2 *Ibid.*, p. 183.

3 Quoted by John Reeves from a pamphlet: '*Rothschild et les états européens*'. *op. cit.*, p. 101

4 Count Corti, *Reign of the House of Rothschild*, pp. 245–6.

5 Heinrich Heine, *Gedanken und Emfallen*, Vol. VII, Berlin 1909, p. 430.

6 Monypenny and Buckle, *op. cit.*, Vol. II. p. 51.

7 Frederick Morton, *The Rothschilds*, London 1962, pp. 73–4.

8 Balla, *op. cit.*, pp. 180–1.

9 Corti, *Reign of the House of Rothschild*, p. 89.

10 *The Greville Diary*, Vol. I, edited by Philip Whitwell Wilson, New York 1927, p. 321.

11 Corti, *Reign of House of Rothschild*, p. 97.

12 Ludvig Borne, *Gesammelte Schriften* Vol. III, Stuttgart 1840, p. 354.

13 *The Greville Diary*, Vol. I, p. 321.

14 *Constitutional*: October 14, 1840.

15 Corti, *Reign of the House of Rothschild*, p. 197.

16 *The Greville Diary*, Vol. II, p. 110.

17 *Ibid.*, Vol. I pp. 205–6.

18 Corti, *Reign of the House of Rothschild*, p. 258.

19 *Mémoires de Caussidière*, Paris 1849, p. 92.

20 *Tocsin des Travailleurs*, 28 June 1848.

21 Corti, *Reign of House of Rothschild*, p. 274.

Chapter VI
THE CHALLENGE

1 Reeves, *op. cit.*, pp. 377–81.

2 A. Ayer, *A Century of Finance*,

3 Cecil Roth, *The Magnificent Rothschilds*, London 1939, p. 45.

4 *Annual Register*, London 1848, pp. 90–1.

5 Corti, *Reign of House of Rothschild*, p. 283.

6 *Ibid.* p. 286.

7 *Ibid.* p. 355.

8 Ravage, *op. cit.*, p. 316.

9 *Furst Bismarck Briefe an Seine Brant und Cutten*, May 1851.

10 Morton, *op. cit.*, p. 92.

11 Corti, *Reign of House of Rothschild*, pp. 342–3.

12 *Die Rheinpolitik Kaiser Napoleon III und der Ursprung des Krieges*, Vol. II, Berlin 1926, p. 113.

13 Victor Fournel, *Paris Nouveau et Paris Futur*, Paris 1865, pp. 47–8.

14 Roth, *op. cit.*, p. 60.

15 C. de B. to Salomon Rothschild, Feb. 21, 1865; quoted by Corti, *Reign of the House of Rothschild*, p. 324.

Chapter VII
VICTORIAN HIGH NOON

1 Roth, *op. cit.*, pp. 122–3.

2 A. Hyamson, *Transactions of the Jewish Historical Society*, Vol. XVII. p. 98.

3 Frances, Countess of Warwick, *Life's Ebb and Flow*, London 1942, pp. 74–5.

4 *Letter from Paris*, edited by Robert Henrey, London 1942, p. 14.

5 Lucy Cohen, *Lady Louisa de Rothschild and Her Daughters*, London 1935, p. 145.

6 Corti, *Reign of House of Rothschild*, pp. 417–8.

7 Cohen, *op. cit.*, p. 147.

8 Mrs James de Rothschild, *Waddesdon and the Rothschild Family*.

9 *Ibid.*

10 An unpublished letter, copyright owned by Lord Rosebery.

Chapter VIII
MAGNIFICENT BROTHERS

1 Randolph S. Churchill, *Winston S. Churchill*, Vol. I. London 1966, p. 285.

2 Roth, *op. cit.*, pp. 98–9.

3 J. Clapham, *The Bank of England*, Vol. I. Cambridge University Press 1944, pp. 328–9.

4 Roth, *op. cit.*, p. 106.

5 Palin, *op. cit.*, p. 22.

6 *Ibid.*, p. 72.

7 Roth, *op. cit.*, pp. 149–50.

8 Lord Asquith and Oxford, *Memoires & Reflections* Vol. II. London 1928, p. 200.

9 Frances, Countess of Warwick, *Afterthoughts*, London 1931, p. 87.

10 Lily Langtry, *Days I knew*, London 1925, p. 235.

11 Palin, *op. cit.*, p. 43.

12 Langtry, *op. cit.*, p. 159.

13 Warwick, *Afterthoughts*, p. 89.

14 *Ibid.*, p. 89.

15 Cohen, *op. cit.*, p. 232.

16 *Ibid.*, p. 235.

17 G. Kressel, *Father of the Yishuv*, translated from the Hebrew by I. M. Lask. Unpublished manuscript, p. 23.

18 David Druck, *Baron Edmond de Rothschild*, published privately, New York 1928, pp. 123–6.

19 *The Diaries of Theodor Herzl*, edited by Marvin Lowenthal, London 1958, p. 19.

20 *Ibid.*, p. 187.

21 Isaac Naiditch, *Baron Edmond de Rothschild*, Unpublished manuscript, British Museum 1945, pp. 25–6.

22 Corti, *Reign of House of Rothschild*, p. 436.

Chapter IX

THE END OF AN ERA

1 *The Diaries of Theodor Herzl*,
pp. 47–8.

2 *Ibid.*, 364.

3 André Maurois, *The Edwardian
Era*, New York 1933, p. 309.

4 Martin Harper, *Mr Lionel*,
London 1970, pp. 63–4.

5 Baron von Eckardstein,
*Ten Years At the Court of St.
James*, London 1921, pp. 170–1.

6 Roth, *op. cit.*, p. 165.

7 Kressel, *op. cit.*, p. 1.

8 *Ibid.*, p. 68 and p 4.

9 Chaim Weitzmann, *Trial and
Error*, London 1949, p. 177.

10 *Ibid.*, p. 178.

11 *Ibid.*, p. 165.

12 Roth, *op. cit.*, pp. 276–7.

Chapter X

THE YEARS BETWEEN

1 An extract from a paper on
Walter Rothschild written by
his niece, Miriam Rothschild.

2 Miriam Rothschild. Foreword
to *Illustrated Catalogue of the
Rothschild Collection of Fleas*,
Vol. 1., British Museum, London
1953.

3 Extract from Lord Rothschild's
address to the Empire Club of
Canada, 4 March 1965.

4 Foreword to *Illustrated Catalogue
Rothschild Collection of Fleas*,
Vol. 1.

5 Extract from Lord Rothschild's
address to the Empire Club of
Canada, 4 March 1965.

6 Palin, *op. cit.*, p. 187.

7 *Ibid.* p. 63.

8 *The Times*, 12 November 1938.

9 *L'Expansion*, December 1967:
Guy de Rothschild in an
interview with Roger Priouret.

Chapter XI

THE SECOND
WORLD WAR

1 E. de Rothschild, *Window on
the World*, pp. 172–3.

2 Speech for the League of
Human Rights of B'nai B'rith,
Toronto, December 11, 1971.

3 *Ibid.*

4 Letter to the author.

5 *Ibid.*

6 *Daily Telegraph*, 13 April 1946.

7 James Rorimer, *Survival*,
New York 1950, p. 260.

8 *Ibid.*, p. 262.

9 *Ibid.*, pp. 185–6.

10 Frederick Morton, *op. cit.*,
pp. 237–8.

Chapter XII

THE ROTHSCHILDS
TODAY : THE BANKERS

1 *Daily Sketch*, 3 August 1955.

Chapter XIII

THE ROTHSCHILDS
TODAY : THE OTHERS

1 1 November 1970.

2 *Daily Express*, 10 June 1967.

3 *Apollo*, September 1963.

Index

Note: Entries in italics indicate illustrations

Aachen Congress 56
'Albert Memorial' of Albert von Rothschild 187, *188*
Alexander I, Tsar 45, 53
Alexander II, Tsar, assassination of 181
Alexander III, Tsar, anti-Semitism of 181–2, 201
Alliance Insurance Company 60, *61*, 197, 199, 229, 261
Ascott House 155, 170, *221, 224*, 250, 292
Ashton Wold, home of Miriam Lane, Lord Rothschild's sister 235, 279
Asquith, Herbert Henry 166, 173, 197
Astronomer, The (Vermeer) 147, *160*, 292
Austerlitz, Battle of 26
Austria, anti-Semitism in, 63, 104, 127, 187; and anti-French coalition, 21–2, 26; and Austro-Prussian war, 149; and Franco-British entente 203; life in Second Empire 149; and Napoleonic Wars 23, 26, 39; railways of 130–1, 132, 135; and revolution of 1848 108; Rothschilds accepted in 64, 187, 189; Rothschild activities in 132–3, 148, 149, 203, 208–10, 229–30, 247, 253; Rothschild loans to 54, 62, 64, 65–6, 67; and war with France (1859) 135–6; and World War I 246–7; and World War II 228–30, 246–7; *see also* Vienna
Aylesbury, Rothschilds at, *112*, 118–19, 155, 156–8, 164, 175

Baldwin Fund for German Refugees 228
Balfour, Arthur 166, 194, statement of Britain's intent in Palestine 207
Balzac, Honoré de 97, 98–9
Baring, Alexander 56
Barings of London 72, 73, 118, 125, 254; 'saved' by the Rothschilds 168–9
Bastille Column, Throne, burning of *107*
Bergerie, La 285
Bernstein, Henry, as a boy (Manet) *270*

Bethmann, Moritz von, on the Rothschilds 63, 88
—— Brothers, bankers 16, 26, 35, 36
Bismarck, Otto von, ambitions for Prussia 148, 149, 150; occupies Ferrières 152–3, *153*; and the Rothschilds 103, 128, 130, 153–4; peace terms of 153; visitor to Ferrières 147–8
Bleichröder, Herr, banker 149, 153
Bonham Carter, Lady Violet 227
Boussac, Marcel 250
British Newfoundland Corporation (Brinco), founded by Baron Anthony 251
Buderus, Carl (later Baron Buderus von Carlhausen), financial adviser to Prince William of Hesse-Cassel 19, 26; appoints Mayer Amschel chief banker 30, 32; bribes King Jerome, 35; becomes secret partner of Mayer Amschel 24; deals with Mayer Amschel 22, 37; death of 69; ennobled 31; fight to keep Elector William's patronage 36–7; Gentz's account omits 74; investments in England 37–9, 41; made Privy Councillor 50; visits William in Denmark 31–2, 36–7; saviour of the Hesse-Cassel treasures 29

Capability Unit ('Think Tank') of Edward Heath, Lord Rothschild heads 274, 277–8
Carlhausen, Buderus von. *See* Buderus, Carl
Carpentier, Rothschild chief accountant, absconds with £1,200,000 132
Castiglione, antagonist of Baron Louis of Paris 208, 210; Comtesse de 135, 147, *147, 159*
Catholic bank, in opposition to the Rothschilds 185
Cavaignac, General Eugène 110
Cavour, Sardinian Minister of Finance 135
Chamberlain, Joseph 201, 202
Changarnier, General 124, *124*, 125
Charles X of France 75–6, 81

Churchill, Winston 166, 237, 250, 251; antagonism to Lord Rothschild 276; food of, scrutinized for poison 240–1; friendship with Baron Anthony 251
Clary, Prince Edmond de 88, 94
Clock, of Alfred de Rothschild *173*
Cohen, Albert 181
Cohen, Levi 30
Compagnie du Nord 266, 267
Compagnie Financière 282
Compagnie Française de Minéraux d'Uranium 266
Connolly, Cyril 237
Crédit Mobilier 185; demise of 138–9; dividends of 131; founding of 124, 125–6, *126*; and fraud scandal 136; rivalry with the Rothschilds 129–31, 132, 135, 136, 138–9, 234
Crimean War 118, 130, 181
Custine, General 21

Dairnvaell, Georges Mathieu 50
Dalberg, Grand Duke Carl von, friendship with Mayer Amschel 32–5, 39, 40, 43
Dali, Salvador 272, 286
de Gaulle, General Charles de 235, 236, 267
Delacroix, Eugène 97
Denmark, involvement in Napoleonic wars 24; William of Hesse-Cassel flees to 29
Diomedea immutabilis rothschildia 215
Disraeli, Benjamin 55, 92, *94*; attends his last Rothschild wedding 166; friend of the Rothschilds 94, 96–7, 121, 122, 135, 155, 161, 162, 164; and Suez Canal shares 162, *163*; at the wedding of Ferdinand von Rothschild and Evelina 148–9
Dollfuss, Austrian Chancellor, assassination of 228
Donnersmarck, Count Henkel von 149–50, 153
Dreyfus, Captain Alfred 181, 185
Drumont, Édouard 185, *185*

East India Company 42, 86
Eckardstein, Baron von 201, 202

Edward, Prince of Wales, later Edward VII, comes to throne 200; friendship with the Rothschilds 140–4, 147, 161, 166, 173, 176, 179; and R.A.C. 170
Einstein, Albert 246
Elizabeth, Empress of Austria, assassination of 189
Elysée Palace ball *127*
Ems telegram 151
Estorff, General von 11, 13, 14
Evelina de Rothschild Hospital for Sick Children, London 156
Exbury House 219–20, 250, *264, 265*
Eyethrope 180, 292
Eugénie, Empress (Eugénie de Montijo) *126*, *126*, 127, 147

Ferdinand, Duke of Brunswick 11
Ferdinand, Emperor of Austria 100–1, 104, 108, 109
Ferdinand I of Italy 65, 66
Fergusson, Lady Colyer 48–9
Ferrières, home of Baron James 119, 136, *137, 142*, 146, 147–8, 158, 190, 242; contemporary balls at 272; as storage house of recovered treasures 249; occupied by the Prussians 152–3, *153*; ransacked by the Nazis 248; Salon Bleu *116*
Fillon, M., former tutor to Baron Guy and employee of the bank 266, 267
Fitzroy, Henry, marries Hannah de Rothschild 94–5
Flea, Miriam Rothschild's diagram of *279*
Fould, Achille 123, *123*, 124, 125, 127, 129, 136, 137, 139, 234
France, anti-Semitism in 181, 184–5; British entente with (1905) 202; fall of, to Prussia 151–2, 153; national debt, conversion of, in 1824 72; in World War II 234, 237, 242, 283
Francis II, Holy Roman Emperor (Francis I, Emperor of Austria) 22, 25, 26
Franco-Austrian war of 1859 135
Franco-Prussian war, peace terms of 153; Rothschild moves to prevent 150

Frankfurt on the Main 12; anti-Semitism in 61–2, 191; Bourse of 128; closure of Rothschild bank in 200; Ghetto of see Judengasse; revolution of 1848 in 108–9; Staatsbibliothek in 191

Franz Joseph, Emperor 187, 189

Frederick the Great of Prussia, and the Seven Years' War 11

Frederick II, Landgrave of Hesse-Cassel 9, 11, 13, 16; army of 17

Frederick William II of Prussia 21

French Revolution 19–21, 53, 105

Frederick William IV of Prussia 109, 111, 129, 130

Generalpümpe, Die 70, 71
Gentz, Friedrich von 55; and Austrian lottery 62; biography of the Rothschilds 74–5; greed of 67; and Neapolitan rising 66; power over Metternich 55; and recognition of Rothschilds 54, 64; on the Rothschilds 53, 65, 128

German Confederation of the Rhine 26, 32, 27;

Gladstone, William Ewart 140, 151

Goering, Hermann 231, 241, 245, 283

Goethe 10, 87

Goldsmith, James 267–8

Gompertz, Benjamin 60

Grape-harvester, figure of, Mouton 289

Gunnersbury Park 92, 94, 136, 155, 170, 213; 93, 171

Greville, Charles 99–100, 102, 103, 104–5

Halton House, of Baron Alfred 173–4, 206, 213

Hanadiv, Rothschild support for 293

Harris, Frank 168

Haussmann, Baron Eugène 131

Heath, Edward 274, 277

Heine, Heinrich, friend of the Rothschilds 72, 96, 97, 99, 123; 96

Herries, John 42, 45, 46, 47, 74

Herzl, Theodor 186, 192–3, 204, 205

Hesse-Cassel, Principality of 11, 16; family of, supporters of Hitler 238; incorporated into Westphalia 32, 37; mercenaries of 16, 17, 21–2, 23–4, 39; Napoleon siezes 28–9, 30, 32; See also William, Prince of Hesse-Cassel

Himmler, Heinrich 228, 231–2
Hitler, Adolf 227, 228, 230, 237, 238, 242, 253
Holy Alliance 53
Hope and Co., of Amsterdam 56
House of the Green Shield, home of Mayer Amschel 17–18, 29, 69, 89, 104, 111; 17
—— of the Saucepan, home of Mayer Amschel 10, 15
Hübner, Count 127, 130, 135–6
Hyde Park Corner, showing Lionel de Rothschild's house in Piccadilly 117

Israel, first Baron Edmond's interest in 181–4, 203–4, 280, 293; contemporary Rothschilds' interest in 282, 293; meeting-ground for the Rothschilds 280; and Six-Day War 264, 280, 293

James Mayer de Rothschild Hospital in Jerusalem 181
Jerome Bonaparte, King of Westphalia 35
Josso, Nathalie, grand-daughter of Baron Robert 291
Judengasse, Frankfurt 9–10, 17–18, 22, 69, 89, 96, 104–5, 190; 8, 90
July Revolution of France 81–2, 95

Kahn, Zadok, Chief Rabbi of France 182, 184
Kreditanstalt, the 132, 133, 185, 187, 229

Laborde, Hôtel de (Hôtel Fouché) 72; 54
Lafite, Château, of James de Rothschild 82, 139, 258, 294 vineyard 120, 139, 183, 280, 283n, 292
Laffitte, Jacques, financier 72, 73, 81, 82, 125; 76
Lagrange, General 28, 29
Lane, Charles, son of Miriam 278, 291
—— George, marries Miriam Rothschild 236
Landau, Hermann 192
Langtry, Lily 174, 176; 174
Lawaertz, middleman in anonymous loan to the King of Denmark 24
Leach, Rodney 261
Leopold II, Holy Roman Emperor 21
Lloyd George, David 194–7, 206
Louis XIV cabinet 261
Louis XVIII 47, 53, 55, 72, 73 75

Louis Napoleon, President of the French Republic 110, 123, 124–5; 111; becomes Emperor Napoleon III 125; see also Napoleon III
Louis-Philippe, Duke of Orleans, King of France 81, 82, 83, 95, 96, 103, 106, 110
Louvre, the 191, 242
Lunéville, peace treaty of 23

Mafalda, Princess of Hesse-Cassel 238
Marie Louise, Archduchess 43, 64, 82
Marigny, Avenue de, residence of Baron Alain 241–2, 271–2
Marx, Karl 95, 124
Mehemet Ali Pasha 103
Mentmore Meet 120; 111
—— Towers 119, 155, 158, 291; 111
Metternich, Count Clemens, later Prince 40, 54; and anti-Semitic demonstrations 62; Gentz's power over 55; and Italian uprisings 82–3; and Marie Louise 64; and Neapolitan insurgency 65–6; power of 53, 61; and recognition of the Rothschilds 54, 64; relations with the Rothschilds 62, 65, 67, 70, 83, 89, 96, 100–1, 103–4, 105, 108, 109; and revolution of 1848 105, 108, 109, 110; resignation of 108; and ultimatum of Egypt 103–4
—— Richard, son of the Austrian ambassador 135, 149
Miferna 266
Milhaud, Darius 286
Moccand, M., discovers hidden Rothschild securities in France 247–8,
Mohilever, Samuel, Russian rabbi 182, 184
Montijo, Eugénie de see Eugénie, Empress
Morgan, J. P., of New York 210
Morny, Duc de 125, 126, 130
Mouton Baron Philippe 285
—— Rothschild 120,139, 237,283, 285, 286, 292; 284, 287, 290; life at 289–90; wine museum at 286–9; 284, 287, 288

Naples 66; Carl Rothschild settles in 67; revolt in 65–6; Rothschilds leave 138
Napoleon Bonaparte 23; 27; approaches Prince William of Hesse 25; annexes German territory 23; and England 24, 25, 29, 39, 41–2, 43, 45; enters Berlin 27; escape from Elba 47;

European wars of 23–4, 25–9, 32, 37, 39, 45; marriage of 43, 64; rout of 45; and the Rothschilds 30, 32, 35, 110; seizes Hesse-Cassel 28–9, 30, 32; victory at Austerlitz 26
Napoleon III, Emperor 110, 111, 290; 127; Baron Alphonse's access to 147, 150; and Baron James 127, 135, 136; 136, 137; and Crimean War 130; fall of 151; and Franco-Prussia war 150–1; and Haussmann 131; marriage of 126, 127; and Mexican throne 138; and treaty with Cavour 135
National Anti-Semitic League 185
Nautilus cups 190, 288
Neipperg, Count Albert von 64
Nelson, Horatio 24
Neuschwanstein castle, war-time hiding-place of the Rothschild art treasures 245; 245
New Court 47, 85, 87, 94, 164, 173, 174–5, 191, 192, 193, 225; 54; demolished and rebuilt 254, 255; during World War II 239, 253; headquarters of Central British Fund for German Jewry 227; Partners' Room 252; post-war 250; Walter dismissed from 199; working conditions at 169–70, 170–1, 175, 225
New Court Investment Trust 266
Nicholas I, Emperor 110–11
Nicholas I, Tsar 130, 181

Odhams, take-over by Mirror group, failure of Rothschilds to prevent 261
Ouvrard, Gabriel-Julien 55, 73, 76

Païva, La 149–50; bed of 150
Papacy, the 67, 86, 101, 127, 185, 272
Paris-St Germain railway 101, 101
Parliament, Jews barred from 121
Paxton, Joseph 119, 136
Pereire, Émile, betrays James de Rothschild 123, 123; and fall of Crédit Mobilier 138, 139; founds Crédit Mobilier 124, 125; rivalry with Baron James 127, 129–30, 136
—— Isaac 125, 130, 136, 138, 139, 185; 123
Périer, Casimir, French Minister of Finance 76, 82, 82, 83
Philip, Prince of Hesse-Cassel 238

PLM (Paris-Lyons-Mediter-
ranean railway) 268
Polignac, M.de, French chief
minister 75–6; —— decree,
signed by Charles X in Paris
76
Pompidou, Georges 266–7, 271
Prussia, joins with Austria
against the French 21; pact
with France 21; wins the
war against France 151, 152
Puckler-Muskau, Prince of, on
Nathan Rothschild 85–6, 87

Raikes, Thomas 49–50
Revolution of 1848 105–10,
187
Rhodes, Cecil 163
Rorimer, James 243–6, 249
Rosebery, Lord, marries
Hannah de Rothschild 158–
61
Rosebery, Lord (contemporary)
291
Rosenberg, Alfred 242–3
Rossini, Gioachino 90, 97, 136
Roth, Cecil 226
ROTHSCHILD
Adelheid, (née Herz) wife of
Baron Carl 67, 105; 51
Adolph of Naples 138, 189
Alain, Baron, son of Baron
Robert of Paris 234, 241,
268, 272, 283, 293
Albert, Baron, son of Anselm
of Vienna 156, 187, 203,
208; 187
Alfred, son of the first
Lionel 144, 164, 165, 166;
143; builds Halton House
173–4; characteristics of
170, 171–3, 174–5; 172;
death of 207; director of
the Bank of England 175;
hatred for Russia 201;
interest in foreign affairs
200–1, 202; natural
daughter Almina Womb-
well 212; patron of the
arts 174; pet goat of 169,
197; role in World War I
206; social life of 190;
university education 143
Alice, 'The All-Powerful',
sister of Baron Ferdinand
165, 179–80, 292; 181;
death of 213; succeeds
Ferdinand 203
Alix, first wife of Baron Guy
272–3, 292, 293; 292
Alphonse, Baron, son of
James Mayer of Paris 130,
135, 136, 139, 144–6, 148, 149,
150, 181, 183, 190, 191;
145, 193; and anti-Semit-
ism 184; death of 203; and
Franco-Prussian war 150–
1, 152, 153–4, 154–5;
house of, during Com-

mune 154; 154; marries
Leonora, daughter of
Lionel 133; 136; social
life of 146–7
Alphonse, son of Baron
Albert 208, 229
Amschel, son of Victor,
present Lord Rothschild
278
Amschel Mayer of Frankfurt,
son of Mayer Amschel 16,
25, 32, 46, 53, 54, 61, 62, 65,
132; 68; adopts his nephew
Mayer Carl as his son 129;
and Bismarck 128;
caricature of 108; consul
general of Prussia 108;
and Crimean War 130;
death of 131, 200; grieves
over his childlessness 128–
9; marriage of 41; and
Metternich 67, 104;
prestige of 128; and railways 101; and revolution
of 1848 108; 108; Solicitor
in the cause of Jewry 87,
127–8; success of 68–9, 95
Anselm, son of Salomon of
Vienna 132–3, 135, 156,
191; death of 156; founder
of the Kreditanstalt 132,
133; influence on Austrian
affairs 148, 149; marries
Charlotte, sister of Lionel
132; 133; 'peace-monger'
148
Anthony, son of Leo 219
220, 225, 226; death
of 254, 255; founds the
British Newfoundland
Corporation (Brinco) 251;
gives Ascott House to
National Trust 250; keeps
the bank going during
World War II 239, 250;
personal friend of Winston
Churchill 251
Anthony, son of Nathan
118, 119, 120, 144, 163,
213; 112–3
Barbara (née Hutchinson), first
wife of Victor, present
Lord Rothschild 219
Benjamin, son of Baron
Edmond 283
Betty, daughter of Salomon,
wife of Baron James 63,
88, 106, 127; 72, 77;
Changarnier in love with
124; as hostess 96–7, 126;
marriage of 72
Carl Mayer of Naples, son
of Mayer Amschel 32, 43,
46, 53, 61, 65, 89, 104, 127,
129; 68, 133; death of
131; and Neapolitan revolt
65–6; and railways 101;
and revolution of 1848
105; settles in Naples 67;

success of 95
Cécile, daughter of Baron
Édouard 241, 242, 292; 292
Charles, son of Nathaniel
('Natty') 199, 214, 215,
291; acquires Ashton
Wold from his father 279;
death of 217; house of
250; interest in natural
history 199, 217
Charlotte, wife of Baron
Lionel 89, 92; 93
Charlotte, wife of Anselm
132, 135, 148; 133
Claude, wife of Baron
James, war decorations of
237
Constance, Lady Battersea,
daughter of Baron
Anthony 120, 132, 151,
161, 179–80, 193
David, son of Baron Guy,
266, 272–3; 273
Dorothy (née Pinto)
('Dollie'), wife of James
213, 227, 278, 283, 292,
293; 278
Edmond, Baron, son of
James Mayer of Paris 136,
181, 203; characteristics of
186, 205; collection of
191; and education of his
son 213; embraces the
cause of Zionism 206;
future 'Father of Israel'
181–4, 182, 186; Palestine
interests 182–4, 186, 192,
203–4, 205–6, 282; 204;
revisits Palestine in 1914
205; 205
Edmond, Baron, son of
Maurice of Paris 212, 283,
292; business interests 282;
childhood 281; 'Father of
Israel' 282, 293; invests in
mass tourism 282; marries
Nadine Lhôpitalier 283;
richest Rothschild 280;
281
Edmund, ('Eddie'), son of
Lionel 250; 264; assumes
responsibility for Brinco
251; interests of 263; 265;
modest social life of 265;
race-consciousness of 263–
4, 293; senior partner 254;
war activities of 237–8
Édouard, Baron, son of
Alphonse of Paris 203,
230, 242; after World
War I 210; after World
War II 247; death of 248;
flees to New York 234
Élie, Baron, son of Baron
Robert of Paris 234, 283;
268; house of 271;
marries Liliane Fould-
Springer, great-niece of
Achille Fould, by proxy

234; moves from Marigny
271; president of PLM
268; prisoner-of-war 234;
235; runs Château Lafite
292
Emma, daughter of Victor,
present Lord Rothschild
278, 291
Emma Louise, daughter of
Mayer Carl of Frankfurt,
wife of Nathaniel ('Natty'),
first Lord Rothschild 166,
213, 214
Éric, son of Baron Alain of
France 266
Eugene, Baron, son of Baron
Albert of Vienna 206, 208,
229, 264; 228; eldest living
Rothschild 291; improves
on Einstein 246; marries
Jeanne Stewart 247;
returns from America to
Europe 247; settles in
America 246
Evelina de, wife of Baron
Ferdinand 48, 148, 156
Evelyn, son of Anthony
of London 254, 292,
293; activities of 263,
265–6; brings changes to
the London bank 255;
Chairman of the Board of
Governors, Israel's Insti-
tute of Technology 293;
Director of the Paris bank
266; presented by the
Queen with the Queen's
Cup for polo 263
Evelyn, son of Leo
206
Ferdinand, Baron, son of
Baron Anselm of Vienna
132, 144, 165, 191; 176;
becomes naturalized
Englishman 175; builds
château near Aylesbury
156–8; death of 181, 203;
early widowerhood of
156; marries Evelina,
daughter of Baron Lionel
148; philanthropy of 156,
180–1; social life of 175–6,
179
George, Baron, son of Baron
Albert of Vienna 203
Gustave, Baron, son of
James Mayer of Paris 136,
139, 181, 183, 184, 190,
203; 193
Gutle, wife of Mayer
Amschel 15, 18, 39, 45,
69, 89, 104–5, 111; 69
Guy, Baron, son of Baron
Édouard 119, 234, 248–9,
267, 283, 293; 236, 273;
Director of the London
bank 266; divorce and
remarriage 272; recon-
structs the Rothschild

stables in France 250; war activities of 234–5; wife and son held to ransom 272–3

Hannah (Fitzroy), daughter of Nathan 88, 90, 237; marries outside the faith 94–5

Hannah (Lady Rosebery) daughter of Mayer of London 158–61, 165; *161*

Hannah (née Cohen), wife of Nathan 30, 58, 87, 89, 90, 92, 94–5, 118, *133*; funeral jewel of *91*

Henri, Baron, of France, grandson of Nathaniel 199, 206, 211, 242, 248, 283; *199, 211*

Hilda, Countess von Auersperg, marries Louis, son of Baron Albert of Vienna 246

Jacob, heir of Victor, present Lord Rothschild. *See* Nathaniel Charles Jacob

James Mayer of Paris, son of Mayer Amschel and later Baron de Rothschild 32, 39, 41, 46, 53, 61–2; *44*; activities in the July Revolution of Paris 81–2; attacks on 70–1, 102–3; awarded Grand Cross of the Legion of Honour 83; buys vineyard in the Médoc 139; character of 97–9; and Charles X 75, 76, 81; and chateau at Ferrières 119, 158, 190; *137*; and Crédit Mobilier 125–6, 127, 129–30, 138–9; death of 139; defends Nathan's reputation 50; finances Louis XVIII 46–7, 72; fortune of 97; founder of the Chemin de Fer du Nord 102, 123, 249; and French national debt 72–3; head of Paris *haute finance* 95–6; interest of in Israel 181; and Italian uprisings (1831) 82–3; in late years *138*; and Louis-Philippe, 82, 83, 96, 103; marries his niece Betty 72; and Metternich 107; and Pereire 123; Napoleon III, (Louis Napoleon) 123, 124, 126–7, 135, 136; *136, 137*; railway tycoon 99, 101–2, 118, 123; secures passage through France of British gold 43; social life of 88, 96–7; stays in Paris during the 1848 revolts 106–8, 109–10; town house of 147

James ('Jimmy'), son of

Baron Edmond 205–6, 213, 236, 180; *211, 213*; character and life of 213–14; death of 293; and Hanadiv 293; helps Jewish orphans 227; marries Dorothy Pinto 213

Jeanne (Stewart), second wife of Baron Eugene of Vienna 247, 291

Julie, daughter of Baron Anselm of Vienna 189

Kitty, first wife of Baron Eugene of Vienna 246; *229*

Leopold (Leo), the first, son of the first Baron Lionel 47–8, 144, 164, 165, 170, 191, 207; death of his son 206; house of 250; kindness of 170, 171, 181; marries Maria Perugia 166; *167*; motor racing activities of 170; *171*; turf activities of 170

Leo, the second, son of the second Lionel 254, 263, 265

Leonora de, wife of Baron Alphonse 133–5, 148, 190; *134, 141, 145*; 'Englishness' of 146; and Franco-Prussian war 151

Liliane de (née Fould-Springer), wife of Baron Élie 234, 267; authority on Rothschildiana 292; *293*

Lionel, the first, son of Nathan Mayer and later Baron 103, 104, 151, 156; *92, 113, 133*; acquires land in Buckinghamshire 155; artistic interests of 191; banking activities of 118, 135; barony bestowed upon by Queen Victoria 92; builds 148 Piccadilly 112, 117, 136–8, 148–9; *117*; buys Suez Canal shares 162–3; caricature of *141*; and Crimean War 130; death of 163; and Disraeli 94, 121, 148–9, 162; enters Parliament 121–2, 155; *122*; family of 143, 148–9; *93*; hunting activities of 120; marries his cousin Charlotte 89; philanthropy of 118; and Prince of Wales 144; and revolution of 1848 106

Lionel, the second, son of Leo of London 219–20, 239

Lionel Walter, ('Walter'), son of 'Natty', first Lord Rothschild 197, 291; *198*; becomes second Lord Rothschild 207;

characteristics of 198–9, 214; death of 227; dismissed from the family bank 199; embraces the cause of Zionism 207; member of Parliament 198; motor racing activities 199–200; zoological collection of 197–8, 199, 207, 214–15; *198*;

Louis, Baron, son of Baron Albert of Vienna 203, 208, 210; *207*; death of 247; dictates his own ransom terms to the Nazis 231; leaves Vienna for Paris 232; marries Hilda, Countess von Auersperg 246; and Nazism 228, 229–32; re-visits Austria 246–7

Louise (née Montefiore), wife of Baron Anthony 120, 165

Maria de (née Perugia), wife of Baron Leo 166, 170, 207; *167*

Marie Hélène, second wife of Baron Guy 272; *273*

Marie-Louise (née Beer), wife of Baron Lionel 220

Mary (née Chauvin de Treuil), wife of Baron Alain 268

Maurice, Baron, son of Baron Edmond of Paris 211–12, 242, 280; *211*

Mayer Amschel, founder of the banking dynasty 9, 10, 190, 293; *10, 40*; advises Elector William 26; apprentice in the Oppenheimer bank 11; and British bullion 43; business during the Napoleonic wars 22, 26; chief banker to William of Hesse-Cassel 30, 35–6; children of 16; collects interest on loans of William of Hesse-Cassel 32–5, 38; conceals Hesse-Cassel treasures 29; Crown Agent to William of Hesse-Cassel 14–15, 24; death of, in 1812 45; family life of 18; first foot in the finances of the Landgraves of Hesse 19; friendship with the Grand Duke Carl von Dalberg 35, 43; Gentz's account of 74; is sent to a *yeshiva* 11; marries Gutle Schnapper in 1770 15; middleman in loans to the King of Denmark 24; moves to the House of the Green Shield 17–18; Napoleon

investigates 35; prepares new deed of settlement 40–1; returns to Frankfurt 12–13; sells coins to William of Hesse 14–15; under 'room' arrest 39; William's suspicions of 35–6, 37–8

Mayer Amschel, son of Nathan 118, 119, 120, 121, 144, 155, 158, 163, 191; *112–3, 155*

Mayer Carl, son of Carl Mayer of Naples 129, 135, 161, 166, 191, 200

Miriam, sister of Victor, present Lord Rothschild, and wife of George Lane 214, 216–17, 235, 278, 293; at seventeen *217*; helps Jewish refugees 227; homes of 280; honorary degrees of 279; marries George Lane 236; scientific interests of 218, 279, 291; war activities of 235–6

Nadine (née Lhôpitalier), wife of the second Baron Edmond of Paris 283

Nathan Mayer ('N.M.'), son of Mayer Amschel 16, 92, 190, 237; *31, 86, 133*; acquires Spanish mine 89; approaches Hessians for loan 35–6; and attacks on Rothschilds 70, 73–4; and Austrian government 53–4; and Battle of Waterloo 47–50; becomes Austrian Consul in London 62; —— naturalized Englishman 42; buys the defeated Napoleon's gold 46; caricature of *58, 91*; characteristics of 30, 57, 60, 84–6, 87–8; courier system of 47–8, 71 death of 90–1; despatches money to Wellington 42–3, 45–6, 47; directs affairs of his brothers 54, 61, 62, 76; establishes own bank 42; family of 87–8, 89, 90, 94; *78*; finances Louis XVIII 46–7; and French national debt 73; gambles with Elector William's money 38–9, 41, 42, 50, 74; goes to England 23, 30; handles Carl Buderus's English investments 37–8, 41; subsidy payments to British allies 46, 54; and July Revolution 81, 82; marries Hannah Cohen 30; meets Levi Cohen in London 30; moves to

Piccadilly 87; raiser of government loans 60; refuses baronetcy 64, 92; 'saves' the Bank of England 60; skill in banking and business 30, 37, 38–9, 42, 46, 60, 83–4; will of 90, 95

Nathaniel Mayer ('Natty'), first Lord Rothschild and son of the first Lionel of London 164, 165, 166; *143, 165*; attitude of to business 167–9, 170; attitude of to his sons 198–9, 214; character of 166–7; death of 207; friendship with Prince of Wales 144; in House of Lords 164, 175, 194; lay head of world Jewry 191–2, 207; and Liberal government 194–7, 206; marries Emma Louise, daughter of Mayer Carl of Frankfurt 166; philanthropic activities of 169, 190, 192; refuses to insure the *Titanic* 197; on Royal Commission on Alien Immigration 192–4; saves Barings 168–9; university education of 143; and Victor 216–217

Nathaniel, Baron von, son of Baron Anselm of Vienna 156, 187, 191

Nathaniel, son of Baron Élie of Paris 266

Nathaniel, son of Nathan 94–5, 118, 120; moves to France 120

Nathaniel, son of Nathaniel Charles Jacob ('Jacob') of London 262, 291

Nathaniel Charles Jacob, heir of Victor, present Lord Rothschild (referred to as Jacob) 219, 255–6, 291, 292; *256*; family of 262; joins the family bank 256; management of bank 261–2

Nelly, wife of Baron Robert of Paris 227

Nicholas, son of Edmund de Rothschild 264

Naomi de (née Halphen), wife of Baron Maurice of Paris 281

Oskar, son of Baron Albert of Vienna 203

Pauline (née Potter), second Baroness Philippe 285–6, 290

Philippe, Baron, son of Baron Henri of Paris 264, 291; *284*; life at Mouton 289–90; literary works of 286; marries Pauline Potter

of Baltimore 285–6; produces talking-picture 211; vineyards of 237, 283, 285, 292; war activities 236–7; war decorations 237; wine museum of 286–9

Philippe, Baroness, the first 285 the second (Pauline) 285; *284*

Philippine, daughter of Baron Philippe 285, 292

Robert, Baron, of Paris, son of Baron Gustave 203, 210; *210*; after World War II 247; death of 248; flees to New York 234; Paris house of 241, 242; president of Jewish refugee organization 227; house of, taken over by Lord Rothschild in 1944 241

Rozsika von Wertheimstein, wife of Charles de Rothschild 215, 216; *216*

Salomon Mayer of Vienna, son of Mayer Amschel 16, 32, 39, 43, 53, 61, 65, 67, 89, 129, 229; *63*; and Anselm 132, *133*; attacks on, 70–1, 72, 73–4; character of 63–4, 83; death of 131; on death of Gentz 75; financial adviser to Archduchess Marie Louise 64; flees from Vienna (1832) 83, (1848) 109; gains right to own land 104; and July Revolution 81; and Metternich 96, 103–4, 105, 108, 109; philanthropic activities in Austria 104; position of in Austria 54, 95, 96, 104, 127; railway 'king' of central Europe 99, 100–1, 104; raises money by public lottery 62; and revolution of 1848 108, 109; settles in Vienna 62–3

Salomon, son of James Mayer of Paris 136, 138

Serena (née Dunn), wife of Baron Jacob 262

Tess (née Mayor), wife of the present Lord Rothschild

Victor, third (and present) Lord Rothschild, son of Charles and nephew of Baron Lionel Walter 216–17, 255, 292, 293; *216, 275*; accompanies Churchill to Paris in 1944 241–2; career of 276–7; characteristics of 218, 274, 277–8; enters the family bank 218 homes of 278, 291; interest in German Jews

227–8; marries, first, Barbara Hutchinson 219; —— second, Tess Mayor 276; politics of 276, 277; scientific interests of 276, 278, 291; sells 'Natty's' house in Piccadilly 232–3; succeeds to the title 227; supports Israel 280; and 'think-tank' 274, 277–8; war activities of 239–40, 241–2, 276

Victoria, daughter of present Lord Rothschild 278

Walter. *See* Lionel Walter, son of 'Natty'

Wilhelm Carl, Baron, of Frankfurt 191, 200, 232

Yvonne (née Cahen d'Anvers), wife of Baron Anthony 225, 226, 239, 292; work for German Jews 227

Rothschild art treasures, German war-time custody of 243

Rothschild banks; end of supremacy of 253; first 18; Frankfurt branch (M. A. Rothschild und Söhne) 40; closure of, in 1901 200 London branch (N. M. Rothschild & Sons Ltd) 42; attitude to employees 225; autocracy of 220, 225; becomes a limited company 255; corporate finance department 261; during 1920s and 1930s 219, 225–6; first outsider admitted as partner 255; and foundation of Brinco 251; handles indemnity after Franco-Prussian war 155; Jacob's management of 261–2; launches New Court Investment Trust 266; modernization of 254–5; post-war difficulties 250; *see also* New Court; Naples branch 67, 138, 200; Paris branch (Messieurs de Rothschild Frères), change of name to La Banque Rothschild 267; management of 181; combines with J. P. Morgan of New York 210; post-war reorganization of 247–8, 266–8; post-World War II apparent decline in influence of 226; rivalry with Crédit Mobilier 129–31, 132, 135, 138–9; theft of shares 132; renaissance of 254; and revolutions of 1848 106–8, 111; 'saves' Barings 169; split into three entities 208 Vienna branch (S. M. Rothschild und Söhne) 187; *221*;

revived after World War I 208, 210

Rothschild Cameo *270*

Rothschild Continuations Ltd 239

Rothschild family; accepted in Austria 187; aid for German refuge Jews 227; anti-Semitism directed against 102, 144, 148, 181, 184–5, 186; attitude to Zionism 186, 192–3, 205–6, 207; Austrian branch *189*; philanthropic activities of 187, 189; settle in America 246; baronies conferred, by Prince Metternich 64; befriended by the Prince of Wales 140, 143; characteristics 291; coat-of-arms, of Frankfurt branch 54–5; *64*; collections of 190–1, 197–8, 220, 242–6, 249, 253; connection with the Duke of Wellington, caricature on *87*; contribution to the Six-Day War 293; convert the French national debt 72; country houses 291; courier system of 47, 65, 71–2, 81–2, 103, 147; creative urge of 291; critics of 70, 73–4, 102–3; English branch, during World War II 237–41; industrial magnates 163; London 'ghetto' 165; personal characteristics 263; reduced resources after World War I 212; sell off property after World War II 213, 250, 291; vitality of 291; exclusion from French loan of 1817 55; fate in the 1848 revolution 106; female 292; exclusion of, from the company 41, 44; following the hounds in the Vale of Aylesbury *113*; fortune, founding of *33*; Frankfurt branch, coat-of-arms 54, *64*; French branch, and anti-Semitism 181, 184–5; during World War II 234–7, 241–3, 285; property of, attempts to save from the Nazis 242; recovery from World War I 210–12; return to France after World War II 246, 247, 248–50, 285; harmony of 88, 292, 293; hunting activities of 118, 120, 146, 180–1, 213; *113*; intellectual 291; internationalism of 53–69; interrelationships of 135, 166; invade the Chilterns 118; inventors of *haute finance* 50; marriages outside the faith 161; non-banking 274; origin of the name 10; in

World War II 206, 234; 'peace-mongers' 103, 130, 149, 264; philanthropy of 118, 120, 169–70, 181, 182, 188–9, 190, 192, 211, 227, 264, 282, 293; present count of 290; racing activities of 121, 155, 161, 170, 187, 211, 214, 250; railway tycoons 99–102, 146; refused peerage by Queen Victoria 140; reverses of, in July Revolution of Paris 81; solicitors for the Jewish cause 86–7, 127, 182, 293; third generation 135; Victorian, opulence of 164–6, 190; von Gentz's biography of 74–5; and World War I 206–7, 210–11, 212, 226, 236, 253, 283; and World War II 227–33, 234–46, 253, 283
Rothschild Investment Trust 262
Royal Automobile Club, founding of 170
Royal Commission on Alien Immigration 192
Ruppell and Harnier, bankers 16, 26, 35–6

Saint-Jacques, Hôtel 268; 268
Sand, Georges 97, 99
Schiff family, neighbours of Mayer Amschel 17
Schillersdorf 187; 188
Schlotheim, Countess von, mistress of William of Hesse-Cassel 31
Schuschnigg, Kurt von 228, 229, 230, 231
Seamore Place, home of Baron Alfred 173, 174, 213; 172
Seven Years' War 11, 13
Shirer, William 231
Snuff-box from Baron Ferdinand's collection 178
Stadnick, Joseph, threatens Alix and David de Rothschild 272–3
Standard Bearer, The (Rembrandt) 271
Suez Canal shares, bought by Lionel de Rothschild 162; 163
Sutton, Denys 289

Talleyrand, Prince de 81, 147
Tapestry, Mouton wine museum 287
Tennant, Henry 174
Thurn and Taxis, Prince of, postmaster of Europe 44
Tring Park 155, 166, 207, 213, 214, 218
—— Zoological Museum 197–8, 199, 214–15, 218, 279
Truman, President Harry S. 242

Tuthankhamen discovery, Rothschild part in 212

Union Générale 185

Valland, Rose 245
Vernet, Horace 97–8; On the Way to Smala 98
Victoria, Queen 67, 92, 162, 190, 290; death of 202; and Franco-Prussian war 151; on Jews and peerage 140, 164; Jubilee celebrations of 192; and Prince Edward's education 144; visits Alice Rothschild in Grasse 179–80; visits Waddesdon, home of Baron Ferdinand 179; 180
Vienna, cholera epidemic in 83; importance of to Rothschilds 53, 61, 62; Nazis in 228, 231; post-war 208; rioting in (1848) 108; 109; Rothschilds in 62, 187–9, 19, 203, 229; Russians in 246
Villèle, M. de, French chief minister 72–3, 75
Vitkowitz, iron and steel works, transfer from Austrian to British ownership 229, 231, 232
Voltaire, on the Holy Roman Empire 10

Waddesdon Bequest 191
—— Manor 158, 173, 175–6, 179, 180, 203, 213, 214, 280; 157, 177; Jewish orphanage at 297; visited by Queen Victoria 179; 180
Warwick, Frances Countess of 146, 174, 175, 176–7
Waterloo, Battle of 47, 48, 49, 50; 48
Weill, Alexandre 95–6
Weizmann, Chaim 205, 207
Wellington, Arthur Wellesley, Duke of 39, 92, 99; Rothschild connection with 42–3, 45–6, 47, 70, 170, 263; 87
Wessenberg, Baron von, Austrian ambassador 26, 28
Wilhelmshöhe, Palace of 21, 28–9, 35, 50; 34
William, Prince of Hesse-Cassel (and Hanau), later William IX, Landgrave, later Elector 11–12, 16, 92; 20; army of 17, 21–2, 25, 39; attacked by Napoleon 28; bastards of 14, 19, 31; builds Wilhelmshöhe 21; created 'Elector' by Napoleon 23; death of 69; exile of in Denmark 28–9, 30, 31–2, 35; financil arrangements with England 22, 23–4; flees from Napoleon to Prague 37; Gentz's account of 74; helps

found the Rothschild fortune 32, 33–34; investments in England 38–9, 41, 50, 74, 75; loans of 26, 32; marriage of 13–14; Mayer Amschel Rothschild does business with 14–15, 19, 24, 25, 26; moves to Cassel 17; and Napoleonic Wars 25–6, 27; returns to Wilhelmshöhe Castle 50; riches of 17, 23, 24, 25, 28, 29, 35; suspicions of Buderus and Rothschilds 35–6, 38, 39, 41; wooed by opposing factions in the Napoleonic wars 25–6, 26–7
William II, Emperor, King of Prussia 129, 152, 153
William II, Kaiser 200, 202
William X, son of William IX, Elector of Hesse-Cassel 69
Windsor, Duke of 187n
Wombwell, Almina, Countess of Carnarvon 212
Wood, Nicholas 99
World War I 206–7, 208, 210–11, 212, 226, 236, 253, 283
World War II 227–33, 234–46, 283

Zichy-Ferraris, Countess Melanie 104
Zionist Congress, first 186